P9-BYB-804

Hawai'i the Big Island

Luci Yamamoto
Alan Tarbell

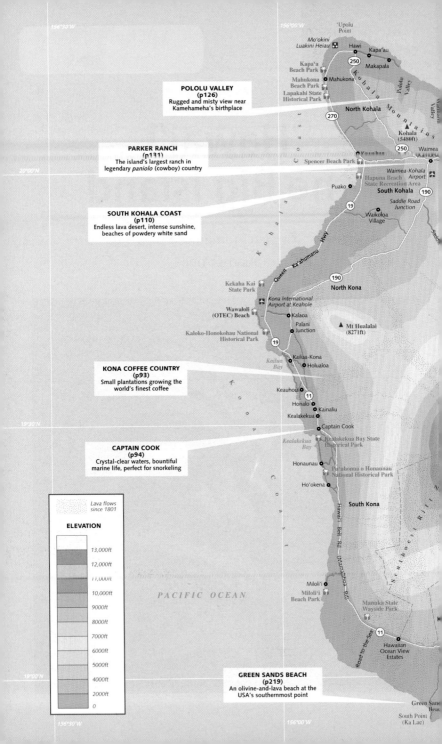

POLOLU VALLEY
(p126)
Rugged and misty view near
Kamehameha's birthplace

PARKER RANCH
(p131)
The island's largest ranch in
legendary *paniolo* (cowboy) country

SOUTH KOHALA COAST
(p110)
Endless lava desert, intense sunshine,
beaches of powdery white sand

KONA COFFEE COUNTRY
(p93)
Small plantations growing the
world's finest coffee

CAPTAIN COOK
(p94)
Crystal-clear waters, bountiful
marine life, perfect for snorkeling

GREEN SANDS BEACH
(p219)
An olivine-and-lava beach at the
USA's southernmost point

'Upolu
Point
*Mo'okini
Luakini Heiau* 🏯 Hawi
Kapa'au
250 Makapala
Kapa'a
Beach Park
Mahukona ● Mahukona
Beach Park
Lapakahi State
Historical Park
North Kohala
270

Kohala Mountains

Pololu
Valley

Waimea
Valley

Kohala
(5480ft)
250 Waimea
(Kamuela)
● Kawaihae
Spencer Beach Park 🏖
Waimea-Kohala
Airport
Hapuna Beach
State Recreation Area
190
South Kohala
Puako ●
Saddle Road
Junction
19
Waikoloa ●
Village

Kohala

190

North Kona

Kekaha Kai
State Park
Kona International
Airport at Keahole
Wawaloli ● Kalaoa
(OTEC) Beach
Palani
Junction
▲ Mt Hualalai
(8271ft)
Kaloko-Honokohau National
Historical Park
19
Kailua
Bay Kailua-Kona
● Holualoa
Keauhou ●
11
Honalo ●
● Kainaliu
Kealakekua ●
● Captain Cook
*Kealakekua Bay State
Historical Park*
Kealakekua
Bay
Honaunau ●
Pu'uhonua o Honaunau
National Historical Park
Ho'okena ●
South Kona

Southwest Rift

Miloli'i ●
Miloli'i
Beach Park
Manuka State
Wayside Park

Hawaiian
Ocean View
Estates

11

PACIFIC OCEAN

Green Sands
Beach
South Point
(Ka Lae)

ELEVATION

Lava flows
since 1801

	13,000ft
	12,000ft
	11,000ft
	10,000ft
	9000ft
	8000ft
	7000ft
	6000ft
	5000ft
	4000ft
	2000ft
	0

156°30'W
156°00'W
20°00'N
19°30'N
19°00'N
18°00'N

WAIPI'O (p151) & WAIMANU VALLEYS (p153)
Magnificent valleys well worth the hike down

MAUNA KEA (p137)
Stargazing atop a 13,700ft mountain

HILO (p159)
Scenic 'old town' capital, known for rain (and rainforests and rainbows)

PUNA COAST (p181)
Catching waves over a lava reef, soaking in a 'hot pond'

KILAUEA CALDERA (p197)
Home of Pele and the world's most active volcano

PACIFIC OCEAN

Kukuihaele

240

Honoka'a

19

Hawai'i Belt Rd

Kalopa State Recreation Area

Laupahoehoe Point Beach Park

Mauna Kea (13,796ft)

19

Kolekole Beach Park

Honomu

Akaka Falls State Park

Onizuka Visitor Information Station

Hilo

200

Saddle Rd

Hawaii Tropical Botanical Garden

Hilo Bay

Hilo

Hilo International Airport

200

11

Kea'au

Kurtistown

Steinback Hwy

Mountain View

130

Lava Tree State Monument

Cape Kumukahi

Kapoho

132

Hawai'i Volcanoes National Park

Hawai'i Volcanoes National Park (Ola'a Tract)

Glenwood

Puna

Pahoa

Mauna Loa (13,677ft)

11

Volcano

Pu'u 'O'o Crater

Isaac Hale Beach Park

MacKenzie State Recreation Area

Kehena Beach

Kilauea Caldera

130

East Rift Zone

137

Chain of Craters Rd

Hawai'i Belt Rd

Ka'u Desert

Southwest Rift Zone

Pahala

Punalu'u

Punalu'u Beach Park

Whittington Beach Park

ohinu

Na'alehu

0 ⸺ 20 km
0 ⸺ 12 miles

Destination
Hawai'i the Big Island

Why is Hawai'i nicknamed the 'Big Island?'

The island's 'bigness' lies first in its sheer size. The other seven major Hawaiian Islands can fit within its borders *twice*. It is a microcosm of a continent with astounding geographical diversity. Within an hour or two, the landscape morphs from lava desert to rain forest, from rolling pastureland to snowy mountaintop.

Here, you'll find stunning extremes in climate. In east Hawai'i, Hilo is the rainiest town in the USA, with over 130 inches of yearly rainfall. The whole windward side is stunningly lush and green, with overgrown jungles hiding unexpected waterfalls and dramatic gulches zigzagging the shore. In contrast, the western Kona Coast boasts guaranteed sunshine, brilliant and blinding, but tempered by the cobalts, emeralds and ivories of perfect crescent-shaped beaches.

The island boasts many outdoor adventures: diving and snorkeling in glassy waters, trekking in rugged valleys, stargazing in pristine air. The island's biggest phenomenon is Kilauea volcano. Depending on nature's whims, you can see fiery-red molten lava – earth in the making.

Big, too, is the range of people. From ancient times, the island has attracted those seeking spiritual power from the land. Many come to visit but can't leave. Of course, many longstanding locals remain, and while few speak Hawaiian exclusively, the lyrical sounds of the language are heard daily: in street and place names, in island music, in casual conversations.

On an island big enough to remain quite rural, a relaxed, 'hang loose, brah' atmosphere still prevails. Here you'll find miles of undeveloped land and remote spots void of other humans. That's the beauty of the Big Island – it's a vast frontier.

LINDA

Highlights

Laze away the day at Kauna'oa Bay (p117)

Satisfy your daily caffeine fix
at one of Kona's famous coffee
plantations (p93)

OTHER HIGHLIGHTS

▪ Hilo (p159) is a well-kept secret and exploring
  its restaurants, museums and art galleries, not
  to mention the excellent farmers' market, will
  reward those who make the trek out to the
  'rainy' side of the island.

▪ Kohala Ditch (p124), an intricate series of
  ditches, tunnels and flumes, is the perfect place
  for a kayak adventure.

Gaze in awe at Kilauea Caldera (p197),
the summit of the most-active volcano
on earth

6

Stunning greenery and towering
waterfalls await those who trek to the
stunning Waipi'o Valley (p151)

KARL LEHMANN

JOHN BORT

Hike your way to the clifftops above Green Sands
Beach (p219)

ANN CECIL

Thrill seekers can trek to the snowcapped peaks of
Mauna Kea (p137) and Mauna Loa (p144)

Watch the sun slide majestically into the ocean at Pu'uhonua o Honaunau National Historical Park (p100)

Amble around the easily accessible Akaka Falls State Park (p158)

Marvel at Puako's giant tide pools (p116), which provide a haven for prolific marine life and and live coral

ANN CECIL

Take in a traditional *kahiko* hula (p37)

ANN CECIL

Slurp on shave ice (p63) to beat the heat

Stroll through the tranquil Lili'uokalani Park (p167) in Hilo

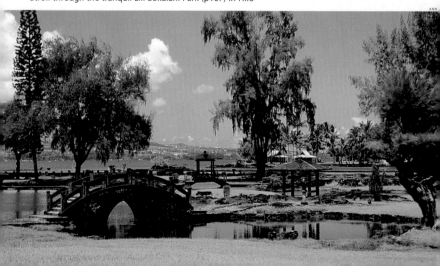

ANN

Contents

Lonely Planet books provide independent advice. Lonely Planet does not accept advertising in guidebooks, nor do we accept payment in exchange for listing or endorsing any place or business. Lonely Planet writers do not accept discounts or payments in exchange for positive coverage of any sort.

Regional Map Contents

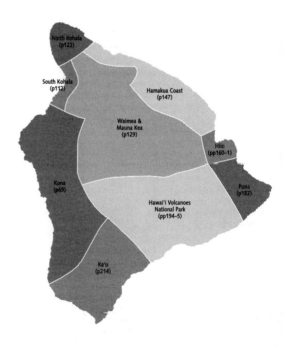
North Kohala (p122)
South Kohala (p112)
Hamakua Coast (p147)
Waimea & Mauna Kea (p129)
Hilo (pp160–1)
Kona (p69)
Puna (p182)
Hawai'i Volcanoes National Park (pp194–5)
Ka'u (p214)

The Authors

LUCI YAMAMOTO   Coordinating Author

Luci is a fourth-generation native of the Big Island. Having grown up in Hilo, she's not fazed by rain, pidgin or Hawaiian street names. After college in Los Angeles, she moved to Berkeley for law school and spent two summers working in Honolulu, contemplating practicing land-use law there. Ultimately she remained in California, where she's now a freelance writer. From childhood, she's known that Hawaii people are quite distinct from mainlanders and she remains fascinated by differences (and similarities) among cultures. Her writings on Hawaii culture have appeared in the *Honolulu Advertiser, San Francisco Chronicle, Threepenny Review* and *ascent*. At least once a year, she returns to Hilo, the only place she's ever called 'home.' For this book, Luci wrote the Destintaion: Hawai'i, Getting Started, Itineraries (West Hawai'i, Back to Nature, Just For Keiki), The Culture, Environment (National, State & County Parks), Food & Drink, Kona (Kailua-Kona, South Kona), South Kohala, North Kohala and Hilo chapters.

My Big Island

I first realized my hometown, Hilo (p159), was unusual when I lived in Illinois for six months and my third-grade teacher pronounced it 'high-low.' Over the years I've grown to appreciate Hilo's low-key charm, and now it's my favorite Big Island base. The climate is balmy (with many sunny days, believe me!), the farmers'-market papayas are incomparable, and Hilo remains largely devoid of tourists. After a day strolling downtown (p169) and picnicking at Lili'uokalani Park (p167), I guarantee you'll swear that time passes more slowly here. Take day or overnight trips to Hawai'i Volcanoes National Park (p192), Waipi'o Valley (p151) and Waimea (p129). For sun and sea, go snorkeling in Kona: Kahalu'u Beach Park (p86) is crowded but it's also convenient with easy, walk-in access. Offshore, Kealakekua Bay State Historical Park (p94) is most popular but other, less-trafficked coves along the coast are accessible through tours (p96).

Waipi'o Valley · Waimea · Hilo · Kahalu'u Beach Park · Kealakekua Bay State Historical Park · Hawai'i Volcanoes National Park

ALAN TARBELL

Early jaunts to Kaua'i and O'ahu made for tropical dreams in Alan's formative years. Family history also played a role in shaping what would become a strong feeling of aloha for this California native. Stories of waterfalls, misty trails, cliff jumps and pounding surf sent Alan back on numerous occasions to visit friends and enjoy the true nature of Hawaii. This trip turned into a re-acquaintance with a lost love, and a fresh introduction to Big Island splendor. For this book, Alan wrote the Itineraries (East Hawai'i, Waterlogged, Land Ho), Hawai'i Outdoors, Kona (North Kona), Waimea & Mauna Kea, Hamakua Coast, Puna, Hawai'i Volcanoes National Park and Ka'u chapters.

CONTRIBUTING AUTHORS

Nanette Naioma Napoleon wrote the History chapter and the Language chapter. Nanette is a freelance researcher and writer from Kailua, O'ahu. She has written a daily history column for the *Honolulu Star-Bulletin* newspaper and currently writes historical features for the *'Oiwi Files*, a native-Hawaiian news journal. She is also the state's leading authority on historic graveyards.

Dr Scott Rowland wrote The Land section of the Environment chapter. Scott is a volcanologist in the Department of Geology & Geophysics at the University of Hawai'i at Mānoa. Born and raised in Honolulu, he has been studying and teaching about volcanoes for the past 20 years. As an avid outdoor volunteer, he also works to protect the beautiful Hawaiian ecosystem.

Dr Samuel M 'Ohukani'ōhi'a Gon III wrote the Wildlife and Environmental Issues sections in the Environment chapter. Sam is the Senior Scientist and Cultural Advisor for the Nature Conservancy of Hawai'i. With a PhD in zoology, he has been working in conservation biology in the Hawaiian Islands for 29 years, exploring every mountain of the archipelago. As a cultural practitioner, he is trained traditionally in native Hawaiian chant and protocol, and is deeply devoted to the land of his birth.

The Health chapter in this book is adapted from material written by Dr David Goldberg, who completed his training at Columbia-Presbyterian Medical Center in New York City. He is an infectious diseases specialist and the editor-in-chief of www.mdtravelhealth.com.

Getting Started

If you have a week, you can easily tour the entire island. For a brief island-hopping trip, stick either to east or west Hawai'i. Avoid the temptation to dash around the island in a madcap attempt to see everything. The island varies greatly from place to place, so if you have specific expectations, choose wisely and you won't be disappointed.

Hawai'i is a financial splurge only if you cannot live without chichi resorts and restaurants. Touring the island on a more-moderate budget is possible, especially if you plan in advance. Avoid paying rack rates by booking accommodations online.

WHEN TO GO

The Big Island climate is balmy year-round, so there is no off-season in terms of weather. It's cooler and rainier in winter (mid-December through March) than in summer (June through August), but both are relatively mild, with consistent trade winds.

A bigger consideration is the tourist season: the winter high season means higher prices for many hotels and condos, plus larger crowds at main attractions. The best times to visit are fall (September through early December) and spring (mid-April through June), when prices drop and summer vacationers are gone.

See climate charts (p225) for more information.

During major holidays like Thanksgiving, Christmas, and around the New Year (see p230) lodging vacancies are tight and prices a bit higher. But the busiest travel period on the Big Island falls around the annual Merrie Monarch Festival (p171), for which you must buy tickets four months in advance and book accommodations a year ahead. The annual Ironman Triathlon World Championship (p77) also means few vacancies and snarled traffic along the Kona Coast. For more on festivals and events, see p229.

COSTS & MONEY

Your minimum budget depends on your traveling style. If you sleep at hostels and eat plate lunches, you can stretch your dollars a fair way, but for a luxury jaunt in South Kohala the sky's the limit.

Not surprisingly, your airfare is the heftiest expense. Fares vary greatly, particularly from the US mainland, where you should expect to pay about

---

DON'T LEAVE HOME WITHOUT...

- Hiking boots or shoes, already broken in
- Top-quality, polarized sunglasses to stop glare atop Mauna Kea and offshore
- Checking on current visa requirements (p234), just in case
- A copy of your travel-insurance policy (p230)
- Lightweight rain gear for sudden downpours
- A wide-brimmed sunhat for shadeless treks across lava
- A sweatshirt for chilly evenings (think lots of layers)
- Binoculars for whale watching and birding, and flashlights for exploring lava tubes
- Snorkel gear if you're going to be underwater more than a day or two

$400 round trip from the west coast and $600 from the east coast. Inter-island flights cost about $100 one way, but online discounts are available (p236) and, as ever, timing is everything.

The Big Island's Hele-On Bus (p239) is quite limited and, frankly, you can't see Hawai'i properly without a car. Renting a car usually costs between $175 and $250 a week, plus taxes and fees. To visit Mauna Kea and other remote places, you'll need either to shell out more than $100 per day for a 4WD or to join a tour (a safer option if you're a novice 4WD driver).

Accommodations (p222) run the gamut: dorm beds cost under $20 and Spartan, motel-like rooms range from $45 to $55. Midrange condos, B&Bs and hotels start from $80 to $100 but typically cost around $125. For anything on the beach, expect to pay $200 nightly, while you're out $400 a night for the cheapest room at a top-end resort.

To cut costs, weekly and monthly condo rates are unbeatable. Better condos include a full kitchen, plus a washer and dryer. If you prefer the amenities of hotels or the personal touch of B&Bs, note that some extend discounts for multiple-night stays.

Since many grocery items are imported from the mainland, prices average 20% higher than on the mainland. Still, eating in is always cheaper than eating out. Fresh produce at farmers' markets can be a steal (like succulent papayas selling at $1 for four).

Many sights and activities are discounted (p228) for kids and seniors.

HOW MUCH?

Condo per night $100-150

Pound of 100%
Kona coffee $20

Gourmet 'Hawaiian
Regional Cuisine' dinner
for two $75+

Local phone call 50¢

Half-day snorkeling
tour $80-100

**LONELY PLANET
INDEX**

Gallon of gas $2.50

Liter of bottled water
$1.75

Bottle of Kona Brewing
Company's Longboard
Lager $1.75

Souvenir T-shirt $12

Local-style plate lunch $5

TRAVEL LITERATURE

For a good background on Hawaiian history, Gavan Daws's *Shoal of Time: A History of the Hawaiian Islands* is almost required reading (which is actually often the case for local high-school students). It covers the period from Captain Cook's arrival to statehood. For a personal account, read *Hawaii's Story by Hawaii's Queen* by Queen Lili'uokalani, which details the dastardly circumstances surrounding her 1893 overthrow.

Renowned artist-historian Herb Kawainui Kane's gorgeous full-cover books, *Pele: Goddess of Hawaii's Volcanoes* and *Ancient Hawaii,* are also compelling introductions to Hawaiian culture.

The genre of Hawaii literature, written by locals, has hit the national radar since the 1990s. Hilo native Lois-Ann Yamanaka introduced pidgin to literary circles with her debut book of poetry, *Saturday Night at the Pahala Theatre,* winner of the 1993 Pushcart Prize for poetry. Her critically acclaimed novels, including *Wild Meat and the Bully Burgers* and *Heads by Harry,* depict 'real' island life, not romantic tales that merely use Hawaii as an exotic setting. Highly recommended as an introduction to local literature is *Growing Up Local: An Anthology of Poetry and Prose from Hawai'i,* a compendium that captures both the pidgin vernacular and local perspectives. The book is widely used in high school, college and university classes on multi-ethnic literature. For more on Hawaii literature, see p37.

To learn more about modern-day island life, *Things Hawaii* by Carrie Ching is both encyclopedia and picture book, covering landmarks, trends and traditions that make the islands unique. Introduce children to the local scene with *hide & Seek in hawai'i: A picture game for keiki,* a stunningly photographed series of 'find-the-object' books by Jane Hopkins and Ian Gillespie.

If phrases like *da kine* and *stink eye* perplex you, a must-read is *Pidgin to da Max* (and its sequel, *Pidgin to da Max Hana Hou*) by Douglas Simonson, illustrated pidgin dictionaries guaranteed to make you laugh till you hurt.

TOP TENS

Festivals & Events

Game enough to brave crowds of tourists and locals alike? Visit during one of the island's main attractions and you're bound for an unforgettable experience. For more listings, see p229.

- Kona Brewers Festival (p77)
- Merrie Monarch Festival (p171)
- Hamakua Music Festival (p148)
- Big Island Hawaiian Music Festival (p171)
- Aloha Festival (p229)
- Hawai'i County Fair (p171)
- Ironman Triathlon World Championship (p77)
- Big Island Festival (p229)
- Kona Coffee Cultural Festival (p77)
- Waimea Ukulele & Slack Key Guitar Institute (p132)

Hidden Big Island

If you're seeking solitude, just veer off the main paths and you'll find an island almost all to yourself. A few destinations require a 4WD or a challenging hike.

- Hawai'i Volcanoes National Park (p206)
- Mo'okini Luakini Heiau (p123)
- Sushi Rock (p124)
- Hakalau Forest National Wildlife Refuge (p138)
- Hobbit House B&B (p218)
- Kekaha Kai State Park (p106)
- Bicycle tour (p59)
- Kona Village Resort (p107)
- Yoga Oasis (p187)
- Mauna Kea (p141) or Mauna Loa (p144 and p206)

Outdoor Activities

Whether your style is strenuous or languorous, the Big Island has an activity just right for you. For more ideas, see p50.

- Snorkeling, Kahalu'u Beach Park (p86)
- Hiking, Hawai'i Volcanoes National Park (p203)
- Kayaking, Kealakekua Bay State Historical Park (p97)
- Surfing, Honoli'i Beach Park (p167)
- Snorkeling, near Captain Cook (p95)
- Hiking, Waipi'o Valley (p152)
- Windsurfing, 'Anaeho'omalu Beach Park (p111)
- Scuba diving, off the Kona Coast (p75)
- Horseback riding, Waimea (p132) or North Kohala (p121)
- Golfing (p59)

INTERNET RESOURCES

Agricultural Tourism (www.hawaiiagtourism.com) Extensive listings of farms, ranches and tours, plus information on local agriculture.

Culture Hawaii (www.hawaii-culture.com) Ideal 'intro' site on Big Island towns, sights, culture and more, sponsored by the Hawaii Island Economic Development Board.

Hawaii Visitors & Convention Bureau (www.gohawaii.com/bigisland) The Hawaii Visitor & Convention Bureau site.

KonaWeb (www.konaweb.com) News, events and online forums on the entire Big Island.

LonelyPlanet.com (www.lonelyplanet.com) Succinct summaries on traveling to Hawaii.

Ulukau: The Hawaiian Electronic Library (www.ulukau.org) Online Hawaiian-to-English (and vice versa) dictionaries and key Hawaiian texts.

Itineraries

CLASSIC ROUTES

WEST HAWAI'I   Five Days

To explore the Kona Coast, you'll need a car. The main city is Kailua-Kona, a convenient hub. See Transportation (p235) before going on the road.

Starting in **Kailua-Kona** (p69), get your feet wet by snorkeling at **Kahalu'u Beach Park** (p74). Then go 'upcountry' to the **Holualoa art galleries** (p90).

The next morning head to Captain Cook and cruise to a crystal-clear cove such as **Kealakekua Bay State Historical Park** (p94). Watch the sunset from **Pu'uhonua o Honaunau** (p100), an ancient 'place of refuge.'

On day three, traverse the lava desert in **South Kohala** (p110) to reach a magnificent beach, such as **Kauna'oa Bay** (p117) or **Hapuna Beach State Recreation Area** (p117). End by trekking to the **Puako Petroglyph Preserve** (p115).

Explore *paniolo* (cowboy) country in **Waimea** (p129) the next day. Learn about Parker Ranch, the second-largest private landowner on the island, at the **Parker Ranch Museum & Historic Homes** (p131). Go horseback riding at **Dahana Ranch** (p132) and indulge at one of Waimea's renowned restaurants.

On day five, drive up scenic Hwy 250 through rolling pastureland to rural North Kohala. Visit **Mo'okini Luakini Heiau** (p123), poke around in tiny **Hawi** (p122) and **Kapa'au** (p125) and hike down **Pololu Valley** (p126).

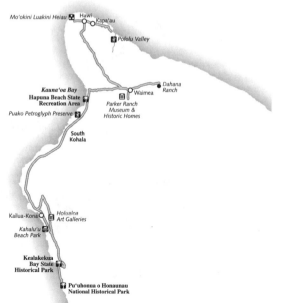

A journey through west Hawai'i includes lush coffee country, swaths of lava desert, mystical valleys – and, of course, any visitor's fantasy beaches. Starting and ending in Kailua-Kona, this 100-mile trip is feasible in five days, but deserves a week or more.

EAST HAWAI'I   One Week

Hilo (p159), Hawai'i's cultural center and windward port, makes a perfect hub. Start with the easternmost tip of the island by taking Hwy 11 to the coast, to enjoy laid-back **Pahoa** (p183). Catch the waves at **Pohoiki Bay** (p187) or snorkel at **Kapoho tide pools** (p187) and then relax in a **hot pond** (p187).

Continue to the southernmost point in the USA at **Ka Lae** (p219). Take a hike to **Green Sands Beach** (p219) or follow the isolated **Road to the Sea** (p221) and stay in a unique **rural B&B** (p217). On your way back north view sea turtles at **Punalu'u Beach Park** (p215).

On the way back to Hilo spend a couple of days at **Hawai'i Volcanoes National Park** (p192). Visit **Kilauea Caldera** (p197), summit of the world's most active volcano. Hike the **Kilauea Iki Trail** (p204) for a taste of the park's varied climate or hike to see the active **P'u 'O'o vent** (p206). Then go to the end of **Chain of Craters Rd** (p201) for the possibility of glimpsing flowing lava.

Pass through Hilo again for a meal and a movie at the classic **Palace Theatre** (p177) or **Kress Cinemas** (p177). Be sure to venture atop the 13,796ft **Mauna Kea** (p141) for the world's clearest stargazing. Then head up the Hamakua Coast, driving the **Pepe'ekeo 4-mile scenic drive** (p158) on your way to the impressive **Akaka Falls** (p158). Stay in an **ocean view B&B** (p148) before checking out majestic **Waipi'o Valley** (p151).

From rugged black- and green-sand beaches to smooth flowing lava, from desert solitude to towering waterfalls, from volcanically heated hot ponds to sub-arctic cinder cones...all included there are close to 200 miles of back roads that demonstrate the hidden gems on this windward coast. In one week it's easy to get distracted, but you'll never be bored!

TAILORED TRIPS

BACK TO NATURE

Start an ecotour in South Kona, where you can share the sea with *honu* (green sea turtles) at **Kahalu'u Beach Park** (p86). Visit the **Amy BH Greenwell Ethnobotanical Garden** (p92) to see traditional Hawaiian flora and the **Original Hawaiian Chocolate Factory** (p87) for the only 100% Hawaiian cacao. Stay at **Rainbow Plantation B&B** (p92), a tropical 'Old MacDonald's farm,' or at **Cedar House** (p98), a coffee plantation. Visit during the **Kona Coffee Cultural Festival** (p77) to tour farms, watch coffee-bean picking and more.

Down in Ka'u, stay at **Macadamia Meadows B&B** (p218) for a free guided tour of an 8-acre mac-nut farm. Head up to **Hawai'i Volcanoes National Park** (p192) and walk along **Devastation Trail** (p201) to see nature's power to destroy and to renew. Keep your eyes peeled for nene, the state bird (frequently seen at the Volcano golf course). In Hilo, forage at the vibrant **farmers' market** (p166) and visit **Hawaii Tropical Botanical Garden** (p158), featuring plants introduced by Westerners.

Ascend **Mauna Kea** (p137), where a colony of astronomical observatories juxtaposes pristine nature and modern science. See the vast Big Island ranchland by **horseback riding** in North Kohala (p121) or in Waimea (p132). Or envision sugarcane-plantation life by **'fluming'** (p124) the old irrigation canals.

JUST FOR KEIKI

It's impossible for *keiki* (children) to be bored on the Big Island, a giant playground. In Hilo, picnic at **Lili'uokalani Park** (p167) and walk across a bridge to **Mokuola (Coconut Island)** (p167). Indulge in **ice shave** (p175) and teach toddlers to swim at **Onekahakaha Beach Park** (p167). Visit during the **Hawai'i County Fair** (p172), featuring carnival rides, game booths and local concession food.

Along the Hamakua Coast, the **World Botanical Gardens Children's Maze** (p156) will fascinate tykes (under 5ft tall!) into finding that one way out.

In Hawai'i Volcanoes National Park, walk through a 'spooky' **lava tube** (p200) and peer into the spectacular Kilauea Caldera. Another adventure for budding scientists is **star gazing** (p141) atop Mauna Kea. Nearby in Puna, dunk in a **thermal pool** (p187) and explore the **Kapoho tide pools** (p187).

For ocean sports, head to Kona and snorkel at **Kahalu'u Beach Park** (p86), safe, shallow and teeming with marine life. Older kids can kayak in the **Kealakekua Bay State Historical Park** (p94) or boogie board at **White Sands Beach Park** (p74). In Waikoloa, you can guarantee an up-close **dolphin encounter** (p112).

In rural North Kohala go **horseback riding** (p121) and hike down **Pololu Valley** (p126). Or, try a retro kid pastime of **'fluming'** (p124) in old irrigation canals, a slow but splashy ride.

WATERLOGGED

Hawai'i's opposing coasts offer a different twist for the water lover. For a calm, clear ocean to dive and snorkel try **Kealakekua Bay State Historical Park** (p95) on the Kona Coast. Another thrilling option is a night dive to see **manta rays** (p75). Being on the leeward side, sun worshipers can bask on white sand beaches and swim in protected coves at **Kauna'oa Beach** (p117) or **Kekaha Kai State Park** (p106). Those who follow the swell, surf's up at **Pine Trees** (p105) or **Banyans** (p75), two local favorites. Fisherfolk and kay-

akers, they do not call this the Gold Coast for nothing: anywhere is game!

The windward side has more fresh-water options, like a swim among cascading water falls on the **Umauma Stream** (p157) on the Hamakua Coast, or a relaxing soak at the **hot pond** (p187) in Puna. The ocean on the east side has adventurous surf at the **Kolekole** (p156) river mouth in North Hilo and reef at **Pohoiki Bay** (p187) in Puna.

LAND HO

With sweltering tropical climes, lava cliffs, desert expanses, coastal valleys, steep gulches and sub-arctic moonscapes, Hawai'i's vast number of microclimates is impressive and easy to access. In Hawai'i Volcanoes National Park hike the **Mauna Loa Trail** (p205) to the top of the world's most massive mountain, or head to the coast and camp at **Halape Shelter** (p208), a secluded cove flanked by lava cliffs and basking sea turtles.

On the Hamakua Coast intrepid hikers can overnight to hidden waterfalls and sacred backcountry beaches in **Waimanu Valley** (p153). Day hike from the **Kohala Forest Reserve** (p136) to the back of **Waipi'o Valley** (p152) or explore the valley floor on horseback.

Waimea is cowboy country, so explore the Hawaiian plains on horseback at **Parker Ranch** (p131) and learn from the famous *paniolo.*

The North Kona Coast follows secluded white-sand beaches, fresh-water oases and exposed lava shore from **'Anaeho'omalu Bay** (p111) to **Keawaiki Beach** (p108).

A walk in the wind at **Ka Lae** (p219) will tell you of the harsh climate that was endured by the early Hawaiians. Mountain-bike down the **Road to the Sea** (p221) or to **Green Sands Beach** (p219).

Snapshot

While tourists and transplants marvel at the Big Island's natural wonders, locals sense the island changing, for better or worse. Tourism remains the island's most profitable revenue source, coming primarily from visitors to the balmy Kona Coast. While the income-generating power of the luxury resorts is appreciated, some locals are dismayed at the rampant commercial development of the island's primo land.

For years, sugar was the largest agricultural industry on the Big Island, but the economy stagnated after its demise (for more information see p26). Today, diversified agriculture is the norm, and crops include coffee, macadamia, anthurium, orchid and papaya, plus vanilla, mushroom, *kalo* (taro) and cocoa.

The most high-tech addition to the island's economy is astronomy. With 13 state-of-the-art telescopes atop Mauna Kea, the Big Island is losing its sleepy, backwoods image. Indeed, the Mauna Kea Astronomy Education Center (p163), launched in 2005, is anticipated to become the island's number-two tourist attraction (after Hawai'i Volcanoes National Park).

As the population booms, especially along the Kona Coast and in Puna, the Big Island now knows the meaning of daily gridlock. The worst stretch, along the Queen Ka'ahumanu Hwy, only points out the problem: locals cannot afford houses close to their jobs, especially along the Kona Coast. The price of real estate is fast becoming out of reach for average locals. But to transplants from places like San Francisco and New York, the Big Island remains quite a bargain. Indeed, the latest newcomers are wealthy mainland transplants – 'gentleman farmers' and second-home millionaires.

More people also means increased environmental threats, such as the introduction of invasive species. Since the 2000s the coqui frog from Puerto Rico has proliferated wildly, becoming an ecological menace, with its deafening shriek and appetite for insects and spiders, and spurring clearing of foliage (p185).

Politically, Hawaii is a middle-of-the-road Democratic state; voters and legislators generally support progressive causes, but they've so far nixed legalized gambling, euthanasia and same-sex marriage. Republicans are gaining in prominence, however, and voters in 2002 elected a Republican governor, Linda Lingle (who's also the state's first female and Jewish governor). On the whole, sexual orientation is a nonissue, but many gays and lesbians remain closeted and there are pockets of extreme conservatives in the islands, especially in rural areas. In 1998, Hawaii made national headlines when a whopping 70% of voters passed a measure granting the legislature, not the courts, the power to define marriage – essentially advocating the prohibition of same-sex marriage.

In 2005, Senator Daniel Akaka's long-stalled Native Hawaiian Government Reorganization Act, to establish a native Hawaiian governing body, was set to reach the US Senate floor. Pushed by Hawaii's two longstanding senators, Akaka and Daniel Inouye, both Democrats, the bill is also supported by the Office of Hawaiian Affairs and almost all state politicians. But some prominent native Hawaiians vehemently oppose the bill, charging that it cedes too much power to the US government. This conflict illustrates that native Hawaiians are not a single, cohesive group but rather a diverse community, adding another layer to Hawaii's multiculturalism.

FAST FACTS

Population: 158,000

Residents born in state of Hawaii: 63%

Median household income: US$40,000

Unemployment rate: 5%

Miles of coastline: 266

Land area: 4028 sq mi

Visitors annually to Hawai'i Volcanoes National Park: 2.4 million

Average work commute, Hilo residents: 18 min

Average work commute, Hawaiian Ocean View Estates residents: 60 min

History

ANCIENT HAWAI'I

Ancient Sites of Hawaii, by Van James, is an in-depth survey of ancient temples, shrines, petroglyphs, fishponds, and other historic sites.

Hawai'i is the northern point of the huge triangle of Pacific Ocean islands known as Polynesia, which means 'many islands.' The other two points of the triangle are Rapa Nui (Easter Island) to the southeast and Aotearoa (New Zealand) to the southwest. Island cultures within this region share many similarities of language, religious beliefs, social structure, legends, myths, musical traditions and tools.

The exact origins of the first settlers in Hawai'i is unknown. Whether they had their roots in Southeast Asia, as has been thought traditionally, or whether they originated in Melanesia, as archaeologists now believe, is a matter of ongoing debate. Either way, their eastward migratory path took them to the southern Polynesian islands of Tonga and Samoa in about 1000 BC. Over the next 1500 years, they migrated to more far-flung areas of Polynesia, with Hawai'i being the last region settled.

Hawaii Island Legends: Piikoi, Pele and Others, by Mary Kawena Pukui and Caroline Curt, is suitable to read to young children or for independent reading by older children and adults.

Even though the early Hawaiian explorers did not know for sure if they would find new islands to settle, they bravely traversed more than 2000 miles of open ocean aboard large, double-hulled voyaging canoes with sails, bringing along many plants and animals – and dreams for a new future.

Once the islands were settled, the Hawaiian people and culture flourished in isolation from the rest of the world for more than 1500 years, until the coming of the first European explorers in the late 18th century.

KAMEHAMEHA THE GREAT

Kamehameha I, 'The Lonely One,' was born in Kohala on the Big Island sometime around 1753. It is said that when he was born a comet appeared in the sky, interpreted by *kahuna* (priests) to mean that he would later be a threat to the ruling chiefs. Because of this his parents sent him away to be raised, to protect him from harm.

Kamehameha grew into a strong warrior and respected leader under the guidance of his powerful uncle, chief Kalaniopu'u. As a teen, Kame-

HOKULE'A: STAR OF GLADNESS

Until about three decades ago, most anthropologists did not think it was possible for ancient people from the western Pacific to make long-distance ocean journeys, since ocean voyaging by most Europeans did not begin until the 15th century with the aid of navigational equipment such as sextons, chronometers and other instruments for plotting and mapping.

This prevailing theory was shattered in 1976 when the Polynesian Voyaging Society, based in Honolulu, launched the *Hokule'a*, a modern reproduction of an ancient Hawaiian voyaging canoe. The *Hokule'a* made a 4800-mile return voyage to Tahiti using only traditional Polynesian navigational aids such as the sun, the moon and the stars, wind directions, ocean current systems, and cloud and wave patterns.

Today the *Hokule'a*, which has sailed more than 100,000 miles on eight major voyages across the Pacific, has become an important symbol of cultural pride for Hawaiians and other Pacific Islanders.

TIMELINE

1778	1779
Captain James Cook, the first Westerner to 'discover' Hawai'i, lands	Captain Cook killed at Kealakekua Bay on the south Kona Coast

hameha was allegedly able to lift the Naha Stone (p167), thereby fulfilling a prophecy that the man who could move this great monolith, originally cut for the tomb of 15th-century chief 'Umi, would ultimately rule the land. As a young man, Kamehameha was with his uncle at Kealakekua Bay in 1779 during the battle with Captain Cook (p96), in which Cook was killed and Kamehameha learned the strategic value of Western firearms.

Before he died in 1782, Kalaniopu'u designated Kamehameha to be the next guardian of the sacred feather idol representing the war god Kukailimoku (Ku), which was a great honor. Still, for the next eight years, Kamehameha fought for supremacy over the Big Island, finally winning out in 1790. Next he set his sights on the island of Maui.

In 1791, on the advice of his priests, Kamehameha built a massive *luakini heiau* (sacrificial temple) at Kawaihae (p118), in the district of Kohala, called Pu'ukohola ('Whale Hill'). There he prayed and sacrificed several of his enemies to gain the support of the great war god Ku. With the belief that Ku was at his side, Kamehameha departed the Big Island with a fleet of war canoes – some mounted with Western cannons – to battle Kahekili, the ruler of Maui and O'ahu. The two forces fought one of the largest battles in Hawaiian history, after which Kahekili was forced to retreat to O'ahu.

Kamehameha prepared his forces for an all-out assault on O'ahu. While Kamehameha was still on Maui, Kahekili died at Waikiki and rule of that island went to his son, Kalanikapule. In 1795, Kamehameha invaded O'ahu in a bloody campaign that started at the shore at Waikiki and ended several days later on a ridge in the Ko'olau mountain range at Nu'uanu, where hundreds of Kalanikapule's warriors were pushed to their death over the towering cliffs. Although Kalanikapule survived the battle, control of the island went to Kamehameha.

Not wanting to stop there, Kamehameha prepared to invade Kaua'i, which was under the rule of Kaumuali'i. Over the next six years, Kamehameha mounted two campaigns against Kaua'i, the first ending when most of his fleet was lost at sea during a violent channel crossing and the second when most of his warriors died from a devastating plague. Although Kamehameha never took Kaua'i by force, Kaumuali'i, seeing that he would not be able to hold off Kamehameha forever, ceded the island to him in 1810, making Kamehameha the *mo'i* (ruling chief) of all the islands.

For nine years while Kamehameha ruled over the islands, the Kingdom of Hawai'i (as the island group was now called) was at relative peace. Kamehameha I established his royal court on Maui at Lahaina (where it remained until 1845, when King Kamehameha III moved the capital to Honolulu on O'ahu). In 1819 he died at his Kamakahonu home in Kailua-Kona (see p73). As tradition demanded, his body was entrusted to two loyal chiefs who buried him in a secret place so rivals couldn't rob the grave to obtain his bones, which were believed to have great *mana* (spiritual power). Nobody knows where Kamehameha's bones are resting, but most speculate that his burial place is somewhere in Kohala, near Kapa'au (p125).

Kamehameha the Great, by Julie Stewart Williams, is a well-researched and written account of the life of this great king. Not too scholarly, not too lightweight – just right.

www.kohala.net/historic /mookini/ Learn more about Mo'okini Luakini Heiau in Kohala, one of the most important ancient temples in Hawai'i.

THE FOREIGN INVASION
The Explorers

In July of 1776, Captain James Cook of the British Navy set out on his third voyage to the Pacific in search of the elusive Northwest Passage,

1790	1793
Kamehameha I wins control of the Big Island	Captain George Vancouver introduces horses and cattle to the island

which reputedly ran from the northern Pacific across the North American continent to the Atlantic. Quite by accident, on January 18, 1778, Cook and his crews aboard the HMS *Resolution* and *Discovery* sighted the islands of O'ahu, Maui, Kaua'i and Ni'ihau, thus becoming the first Westerners to 'discover' the islands.

Cook promptly named the Hawaiian archipelago the Sandwich Islands in honor of his patron, the Earl of Sandwich. Cook made his first landing at Waimea on the island of Kaua'i. Coincidently, this occurred at the time of year when the Hawaiians celebrated the *makahiki*, the annual festival honoring the great god Lono. Cook was seen as the *kinolau*, or earthly manifestation of the god, and he and his crews were welcomed with open arms.

How 'Natives' Think: About Captain Cook, for Example, by Marshall Sahlins, is a controversial look at recent ethnohistorical interpretations of Captain Cook's death in Hawaii.

Tragically, 13 months later, while at Kealakekua Bay on the Big Island, Cook, along with some of his crew and many Hawaiians, was killed in a battle spawned by growing tensions between the two groups (see p96). After Cook's ships returned to Great Britain without him, news of his discovery quickly spread throughout Europe and the Americas, opening the floodgates to a foreign invasion of other explorers, traders, adventurers, missionaries and fortune seekers.

The next explorer to have an impact on the islands was Captain George Vancouver, who sailed with Captain Cook on his second and third voyages. In 1789, Vancouver was appointed to head another voyage to the Pacific to take up where Cook had left off searching for the Northwest Passage. During the course of his Pacific explorations, Vancouver visited Hawai'i three times in the 1790s.

On his second visit in 1793, his ships brought beef cattle, horses and sheep, as well as goats and geese. Because they were designated *kapu* (off limits) for 10 years, the animals thrived, but the landscape they inhabited did not. Unrestricted grazing upset the delicate balance of the ecosystem, leading to deforestation, erosion and the extinction of many native plants and birds.

With the introduction of cattle and horses to the Big Island, ranching emerged as the economic mainstay. Long before American cowboys roamed the west, Hawaiian *paniolo* (cowboys) were ranching on the Big Island. Numerous ranches were established during the 19th century. The largest of these is Parker Ranch (p131), founded in 1847 by John Palmer Parker, which includes 175,000 acres of lush pasture lands and tropical forests. It is one of the largest ranches in the USA.

DID YOU KNOW?

It takes seven years for a macadamia nut tree to produce edible nuts.

The China Trade Route

Like their explorer counterparts, the American, British, French and Russian merchant traders – who began arriving in the islands in the late 18th century – had different ideas about the value of the islands to themselves and their home countries. For them, Hawai'i became a key factor in the development of the China trade route. Traders typically picked up furs on the Pacific Northwest coast of America and sandalwood in Hawai'i, then traded them in China for exotic spices, silk cloth and furniture, which in turn commanded high prices in their European home ports.

'Iliahi, or sandalwood, a tree with highly fragrant heart wood, was abundant in the Hawaiian islands prior to the arrival of Westerners. The

1810	1820
Kamehameha the Great completes the unification of the islands and becomes king	First missionaries to Hawai'i arrive at Kailua Bay

Hawaiians used it to scent *kapa* (bark cloth), but it was not harvested on a wide-scale basis. Once news of this coveted tree reached America and Europe, traders flocked to the islands to fill their ships with the precious and highly profitable wood. To meet the demand, many chiefs ordered their people to leave their work in the taro fields and fishing areas to harvest the trees in the upland forests, a laborious task that required many man hours of back-breaking work. Some chiefs sold their trees for items the islands did not have, such as iron nails and weapons, while other chiefs traded them for cold, hard cash. Because of greed on the part of both Hawaiians and traders, native sandalwood trees were all but wiped out and many farming areas were left in ruins, never to recover.

'Thar She Blows!'

Like the 19th-century traders, whalers found Hawai'i to be the perfect mid-ocean waystation. Here they could transfer their catch to trade ships bound primarily for the eastern seaboard of America. Pausing in the islands allowed them to stay in the Pacific for longer periods of time without having to return home with their payload, resulting in greater catches during the whaling season and higher profits.

By the 1840s, Hawai'i had become the whaling capital of the Pacific, with hundreds of ships stopping in island ports each year. Although migrating whales are still abundant in Big Island waters, the mostly rocky shores prevented most whaling ships from establishing ports on the island.

DID YOU KNOW?

Parker Ranch in Kohala is one of the largest ranches in the USA.

Soul Savers

On April 19, 1820, the brig Thaddeus, out of Boston, arrived at Kailua Bay on the Big Island with the first group of Christian missionaries, who were Protestant. By a twist of fate, these missionaries arrived just 11 months after the death of King Kamehameha I, an event that had precipitated the overthrow of the traditional kapu system of religious laws, resulting in a great upheaval of Hawaiian society.

Into this religious chaos came missionaries, who were determined to save the natives from themselves. They prohibited the dancing of hula because of its 'lewd and suggestive' movements. They prohibited most of the traditional Hawaiian chants and songs because they paid homage to 'heathen' gods. They taught the women to sew Western-style clothing so they could cover their mostly naked bodies. And the missionaries abolished polygamy, despite the fact that it was accepted – and necessary – in the isolated island group.

The missionaries were zealous in their efforts to teach Hawaiians how to read and write, and they built as many schools as they did churches.

SAFE HARBOR FOR WHALES

Before the arrival of Westerners, Hawaiians did not hunt whales, but they did salvage the bones from dead or sick whales that washed ashore to make jewelry, spearheads and fishing lures. Pu'ukohola Heiau in Kawaihae (p118) translates as 'whale hill,' referring to the shape of the hill itself or possibly to the fact that this site has a great view of the ocean where whales can often be seen swimming close to shore.

1828	**1838**
First coffee trees planted on the island	Hulihe'e Palace built by Governor Kuakini

As the Hawaiians had no written language, the missionaries established one using the Roman alphabet, allowing them to translate the Bible. Hawaiians took these reading lessons in great numbers, leading to a higher literacy rate in the islands than on the US mainland at that time.

Outside of their church duties, many missionaries became influential advisors to the monarchs and were granted large tracts of land in return. Many missionary families left the church altogether to turn their land into sugar plantations or to start other enterprises. It is often said that the missionaries came to do good – and did very well.

The Rise of King Sugar

In the 1840s, sugar growing began to emerge as a second economic force behind whaling in Hawai'i, and the Big Island played a major role in the development of this industry. At its height in 1936, the island had 16 sugar mills that provided 34% of the total sugar produced throughout the kingdom.

The first sugar plantation to be established on the island was the Kohala Sugar Company, started in 1863 by Reverend Elias Bond, who wanted to create employment for the Hawaiians who were leaving the island in large numbers in search of better opportunities on Maui and O'ahu. Many other plantations and mills soon followed.

The last surviving company was the Ka'u Agribusiness Company (formerly Ka'u Sugar Company), which closed its doors in 1996. Rising US labor costs versus cheaper labor markets in Mexico and the Philippines led to the industry's demise. Remnants of Hawai'i's sugar days can still be seen in abandoned mills, railroad trellises, cane-haul roads and rural plantation towns that dot the landscape of the Big Island.

THE MONARCHY ERA

Throughout the monarchy period (1810–93), the ruling sovereigns of Hawai'i fought off continual efforts by European and American settlers to gain control of the kingdom. In 1836, the French threatened to take over if the persecution of the Catholics by the ali'i (chiefs) didn't end. The chiefs, led by Queen Ka'ahumanu (wife of Kamehameha I), had been strongly influenced by the Protestants, the first missionaries to arrive in the islands, who had become close advisors to the royal inner circle. In 1843, the British naval captain Lord George Paulet succeeded in taking

---

KING SUGAR

Ko (sugarcane) arrived in Hawai'i with the early Polynesian settlers. While Hawaiians enjoyed chewing the cane for its juices, they never refined it into sugar. The first known attempt to produce sugar in Hawai'i was in 1802, when a Chinese immigrant on the island of Lana'i boiled crushed sugarcane in iron pots. Other Chinese immigrants soon set up small sugar mills on the scale of neighborhood bakeries. In 1835, a young Bostonian, William Hooper, founded the islands' first sugar plantation, Koloa Plantation on Kaua'i, which operated for 113 years. By 1850, the number of plantations in Hawai'i had grown to seven, and the industry was beginning to take off. Less than four decades later, there were 80 plantations in the islands and 'King Sugar' was the backbone of the Hawaiian economy.

1863	**1881**
Kohala Sugar Company, the island's first sugar plantation, is founded	First macadamia nut farm established in Honoka'a

over the kingdom, but this action was rescinded within six months by Admiral Richard Thomas, who concluded that Paulet had acted without the authority of the crown.

In 1848, because of pressure from foreign residents who wanted to own their own land, a sweeping land reform act called the Great Mahele was instituted. This act allowed, for the first time, the fee simple ownership of land. Each island had been divided into several large districts, with each district subdivided into smaller pie-shaped wedges of land called *ahupua'a* that ran from the top of the mountains to the sea. The chiefs had not owned the land, in the Western sense, but were considered to be the caretakers of the land and the people who lived there.

The reforms of the Great Mahele had far-reaching implications. For foreigners, who had money to buy land, this meant greater economic and political power. For Hawaiians, who had little or no money, this meant a loss of land-based self-sufficiency and forced entry into the low-wages labor market, primarily run by Westerners.

Because of the economic stranglehold of King Sugar, virtually all of the planters (who were mostly US citizens) became highly influential in the business community and government circles. These 'sugar barons' made concerted efforts to bring the independent kingdom of Hawai'i into the political and economic sphere of the USA, which would greatly enhance their bottom line. In 1876, the planters successfully lobbied the USA to ratify a reciprocity treaty, which allowed sugar from Hawai'i to enter the USA duty-free.

On January 17, 1893, a group of sugar planters intent on annexation, supported by both the US minister in the islands and a small contingent of US marines aboard a visiting warship, forcibly arrested Queen Lili'uokalani and took over 'Iolani Palace in Honolulu on O'ahu, resulting in a tense but bloodless coup d'état against the kingdom.

In 1895, while annexation was debated in Washington, a group of Hawaiian royalists attempted a counterrevolution, which was quashed. The deposed queen was accused of being a conspirator and sentenced to five years of hard labor, later reduced to nine months under house arrest at 'Iolani Palace and a $5000 fine. After serving her term, Lili'uokalani lived out her days at her husband's family home. Although she continued to lobby for the restoration of the monarchy, her efforts were in vain. She died in 1917, a tragic but heroic figure to the Hawaiian people and other supporters.

DID YOU KNOW?

In 1993 more than 10,000 native Hawaiians attended protest ceremonies at 'Iolani Palace in observance of the 100th anniversary of the overthrow of the Kingdom of Hawai'i.

ANNEXATION, WORLD WAR II & STATEHOOD

Although annexation had been sought by factions of resident foreigners since the 1870s, it was not until April 1898, when the USA declared war on Spain to redress the Spanish occupation of Cuba and the Philippines, that Hawai'i, in particular Pearl Harbor, became a strategic military focal point in the Pacific. With the tide of 'Manifest Destiny' still in motion, the USA easily rationalized its colonial presence in the Pacific Rim and Asia. However, even with annexation a fait accompli, the next logical push, for statehood, would be a long and arduous one.

In 1897, as a protest of the queen's overthrow and the application for annexation, more than 21,000 people – almost half of the population of

1898	1946
Republic of Hawai'i formally annexed by the USA	Tsunami hits the island, killing 61 people and destroying dozens of buildings in Hilo

Nation Within: The Story of America's Annexation of the Nation of Hawaii (2003), by Tom Coffman, provides compelling historic details about the overthrow of the Hawaiian monarchy, annexation and the drive for statehood.

Hawai'i at that time – signed an anti-annexation petition that was sent to Washington. Despite this overwhelming show of support for home rule, President William McKinley signed a joint Congressional resolution approving the annexation of the five-year-old Republic of Hawai'i on July 7, 1898.

Between 1900, when Hawai'i became a territory, and 1959 when Hawaii was finally declared a state, numerous statehood bills were introduced in Congress, only to be shot down. One of the primary reasons for this lack of support was racial prejudice against Hawai'i's multicultural population. Congress also thought that Hawai'i's remote location in the middle of the Pacific Ocean would make it almost impossible to conduct essential government business in a timely and efficient manner. Hawai'i's growing labor unions were a further cause for concern.

Several historical events helped to turn the tide in favor of statehood in Congress. In 1936, Pan American airlines launched the first commercial flights from the US mainland to Hawai'i, an aviation milestone that ushered in the transpacific air age and the beginning of mass tourism. The installation of wireless telegraph and, later, telephone service between Hawai'i and the mainland also put the territory in a better position for statehood. But it was the strategic military role of Pearl Harbor in WWII and the Korean War, and the heroism shown by Americans of Japanese ancestry in those wars, that was probably the impetus for statehood.

http://starbulletin
.com/1999/10/18/special
/story4.html
Photos enhance this feature story published by the *Honolulu Star-Bulletin* about Hawaii's long road to statehood.

On August 21, 1959, Hawaii was officially admitted to the union as its 50th state.

HAWAIIAN RENAISSANCE

In the early 1970s, Hawai'i began to experience a resurgence of Hawaiian cultural pride and ethnic identity, not seen since the reign of King Kalakaua in the 1880s. It is difficult to pinpoint a single event or activity that caused this, but the building of the long-distance voyaging canoe, *Hokule'a* (p22),

PEARL HARBOR ATTACKED

The surprise attack on Pearl Harbor and other military installations on the island of O'ahu on December 7, 1941, will always be remembered as the 'day of infamy' in US history. On that quiet Sunday morning, 354 Japanese aircraft, launched from six aircraft carriers stationed 230 miles north of O'ahu, invaded Hawai'i, killing more than 2000 US military personnel and 48 civilians. This devastating attack propelled the USA into the Pacific theater of WWII against Japan.

Unlike the US mainland, Hawai'i was placed under Marshall Law and actions 'vital to national security' were initiated. Many of Hawai'i's beaches were lined with barbed wire to prevent the Japanese troop landings via submarines. About 300 to 400 Japanese residents in Hawai'i were arrested as enemy sympathizers and sent to mainland interment camps, some for the duration of the war. Although the Japanese community, many of whom were born and raised in the islands and were loyal US supporters, vehemently protested this action, their protests fell on deaf ears.

Hundreds of men of Japanese ancestry enlisted in the US armed forces, forming the all-Japanese 442nd Regimental Combat Team and 100th Infantry Battalion (both of which comprised mostly soldiers from Hawai'i), which became the most highly decorated unit of its size in US military history. This went a long way toward changing mainstream American attitudes toward the resident Japanese population, both in the territory and on the mainland.

1959	1960
Hawaii becomes the 50th state of the USA	Another tsunami hits the island, killing 159 people and destroying more than 1000 buildings

---

HAWAIIAN HOME LANDS

In 1920, under the sponsorship of Prince Jonah Kuhio Kalaniana'ole, the Territory of Hawai'i's Congressional delegate, the US Congress passed the Hawaiian Homes Commission Act. The act set aside almost 200,000 acres of land for homesteading by native Hawaiians, a small fraction of the crown lands that were taken from the Kingdom of Hawai'i when the USA annexed the islands in 1898.

Under the legislation, people of at least 50% Hawaiian ancestry were eligible for 99-year leases at the rate of $1 a year. Originally, most of the leases were for 40-acre parcels of agricultural land. Hawai'i's prime land, already in the hands of the sugar barons, was excluded from the act. Much of what was designated for homesteading was on far more barren turf. Still, many Hawaiians were able to make a go of it.

Presently, there are about 6500 native Hawaiian families living on about 30,000 acres of homestead lands. As with many projects intended to help native Hawaiians, administration of the Hawaiian Home Lands has been controversial. The majority of the land has not been allocated to native Hawaiians but instead has been leased out to big business, ostensibly as a means of creating an income for the administration of the program; in reality, most of these revenues go into the state general fund.

In 2003, after years of lobbying, State Senate Bill 476 was enacted, mandating the state to pay the Office of Hawaiian Affairs an amount equivalent to the pro-rata share of ceded land-lease revenues obtained from Honolulu International Airport. Revenues from other homestead lands being leased out are still in dispute.

---

was a catalyst. This project required the learning of ancient navigational skills and sailing techniques that had been nearly forgotten.

Simultaneously, concern by a small group of people throughout the islands about development cutting off access to traditional gathering grounds led to the formation of the Protect Kaho'olawe 'Ohana (PKO), which protested the US Navy's target practice on the nonpopulated island of Kaho'olawe. The 'Ohana rapidly gained local and national support, partly by invoking a lawsuit against the federal government, and became a focal point of political awareness and activism.

From the Skies of Paradise: Maui, by Douglas Peebles, provides stunning aerial photographs, historical information and a look at contemporary community life.

Greater interest in the hula also began to be seen in the 1970s, especially among young men. New hula *halau* (schools) began to open, many of which revived interest in ancient hula techniques and dances that had been subjugated in favor of more modern, Western-style hula dances. The Merrie Monarch Festival (p171), which takes place in Hilo on the Big Island, has become the Olympics of hula and has an international following. Today, there are many hula festivals on all of the islands, featuring dozens of hula *halau* and thousands of dancers of all ages.

Revival of the Hawaiian language has also been a focal point of the Hawaiian renaissance. By the 1970s, the pool of native Hawaiian speakers had dropped to under 1000 individuals statewide. In an effort to reverse this trend, Hawaiian-language immersion schools began to emerge. The University of Hawai'i began offering Hawaiian-language classes for the first time in the 1970s. In 2003 the university graduated its first student with a master's degree in Hawaiian-language studies.

www.lymanmuseum.org The official site of the Lyman Museum in Hilo lists current exhibits and special events.

Contemporary music has also been affected by the ongoing Hawaiian renaissance. There is interest in preserving old songs, particularly

1963
Merrie Monarch Hula Festival begins

1978
Ironman Triathlon starts in Kona

protest songs, as well as creating new compositions. Many people have also become interested in relearning nearly lost arts, such as the making of *kapa*, drums, gourds, feather lei, fish hooks, wooden bowls and other items. Some folks feel that if this renaissance had not occurred, Hawaiian language and culture would have been nearly extinct by now.

Recently there has also been a resurgence of interest in genealogy and in traditional ancestral connections. In 1990, the Native American Grave Repatriation Act, which allows claims for repatriation of designated human remains and artifacts from museums and other public repositories around the world, was enacted after considerable work on the part of various Hawaiians, Native American Indians and Native Alaskans. Statewide burial councils now oversee the disposition of human remains found during construction projects or land erosion.

Beginning in the early 1990s, the topic of Hawaiian sovereignty (or self-determination) has become a highly debated and controversial issue, not only for Hawaiians but for the general community as well. It has been a hot topic of media coverage, local meetings and household discussions. Many groups have formed, with differing ideas about what model of sovereignty, if any, should be adopted.

Eddie Would Go (2002), by Stuart Holmes Coleman, is a biography of notable professional surfer and lifeguard Eddie Aikau, including his tragic death. It describes the Hawaiian renaissance of the 1960s and '70s from a personal perspective.

1983	1996
Kilauea Volcano starts its latest eruption (which is still ongoing)	Last sugar mill closes on the island

The Culture

The Big Island occasionally endures an identity crisis. Yes, it's the *biggest* island, but it's neither the most populous nor the site of the state capital, Honolulu. Instead, the Big Island retains a rural and down-home flavor. Sure, it boasts the second-largest town statewide, the only Neighbor Island campus of the University of Hawai'i, swanky resorts and the gamut of big-box retailers. Sure, its two active volcanoes, premier astronomical site on Mauna Kea and vast stretches of undeveloped land attract scientists, environmentalists, farmers, investors and sightseers alike. But look for the heart of the island in the longtime locals.

REGIONAL IDENTITY

At first glance, being 'local' in Hawaii means talking pidgin and wearing a T-shirt and *rubbah slippah*. But underneath it's a mindset that comes from living 2500 miles from the nearest continent, in communities where everyone knows everyone. Here, family background and connections are important – not to be snooty, but to find common bonds. Especially in long-standing towns like Hilo, folks can't leave the house without bumping into long-ago schoolmates or a spouse's colleagues. Forget about anonymity!

But don't lump all locals in one category. Underlying a statewide identity are quirks particular to each island and town: Honolulu is 'big city' and much faster paced than any other place. Neighbor Islands have traditionally been considered the backward 'country,' if not *da boonies* (the boondocks). Hilo is considered a remote, leisurely, predominantly Japanese and rainy town. Indeed, compared to O'ahu people, Hilo people tend to dress more casually, talk more pidgin, wear less makeup, differentiate more between local and nonlocal, and fend off yuppie trends for a few years longer.

But everything is relative: on the Big Island itself, Hilo was traditionally considered 'town' and everyplace else, 'country.' Hilo people were assumed to be honest and hardworking (if rather staid), with college-bound kids attending the island's two top public high schools. Since the 1980s, however, Kona has risen to economic prominence and is now associated with new money, fun-loving transplants and travelers, expensive real

DID YOU KNOW?

In 1874 King David Kalakaua wrote 'Hawai'i Pono'i,' which in 1967 became Hawaii's state song (and the only state song not in English).

WHO'S WHO

Hawaiian People of native Hawaiian ancestry. It's a faux pas to call any state resident 'Hawaiian' (as you would a Californian or Texan)! Note that in this book, Hawai'i refers to the island of Hawai'i or to the pre-statehood Hawaiian Islands. Locally this spelling is official and ubiquitous both for the state and for the island. But in this book, Hawaii refers to the state (to differentiate it from the island).

Local People who grew up in Hawaii. Locals who move away retain their local 'cred,' at least in part. But longtime transplants (see below) never become local. To call a transplant 'almost local' is a welcome compliment, despite its emphasis on the insider-outsider mentality.

Kama'aina Literally defined as 'child of the land,' *kama'aina* are people native to a particular place. A Hilo native is *kama'aina* of Hilo and not of Kailua-Kona, for example. It assumes a deep knowledge of and connection to the place.

Haole A Caucasian person. Often further defined as 'mainland haole' or 'local haole.'

Transplant People who move to the islands as adults.

Neighbor Island resident People who live on the Hawaiian islands other than O'ahu.

estate, luxury resorts and traffic. Like Honolulu and parts of Maui, Kona has become more 'haole-fied' and less traditionally local on the surface.

Compared with Honolulu people, Big Islanders tend to be more easygoing and low-key. Rarely will Hilo people honk their car horns, complain to waiters or neglect to smile or thank you. Most avoid embarrassing confrontations and prefer to 'save face' by keeping quiet. Public conversations, both among friends and strangers, are typically kept to casual topics; if you hear an intense discussion on international politics, Greek philosophy or sex and relationships, it's likely the speakers are mainland transplants or tourists. That said, locals do have opinions – they just don't broadcast them.

'Kids watch the same TV and listen to the same music – and they emulate hip-hop stars'

Despite a unique identity, however, locals are drawn to mainstream American culture and follow national trends. Kids watch the same TV and listen to the same music – and they emulate hip-hop stars, to the chagrin of those who see local culture getting diluted. The highly educated and upper-income classes also fall outside the usual definition of 'local-ness,' as they speak no pidgin and aspire to the same Ivy League dreams as their mainland counterparts. Nevertheless, even those with little in common will band together to support fellow locals. If an athlete or musician from any island becomes a national celebrity, everyone rejoices over the coup. During the 2004 season of the Fox network's *American Idol,* thousands of Hawaii fans went wild and catapulted O'ahu native Jasmine Trias to the top three.

Underlying local consciousness are long-standing native Hawaiian issues. The 1970s Hawaiian cultural renaissance initiated changes hailed by all locals. In 1978, the state re-established Hawaiian as an official language, and the US government stopped bombing Kaho'olawe. But there is no cohesive political group and no consensus regarding larger sovereignty issues. In the islands, only native Hawaiians are called 'Hawaiian,' to recognize the existence of the indigenous people. Hawaiian identity and local identity are related, but be careful not to confuse the two.

LIFESTYLE

Family is the predominant force. The *'ohana* (family) is central to islanders' interactions with each other and with outsiders. Weekends are generally reserved for family – you'll often see locals gathered together for all-day picnics and cookouts. You need not be related by blood or

---

GOT LUCKY?

When locals go on vacation, they go to…Las Vegas. Perhaps blasé about tropical scenery, a surprising number enjoy the artificial glitz, theme-park casinos, nearby golf courses, all-you-can-eat buffets and chance to win big (gambling is illegal only in two states: Hawaii and Utah).

Mostly, however, Hawaii people go to Vegas to hang out with other locals. On any given trip, locals are bound to spot folks they recognize from home. While the Vegas habit crosses ethnic and age lines, seniors are particularly frequent returnees.

The Honolulu–Vegas circuit has become a well-oiled machine, and companies such as Sam Boyd's Vacations–Hawaii offer discounted packages that keep locals coming back – often multiple times a year. Most stay downtown at the California Hotel, rather than at the upscale resorts on the Strip.

Over the years, Hawaii has considered ending its gambling ban, but opposition abounds from a bipartisan coalition of politicians, religious groups and the general public. Despite the state's financial woes and the local penchant for playing the slots, island gambling remains taboo.

A sizable community of Hawaii expatriates lives in Vegas, largely due to the low cost of living. But most locals shake their heads in disbelief. Vegas is fun but there's no place like Hawaii.

marriage to be considered *'ohana,* and lots of 'uncles' and 'aunties' are not relatives at all. While locals are friendly and approachable, however, those looking to hook up with an island girl or guy might find it hard to penetrate their tight social circles.

The workday starts and ends early, and most find a comfortable work-home balance. Childcare is shared with grandparents and relatives, typically eager babysitters. Retirees often congregate in friendly gangs for morning golf or coffee, and virtually all homeowners grow fruits and vegetables in their backyards. But you might be surprised at how much daily life resembles that in any suburban mainland town, with long hours at the office, shopping trips to Wal-Mart and Costco, killing time in traffic jams, poverty and homelessness and, yes, wearing long pants and leather shoes.

Throughout the state, the business 'uniform' for men is a cotton Reyn Spooner aloha shirt with dark slacks. (Believe it or not, lawyers and businessmen always wear their aloha shirts tucked in, while the untucked style is favored by retirees, blue-collars and the with-it young crowd.) For women, the muumuu has been passé since the 1980s, unless worn by Hawaiian *tutu* (grandmothers) or hula teachers.

Much of what's considered the local lifestyle are working-class customs lingering from plantation days. Today, socioeconomic class determines whether a Big Islander follows the typical pattern (which parallels the mainstream 'American dream') or adopts more-cosmopolitan mores. The less educated usually marry early and stick to traditional male and female domestic roles (it's still odd for a wife not to take her husband's surname). But those who study or travel outside the islands are less likely to fit the mold.

Pakalolo (marijuana) remains a billion-dollar underground industry (and the state's most profitable crop) and the use of 'ice' (crystal meth-amphetamine) has become rampant since the 1990s, especially in rural communities like Miloli'i. Some attribute the ice epidemic to dropping prices for the drug and crackdowns on marijuana cultivation. Whatever the cause, ice-related crime is rising and social service agencies are struggling to provide treatment for addicts.

The Aloha Shirt: Spirit of the Islands by Dale Hope and Gregory Tozian is a gloriously illustrated picture book that reveals the rich history behind this modern Hawaii icon.

DID YOU KNOW?

Captain Cook wrote Hawai'i as Owy-hee, Maui as Mowee, O'ahu as O-ahoo, Kaua'i as Atowai and Ni'ihau as Neehau.

POPULATION

The state's population of 1.2 million is heavily concentrated on O'ahu, where Honolulu remains the state's only 'city.' The Big Island is the second-most populated island, but due to its size, the island's population density is miniscule. Just compare: roughly 1470 people per sq mile on O'ahu; 162 on Maui; 106 on Kaua'i; and only 37 on the Big Island.

With a population just above 40,000, Hilo is undoubtedly the largest town on the island. Kailua-Kona hovers around 10,000, but if you count its suburbs, the Kailua vicinity numbers almost 30,000. Waimea, at 7000, is the only other concentrated town, as the others are around 3000.

In the Big Island's ethnic mix, there's no majority. The haole (Caucasians) comprise the largest ethnic group at just over 30%, reflecting the influx of mainlanders to the island. The Japanese are the second-largest unmixed group at almost 14%, followed by native Hawaiians at 10% and Filipinos at 9%. Mixed-race people comprise 28% of the population. The 2000 US Census introduced the mixed-race category in 2000, allowing respondents to select more than one race. Statewide, the multiracial population is 24% (compared to only 2.4% nationwide). Most of these mixed-race individuals have Asian (mainly Chinese) and Hawaiian ancestry, or that combination plus Caucasian. Half of all marriages in Hawaii are mixed race.

The number of 'pure' native Hawaiians has dropped steadily ever since Captain Cook's arrival, and while a sizable number identify themselves as Hawaiian or part-Hawaiian, experts estimate the number of pure native Hawaiians to be under 5000 nationwide.

SPORTS

The Big Island isn't populous enough to offer major big-ticket sports, like football or basketball. Instead, the main spectator sports on the Big Island include triathlons, sport fishing and canoe paddling. The headliner is the legendary Ironman Triathlon World Championship (p77), which attracts over 25,000 spectators in Kona and 50 million TV viewers worldwide each October.

The internationally famous Hawaiian International Billfish Tournament (p77), held each August since 1959, is another big draw. Numerous other fishing tournaments take place year-round, including the **Hawaii Marlin Tournament Series** (www.konatournaments.com) and **Hawaii Big Game Fishing Club** (www.hbgfc.org) events.

Canoe paddling is exciting to watch, and races are held year-round in waters off Hilo, Kailua-Kona, Keauhou and Kawaihae. Check with the **Hawai'i Island Paddlesports Association** (hotline ☎ 969-6695; www.kaikahoe.org) for a race schedule.

An ancient Hawaiian 'extreme' sport is *he'e holua,* sledding down mountain slopes and lava fields at speeds up to 50mph. *He'e holua* is meant to honor Pele, the mythical goddess of the volcano, by demonstrating one's willingness to risk life by riding the 'waves of Pele.' Tom 'Pohaku' Stone, a native Hawaiian expert surfer and waterman, singlehandedly revitalized the 2000-year-old sport when in the 1990s he rode a *holua* (sled) for the first time in 100 years. Today he handcrafts both sleds and surfboards from native hardwood (check out his website at www.hawaiibc.com). Bear in mind, the sport remains quite esoteric and you're unlikely to catch a glimpse of a random sledder as you cruise around the island.

Statewide, there are no professional sports teams, probably due to the islands' remoteness and relatively small population. Thus Big Islanders, like all locals, rally around the University of Hawai'i at Manoa, especially for women's volleyball and men's basketball and football. In addition, Hiloans enjoy UH-Hilo games, especially men's basketball, which draws lively crowds during winning seasons.

See the Hawai'i Outdoors chapter on p50 for more on sports.

MULTICULTURALISM

It's a common misconception that Hawaii is a 'melting pot' of races and ethnicities. Certainly the island population is diverse, with no ethnic majority, and locals are generally tolerant of differences. But lines do exist. The old plantation stereotypes and hierarchies continue to influence social interaction in Hawaii. Caucasians have historically held the most power, but early immigrant groups, particularly the Chinese and Japanese, have proven upwardly mobile. Later immigrants, including Filipinos, Southeast Asians and other Polynesians, have had less time to advance and often hold low-level service jobs.

Among themselves, locals good-naturedly joke about what are admittedly island stereotypes: Portuguese talk too much, Chinese are tight with money, Japanese are uptight do-gooders, haole act like know-it-alls, Hawaiians are huge and lazy, Filipinos eat dog and so forth. Hawaii's much-loved comedians of the 1970s and 1980s – Andy Bumatai, Frank

---

For an insider's look at surf culture, don't miss Stacy Peralta's 2004 Sundance Film Festival opener, *Riding Giants,* which features three titans of big-wave surfing: Greg Noll, Jeff Clark and Laird Hamilton.

Hawaii's Sports Hall of Fame (www.alohafame.org) honors the state's champion athletes and outstanding coaches.

To hear pidgin spoken by *fo' real kine* locals, go to www.extreme-hawaii.com/pidgin.

DeLima and Rap Reiplinger – used such stereotypes to comic effect appreciated by all. Locals seem slightly perplexed at the emphasis on 'political correctness' on the mainland.

Interestingly, while locals recognize the different Asian ethnicities, they lump all whites into one group: haole. If someone calls you haole, don't worry. There's usually no negative subtext. But depending on the tone of voice (and any accompanying adjectives), it can be an insult or a threat. Generally, prejudice against haole depends on personal factors, such as whether they are local or longtime residents and, above all, whether they respect island ways.

RELIGION

Religion in ancient Hawaiian civilization was the cornerstone of society. All individual, family and community activities were governed by strict religious laws, known as the *kapu* (taboo) system. These laws governed what people ate, how they prayed, whom they married and just about every other aspect of daily living.

The breaking of a *kapu* could result in banishment for a brief period of time if it was a minor infraction – such as stealing or eating a prohibited food – or death, if it was a major infraction, such as murder or temple desecration.

When King Liholiho broke the *kapu* by dining with Queen Ka'ahumanu yet suffered no divine punishment, many Hawaiians rejected the entire tradition and were willing converts to Christianity (see p25). But others took the Hawaiian religion underground. While the traditional beliefs never regained their former command, the philosophy endured, often expressed as *aloha 'aina* (reverence for the land's sanctity). In part, the Hawaiian sovereignty movement is rooted in *aloha 'aina*, to reclaim the land regarded as abused by outsiders.

Almost all the ancient historical sites in the islands – *pu'uhonua* (place of refuge), heiau (place of worship), petroglyphs – are religious sites, chosen for the mana of the land. Some sites have little or no constructed adornment, such as Halema'uma'u Crater (p199), where traditionalists perform rituals and leave offerings.

Today, most Hawaii people remain devoted Christians, with Roman Catholics being by far the largest denomination. Mainstream Protestant

DID YOU KNOW?

If you spot a Union Jack lookalike in the Hawaii state flag, you're right. It symbolizes the friendship between the British and King Kamehameha I, who commissioned the flag in 1816.

Translate your name into Hawaiian at www.alohafriends.com/names.html.

ANCIENT PANTHEON

Ancient Hawai'i was a polytheistic society. The four major gods were Ku, the god of war and male generating power; Kane, the god of fresh water, sunlight and procreation; Kanaloa, the god of the ocean and ocean winds; and Lono, the god of peace and agriculture.

There were also dozens of demigods and deities who reigned over the natural and supernatural worlds. Among those who are still worshipped today are Pele, goddess of volcanoes (p200); Laka, goddess of the hula; and Hina, goddess of the moon.

Most of the deities had earthly counterparts *(kinolau)*, which could be animate or inanimate objects, such as rocks, animals and trees, or other natural elements, such as wind and rain. Virtually all things in the earthly world were the *kinolau* of a deity, therefore all things were considered to have mana, to one degree or another.

Ancient Hawaiians believed that when humans die, their spirits live on in the form of *'aumakua* (guardian spirits) that protect living family members. *'Aumakua* adopt earthly forms such as sharks, geckos, birds or fish. A reciprocal relationship existed: *'aumakua* would provide guidance and protection to the living, who in turn were duty-bound to revere and protect their guardian spirits on earth.

Christianity is struggling with declining membership, while evangelical churches are burgeoning. Buddhists number an estimated 100,000 in Hawaii, the highest statewide percentage of Buddhists in the USA, but the number of younger adherents is dwindling.

ARTS
Music

Integral to Hawaiian music is the guitar, first introduced to the islands by Spanish cowboys in the 1830s. The Hawaiians made the guitar their own during the 19th century by adopting steel strings and the slack-key method (*ki ho'alu*, which means 'loosen the key'). For *ki ho'alu*, the six strings are slackened from their standard tuning to facilitate a full sound on a single guitar – the thumb plays the bass and rhythm chords, while the fingers play the melody and improvisations, in a picked style.

The most influential slack-key artist was Gabby Pahinui (1921–80), who launched the modern slack-key era with his first recording in 1946. Over the years, he played with the legendary Sons of Hawaii and later formed the Gabby Pahinui Hawaiian Band with four of his sons; his home in Waimanalo on O'ahu was a mecca for backyard jam sessions. Other pioneering slack-key masters were Sonny Chillingworth, Leonard Kwan and Atta Isaacs.

The instrument most commonly associated with Hawaii is the ukulele, though it's derived from the *braguinha*, a Portuguese instrument introduced to Hawaii in the late 19th century. Ukulele means 'jumping flea' in Hawaiian, referring to the way players' deft fingers would swiftly 'jump' around the strings. Hawaii's ukulele masters include Eddie Kamae, Herb Ohta and Jake Shimabukuro.

Over the years, Hawaiian music has progressed from the lighthearted, novelty music of the 1930s to '50s, such as 'Lovely Hula Hands' and 'Sweet Leilani,' to a more sophisticated sound. In the 1970s, Hawaiian music enjoyed a rebirth, and artists such as the Sunday Manoa, Cecilio & Kapono, Hui 'Ohana and the Beamer Brothers remain icons in Hawaii. Perhaps the most famous island musician is the late Israel Kamakawiwo'ole,

Slack-key guitar fans: www.dancingcat.com is a good introduction to the genre and includes a schedule of performances across the USA. www.taropatch.net is geared toward guitarists, with reviews of instructional materials and online discussion boards.

BIG ISLAND SOUNDS

The Big Island has spawned top musicians too numerous to list. But here's a sample.

Darlene Ahuna is a traditional Hawaiian vocalist who started singing professionally in 1979 and, 15 years later, got her big break in 1994, when she won a talent contest sponsored by the Hilo Hawaiian Hotel to become its headline performer. Since then she's won multiple Na Hoku Hanohano awards (given annually by the Hawai'i Academy of Recording Artists) and her renditions of hula classics remain local favorites.

Brittni Paiva (www.brittnipaiva.com), a Hilo teen and an up-and-coming musician, plays the ukulele, slack-key guitar and bass on her 2004 debut release *Brittni x 3*. A home-schooled student who practices four to six hours daily, she's already won top honors at local competitions.

Ledward Ka'apana is perhaps the Big Island's most acclaimed slack-key artist. Ka'apana (www.ledkaapana.com) grew up in Kalapana and as teenagers, he and his twin brother Nedward and cousin Dennis Pavao formed the acclaimed Hui 'Ohana.

A falsetto virtuoso, Kalapana-native Dennis Pavao, died of a brain aneurysm at age 50 in 2002. He recorded both with Hui 'Ohana and as a soloist. His second posthumous release, *Dennis Pavao: The Golden Voice of Hawai'i Vol 1*, which he recorded only a few weeks before his death, is a gem.

Kainani Kahaunaele was the winner of three 2004 Na Hoku Hanohano awards and was born on Kaua'i but moved to the Big Island to study the Hawaiian language at UH-Hilo, where she's now an instructor. Her debut CD, *Na'u 'Oe*, features her original Hawaiian compositions.

whose *Facing Future* is Hawaii's all-time bestselling album. 'Bruddah Iz' died in 1997 at age 38, due to morbid obesity, but he remains a driving force in putting Hawaiian music on the map. The genre is now breaking out of the niche market, with online sales mounting and a new Grammy Award for Best Hawaiian Music Album established in 2005.

Hula

In ancient Hawaii, hula was not entertainment, but religious expression. Dancers used hand gestures, facial expression and rhythmic movement to illustrate historical events and legendary tales and to venerate the gods. They wore *kapa* (bark cloth), never the stereotypical grass skirts. When the Christian missionaries arrived, they viewed hula dancing as too licentious and suppressed it. The hula might have been lost forever if the 'Merrie Monarch' King Kalakaua, the last king of Hawai'i, had not revived it in the late 19th century.

Today's commercial hula shows, which emphasize swaying hips and nonstop smiling, might be compelling but they're not 'real' hula. Serious students join a hula *halau* (school), where they undergo rigorous training and adopt hula as a life practice. Dancers learn to control every part of the body, as subtle differences in gestures can change the meaning entirely.

For authentic hula, the best venues are the Merrie Monarch Festival (p171) and the Na Mea Hawaii Hula Kahiko Series (p209).

Holo Mai Pele, a mesmerizing performance of ancient hula, premiered on *Great Performances* in 2001. For a video or book, go to www.pbs.org/holomaipele, which also features excellent photo clips and background information.

Hawaiian Arts & Crafts

Ancient Hawaiians relied on manual handiwork for everything, from clothing to canoes. Thus almost all traditional objects have an aesthetic component, being handmade according to exacting detail. Nowadays, a small group of artisans and craftspeople perpetuate the old traditions, such as woodworking, which ideally uses prized koa to create hand-turned wooden bowls and furniture, impossibly smooth and polished. Today a variety of hardwood is used since koa has grown scarce.

Lauhala weaving is another craft perpetuated only by a few. Weaving the *lau* (leaves) of the *hala* (pandanus) tree is actually the easy part, while preparing the leaves, which have razor-sharp spines, is difficult, messy work. Traditionally *lauhala* served as mats and floor coverings, but today smaller items such as hats, placemats and baskets are most common.

Christian missionaries introduced patchwork quilting to Hawaiians. But because they'd only recently adopted Western dress, Hawaiians didn't have a surplus of cloth scraps – and the idea of chopping up fabric simply to sew it back together in small squares seemed absurd. Instead they created their own designs, which typically feature stylized tropical flora on a contrasting background. A handcrafted Hawaiian quilt is painstakingly stitched and costs thousands of dollars.

Lei making remains a popular craft, as people continue to wear lei on a regular basis. Today's popular tourist lei feature flashy or fragrant flowers, such as plumeria or dendrobium orchids. In fact, many orchid lei originate in Thailand and are not Hawaiian at all. Traditionally, lei were more subtle in their beauty, made of *mokihana* berries, *maile* leaves and other greenery. Intricate collectors' lei are sewn with shells and seeds.

For a list of top galleries and shops, see p89. Remember, cheap imitations abound.

To identify almost every Hawaiian lei, all you need is *A Pocket Guide to the Hawaiian Lei* by Ronn Ronck.

Literature

For years, 'Hawaii literature' referred to fiction set in Hawaii, typically by nonlocal writers. Oft-cited examples include *Hawaii,* James Michener's

Kids of all ages will get *chicken skin* (goose bumps) from the classic island legends in *Hawaii's Best Spooky Tales* and its sequels, edited by Rick Carroll.

NO TALK LI' DAT

The Hawaii educational system has traditionally pushed local kids to use standard English and not pidgin in the classroom. State department of education leaders (and many parents) often blame low scores on standardized tests on local kids' speaking, thinking and writing in pidgin. But a movement to legitimize pidgin as a language is afoot. Da Pidgin Coup, a group of University of Hawai'i faculty and graduate students, asserts that pidgin can coexist with standard English and should not be forbidden if its use facilitates the learning process. As the argument goes, *what* you say is more important than *how* you say it.

The most well-known champion for pidgin use is Lee Tonouchi, a lecturer in the English Department at Kapiolani Community College on O'ahu, who was hired with an application written entirely in pidgin. A prolific writer and playwright, he makes an intriguing, subversive argument for legitimizing pidgin. His books include *Da Word* and *Living Pidgin: Contemplations on Pidgin Culture*.

This debate parallels the 1996 debate over Ebonics (black English) in Oakland, California, where the local school board recognized Ebonics, a term derived from ebony and phonics, as a separate language. The board concluded that most African American children come to school fluent in their vernacular, and to condemn it would be counterproductive.

Granted, pidgin use is not universal among locals and is determined by socioeconomic class. But all locals clearly understand it – and they regard pidgin as social glue, bonding them to a shared identity and sense of humor. Most locals straddle the two languages, using either pidgin or standard English when it's most appropriate.

In a lyrical narrative, poet Garrett Hongo rediscovers his Big Island birthplace in *Volcano: A Memoir of Hawai'i*, an exploration of setting, mind, body and soul.

ambitious saga of Hawaii's history, and *Hotel Honolulu*, Paul Theroux's novel about a washed-up writer who becomes the manager of a run-down Waikiki hotel. Also widely read is Isabella Bird, the 19th-century British adventurer, who captures the exoticism of the islands for outsiders. Today, however, a growing body of local writers is redefining the meaning of Hawaii literature.

Local literature doesn't consciously highlight Hawaii as an exotic setting but instead focuses on the lives and attitudes of universal characters. **Bamboo Ridge Press** (www.bambooridge.com), which publishes contemporary local fiction and poetry in a biannual journal, *Bamboo Ridge*, has launched the careers of many local writers including Lois-Ann Yamanaka and Juliet Kono, both from Hilo. See p14 for suggested titles.

Environment

Of all the major Hawaiian Islands, Hawai'i (aka the Big Island) is the youngest, the largest and the only island with active volcanoes that have erupted in recent centuries. Here the story of lava – from molten liquid to glossy, hardened rock and eventually into rich soil for ohia forests – is on full display, presenting a unique opportunity to study the way earth is formed and transformed by other natural forces. Because they are isolated from the continents, the Hawaiian Islands have become the habitat for thousands of endemic species of flora and fauna found nowhere else on earth. The arrival of Europeans upset the balance, however, and today the islands account for 75% of extinct species in the USA and one-third of its endangered plants and animals. Whereas a small sliver of the Big Island is protected as parks, competing interests vie for control of the land. Despite the Big Island's relative size, it remains an island, limited in precious and irreplaceable resources.

http://volcano.und.nodak
.edu/vwdocs/hawaii
_review/VREV3.html
The Teaching and
Learning section of the
VolcanoWorld website
contains explanations
of volcanic features,
diagrams of different
types of volcanoes and
a review of Hawaiian
volcanism.

THE LAND Dr Scott Rowland

A huge natural volcano factory formed the Hawaiian Islands. A key component of this process is the geologic 'hotspot,' a stationary column rising slowly upward from perhaps as deep as the core-mantle boundary, some 2200 miles below Earth's surface. This column is solid rock, but moves upward because it is slightly hotter and therefore less dense than the surrounding mantle rock. Along most of the way, the pressure

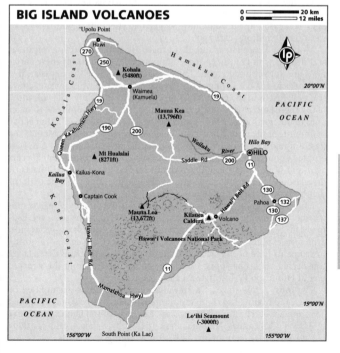

BIG ISLAND VOLCANOES

0 —— 20 km
0 —— 12 miles

'Upolu Point
Hawi
270
250
Kohala (5480ft)
Hamakua Coast
Kohala Coast
20°00'N
Waimea (Kamuela)
19
19
Kona Coast
Mauna Kea (13,796ft)
PACIFIC OCEAN
Queen Ka'ahumanu Hwy
190
200
Wailuku River
Hilo Bay
Mt Hualalai (8271ft)
Saddle Rd
200
HILO
11
Kailua Bay
Kailua-Kona
130
Captain Cook
Pahoa
132
130
Hawai'i Belt Rd
Mauna Loa (13,672ft)
Kilauea Caldera
Volcano
137
Hawai'i Volcanoes National Park
Hawai'i Belt Rd
11
PACIFIC OCEAN
Mamalahoa Hwy
19°00'N
156°00'W   South Point (Ka Lae)
Lo'ihi Seamount (-3000ft)
155°00'W

Inside Hawaiian Volcanoes
(a Smithsonian Institu-
tion video production)
does an excellent job
of explaining the inner
plumbing system of a
Hawaiian volcano. It
includes footage of classic
experiments with gelatin
volcano models.

is so great that, although hot, the rock cannot melt. Only at the very top, around 60 miles below Earth's surface, is the pressure low enough so that the column starts to melt. It is this melted rock (magma) that eventually works its way to the surface to build Hawaiian volcanoes.

Meanwhile, plate tectonics is carrying the Pacific Plate northwestward about 9cm each year. This is the conveyor belt part of the volcano factory. It means that each volcano only gets supplied with magma for one or two million years. Once the plate has carried a volcano off the hotspot, its eruptions cease and erosion, subsidence and reef growth become the dominant geological processes.

The result is a chain of volcanoes that is young and unweathered at one end, yet older and eroded at the other. This progression was noticed by the first Western-trained geologists to visit Hawai'i. Native Hawaiians noted the pattern as well, attributing the progression to the travels of volcano goddess Pele, who was forced by jealous siblings to keep moving on until she eventually settled on the Big Island.

The Hawaiian chain does not end where the large islands stop. Stretching some 900 miles beyond Ni'ihau are the Northwestern Hawaiian Islands – isolated rocks, shoals, and atolls that were once mighty volcanic islands as big as today's major Hawaiian Islands. And the Hawaiian chain of volcanoes doesn't end even there. Beyond Kure are seamounts (mountains on the ocean floor that don't make it up to sea level) that were also once powerful Hawaiian volcanoes. The entire Hawaiian-Emperor volcanic chain stretches some 5500 miles from the north-central Pacific to Russia's Kamchatka peninsula, which is essentially the same distance as that from Florida to Alaska. Each of these volcanoes was once located where the Big Island of Hawai'i is today, but irresistible plate tectonics have carried it to its present position. Thus Meiji, the oldest of the volcanoes, is the island you would have visited had you booked your Hawaiian vacation 80 million years ago!

Along the Hawaiian island chain there are both clusters of volcanoes and regions with volcanoes spaced far apart; the reasons for these variations are not yet understood. The island of Hawai'i (ie the Big Island) is one such cluster, consisting of seven volcanoes, five of which extend above sea level. Just as in the Hawaiian-Emperor chain as a whole, the volcanoes of the Big Island cluster range from young ones in the southeast to older ones in the northwest. From youngest to oldest, they are Lōi'hi (an active seamount southeast of Kilauea), Kilauea (currently erupting), Mauna Loa (last erupted in 1984), Hualalai (last erupted in 1801), Mauna Kea (last erupted about 3600 years ago), Kohala (last erupted around 65,000 years ago) and Mahukona (an old seamount off the west cost of Kohala). A drive around the island allows you to observe the same geologic patterns that both the ancient Hawaiians and early Europeans did.

Lōi'hi (also known as Kama'ehu) can be visited only by research submarines because its summit is approximately 900yd below sea level. Estimates for when Lōi'hi will grow to the surface vary considerably, but most geologists expect that it will be at least 30,000 years from now. Monitoring instruments have been placed at its underwater summit, and the data are transferred via a fiber-optic cable that comes ashore along the wrecked pier at Honu'apo (Whittington Beach; see p216).

The most active stage of a Hawaiian volcano's life is exemplified by Kilauea and Mauna Loa. Both erupt often, produce large volumes of fluid lava, and are barely scarred by erosion. Driving around Crater Rim Drive in Hawai'i Volcanoes National Park (p197) by Kilauea caldera, there are no erosional features in sight – only young lava flows, vents and the caldera. Gazing off towards Mauna Loa (p203) affords a spectacular view of a nearly pristine Hawaiian volcano, with a smooth profile almost unbroken by valleys or gullies. When you are at the Kilauea caldera, only one to two miles below your feet is a network of magma-filled voids and conduits, collectively called the magma chamber. Magma from the hotspot collects in the chamber prior to and during eruptions. Gases bubbling out of the magma percolate to the surface, giving the place a sulfurous odor. Swelling and contracting of the magma chamber likewise results in rising and falling of the volcanic summit, and these very slight movements are carefully monitored by the staff of the USGS Hawaiian Volcano Observatory to keep tabs on Kilauea's subterranean activity.

Mauna Kea is also visible from Kilauea, but its profile is clearly different from that of Mauna Loa. Instead of a smooth, rounded shape, Mauna Kea (and Hualālai volcano, which is visible from most points along the northwest coast of the island) is bumpy and steeper. Those bumps are large scoria (cinder) cones, indicating that in the later stages of a Hawaiian volcano's life, the lava fountains are spectacularly high. This happens because by this late stage, the magma chamber has solidified and the (now infrequent) batches of rising magma have no place to pause and allow gas bubbles to escape prior to the volcano erupting. With all its original gas still present upon reaching the surface, the magma is capable of producing very high fountains.

When you cross the Wailuku River heading north from Hilo on Hwy 19, you pass from Mauna Loa to Mauna Kea, and immediately you can see the power of erosion and weathering. The soil in the road cuts is thick and reddish-brown in color; as you continue north, you will cross almost innumerable gullies, streams and gulches. These all indicate that this surface has been attacked by rain, flowing water and chemical alteration for a long time. In a few places you'll also notice that there is a cliff at the coastline, the product of relentless pounding by ocean waves. But Mauna Kea didn't just die completely one day – erosion and eruptions have occasionally occurred simultaneously. Farther north, off Hwy 19 about halfway between Hilo and Hamakua, Laupahoehoe Point was produced when lava flowed to the coast down a large, rain-cut gulch.

To really see the effects of erosion, go to Waipi'o Valley lookout (p152) and gaze at the deeply dissected slopes of Kohala. Waipi'o Valley is being cut into the flanks of Kohala by flowing water. Typically stream-cut valleys are V-shaped, with the stream at the bottom point of the vee. Waipi'o Valley, however, has a flat floor of muddy sediments. This is the result of the sea level rising, Kohala volcano subsiding, or both. The flat floor is perfect for growing *kalo* (taro), a staple of the Hawaiian diet; in ancient times fertile Waipi'o was an important center of Hawaiian culture. The sheer cliffs forming the far coastline are the headwall of a giant avalanche that collapsed much of Kohala into the ocean during ancient times.

Your drive around and across the Big Island (and back through time) may leave you exhausted and out of gas. But Pele and plate tectonics have no time for rest. Come back in a few hundred thousand years. Today's volcanoes will be off toward where Maui is today, and one or two new volcanoes will be seen poking their heads above the waves.

WILDLIFE   Dr Samuel M 'Ohukani'ōhi'a Gon III

The Hawaiian Islands are already world-renowned as a hotbed of plant and animal life found nowhere else on the planet, and the island of Hawai'i is no exception. In fact, being the largest of the island chain with twice the land area of all other islands combined, the so-called Big Island

DID YOU KNOW?

The Hawaiian words *pahoehoe* (smooth-surfaced, glassy lava) and *'a'a* (rough-surfaced lava) have been adopted by geologists all over the world, except in Iceland, where they say *helluhraun* (pavement lava) and *apalhraun* (rough lava) instead.

DID YOU KNOW?

Statistically speaking, Kilauea is actually more explosive than Mt St Helens.

stands by itself as an epitome of biological exemplars. With everything from the driest desert regions to perennially soaked montane wet forest, and from sun-baked beaches to glistening snowfields, the sheer number of ecological zones on the island of Hawai'i exceeds the entire country of Brazil! US Forest Service scientists say that acre for acre, Hawai'i has the highest concentration of life zone types on Earth. From tropical to alpine, desert to bog, all find their niche on this island.

With this kind of habitat diversity, it's no wonder that the lucky colonists who originally arrived in Hawai'i millions of years ago were able to find a place to live. Low, dry atolls, typical in the central Pacific, could never support the thousands of native species we have here. Windborne seeds and spores brought plants to the originally lifeless volcanic island, and migratory birds, such as the Pacific golden plover, brought passengers in the Alaskan mud caked on their feet. Ocean waves carried floating seeds onto our shores. Sometimes huge logs from the Pacific coast would wash ashore, after which the living passengers under bark and in crevices could crawl out and start a new life.

Given the huge opportunities offered by the welcoming and rich Hawaiian environment, these ancestral colonists rapidly diversified in an evolutionary explosion called adaptive radiation, meaning species generation in an array of different ecological directions, like beams emanating from a source of radiant light. One finchlike ancestor underwent this kind of diversification and created the Hawaiian honeycreepers, a unique subfamily of birds (the Drepaninae) known nowhere else.

Being 2500 miles from the closest continent or high island (ie those with cloud-forming elevations over 3000ft) system meant that many kinds of animals could never get to the Hawaiian islands via natural means. Picture a cow swimming 2500 miles, or indeed any large land mammal, and it is immediately apparent that Hawai'i before the arrival of humans was a tropical ecosystem unlike anywhere else on Earth. There was lush tropical forest, but not a single monkey, browsing animal (ie one that primarily grazes on low-lying vegetation), large predatory jungle cat, snake – not even a mouse! And of course, without such large animals to bother, there were no biting flies, mosquitoes, or leeches either. Indeed, the native animal life of Hawai'i in the distant past was entirely dominated by three main groups: birds, arthropods (such as insects and spiders) and snails. Our only wholly terrestrial mammal is one that indeed could get here on its own: the 'ope'ape'a (Hawaiian hoary bat). Today the island of Hawai'i is one of its strongholds. On the coasts and lowlands in the hours just after sunset, the bats' erratic silhouettes might be seen, darting after emerging moths and night insects.

WHAT'S IN A NAME?

An indigenous species is one found naturally in a place, but is not necessarily restricted to that place. *Naupaka kahakai*, a coastal plant, is indigenous to the Hawaiian Islands, but is also widespread on the coasts of the tropical Pacific and Indian oceans. An endemic species is a special kind of indigenous species. Not only is it native to a place, but it is restricted to that place. *'Io*, the Hawaiian hawk, is endemic to the island of Hawai'i.

A Polynesian introduction is one of only dozens of plants and animals that were brought to the islands by the voyaging ancestors of Hawaiians. Kukui, our state tree, is a Polynesian introduction.

Finally, an alien or non-native species is one introduced after the arrival of early Europeans to Hawai'i, either purposefully or accidentally. Most of our pests are alien species, although many of our beneficial crops and ornamental plants also fall into this broad category.

Animals

MARINE MAMMALS

Whale watching (p55) has become one of the paramount wildlife activities to pursue while in Hawaiian waters. The highlight is the winter calving of migrating Pacific humpback whales. On the island of Hawai'i, the best viewing locations are along the calm northwest coast and at small shallows near Ka Lae (South Point; see p219), where the whales (and their human audience) concentrate. While these showy baleen whales receive the most press, there is actually a broad diversity of whales that have been seen in Hawaiian waters. Fin whales and blue whales are known to pass through Hawaiian waters on trans-oceanic migrations, though their deep water passage makes viewing from land a highly unlikely event. Much more commonly seen are smaller whales and dolphins, such as rough-toothed dolphin, spotted dolphin, bottlenose dolphin, spinner dolphin, melon-head whale, pygmy killer whale, false killer whale, pilot whale and others. Spinner dolphins are a particular treat, with their acrobatic leaps accompanied by rapid mid-air twirls designed to impress observers. Sometimes there are beachings of large toothed whales; in ancient times, such events were considered sacred, and the teeth of beached whales were considered *kapu* (restricted) for chiefly use. The teeth in particular were carved into pendants worn only by the *ali'i* (royal class).

Today, marine mammals of all kinds receive protection from harassment, and it is not good practice to disturb resting animals in quiet bays, whether you are in a kayak or swimming in the water. If they come to you, however, that is another matter, and you could find yourself part of a small pod for an unforgettable moment.

The only nonwhale marine mammal, the Hawaiian monk seal, is concentrated in the Northwestern Hawaiian Islands, far from the island of Hawai'i. In recent years, as recovering populations have expanded their northern range, more and more sightings have been made among the main islands. Because the island of Hawai'i has a huge coastline with many remote beaches, monk seals have been coming ashore to rest and sun themselves. It is rare, however, for one to rest on a popular beach. Hawaiians named the monk seal *'ilio kai* ('dog of the sea'), recognizing its ancestral land-predator heritage. Another Hawaiian name for the seal is even more fun: *'ilio holoikauaua*, which can be translated as 'the dog that runs in a glutinous way,' which, if you've ever watched a seal or sea lion bounce like jelly down sandy slopes into the waiting ocean, is a perfect description of this rare Hawaiian seal.

Hawai'i's Native & Exotic Freshwater Animals by Mike N Yamamoto and Annette W Tagawa This definitive guide to the world of Hawaiian freshwater ecosystems tells the story of animals that evolved out of the sea to colonize freshwater streams pouring down volcanic flanks – and how some can climb up waterfalls hundreds of feet high!

THE LIFE AQUATIC IN HAWAIIAN STREAMS

How do you evolve native fresh-water wildlife when you are surrounded by thousands of miles of ocean? It turns out that several species of Hawaiian fishes, shrimps, and snails have left the sea behind for a fresh-water existence. Even a native sponge has found its way from the sea upstream, painting some stream boulders of Hamakua and Kohala with dabs of bright green. Hawaiians considered one of the native fish, a goby with a bright red tail, as a sacred manifestation of water spirits called *mo'o*, and these rarest of our native stream fishes were not eaten or molested. Most of the Big Island's streams are found along its northern flank, where large streams such as in Waipi'o Valley offer the curious a glimpse of the life aquatic. Keep your eyes open for our native dragonfly, *pinao*. It is the largest dragonfly species of the United States and can sometimes be seen in large numbers at valley overlooks, such as at Pololu, in the Kohala Mountains, swooping acrobatically after small insects that are caught on the fly.

LAND MAMMALS

If you are looking for native land mammals, the island of Hawai'i is one of the best places to view the only native Hawaiian terrestrial mammal, the 'ōpe'apēa (Hawaiian hoary bat). Small enough to fit in the palm of your hand, this insect-eating bat roosts in trees during the day and emerges at dusk to pursue moths and other night-flying insects. This reddish-brown bat is sometimes marked by pale hairs that give it a frosted, hoary look. You can catch a glimpse of this strong flier's acrobatic aerial loops and dives anywhere from coast to treeline, but the lowlands of Kona seem to be the best place to view this endangered Hawaiian mammal.

DID YOU KNOW?

The wings of the Hawaiian hoary bat are like the sails of a Hawaiian voyaging canoe, and probably gave the bat its name.

The wilds of Hawai'i are also home to hoofed foreign invaders, including wild cattle, feral pigs, mouflon sheep and feral donkeys (called 'Kona nightingales' in a lampooning reference to their oh-so melodic braying in the evening hours). Though these ungulates (hoofed browsing mammals) have been consciously introduced in past years to augment game hunting opportunities, conservationists recognize that they are incompatible with native vegetation and their continued presence contributes to the long-term degradation of native plants and animals. The best wilderness areas on the island, such as Hawai'i Volcanoes National Park, have a zero-tolerance policy for these alien ungulates; indeed, where they have been excluded, native forest is recovering and the true wilderness of Hawai'i can be best enjoyed.

BIRDS

Hawai'i is a birder's paradise, with many species that can not be seen anywhere else. The islands boast several areas where native forest birds are concentrated, and at least two of them can be readily visited (but you might need to rent a good 4WD vehicle).

Hawaii's Birds by the Hawai'i Audubon Society This classic field guide has ably served birders from all over the world on their Hawaiian peregrinations – perfect when you want to identify that brilliant visitor to your breakfast courtyard.

On the windward side of the island near Mauna Kea is Hakalau Forest National Wildlife Refuge (p138), the first US Fish and Wildlife Service refuge established not for migratory waterbirds, but for forest birds. There you can see some of the birds found only on the Big Island, for example the Hawai'i Creeper, Hawai'i 'ākepa and Akiapōlā'au species. For most forest birds, a large ohia tree in full bloom is an irresistible attraction. If you can find such a tree, spend some quality time there with your binoculars at the ready, and you will surely be rewarded.

Another concentration of forest birds can be found in the vicinity of Kilauea Volcano, where the birding is likewise rich. Catch common native forest birds, such as the bright red 'apapane and the green 'amakihi, along the many trails in Hawai'i Volcanoes National Park (p203). Or scan for these and rarer species along the Mauna Loa Rd (p203), running

---

BOUNTIFUL BIRDING ON THE BIG ISLAND   Dr Samuel M 'Ohukani'ōhi'a Gon III

Whether you want to admire a Hawaiian hawk soaring in the calm skies of Kona, or catch the melodious conversations of red and green honeycreepers flitting through native rainforest in Ka'ū, the Big Island offers some of the best bird-watching opportunities of any island in the archipelago. So much of the forest remains a native ecosystem and prime forest-bird habitat; major roads and trails take you through the heart of some of these places. Despite being the youngest island, there are several species of native birds that occur only on the island of Hawai'i. 'Io, the Hawaiian hawk, is one of the Big Island endemic species, as is the endangered 'alala (Hawaiian crow), today found in the wild only in Kona. The montane forest-bird refuge at Hakalau (p138), on the windward flank of Mauna Kea, is a superb place to view rare native forest birds in their habitat, as are the forests along the trails in Hawai'i Volcanoes National Park (p203).

through Kīpukapuaulu, an island of older vegetation surrounded by the recent Keʻāmuku lava flow, where large trees and rich vegetation attract a diversity of birdlife.

NATIVE INSECTS & INVERTEBRATES

Scientists estimate that there are about 10,000 native species of plants and animals in Hawaiʻi, and of that, the majority are invertebrates of various kinds: insects, spiders and other microfauna that most visitors easily ignore. Yet among them are some world-class symbols of Hawaiʻi's biodiversity and uniqueness, symbolized by the Hawaiian happyface spider. Here is the poster-child of Hawaiian conservation – a bright yellow body with cheerful markings in red and black that bear an uncanny resemblance to a smiling face. You might run into a Hawaiian happyface spider in wet forest in Hawaiʻi Volcanoes National Park, where you can examine a series of photos of these remarkable arachnids at the park's visitor center. So symbolic of Hawaiian native species is this endemic spider that U-Haul vans celebrating each of the 50 states selected the happyface as the symbol of Hawaii. But among its Hawaiian colleagues are many other remarkables: flightless flies, stinkless stinkbugs, blind cave leafhoppers that have evolved into roothoppers, antless antlions (because Hawaiʻi has no native ants), giant dragonflies and snowfield bugs with antifreeze blood, to name just a few. Books such as *Hawaiian Insects and their Kin* by Frank Howarth and Bill Mull showcase Hawaii's remarkable microfauna.

Plants

Wherever you travel in the world these days, our human-transported landscapes of familiar plants have been firmly established, and the island of Hawaiʻi is no exception. In the tropical streets of Hilo, nearly all of the bright flowers and lush landscaping is a pantropical mix of introduced horticultural standards everywhere from the Philippines to the Caribbean and Southeast Asia to Central America.

Even in our wild places, plants that have naturalized (ie escaped cultivation and established themselves without human care) have gained a solid footing, so that for the roster of 1200 flowering plants and ferns that are native to Hawaiʻi, there are perhaps 1500 different species of non-native plants that have escaped into our ecosystems and now compete with them. From sea level to about 2000ft, the aliens are dominant,

http://pacificislands.fws
.gov/wnwr/bhakalaunwr
.html
The US Fish and Wildlife Service website showcases the amazing diversity of endangered Hawaiian honeycreepers and other birdlife of the region.

http://www.hawaii-forest
.com/index.html
A first-class, commercial website that provides a whirlwind tour of the island by the time you've gone through its colorful and informative pages.

DID YOU KNOW?

The name of the pit crater within Kilauea, Halemaʻumaʻu, refers to the lush proliferation of ferns such as ʻamaʻu that grow in the surrounding rain forest.

HAPUʻU TREE FERN, THE MOTHER OF THE FOREST

When hiking through wet ohia forest on the windward flank of the Big Island (say, while on the many trails of Hawaiʻi Volcanoes National Park, or alongside the Stainback Hwy west of Hwy 11 in the Puna District), you will see not only the dense dark canopy of the ohia trees, perhaps some sparked with brilliant red flowers, but beneath, forming a secondary canopy of huge fronds, our native tree fern, *hāpuʻu*, with its fibrous trunks rising to well above your head before sending out a bright green circle of luxuriant fronds.

Take a moment to examine the trunk, and you will see that it is a cradle of plant life. The rough, organic surface is a bed for windborne seeds and spores, and many of the wet forest trees get their start perched on the sturdy trunk of a *hāpuʻu*. As the trees grow, they send roots down to the ground along the trunk and eventually find rooting in more permanent substrate, outgrowing their fern mother. And when the shorter-lived fern dies, we are left with a tree of two trunks joined several feet above ground, and can imagine its infancy long ago on a tree fern nurse-log.

but as you rise above these elevations, you find more and more natives, such as the ubiquitous, red-blossomed *ohia lehua* tree, the official flower of the island. Indeed the island of Hawai'i may be the best place to view this sturdy tree, symbol of Ku, the Hawaiian god of war and also patron god of the forest.

Walking in the native forests of the Big Island, you are transported into a world that would have been familiar to ancient Hawaiians. Each tree, each shrub and even the tiniest epiphytic ferns on the trunks of trees had a Hawaiian name and a use. At places like Akaka Falls (p158), you can find the native nettle *mamaki*, with its red midribs and large, pale papery leaves. A cottage industry has arisen around the invigorating tea made from the leaves of this plant, but its use in ancient Hawai'i was in more potent and complex mixtures of native herbs that catered to both the symptomatic ailments and the psyche of the patient.

Along Saddle Rd is a small forest sanctuary at Pu'u Huluhulu (p145), a cinder cone of luxuriant forest in an otherwise barren lava setting. There, mighty koa trees and red-blossomed ohia form a canopy over a mix of native shrubs, vines and ferns. During the right time of year (mid-summer), the native raspberry, *'ākala,* is in full fruit, and the large, luscious berries, each like a small plum in size and a wonderful maroon color when ripe, will leave you smiling and your fingers red-stained. On the surrounding reddish lava flows, one of the prominent shrubs is another edible: the famed *'ohelo* berry, sacred to the volcano goddess Pele. After picking the first ripe fruit and tossing them outward with thanks to the volcano goddess (thereby ensuring that seeds are spread to sprout into future plants), more can be collected for eating or for cooking into jams and sauces. Locals will go out of their way for a scoop of vanilla ice cream with hot *'ohelo* berry sauce dribbling down the sides!

Near the highest extent of vegetation, above 9000ft elevation, some very distinctive shrubs and trees provide the fabric of their ecosystems. The yellow-flowered *māmane* tree is essential food for the endangered *palila,* a Hawaiian honeycreeper. The tiny-leafed *pukiawe* shrub, with red, pink or white berries, played an important role in ancient Hawaiian culture as a plant used to nullify the spiritual power of high chiefs, allowing them to interact with their subjects. Both of these subalpine plants can be seen on the cinder slopes of Mauna Kea, the state's tallest mountain.

NATIONAL, STATE & COUNTY PARKS   Luci Yamamoto

On the Big Island, about 13% of the land is protected as national, state and county parks, with additional land protected by nature preserves, marine reserves, botanical gardens and much, much more.

National parks comprise the majority of park land, due to the magnitude of 333,000-acre Hawai'i Volcanoes National Park (p192), established in 1916. The park comprises unique geological features (including two of the world's most active volcanoes) and seven ecological zones, from sea coast to rain forest to alpine. It is the habitat of many endangered species. It also encompasses significant archaeological sites such as Halema'uma'u Crater (p199) that have great cultural meaning to native Hawaiians. In addition the park is a major recreational attraction, with campgrounds and numerous hiking trails. The island's two other national parks, Kaloko-Honokohau National Historical Park (p104) and Pu'uhonua o Honaunau National Historical Park (p100), both protect ancient Hawaiian fishponds, heiau and other cultural sites.

The 15 state parks on the island include both recreational spots such as popular Hapuna Beach State Recreation Area (p117) and historical

DID YOU KNOW?

Luscious *'ohelo* berries, sacred to the volcano goddess Pele, are close relatives of blueberries from North America.

DID YOU KNOW?

In ancient times, Hawaiians only rarely visited the sacred realm of Pele, their volcano goddess, and those who did used a rare plant growing only around the volcano to brand a temporary tattoo onto their skin.

sites such as Moʻokini Luakini Heiau (p123). The waters offshore at Kealakekua Bay State Historical Park (p94) are designated a marine sanctuary and subject to strict rules (eg kayak tours are not allowed within protected waters). On the county level, there are three-dozen parks, mostly at easily accessible beaches. Camping is allowed at 10 beach parks, but deserted or unkempt conditions at some of them might deter even eager campers.

National wildlife refuges (NWR; www.refugenet.org), such as the Hakalau Forest National Wildlife Refuge (p138), near Waimea, also afford protection for natural resources, from koa to endangered birds. Some privately owned nature areas, such as Waipiʻo Valley (p151), under the

Nature Area	Features	Activities	Best Time to Visit	Page
Hawaiʻi Volcanoes National Park	vast lava landscape, active volcanoes, ohia forest, museum	hiking, camping, sightseeing	year-round	p192
Puʻuhonua o Honaunau National Historical Park	ancient Hawaiian 'place of refuge'	walking, snorkeling, sightseeing	year-round	p100
Akaka Falls State Park	path through lush rain forest to two impressive waterfalls	walking	year-round	p158
Hapuna Beach State Recreation Area	popular white-sand beach	boogie boarding, swimming, bodysurfing, camping	year-round; calmer surf in summer	p117
Kealakekua Bay State Historical Park	abundant marine life in clear, protected waters	snorkeling, kayaking, diving	year-round	p94
Kekaha Kai State Park	remote beaches accessible only by 4WD and foot	swimming, bodysurfing, boogie boarding, snorkeling, hiking	year-round; calmer surf in summer	p106
Ahalanui Beach Park	lava-rock hot pond near shore	soaking, swimming	year-round	p187
Honoliʻi Beach Park	consistent surf break conveniently located near Hilo	surfing	year-round	p167
Kahaluʻu Beach Park	life-sized underwater fishbowl, shallow waters	snorkeling, surfing	year-round	p86
Onekahakaha Beach Park	shallow waters, tide pools, picnic tables	swimming, exploring tide pools, picnicking	year-round	p167
Waipiʻo Valley	spectacularly lush valley, taro fields, waterfalls	hiking, camping	year-round	p151
Mauna Kea	Hawaiʻi's highest peak, world-class astronomy site	stargazing, hiking	year-round	p141
Moʻokini Luakini Heiau	ruins of ancient sacrificial temple, spectacular view of horizon and Maui	hiking, whale watching	year-round	p123
Pololu Valley	mystical valley at island's northernmost tip	hiking	year-round	p126
South Point	green-sand beach at the southernmost point in the USA	hiking, swimming	year-round	p218

control of Kamehameha Schools Bishop Estate, are open to the public and subject to other rules. Small, private gardens also help to perpetuate native flora and culture. The Amy BH Greenwell Ethnobotanical Garden (p92) replicates a traditional *ahupua'a* (land division) and features plants that existed on the island before Western contact. Hawaii Tropical Botanical Garden (p158), on the other hand, is sprawling and lush but, while impressive, showcases mainly exotic flora introduced after Captain Cook's arrival.

http://www.nps.gov
/havo/
Get the latest status of the current active lava, plus all the biological, geological and cultural details you might need to get the most out of your visit.

The management of Hawai'i's precious land can be contentious. Often, the state or county clashes with native Hawaiians who believe that their concerns and ancient spiritual sites are misused for recreational, commercial or scientific purposes. Sometimes native Hawaiians and environmentalists are aligned, as in their opposition to additional development on Mauna Kea without adequate environmental studies and public hearings (see p140). Smaller beach parks, like Ho'okena Beach Park (p101), are almost regarded as locals-only spots. Dolphins and other creatures are revered, and some locals fear that an influx of tourists will scare them away.

Hawai'i's parkland might be safe from development, but parks, too, are subject to environmental hazards. Once the government improves access, for example by paving roads and building parking lots and facilities, people inevitably flock to the site. Soon, a paved road will be run to Manini'owali (Kua Bay), a pristine, remote beach at Kekaha Kai State Park (p106). Certainly this will boost the number of visitors and perhaps transform it into a tourist magnet like Hapuna Beach State Recreation Area (p117). The balance of interests – environmental, public access and native Hawaiian rights, among others – is an ongoing challenge.

For more on parks in general, contact the **Department of Land & Natural Resources** (DLNR; on O'ahu ☎ 587-0320; www.state.hi.us/dlnr; Kalanimoku Bldg, 1151 Punchbowl St, Honolulu), which offers publications and online information about safe hiking and conservation. Ask about its Big Island branch offices. DLNR oversees the following programs:

Department of Parks & Recreation (☎ 961-8311; www.co.hawaii.hi.us; Suite 6, 101 Pauahi St, Hilo, HI 96720; ⏲ 7:45am-4pm Mon-Fri) Info on county parks, including camping permits.
Division of Forestry & Wildlife (DOFAW; on O'ahu ☎ 587-0166; www.dofaw.net; 1151 Punchbowl St, Room 325, Honolulu, HI 96813) Supervises public land management of forests and natural area reserves (NARs). Public outreach focuses on outdoor recreation, conservation and watershed protection. Website includes addresses of Big Island branch offices, links to Geographic Information System maps and the Na Ala Hele Trail and Access Program.
Division of State Parks (☎ 974-6200; www.hawaii.gov/dlnr/dsp; PO Box 936, Hilo, HI 96721; ⏲ 8am-noon Mon-Fri) For more on state parks, including camping permits.

ENVIRONMENTAL ISSUES Dr Samuel M 'Ohukani'ōhi'a Gon III

Being the largest of the Hawaiian Islands, there have been few environmental issues that have not risen to prominence on the Big Island of Hawai'i. Alternative energy projects have come and gone, leaving giant windmills rusting on windswept plains along the South Point road. Even geothermal wells (which provide 20% of the island's power) are not problem-free, as they are sometimes clogged with mineral steam deposits. Growing populations have brought urban sprawl and miniature versions of Honolulu rush-hour traffic to the roadways of Kona and Hilo. Speculative land purchases have subdivided some of the last lowland rain forest areas of Puna, while driving property values up so high that native Hawaiians and long-time residents can ill afford the burgeoning tax burden.

New owners with liquid assets but little or no relationship with the land mean that native species and cultural sites alike are dealt with as liabilities, and only strong laws protecting the resources of the land and advocacy organizations such as the **Sierra Club** (www.hi.sierraclub.org) serve to guard such places from the bulldozers of progress. Large resorts along the Kona and Kohala coastlines are a mixed blessing. Some have been sensitive to natural and cultural resources and, by working with local communities, have incorporated culture and natural features to enhance visitors' experiences. Others are the typical transplant of 'fantasy island' onto the landscape, supplanting ancient heritage and features with what investors think tourists want.

The collapse of sugarcane agriculture in the 1990s left entire communities, such as Pahala in the Ka'u District, searching for economic stability, while the huge lowland areas once secure with sugarcane are now in sporadic ventures in diversified agriculture – or are converting into fallow fields bringing new weed threats closer to adjacent native forest reserves. In our increasingly military age, the training areas of the island of Hawai'i, the largest in the state, are increasingly active, and there is friction between military training and endangered species habitats, as well as many native Hawaiians, who hold the land sacred and consider the heavy footprint of the military unacceptable.

Yet for all this, the island of Hawai'i retains some of the largest remaining acreage of Hawaii's native ecosystems to the extent of hundreds of thousands of acres. Thankfully, some of this has long been protected in parks such as Hawai'i Volcanoes National Park, which recently received a 117,000-acre addition of land, formerly belonging to Kahuku Ranch, in cooperation with the **Nature Conservancy** (http://nature.org). There are extensive state forest reserves and special state lands called Natural Area Reserves, where special ecological systems are recognized and protected. For all its unique and irreplaceable native species and ecosystem resources, in addition to a state forest reserve system that is the 11th-largest in the nation, the state budget for forest management ranks 48th, nearly the lowest in the USA.

The conservation-savvy traveler will find that the major nature organizations are very active on the island of Hawai'i. The Sierra Club has a Big Island chapter called Moku Loa (Long Island), which is very active both in the political arena and on land, battling alien infestations (such as Miconia and coqui frogs) as well as challenging the military over its environmental compliance. The **Hawai'i Audubon Society** (www.hawaiiaudubon .com) is also very active on the island – no surprise, as Hawai'i is one of the best strongholds for native birds. The Nature Conservancy has preserves in the Kona and Ka'u districts, but these are in remote areas with no civilized approach. Nonetheless, it is heartening to know that some of the best natural areas on the island are being managed to heal the damage of history and to maintain native ecosystems for generations to come.

Hawai'i Outdoors

Being the Big Island of the chain, the variety of outdoor activities is immense. While it does not get the huge winter swell of O'ahu's North Shore, or gusty winds of Maui's Ho'okipa Beach, the Big Island is unique when it comes to outdoor and adventure activities. Of all the Hawaiian Islands, only in Hawai'i can you snowboard and surf in the same day, find white-, black- and green-sand beaches, test your will in the Ironman Triathlon, stargaze from the world's clearest summit and see active lava flowing into the sea.

From hiking to scuba and horseback riding to surfing, you can do it here. If you've always wanted to tick these activities off your wish list, here is your opportunity. Operators throughout the island will cater to all your desires with affordable instruction, convenience and availability. No time-consuming prior planning here, just feel out what each day calls for, rent the equipment, take the lessons and go for it.

Of course, you can also loll on the beach, go for a swim, golf, snorkel, jog, kayak and mountain bike here. Most people salivate when you mention a trip to Hawai'i, either because they have been or they are itching to go.

Always heed the numerous warning signs dotted around the coast.

WATER SPORTS

Hawai'i, like the rest of the island chain, is surrounded by the vast Pacific Ocean. The ancient Polynesians had to find their way across thousands of miles of open ocean before reaching the Big Island. Through a profound study of the wind, currents and stars the Polynesians had the first vast vessel of navigation called *Hokule'a* (see p22). They were true masters of the sea and even pioneered the modern-day cult of surfing.

Needless to say, one of the main reasons people come to Hawai'i is to get closer to sea, to tap in and experience some local knowledge, and to know a little better the power and wonder of the ocean through modern and traditional sports alike.

SWIMMING

The Big Island has over 300 miles of shoreline, but much of the coast is composed of jagged lava. Only along the Kona Coast will you find plush

---

OCEAN SAFETY

Drowning is the leading cause of accidental death for visitors. If you're not familiar with water conditions, ask around. It's best not to swim alone in unfamiliar places.

Rip Currents Rips, or rip currents, are fast-flowing ocean currents that can drag swimmers out into deeper water. Anyone caught in one should either go with the flow until it loses power or swim parallel to shore to slip out of it.

Rogue Waves Never turn your back on the ocean. Waves don't all come in with equal height or strength, and sometimes one can sweep over a shoreline ledge and drag sunbathers from the beach into the ocean.

Shorebreaks If waves that are breaking close to the shore are only a couple of feet high, they're generally fine for novice bodysurfers. Large shorebreaks, though, can hit hard with a slamming downward force.

Undertows Common along steeply sloped beaches, undertows occur where large waves wash back directly into incoming surf. Swimmers caught up in one can be pulled underwater. Don't panic; go with the current until you get beyond the wave.

For information about tsunami, see p227.

white-sand beaches, lined with palms and tucked among the coves of black lava. The bittersweet side of the Hawai'i coast is accessibility. It may take a 4WD to get there, but then you might just have the beach to yourself.

The best swimming spots are in South Kohala and North Kona, such as popular Hapuna Beach (p117), any of the remote and pristine beaches at Kekaha Kai State Park (p106) and perfect, crescent-shaped Kauna'oa Bay (p117) by the Mauna Kea Beach Hotel. Some folks also like to stroke the 2.4-mile swimming portion of the Ironman Triathlon (p77). The snorkeling areas in South Kona are also good for swimming (p74) and for convenience there are some good beaches close to Kailua-Kona (p74).

On the eastern coast, the seas are often rough and inappropriate for novices but there are a few good options (p168). Otherwise, unique wonders abound, such as a hot pond (p187), black- and green-sand beaches (p219), and countless lava tide pools (p187). The windward side of the island is much wetter, providing abundant waterfalls and hidden streams to take a dip.

There are public swimming pools located in Honoka'a, Hilo, Kapa'au, Kealakekua, Laupahoehoe and Pahoa. For directions and open-swim schedules, call the county **Aquatics Division** (☎ 961-8694).

> 'The waters on the lee-ward coast provide good conditions almost the entire way'

SNORKELING

Rainbows are not only seen above the water in Hawai'i; a myriad of colors present themselves in these clear tropical waters. Just don a mask and snorkel and the ocean is your aquarium of vibrant corals and reef fish.

The waters on the leeward coast provide good conditions almost the entire way, but the spots south of Kailua-Kona are a heaven for snorkelers. On the windward coast, stream runoff and turbulent water leave little visibility but there are a few worthwhile spots.

Rental prices range from $9 to $15 per week. Check out the freebie magazines for coupons. Snorkeling tours, typically from $80 to $100, can make life easy, transporting you to prime spots and providing gear and food. They depart mainly from Keauhou Bay, Kailua Pier or Honokohau Harbor (p96). It's best to book in advance, especially during high season.

DIVING

Along the Kona Coast, diving conditions are excellent, with warm, calm waters and frequent 100ft visibility. Sites range from shallow beginner dives to challenging nighttime and lava tube dives. One of the best spots is Ka'awaloa Cove in the Kealakekua Bay State Historical & Underwater Parks (p94). In Kailua-Kona, you can also arrange a thrilling night dive to see manta rays (p75). The best conditions are in spring and summer, but diving is decent year-round. Other good leeward sites include Place of Refuge and the Old Airport in Kailua-Kona and Puako in South Kohala. On the Hilo side, the water tends to be cloudy from river runoff, and diving conditions are mediocre.

THE BIG ISLAND'S TOP FIVE SNORKELING SPOTS

Kealakekua Bay (p95) For beautiful snorkeling in the pristine 30ft-deep waters.

Pu'uhonua o Honaunau National Historical Park (p101) For convenience, a terrific drive-up snorkeling spot.

Kahalu'u Bay (p86) A popular Kailua-Kona snorkeling haunt and a good place for beginners.

Kapoho Tide Pools (p187) One of the east coast's few protected areas.

Puako Bay (p116) For extensive reef possibilities.

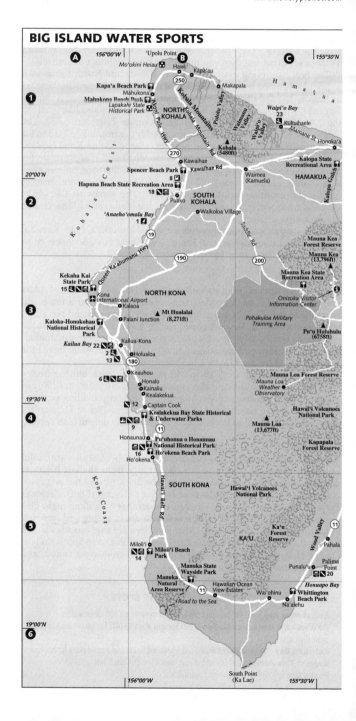

BIG ISLAND WATER SPORTS

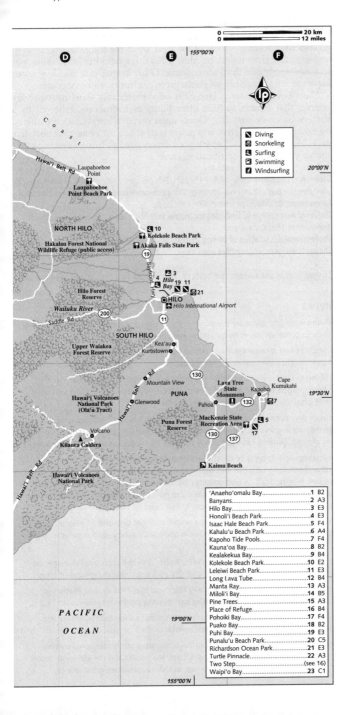

'Almost 700 fish species live in Hawaiian waters, and nearly one-third are endemic'

The marine life here is phenomenal and since the Big Island is such a baby – geologically speaking – most of the reefs are of the fringe variety, close to and accessible from the shore. Almost 700 fish species live in Hawaiian waters, and nearly one-third are endemic. Other magnificent sea life you can expect to see are spinner dolphins, green sea turtles, and moray eels.

Many dive operations (see p73) offer reasonably short introductory courses that usually include three hours of instruction, followed by a shallow beach or boat dive. Open-water certification courses are offered by many companies. Dive-trip prices start at $55 for a one-tank boat dive or $105 for two tanks. Experienced divers needn't bring anything other than a swimsuit and certification card.

Some useful organizations:

Divers Alert Network (DAN; ☎ 800-446-2671, 24hr emergency hotlines ☎ 919-684-8111/4326; www.diversalertnetwork.org) DAN advises on diving emergencies and offers supplemental insurance for evacuation, decompression services, illness and injury.

National Association of Underwater Instructors (NAUI; www.naui.org) This worldwide association certifies scuba divers.

Professional Association of Diving Instructors (PADI; ☎ 800-729-7234; www.padi.com) This worldwide association certifies scuba divers.

If you just want to test the waters, beginners can try 'snuba' (opposite).

RESPONSIBLE DIVING

The popularity of diving is placing immense pressure on many sites. Please consider the following tips when diving to help preserve the ecology and beauty of reefs.

- Do not use reef anchors and take care not to ground boats on coral. Encourage dive operators to establish permanent moorings at popular sites.

- Avoid touching living marine organisms with your body or dragging equipment across the reef. Polyps can be damaged by even the gentlest contact. Never stand on coral. If you must hold on to the reef, only touch exposed rock or dead coral.

- Be conscious of your fins. Even without contact, the surge from heavy fin strokes near the reef can damage delicate organisms. When treading water in shallow reef areas, take care not to kick up clouds of sand. Settling sand can easily smother the delicate organisms of the reef.

- Practice and maintain proper buoyancy control. Major damage can be done by divers descending too fast and colliding with the reef. Make sure you are correctly weighted and that your weight belt is positioned so that you stay horizontal. Be aware that buoyancy can change over the period of an extended trip: initially you may breathe harder and need more weight; a few days later you may breathe more easily and need less weight.

- Take care in underwater caves. Spend as little time within them as possible, as your air bubbles may be caught within the roof and thereby leave previously submerged organisms high and dry.

- Resist the temptation to collect or buy coral or shells. Aside from the ecological damage, taking home marine souvenirs depletes the beauty of a site and spoils the enjoyment of others.

- Ensure that you take home all your rubbish and any litter you may find as well. Plastics in particular are a serious threat to marine life. Turtles can mistake plastic for jellyfish and eat it.

- Resist the temptation to feed fish. You may disturb their normal eating habits, encourage aggressive behavior or feed them food that is detrimental to their health.

- Minimize your disturbance of marine animals. It is illegal to approach endangered marine species too closely; these include many whales, dolphins, sea turtles and the Hawaiian monk seal. In particular, do not ride on the backs of turtles, as this causes them great anxiety.

WHALE WATCHING

Many species of whale are found in Hawaiian waters, including sperm whales, false killer whales, pilot whales and beaked whales. Nonetheless, it's the migrating humpbacks with their acrobatic displays that attract tourists. Peak whale-watching season is from January through March, although whales are usually around for a month or so on either side of those dates.

Luckily for whale watchers, humpbacks are coast-huggers, preferring shallow offshore waters for nursing their newborn calves. Be aware humpbacks are highly sensitive to human disturbance and noise. Coming within 100yd of a humpback (300yd in 'cow/calf waters') is prohibited by federal law and can result in a $25,000 fine. Whale-watching tours depart from Honokohau Harbor (p103).

Snuba

Somewhere between snorkeling and diving, snuba allows divers to breathe through a long hose attached to an air tank, which is floating on a raft at the surface. This is a good introduction for kids (ages 12 and up) and people intrigued by scuba but not yet hooked on the idea. Snuba programs teach elementary dive techniques including clearing your facemask and equalizing ear pressure. Generally, the best snuba experiences are those from boats, because you can reach better dive sites, but snuba from the beach is also available. The cost ranges from $70 to $110, depending upon the outfit and whether it's a shore or boat dive.

SURFING

Big Island surf spots often have rugged lava-rock shorelines that require nimble maneuvering. Another hindrance are *wana* (sea urchins that resemble pin-cushions), which abound at some beaches. Don't expect the monster waves that hit O'ahu's North Shore either. Still, there are a few nice surf breaks where you'll find throngs of dedicated Big Island surfers.

For the most part, like on the other islands, bigger swell comes from the north in the winter, but conditions can be good anywhere and anytime. The leeward coast breaks are generally cleaner, especially in the morning, but the windward side has a few river mouths that spew runoff. Check the local tides and weather with the daily Big Island surf report at www.hawaiisurfnews.com.

Consistent spots on the east side are Honoli'i Cove (p168), Kolekole Beach Park (p156) and Waipi'o Beach (p153), all north of Hilo. Pohoiki Bay at Isaac Hale Beach Park (p187) is a bit heavier, but more experienced surfers will enjoy this lava reef.

Along the Kona Coast, try Kahalu'u Beach (p86) in Keauhou, Banyans (p75) close to White Sands Beach, and Pine Trees (p105) near Wawaloli (OTEC) Beach.

You can rent a surfboard from local surf shops ($10 to $20 per day) in Kona (p76) and Hilo (p168). If you want to learn, try a one-hour or full-day lesson (p168); private and multiple lessons can also be arranged.

Boogie Boarding & Bodysurfing

Top spots for boogie boarding and body surfing include Hapuna Beach (p117), White Sands Beach (p74), and the beaches at Kekaha Kai State Park (p106).

KAYAKING

Out of the way coves and turquoise waters make Hawai'i ideal for sea kayaking. From Mahukona Beach Park in North Kohala to the Manuka

To gain a good understanding about where surfing stands today, from its roots to rise in status as an international cult, see Dana Brown's *Step into Liquid*, an essential classic surf documentary.

Paddling Hawaii by Audrey Sutherland is an indispensable guide for everything from cleaning your fresh octopus dinner to making safe surf landings.

State Wayside Park in Ka'u, the possibilities are seemingly endless on the Kona Coast. Enthusiasts could split this stretch into a multi-week trip of a lifetime.

Kayaking in Kealakekua Bay (p97) is a must. The most popular launching spot is Napo'opo'o Beach, from which you paddle across the bay toward the Captain Cook Monument, where you can snorkel and explore. Pristine coastline along Kekaha Kai State Park provides seclusion while Kailua Bay is a local Kona playground. Another super popular kayak tour called Flumin' launches from Hawi; see p124.

A northern island start in the summer makes a spectacular kayak from 'Upolu Point to the Waipi'o Valley. Down Hilo way, kayakers usually put in at the Hilo Bayfront Beach Park or at Richardson Ocean Park.

You can rent kayaks all along Hwy 11 on the Kona Coast (p97).

A CULT CLASSIC

He'enalu (wave sliding) could only spawn from a culture so steeped in its connection to the sea. From the beginning of their existence the Polynesians have crisscrossed the Pacific following the stars and riding the waves. An integral part of the early Hawaiian lifestyle, surfing was imbued with sacred elements. From the kahuna's selection of the tree and carving of the board, to the special chants to christen the board and instill courage in the man or woman who challenged the waves; from the ritual show of prowess among *ali'i* (chiefs) and commoners alike, to the youthful enthusiasm involved with catching a wave; surfing embodied the Hawaiians' profound love and knowledge of the ocean. Love and lands were won and lost in this test of skill and bravery.

The high status of *he'enalu* as a Hawaiian pastime was evidenced in its strict *kapu*. The Hawaiian hierarchy was evident even down to the board size and shape. There were four basic styles used. Children tended to ride the *paipo* or *kioe* (belly board) measuring 2ft to 4ft long. Commoners generally used two sized boards made from Koa, the 9ft *alaia* or *omo* (stand up board), and the longer *kiko'o*, which could reach up to 18ft. The dense nature of the wood made these boards heavy and a bit awkward. Sometimes weighing 100lb, it took a real master to surf these planks! The *ali'i* on the other hand rode *olo* boards, longer still (up to 24ft) and specially made from *wili wili*, a light balsa-like wood. Certain beaches and breaks were *kapu* to all but the *ali'i*. The Waikiki break, Kalehuaweke, on O'ahu tells of a commoner who dropped in on a Hawaiian chiefess. Oops, this faux-pas meant sure death, but he evaded punishment after offering her his lehua wreath. Looks like local territorialism is nothing new to the sport.

At the arrival of Captain Cook in 1779 at Kealakekua Bay, Lieutenant James King wrote two pages in his journal describing the local pastime he witnessed on the Big Island's Kona coast:

'[T]he great art is to guide the plank so as always to keep it in the proper direction on the top of the swell, and as it alters its direct. If the swell drives him close to the rocks before he is overtaken by its break, he is much prais'd,'…'they seem to feel a great pleasure in the motion which this exercise gives.'

True to its essence, the nature of the ritual was to get naked, gamble and show off.

But the fun soon ended after contact with the Europeans, as disease and death struck the Hawaiians and their sensual culture. With populations decimated, the islands came under a new Calvinistic morality. Replacing the Kapu, these new set of rules banned surfing, music and hula in the interest of modesty, industry and religion. By 1820 surfing, like much of Hawaiian culture, had almost vanished.

He'enalu continued, but mainly underground until the turn of the 20th century, when the sport began to make a comeback. The father of this modern revolution was Duke Kahanamoku, a native Hawaiian who stood out among the resurgence happening at Waikiki. He was one of the few to ride and master the 'bluebirds' (big swells). Following in his ancestral tradition he was the consummate waterman, winning a 1912 Olympic gold medal in swimming. He soon took his notoriety around the world and became known as the ambassador of surfing, a local hero, and a legend in his own time.

WINDSURFING

Might be best to try another island. But there are a few decent spots to mess around. The best area is 'Anaeho'omalu Bay (p111) at Waikaloa where wind consistently funnels down from Waimea. Beginners will find this an ideal spot to learn and you can rent equipment and take lessons. December and January storms bring winds from 18 to 35 knots. This is the season on the Kona Coast but things can get a little more exciting when the spring trade winds kick up; novices are warned off at that time.

KITEBOARDING

A relatively new sport, kiteboarding is gaining popularity. A hybrid between surfing and maneuvering a two-string kite it really resembles wakeboarding more than windsurfing. The difference is there is no boat, just the whims of the wind to power or drag you along. The main thing to get right is controlling the kite, which can be a bit tricky. Handling the board comes easier, especially if you have any experience with board sports.

Being the windy spot of the island, 'Anaeho'omalu Bay is the best place to have a go. First, you learn how to fly the kite, then you practice bodydragging. Ask around for rental and lessons on the beach.

FISHING

Deep-sea fishing is an obsession on the Kona Coast, which is the world's No 1 spot for catching Pacific blue marlin. The waters are also rich with 'ahi (yellowfin tuna) and aku (bonito or skipjack tuna), swordfish, spearfish and mahimahi (dolphin). June to August typically sees the biggest hauls for blue marlin, while January to June is the best for striped marlin. Most of the world records for catches of such fish belong to Kona fishers, with at least one marlin weighing 1000lb or more reeled in virtually every year. For charter tours, see p76.

'June to August typically sees the biggest hauls for blue marlin, while January to June is the best for striped marlin'

LAND ACTIVITIES

These tiny specks of land are actually massive mountains of land jutting more than 30,000ft from the bottom of the ocean. Hawai'i offers some of the richest ecosystems on the planet. Hiking is extraordinary and you can even ski in the winter (p142). But you needn't be limited to your own two feet: try two wheels or a four-legged creature. Or take a swing with racquets and clubs.

HIKING

The hiking in Hawai'i is top-notch, and there's enough diverse terrain to sate even the shortest attention spans. Hikes range from brief, laidback nature strolls to multiday backcountry treks that will set anyone's calves quaking. There are places where you could walk for days without seeing another soul. Just pick your place: blistering desert treks or lush rain-forest walks, nature preserves or botanical gardens, beach strolls or snowy ridgelines – it's all here.

All levels of hikers will find awesome trails on the Big Island. The widest variety of hiking is found at Hawai'i Volcanoes National Park (p203), where trails lead across steaming crater floors, through lush native forests and up to the peak of Mauna Loa.

Along the steep coastal cliffs and deep valleys of the Kohala Mountains, you can take short hikes at Pololu Valley (p126) and Waipi'o Valley (p152), or backpack deep into remote Waimanu Valley (p153).

THE BIG ISLAND'S TOP FIVE HIKES

Waipi'o and Waimanu Valleys (p152) For deep, verdant costal valleys and flowing waterfalls.
Mauna Loa Trail (p205) For its vast volcanic landscapes and unhindered views.
Kilauea Iki Trail (p204) For a condensed look at the intriguing environments in Hawai'i Volcanoes National Park.
Mauna Kea Summit Trail (p141) Hike the sacred white mountain, the islands' highest point.
Napau Crater Trail (p206) See petroglyphs, camp and glimpse the active Pu'u 'O'o Vent in Hawai'i Volcanoes National Park.

North of Kona, you can hike in from the highway to secluded beaches or explore portions of ancient footpaths and petroglyph fields. **Na Ala Hele** (☎ 331-8505; www.hawaiitrails.org), a state-sponsored group of volunteers, is currently working to re-establish the entire 50-mile historic trail system that once ran between Kailua-Kona and Kawaihae. South of Kona, the simple Captain Cook Monument Trail (p98) leads to the spot where he died at Kealakekua Bay, and a jumping-off point for snorkeling.

The most arduous hikes scale the summits of Mauna Kea (p141) and Mauna Loa (p205), where the altitude of almost 14,000ft can be daunting.

For tours, **Hawaiian Walkways** (☎ 775-0372, 800-457-7759; www.hawaiianwalkways .com) and **Hawaii Forest & Trail** (☎ 331-8505, 800-464-1993; www.hawaii-forest.com) are the Big Island's best outfits, each offering guided hikes to places you might not see otherwise. The Sierra Club's **Big Island Moku Loa Group** (☎ 965-9695; www.hi.sierraclub.org/Hawaii/outings.html; suggested donation for nonmembers $3) offers low-cost hiking tours, ranging from trekking over new lava rock in Kalapana to backpacking in Pololu Valley. If you want a particular tour or day, reserve in advance. If you call only a day or two ahead, it might be sold out.

Hike Safety

'Hawai'i has no snakes (although there are some reports of recent sights)'

Hawai'i has no snakes (although there are some reports of recent sights), no poison ivy, no poison oak and few wild animals that will fuss with hikers. But hiking around volcanoes presents a variety of dangers. Fumes can lead to respiratory problems; lava flows can unexpectedly collapse; crevasses can wrench ankles. Heed all posted warnings and hike with a buddy.

Flash floods are a real danger in many of the steep, narrow valleys that require stream crossings. Warning signs include a distant rumbling, the smell of fresh earth and a sudden increase in the river's current. If the water begins to rise, get to higher ground immediately. A walking stick is good for bracing yourself on slippery approaches, gaining leverage and testing the depth of rivers and streams.

Darkness falls fast once the sun sets and ridge-top trails are no place to be caught unprepared in the dark. Always carry a flashlight just in case. Long pants offer protection from overgrown parts of the trail, and sturdy footwear with good traction is a must (and lava will still chew right through it). If you plan to hike one of the volcanoes be prepared for possible winter mountaineering conditions. Pack 2L of water per person for a day hike, carry a whistle and something bright to alert rescue workers, wear sunscreen, tote a first-aid kit and above all, start out early.

GOLF

A destination for its verdant green fairways, challenging design, lava hazards, and greens on the cliffs above the crashing surf, the Big Island boasts over 20 golf courses, including the world-class courses at the South Kohala luxury resorts. There are other quality courses sprinkled around the island providing a variety of options and conditions.

THE BIG ISLAND'S TOP TEN GOLF COURSES

Mauna Kea Golf Course (p117) Experts regard this course as the island's best.

Francis I'i Brown North Course (p115) Exquisitely maintained and less crowded than other top courses.

Francis I'i Brown South Course (p115) Close to the ocean and flanked by stunning lava this is a popular Kona classic.

Hapuna Beach Prince Hotel Golf Course (p117) A narrow course designed by Arnold Palmer, the fairways and greens are exceptionally well kept.

Four Seasons Hualalai Course (p107) A highly regarded course designed by Jack Nicklaus but open only to club members and hotel guests.

Waikoloa Beach Course (p113) Probably the most popular course for the quality, price and location on the water.

Waikoloa Kings' Course (p113) A challenging links-style course weaving among lava.

Hilo Municipal Golf Course (p168) For a sweet deal in Hilo, head to where the locals play, rain or shine.

Volcano Golf & Country Club (p203) Play on the lush forest grounds in a misty mountain setting.

Naniloa Country Club Golf Course (p168) Hilo's other course has only nine holes but the location is very scenic.

Many courses offer *kama'aina* (local) discounts and greens fees are usually slashed by 50% if you take an afternoon tee-off time; definitely ask about discounts. Super-thrifty golf hounds should consider packing a driver and putter and renting the rest at the links of their choice.

HORSEBACK RIDING

The Big Island is *paniolo* (cowboy) country, and the pastureland of Waimea and North Kohala are perfect for horseback riding. Custom rides, cattle drives and tours appropriate for kids and beginners are all possible. For tours see (p132) in Waimea, (p121) in North Kohala, (p98) in South Kona and (p155) on the Hamakua Coast.

MOUNTAIN BIKING & CYCLING

With wide-open spaces, the Big Island is ideal for both road and mountain biking. Generally speaking, local biking communities are well organized, host group rides, build new trails and promote responsible and safe cycling. Road cyclists should be advised that many paved roads are narrow, bordered by jagged lava with no shoulder. The Ironman route on Hwy 19 north of Kailua Kona (p77) is an exception with well-established shoulders.

In addition to established routes, which include the 45-mile Mana Rd loop (p138) circling Mauna Kea and the 6.5-mile beach trail to Pine Trees (p105) on the Kona Coast, there are also miles of 4WD roads and rocky trails. If you are in South Point follow the trail to Green Sands beach and in Hawai'i Volcanoes National park try the Escape Rd.

For bicycle rentals, head to the main towns, Hilo (p178) or Kailua-Kona (p85). The following organizations offer tours and information:

Bicycle Adventures (☎ 800-443-6060; www.bicycleadventures.com; 7-day trip $2400) Based in Washington state on the mainland offering full cycling-vacation packages that traverse the island.

Big Island Mountain Bike Association (☎ 961-4452; www.interpac.net/~mtbike) In Hilo.

Big Island Race & Training Schedule (www.bigislandraceschedule.com) For all manner of annual races including biking, running, swimming and outrigger canoeing.

Kona Coast Cycling Tours (☎ 345-3455, 877-592-2453; www.cyclekona.com; half-day tour $60-75, full-day $100-155) It allows older kids (12 to 16 years) on many rides at a reduced rate. You can also request custom-designed tours ($150 for the tour) on which a guide will accompany you for the ride (and carry all the supplies!).

People's Advocacy for Trails Hawaii (in Kona ☎ 326-9495) Learn more about Big Island mountain biking.

John Alford's *Mountain Biking the Hawaiian Islands* should be your bible.

RUNNING

The Big Island is famous worldwide for its premier endurance test. Each October, Kona hosts the Ironman Triathlon (see the boxed text, p77), which combines a 2.4-mile ocean swim, 112-mile bike race and a full marathon (26.2 miles) into one exhaustive endurance race. Some 1500 men and women from 50 countries compete each year.

The Keauhou-Kona Triathlon is a half-Ironman, held in Keauhou Bay each May as a qualifier for the main event.

You would be hard pressed to find a more beautiful running circuit than the craters and calderas of Hawai'i Volcanoes National Park. Check out the Kilauea Volcano Wilderness Runs. For information, contact the **Volcano Art Center** (☎ 967-7565; www.volcanoartcenter.org; PO Box 104, Hawai'i Volcanoes National Park, HI 96718).

The **Hawaii Race** (☎ 808-538-0330; 9 N Pauahi, No 200, Honolulu, HI 96817) includes statewide running, swimming and cycling race schedules, qualification details and entry forms.

Want to tackle the Ironman Triathlon? Serious competitors won't do less than 40 hours' training per week. Still keen?

TENNIS

Many county parks on the Big Island have municipal tennis courts that are well maintained, with fresh nets and night lighting. Call the **Department of Parks & Recreation** (☎ 961-8311) in Hilo for a list of public tennis courts. Also check with the large hotels as some allow nonguests to rent court time. However, the more exclusive the place, the more likely that only guests are allowed to use them. Prices typically run about $10 per hour.

Food & Drink

In Hawaii, the locals don't eat for survival – they eat for sheer pleasure. You'll find an array of cuisines, introduced by the first Polynesians and the succession of immigrants who followed. It took human settlers to create Hawaii's modern-day cornucopia, as the only indigenous edibles were ferns, *'ohelo* berries and other barely sustaining plants. The Polynesians brought *kalo* (taro), *'ulu* (breadfruit), *'uala* (sweet potato), *mai'a* (banana), *ko* (sugarcane), *niu* (coconut) and mountain apple, plus chickens, pigs and dogs for meat – and they discovered an abundance of seafood.

Bear in mind that 'local' fare is a broad term. You can go highbrow at five-star restaurants serving Hawaii Regional Cuisine, which highlights Pacific Rim flavors and island-grown produce, seafood and meat. Or you can sample everyday *local kine grinds* – hearty, flavorful, and most important, plentiful! Local street food is often fried, salty, gravy-laden and meaty. But a trend toward healthy cooking in Hawaii is afoot, and you can find plate lunches featuring grilled fish and brown rice. Vegetarians will find lots of options: luscious fresh papaya and pineapple, organic greens, tofu delicacies and more. No one in Hawaii goes hungry.

DID YOU KNOW?

Restaurants that top pizzas with pineapple and call it 'Hawaiian' are way off. The pineapple was introduced to Hawaii in 1813 and grown commercially only after 1900.

STAPLES & SPECIALTIES

Nowadays you can find haute cuisine and imported haole (Caucasian) supplies (like olive oil, artisan bread and balsamic vinegar) anywhere in the islands. But at heart, Hawaii is a 'beer and rice' type of place – the 'wine and cheese' crowd has a long way to go. A meal is incomplete without the foremost local staple: sticky, medium-grain, white rice. The rice pot accompanies even pasta or potato meals, and 20lb bags of rice are typical raffle prizes. (Granted, the Atkins low-carb diet is a phenomenon in Hawaii, too.) While ketchup and salsa might be the mainland's top condiments, the local essential is soy sauce, always called by its Japanese name, shoyu.

Native Hawaiian

The centerpiece of a native Hawaiian meal is *kalua* pig, baked underground in an *imu* (a pit of red-hot stones). To cook the pig, layers of crushed banana trunks and *ti* leaves are placed over the stones. The pig, stuffed with hot stones, is laid atop the bed, along with other foods wrapped in *ti* and banana leaves. Everything receives another covering of *ti* leaves, a layer of mats and dirt to seal in the hot steam. To *kalua* means to cook using this method. Cooking time is four to eight hours, depending on the quantity of food. Traditional *kalua* cooking is hard to find now, as few resorts cook pork underground for luau. At home, it's hard to find folks willing to sacrifice their backyard for an *imu*, which scorches surrounding vegetation.

Wetland taro was the Hawaiians' primary starch, usually eaten as poi, a paste pounded from cooked taro. The paste is thinned to a desired consistency by adding water. You might hear locals describe poi texture by the number of fingers needed to scoop it into the mouth: one-, two- and three-finger poi. Poi is highly nutritious, easily digestible and a perfect complement to strongly flavored foods. But many nonlocals find poi bland and describe the texture as akin to 'wallpaper paste,' which strikes locals as not only absurd but also insulting. Taro is a sacred food, considered the root of all life. Traditional Hawaiian households always show respect for taro: when the poi bowl sits on the table, one is expected to refrain from arguing or speaking in anger.

Other commonly eaten Hawaiian foods are *laulau* (bundle of pork, chicken or butterfish, wrapped in taro leaf, which cooks to a soft texture similar to spinach, and steamed in a covering of *ti* leaf); *lomi* salmon (a dish of minced, salted salmon, diced tomato and green onion); baked *'ulu* (breadfruit); raw *opihi* (limpets picked off the reef at low tide); *pipi kaula* (beef jerky); *haupia* (a stiff pudding made of coconut cream and arrowroot); and raw *'a'ama* (black crab).

Local Food

While 'destination' restaurants might show off Hawaii's finest flavors, the soul of island food resides in cheap everyday eats, including the following:

Homesick locals living on the mainland share their recipe collections online at www.alohaworld.com /ono.

Bento A remnant of plantation days, this prepackaged Japanese-style box lunch includes rice and your choice of meat or fish, along with pickles, *kamaboko* (a cake of puréed, steamed fish) and cooked vegetables.

Crack seed A Chinese snack food made with dried fruit, often plums or lemon. Crack seed can be sweet, sour, salty or a combination of all. The most popular – and most overwhelming to the uninitiated – is *li hing mui*. Today locals use *li hing* flavoring to spice up everything from fresh apples to margaritas!

Loco moco For an only-in-Hawaii experience, try this amalgamation of rice, fried egg and hamburger patty topped with gravy and a dash of shoyu. It's surprisingly appetizing, and meatless versions are available.

Okazu-ya If you want to cobble together your own meal, Japanese 'fast food' is sold individually (by the piece) at *okazu-ya* (lunch counters). There are dozens of options, including *musubi* (rice ball), *maki* (hand-rolled) sushi, tofu patties, shrimp tempura, *nishime* (stew of root vegetables) and Japanese-style fried chicken.

For Spam trivia, history, events, recipes and more, go to www.hormel.com (and search the site for Spam).

Plate lunch This fixed-plate meal (akin to a 'blue-plate special') comprises 'two scoop rice,' a scoop of macaroni salad and an entrée, such as beef stew, *tonkatsu* (pork cutlets), grilled mahimahi or teriyaki chicken.

Pupu *Anykine* snacks or appetizers. An irresistibly savory favorite is *poke* (poh-kay), which contains cubed raw fish (often *'ahi*) typically marinated in shoyu, sesame oil, salt, green onion and chili pepper. Traditional *poke* includes *ogo* (seaweed) and *inamona*, a flavoring made of roasted and ground *kukui* (candlenut), while countless current renditions might use oysters, tofu or fruit. Also worth trying are boiled peanuts in the shell, which are similar to the *edamame* (boiled soybeans) popular at sushi bars and taste fresher than the usual dry-roasted nuts.

Saimin Found only in Hawaii, this noodle soup is garnished with your choice of toppings, such as green onion, dried nori (seaweed), slices of *kamaboko*, egg roll and *char siu* (Chinese roast pork).

COMFORT FOOD IN A CAN

Hawaii is the Spam capital of the USA, and locals consume a whopping four million cans per year, or 10,958 cans per day (3½ times more than any other state consumes). While US foodmaker Hormel's Spam, a pork-based luncheon meat, is the butt of jokes almost everywhere, there's little stigma in Hawaii. Rather, Spam is a comfort food – always eaten cooked, not straight from the can.

Why Spam? No one knows exactly. Some people say it simply goes well with rice, Hawaii's ubiquitous starch. Others claim it's a legacy of plantation cookery, when fresh meat was not always available. Even today, whenever the islands are threatened by a hurricane or dockworkers' strike, locals stock up on water, batteries, toilet paper, 20lb bags of rice and…Spam.

A local favorite is Spam *musubi*: a block of rice with a slice of fried Spam on top (or in the middle), wrapped with a strip of black sushi nori. Originated in the 1960s or '70s, it has become a classic, and thousands of *musubi* are sold daily at grocers, lunch counters and convenience stores. The Spam *musubi* phenomenon has even reached Hormel, which in 2004 released a collector's edition can called 'Hawaiian Spam' with a recipe for you-know-what on the back.

Shave ice Called 'ice shave' on the Big Island, this is a mainland 'snow cone' taken to the next level: the ice is shaved fine like powdered snow, packed into a paper cup and drenched with syrups in eye-popping hues. For a change, try sweet azuki-bean paste or ice cream underneath.

Hawaii Regional Cuisine

Less than two decades ago, Hawaii was not exactly a foodie destination. Sure, locals savored their Spam *musubi* (see opposite) and enjoyed decent ethnic fare, but fine dining typically meant imitation 'continental' fare that ignored the bounty of locally grown produce, seafood and meat.

In the late 1980s and early 1990s, top island chefs finally showed off local ingredients and multicultural influences – and quickly hit the gourmet radar. The movement was dubbed 'Hawaii Regional Cuisine' and the pioneering chefs became celebrities. Roy Yamaguchi is the forerunner who opened his original Roy's restaurant in Honolulu in 1988. Today's culinary connoisseurs seem rather jaded by his ever-growing empire of 30 restaurants across the USA, but you can judge for yourself at his outpost in Waikoloa (p113).

> Never trust a skinny chef? That's the motto of celebrity chef Sam Choy, who shares a few favorite recipes at www.samchoy .com.

DRINKS
Nonalcoholic

The best-known drink in Hawaii is world-renowned Kona coffee, which typically costs $20 per pound. The upland slopes of Mauna Loa and Hualalai on the Big Island's Kona district offer the ideal climate – sunny mornings and rainy afternoons – for coffee cultivation (see p93).

Traditionally, Hawaiians had no alcoholic drinks, but whalers introduced them to liquor and taught them to make their own, *'okolehao,* distilled from the *ti* root. Instead they used *'awa* (kava) as a mild intoxicant, and in recent years, *'awa* 'bars' have popped up. *'Awa* is found throughout the Pacific and used as medicine and for rituals. Typically, the root of the plant is chewed or pulverized and mixed with water to produce a milky concoction that numbs the mouth and has a sharp and earthy flavor. Truth be told, the stuff tastes awful. But the lactones in *'awa* are believed to relieve anxiety, fatigue and insomnia, while fostering restful sleep and vivid dreams. The effect from an 8oz glass is mildly narcotic, but not mind-altering. *'Awa* is not recommended for pregnant women or for daily use. Sample 100% legal *'awa* at the Pahoa farmer's market (p183) and Kanaka Kava (p83) in Kailua.

Fruit drinks are everywhere, but inexpensive canned drinks are generally not pure juice. One native Hawaiian fruit-juice tonic is *noni* (Indian mulberry), which grows with wild abandon throughout the island. Proponents claim that *noni* reduces inflammation, boosts energy and helps cure everything from arthritis to cancer. All that's known for sure: *noni* tastes and smells nasty. Sold commercially, it's usually mixed with other juices.

> **DID YOU KNOW?**
>
> It takes 300lb of pressure to crack the outer shell of a macadamia nut.

Alcoholic

In general, drinking is a social pastime rather than a daily habit. The drinking age in Hawaii is 21, and shopkeepers will card baby faces. Beer is the drink of choice, due to habit and cost (it's cheap). Coors Light, nicknamed 'bullets,' tends to be a local favorite.

The microbrew trend is thriving on the Big Island: Kona Brewing Company (p74) is both a brewery and a lively pub and restaurant. Another Big Island label is Hilo's Mehana Brewing Company, as it supplies its beer to upscale restaurants and even produces a mild ale called 'Roy's Special Reserve' for Roy Yamaguchi's restaurants.

> In *The Best of the Best from Hawaii Cookbook,* Gwen McKee and Barbara Moseley carefully compile 300 recipes from Hawaii's most-popular community cookbooks. With plastic spiral binding, this is a neo-retro masterpiece.

Although Big Islanders are predominantly beer drinkers, wine is gaining in popularity among the upper-income classes. At Volcano Winery (p203), you can sample only-in-Hawaii tropical wines, such as imaginative guava nut and honey concoctions.

As for the kitschy 'umbrella' drinks often associated with Hawaii, be forewarned that no self-respecting local would ever order a *chi chi* or, worse, any blue beverage.

CELEBRATIONS

Almost any occasion calls for lots of food and drink, so you're likely to have ample opportunity to feast with the locals. Island festivals showcase island specialties, such as the Kona Coffee Cultural Festival (p77), the Hapuna Beach Prince Hotel's Poke Festival (p118), and the Kona Brewers Festival (p77). Discriminating palates can find high-end culinary events, such as the Big Island Festival (p229), when internationally acclaimed chefs show their stuff (for $70 to $125 per person).

Locals also find lots of informal occasions to celebrate, and you're bound to see large family gatherings at beaches and parks. Families and other groups often reserve a park pavilion for potluck dinners, where numerous tables are literally covered with food. All milestone events invariably involve a massive spread. You'll also see locals celebrating the standard American holidays much as mainlanders do, with elaborate birthday and wedding cakes, Easter egg hunts, Super Bowl beer parties and Thanksgiving turkey dinners. The difference lies in the nontraditional variety of food served. Sure, you'll see a whole turkey on the table for Thanksgiving, but you'll also see rice (no mashed potatoes), teriyaki-barbecued meat, fried whole shrimp, *maki* sushi and much more.

WHERE TO EAT & DRINK

If nothing else, you'll have the gamut of dining options in Hawaii. For a quick meal, the best places are open-air, '70s-style drive-ins or *okazu-ya* lunch shops. Often queued up at lunchtime, the folks in line behind you might get impatient if you dawdle at the counter.

Diner-style restaurants abound. Often with formica tables and vinyl chairs, no view and no decor, these restaurants are the mainstays of everyday

Hawaii's Best Local Desserts, by Jean Watanabe Hee, reveals dozens of recipes for gotta-be-homemade desserts, from *haupia* chocolate pie to macadamia nut angels.

HAWAIIAN FEASTS

The best-known local celebration is the luau, the native Hawaiian feast that's become a household word across the USA. Early Hawaiians celebrated auspicious occasions – such as a child's birth, war victory or successful harvest – with a feast to honor the gods and share their bounty. Called *'aha'aina* (gathering for a meal) in ancient times, the term luau became common much later; it also refers to the young edible taro leaves that traditionally were used to wrap food cooked in the underground *imu* (pit of red hot stones).

Today there are two types of luau: private and commercial. Private luau are family affairs, thrown for a Hawaiian wedding or a baby's first birthday, sans fire-eaters and Tahitian dancers and the rousing 'Aloooooooooooha!' greeting. Guests feast on raw shellfish delicacies never served at commercial luau, and the entertainment is a lively local band, which might spur the *tutu* (grandmothers) to get up and dance hula with their grandchildren.

But unless you have connections, your only option is a hotel luau performance. These are well-choreographed shows that include an all-you-can-eat buffet and flashy Polynesian performances. The food tends to be mediocre, featuring the Hawaiian standards like poi and *kalua* pig – plus roast beef, teriyaki beef, fried rice and motley options designed to please all. Predictably, top-end resorts offer the best luau.

BIG ISLAND TOP FIVE EATS

Budget

- Café 100 (p174)
- Maha's Café (p134)
- Ning's Thai Cuisine (p184)
- KTA takeout (locations in Hilo, Kona, Keauhou and Waimea)
- Sam Choy's Kaloko (p104)

Midrange

- Café Pesto (p175 & p119)
- Miyo's (p175)
- Teshima Restaurant (p91)
- Hilo Bay Café (p176)
- Ocean Sushi Deli (p176)

Top End

- Daniel Thiebaut (p135)
- Merriman's (p135 & p113)
- Seaside Restaurant (p174)
- Kenichi Pacific (p88)
- Restaurant Kaikodo (p176)

---

dining out because you get quick service and decent food at decent prices. If you've got an appetite or want variety, all-you-can-eat seafood and prime rib buffets are a good option. Such buffets are common at hotels, and they're popular for local family gatherings.

If you want to sample Hawaii's finest offerings, top-end restaurants are impressive and distinctive. But don't expect the smooth, sophisticated service you might receive at a comparable place in New York or San Francisco. Hawaii is not a white-tablecloth-and-silver type of place, and service might seem lackadaisical. But the casual demeanor can be refreshing.

The best supermarket is KTA, an islandwide chain with a huge selection of to-go meals. While you'll find bargains on locally found foods (sashimi-grade 'ahi is less than $10 per pound), items shipped from the mainland are surprisingly pricey (a box of cereal might be $5).

For an online restaurant-review blog by a local in the know (complete with photos!), click to http://onokinegrindz.typepad.com.

VEGETARIANS & VEGANS

While most locals are omnivores, vegetarians and vegans can feast in Hawaii, too. The Asian influence in local cuisine guarantees lots of vegetable and tofu options, even when you're 'out country' in rural towns. The vast majority of restaurants offer a variety of entrées (main courses), rather than proclaiming themselves a steakhouse or rib joint. So, even if you forgo the oxtail soup, you're sure to find stir-fried veggies or fresh tossed greens on the menu.

That said, vegetarians aren't the target market: a plate lunch without meat or fish is not quite a plate lunch, and top-end restaurants tend to highlight seafood. An alternative is to look for yourself at the numerous farmers' markets and health-food stores islandwide, but they aren't cheap.

The trend toward meatless diets is growing, mostly among young women and transplants (hippie or otherwise). Most people eat everything in moderation and might view vegetarianism as extreme. Locals have a 'live and let live' attitude and if you start admonishing others about the evils of meat eating, you won't make any friends. As you'd expect, the most ardent supporters of meatless diets and organic, local and sustainable farming are haole newcomers, especially from the west coast.

EATING WITH KIDS

Hawaii's family-oriented, extremely casual atmosphere means kids are welcome almost everywhere. Restaurants are usually quick to accommodate children with high chairs and booster seats, though too much noise or unruliness is inappropriate for the upscale establishments (locals are courteous to the nth degree and might not complain, but why stick out like an obnoxious tourist?).

Families should also take advantage of the daily opportunity to eat outdoors. The balmy weather allows for impromptu plate lunch at the beach or fresh fruit at a roadside stand. If you really want to act local, buy a *goza* (inexpensive roll-up straw mat), pack a picnic and head to the nearest park.

Kids will find lots of treats, such as homemade ice cream, shave ice, sweet bread and an assortment of chips. As for main dishes, the local palate tends toward the sweet and straightforward side, without too much garlic, bitter greens, pungent cheeses and strong spices – which typically agrees with kids' tastes.

At hotel luaus, kids get a discount (and sometimes free admission with a paid adult). Commercial luaus might seem like a cheesy Vegas show to adults, but kids will probably enjoy the flashy dances and fire tricks.

> A hefty community cookbook, *Kona on my Plate: A Hawaii Community Cookbook*, conveniently comprises history, Hawaiian culinary definitions and, of course, hundreds of recipes.

HABITS & CUSTOMS

Locals eat three square meals early and on the dot: typically 6am breakfast, noon lunch and 6pm dinner. Restaurants are jammed around these mealtimes, but they clear out an hour or two later, as locals are not lingerers. If you dine at 8:30pm you might not have to wait at all! But bear in mind that most places shut down by 10pm. In general, locals tip slightly less than mainlanders do, but still up to 20% for good service and at least 15% for the basics.

Home entertainment always revolves around food, usually served potluck style with all guests adding to the anything-goes smorgasbord. Throwaway paper plates and wooden chopsticks make cleanup easy, and the rule is 'all you can eat' (and they really mean it). If you're invited to someone's home, show up on time and bring a dish, preferably homemade (but a bakery cake or pie is always appreciated). Remove your shoes at the door. And don't be surprised if you're forced to take home a plate or two of leftovers.

> For *pau hana* (after work) meals, Joan Namkoong's *Go Home, Cook Rice* features everyday recipes that originally appeared in the *Honolulu Advertiser*, for which she was a food writer.

EAT YOUR WORDS

If someone offered you a *broke da mout' malasada* or *'ono kine poke*, would you try it? Don't miss out because you're stumped by the lingo. Here's a list of common food terms; for pidgin and Hawaiian pronunciation tips, see p249.

Food Glossary

'a'ama black crab
'awa kava, a native plant used to make an intoxicating drink
bento Japanese-style box lunch
broke da mout' delicious (as in, 'it broke my mouth')
crack seed Chinese preserved fruit; a salty, sweet or sour snack
donburi large bowl of rice and main dish
grind to eat
grinds food; *'ono kine grinds* is good food
guava green-yellow fruit with moist pink flesh and lots of edible seeds
gyoza grilled dumpling usually containing minced pork or shrimp

haupia coconut pudding
imu underground earthen oven used to cook *kalua* pig and other luau food
inamona ground and roasted *kukui* (candlenut), used to flavor dishes such as *poke*
kaiseki ryori Japanese multicourse chef's tasting menu
kaki mochi shoyu-flavored rice crackers; also called *arare*
kalo taro
kalua traditional method of cooking in an underground pit
kaukau food
kamaboko a block of puréed, steamed fish
katsu deep-fried fillets
laulau a bundle made of pork or chicken and salted butterfish, wrapped in taro and *ti* leaves and steamed
li hing mui sweet-sour crack seed
liliko'i passionfruit
loco moco dish of rice topped with a hamburger, a fried egg and gravy; nonmeat options available
lomilomi salmon minced, salted salmon, diced tomato and green onion
luau Hawaiian feast
mai'a banana
mai tai alcoholic drink made from rum, grenadine, and lemon and pineapple juices
malasada Portuguese fried dough, served warm and sugar-coated
manju Japanese bun filled with sweet bean paste
mochi Japanese sticky rice, pounded and shaped into a dumpling
nishime stew of root vegetables and seaweed
noni Indian mulberry; a small tree with yellow, smelly fruit that is used medicinally
nori Japanese seaweed, usually dried
ogo seaweed
ohelo shrub with edible red berries similar in tartness and size to cranberries
'ono delicious
'ono kine grinds good food
'opihi edible limpet
pad thai rice noodles stir-fried with tofu, vegetables, egg and peanuts
pho Vietnamese soup, typically beef broth, noodles and fresh herbs
pipi kaula Hawaiian beef jerky
poha gooseberry
poi staple Hawaiian starch made of steamed, mashed taro
poka a fruit in the passionfruit family
poke cubed raw fish mixed with shoyu, sesame oil, salt, chili pepper, *inamona* and other condiments
ponzu Japanese citrus sauce
pupu snack or appetizer; also Hawaiian word for shell
saimin a Hawaiian version of Japanese noodle soup
shoyu soy sauce
soba buckwheat noodles
star fruit translucent yellow-green fruit with five ribs like the points of a star and sweet, juicy pulp
taro plant with edible corm used to make *poi* and with edible leaves eaten in *laulau; kalo* in Hawaiian
teishoku fixed, multicourse Japanese meal
teppanyaki Japanese style of cooking with an iron grill
tonkatsu breaded and fried pork cutlets, also prepared as chicken *katsu*
tsukemono pickled vegetables
'uala sweet potato
'ulu breadfruit; a large, starchy fruit that, when roasted, resembles the texture and smell of bread
ume Japanese pickled plum
wana sea urchin

Kona

From ancient times, the Kona Coast has been the island's *numbah-one* vacation site. The reasons are obvious: guaranteed sunshine, a hang-loose vibe and clear blue waters. Today the vast majority of Big Island visitors focus on the west side of the island.

But don't make the mistake of lumping all of Kona together: Kailua-Kona, once a lazy beach town, is now the commercial center of west Hawai'i, which has flourished with tourism and development since the 1970s. The Ali'i Dr strip resembles a mini Waikiki – tourist-tacky perhaps, but also ideal for oceanfront strolling, dining and people watching at all hours. In contrast, the sprawling outskirts of Kailua resemble mainland suburbs, right down to the big-box proliferation and daily traffic jams.

Up the slopes of Hualalai, you'll find Holualoa, a long-standing artists' community, and a refreshing change in climate. The cooler, rainier 'Coffee Belt' starts there and continues more than 20 miles to the south. South Kona epitomizes the age-old vision of paradise, complete with tangled backyard jungles, quaint family-owned businesses and pristine waters teeming with marine life. Above Kailua town, North Kona encompasses both huge swaths of barren lava desert and idyllic, once-secret white-sand beaches along the coast.

The Kona Coast's cachet comes with a price. As newcomers have flocked to Kona to buy their dream home, real estate values have skyrocketed, making home ownership too expensive for the average local. Now many commute for miles up and down the coastal highway, spurring gridlock for hours. Luckily, you can avoid rush-hour traffic – you're on holiday.

HIGHLIGHTS

- Night diving with giant **manta rays** (p75)
- Imbibing 100% pure **Kona coffee** (p93)
- Taking an 'unwired' (no phone, TV or computer!) getaway at **Kona Village Resort** (p107)
- Snorkeling in a life-sized fishbowl at **Kealakekua Bay State Historical Park** (p94) or **Kahalu'u Beach Park** (p86)
- Imagining life in ancient Hawai'i at **Pu'uhonua o Honaunau National Historic Park** (p100)
- Exploring tide pools at **Wawaloli (OTEC) Beach** (p105)

★ Kona Village Resort

★ Wawaloli (OTEC) Beach

Manta Rays ★

Kahalu'u ★   ★ Kona Coffee
Beach Park

Kealakekua Bay ★
State Historical Park

★ Pu'uhonua o Honaunau
National Historic Park

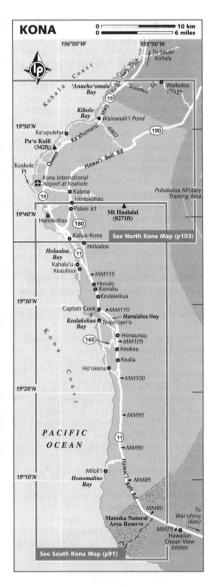

KONA

KAILUA-KONA

pop 10,000

The tropical heat and central location of this town attract hundreds of thousands of visitors annually (which is well over double the number drawn to Hilo). Clearly Kailua

is tourist town, rife with kitschy shopping bazaars, sunburnt sightseers and a nonstop swath of beachfront hotels. While it might feel too commercial, here you'll find afford-able lodging and beaches literally bordering the highway. It's a convenient home base for exploring the entire coast.

HISTORY

Kamehameha the Great lived his last years in Kailua-Kona, worshipping at Ahu'ena Heiau, his own temple. But soon after his death in 1819, his son Liholiho broke the *kapu* by din-ing with women. When no godly wrath en-sued, the traditional belief in Hawaiian gods collapsed. When the first missionaries sailed into Kailua Bay in 1820, the Hawaiian Islands transformed into a Christian society.

In the 19th century, the city was a leisure retreat for Hawaiian royalty. Still standing on Ali'i Dr, Hulihe'e Palace (p73) was a favorite getaway for King David Kalakaua (1836–91), the last king of Hawai'i. Kalakaua, a trained musician and lyricist, was the catalyst for a Hawaiian cultural resurgence, restoring public performance of hula and promoting music, from ancient chant to the waltz. The Merrie Monarch Festival (p171) is named in his honor.

Long considered the fun-loving kid sister to sensible, solid Hilo, Kailua has grown into the island's commercial powerhouse since the 1970s. While Hilo is the governmental seat of the island, Kailua's economic clout has skyrocketed, especially as resorts have mush-roomed along the coast. With the demise of the sugar industry in the mid-1990s, tourism and other crops, including world-renowned Kona coffee, have taken center stage.

ORIENTATION

Kailua-Kona is south of the airport on Hwy 19 (Queen Ka'ahumanu Hwy), which be-comes Hwy 11 (Kuakini Hwy) at Palani Rd, the primary entry to Kailua town. Highways and major roads in Kona parallel the coast-line, so navigating is easy. Locals call the highways by their Hawaiian names, so be familiar with the highway number and name.

Ali'i Dr is Kailua's main street, with the vast majority of hotels and condos abutting the 5-mile coastal road that runs south to Keauhou. Ali'i Dr is usually bustling with pedestrian traffic, a nice change from the

KONA

typical Big Island streets dominated by cars. Kailua's shopping malls and supermarkets are slightly inland, within the 'downtown' area between Ali'i Dr and the highway.

INFORMATION
Bookstores

Bargain Books (☎ 326-7790; North Kona Shopping Center, 75-5629 Hwy 11; ☷ 10am-9pm Mon-Sat, to 6pm Sun) Well-organized selection of new and used books; good for bargain hunters.

Borders Books Music & Café (☎ 331-1668; 75-1000 Henry St, at Hwy 11; ☷ 9am-9pm Sun-Thu, to 10pm Fri & Sat) Largest bookseller in Kailua-Kona, with many US and foreign newspapers.

Middle Earth Bookshoppe (☎ 329-2123; 75-5719 Ali'i Dr; ☷ 9am-9pm Mon-Sat, to 6pm Sun) Indie bookstore tucked in a quiet alley; excellent Hawaiiana and travel sections.

Emergency

Police (☎ 326-4646) For nonemergencies.
Police, Fire & Ambulance (☎ 911) For emergencies.
Sexual Assault Hotline (☎ 935-0677)
Suicide Prevention Hotline (☎ 800-784-2433)

Internet Access

Island Lava Java (☎ 327-2161; Ali'i Sunset Plaza, 75-5799 Ali'i Dr; per 15 min $3; ☷ 6am-10pm) Popular café but computers are inside, where it can get stuffy.

Scandinavian Shaved Ice Internet Café (☎ 331-1626; 75-5699 Ali'i Dr; per 15 min $2.25; ☷ 10am-9:30pm Mon-Sat, noon-9pm Sun) Small, closetlike space, saved by the wafting aroma of ice cream and waffle cones.

Zac's Business Center (☎ 329-0006; North Kona Shopping Center, 75-5629 Hwy 11; per 15 min $2.75; ☷ 8am-6pm Mon-Fri, 9am-5pm Sat) All-purpose center for faxing, copying, scanning and Internet access.

NAME THAT TOWN

Often confusing to nonlocals are Kailua-Kona's alternative names, so here's the scoop. The town started out as simply Kailua. But when the post office discovered there was a Kailua on O'ahu and another on Maui, they renamed the Big Island town Kailua-Kona. Kona means 'leeward' and the Kona Coast refers to dry, sunny west Hawai'i. Locals call the town itself both Kailua and Kona (and also Kailua-Kona). If they refer to Kona, they *usually* mean Kailua, but they *might* mean any of the towns or beaches along the Kona Coast. Got it?

Internet Resources

Big Island Visitors Bureau (www.gohawaii.com/big island) Comprehensive calendar of island events. Listings for eats, sleeps and the like feature only for the bureau's paying members, however.

KonaWeb (www.konaweb.com) Founded in 1995 by Konabob and Shirley Stoffer, this 'mom-and-pop' website feels like a trusted old friend. Start clicking around and you'll find a handy source of general island info, current happenings, webcam views of Kailua, weather updates, and a popular online forum. Sign up for a biannual online newsletter on what's new on the island.

Media
NEWSPAPERS

West Hawaii Today (www.westhawaiitoday.com) Kona Coast's daily newspaper.

See p223 for other listings. Some of the free tourist guides found in sidewalk racks are worth checking out:

101 Things to Do (www.101thingstodo.com) Impressively thorough but beware the many mispelled Hawaiian words.

Coffee Times (www.coffeetimes.com) Decent intro to the Big Island's coffee industry.

This Week Big Island (www.thisweek.com/bigisland) Portable, with various discount coupons.

RADIO

Due to the Big Island's size and mountainous terrain, west Hawai'i stations broadcast only in the vicinity. Often a station will simulcast shows at different frequencies on either side of the island. Check out www.hawaiiradiotv.com/BigIsleRadio for a complete listing.

KAGB 99.1 FM Island hits on station voted the best in *Hawaii Island Journal*.

KAOY 101.5 FM (www.kwxx.com) Island and pop hits.
KKON 790AM Oldies station.
KLEO 106.1 FM (www.kbigfm.com) Hawaii's big hits.
KLUA 93.3 FM 'Kiss FM' contemporary pop.
KRTR 105.5 FM (www.krater96.com) Adult contemporary.

Medical Services

Hualalai Urgent Care Clinic (☎ 327-4357; 75-1028 Henry St; ☷ 8am-5pm Mon-Fri, 9am-5pm Sat) For non-emergency medical care. Appointments recommended.

Kona Community Hospital (Map p95; ☎ 322-9311; www.kch.hhsc.org; 79-1019 Haukapila St, Kealakekua) About 10 miles south of Kailua-Kona, off Hwy 11.

Longs Drugs (☎ 329-1380; Lanihau Center, 75-5595 Palani Rd; ☷ 8am-9pm Mon-Sat, to 6pm Sun) For prescriptions, this one is centrally located.

KAILUA-KONA IN...

One Day
Shake off jet lag by strolling down Ali'i Dr, visiting **Hulihe'e Palace** (p73) and quenching your thirst with **shave ice** (opposite). Then head to **White Sands Beach Park** (p74) to boogie board or to **Old Kona Airport State Recreation Area** (p74) to explore tide pools. In the afternoon, visit the art galleries in **Holualoa** (p90). Divers, a **manta ray night dive** (p75) is a must.

Two Days
Start day two with morning snorkeling. **Kahalu'u Beach Park** (p86) is ideal for beginners or if you're short on time. Otherwise, kayak to **Kealakekua Bay State Historical Park** (p94) or cruise to a less crowded cove nearby. In the afternoon, learn about native Hawaiian plants at the **Amy BH Greenwell Ethnobotanical Garden** (p92), then visit **Pu'uhonua o Honaunau National Historic Park** (p100) for the amazing sunsets.

Three Days
On day three, find a secluded beach at **Kekaha Kai Beach Park** (p106), stopping at **Costco** (p104) if you need beach gear. You might have to rent a 4WD or hike in, but who said desert-island fantasies come easily? For lunch, savor *local-kine grinds* at **Sam Choy's Kaloko** (p104). Watch the sunset at **Wawaloli (OTEC) Beach** (p105) before returning to Kailua.

Money
Bank of Hawaii (☎ 326-3903; Lanihau Center, 75-5595 Palani Rd) and **First Hawaiian Bank** (☎ 329-2461; Lanihau Center, 74-5593 Palani Rd) have branches with 24-hour ATMs.

Post
Post office (☎ 331-8307; Lanihau Center, 74-5577 Palani Rd, Kailua-Kona, HI 96740; ⊗ 8:30am-4:30pm Mon-Fri, 9:30am-1:30pm Sat) Holds general-delivery mail for 10 days. See p232 for instructions.

Tourist Information
Be wary of 'tourist information' booths along Ali'i Dr, because they often are fronts for aggressive salespeople who try to lure visitors into buying a time-share. The best sources include hotel staff and, better yet, B&B proprietors and the Internet resources listed on opposite. Just south of Kailua, the Kona Historical Society (p92) has a small museum and office in Kealakekua. The nearest Big Island Visitors Bureau (p111) is in Waikoloa, but it's no more than a brochure stand.

Travel Agencies
Regal Travel (☎ 329-0536, 800-373-6935; www.regal travel.com; Suite A5, Lanihau Center, 75-5595 Palani Rd; ⊗ 9am-4:30pm) A longtime agency based in Honolulu, buys interisland tickets in bulk, so if the timing's right, you can snag a discount. Check online for the widest selection of travel deals.

DANGERS & ANNOYANCES
Common sense and street smarts should keep you out of trouble in Kailua-Kona. That said, keep to well-trafficked streets and neighborhoods. Try not to look and act too much like an easily targeted tourist. Benign accosters come in the form of timeshare salespeople, who lure vacationers with discounts on island activities and other catchy gimmicks.

The main annoyance around Kailua is daily weekday highway traffic during commute hours. The worst gridlock hours: between 4pm and 6pm going south on the Queen Ka'ahumanu Hwy (Hwy 19) and from 6am to 8am going north on the Kuakini Hwy (Hwy 11). The after-work traffic on the Queen Ka'ahumanu Hwy is especially aggravating and starts all the way from South Kohala, as resort workers start commuting to faraway homes farther south. If possible, avoid landing at the Kona airport during the evening rush hour, if you're staying in Kailua.

During nonrush hours, traffic is relatively light and locals do tend to speed. The roads can be curvy and narrow, especially if you are used to straight, no-brainer, mainland freeways. If you are being tailed, don't speed up and cause an accident; just pull over and let the car pass. Locals will appreciate it.

KONA

KAILUA-KONA

0 — 400 m
0 — 0.2 miles

To Kona Coast Divers (3.5mi);
Kona International Airport (7mi);
North Kona (10mi);
Kohala coast (25mi)

INFORMATION
Bank of Hawaii..............................1 C3
Bargain Books........................(see 50)
Borders Books Music & Café.......2 D3
First Hawaiian Bank......................3 C3
Hualalai Urgent Care Clinic..........4 D3
Island Lava Java....................(see 41)
Kona Natural Foods................(see 43)
Longs Drugs..........................(see 49)
Middle Earth Bookshoppe............5 C4
Post Office.................................6 C2
Regal Travel..........................(see 49)
Scandinavian Shaved Ice Internet
  Café......................................7 C4
Zac's Business Center............(see 50)

SIGHTS & ACTIVITIES
Ahu'ena Heiau.............................8 B4
Big Island Divers..........................9 B2
Club in Kona.............................10 C3
Fun Factory...........................(see 47)
Gold's Gym..............................11 B2
Hulihe'e Palace..........................12 C4
Jack's Diving Locker................(see 42)
Kailua Pier...............................13 B4
Kona Bowl................................14 C3
Kona Brewing Company..........(see 50)
Moku'aikaua Church...................15 C4
Snorkel Bob's............................16 D5

SLEEPING
Hale Kona Kai...........................17 D6
King Kamehameha's Kona Beach
  Hotel...................................18 B4
Kona Billfisher...........................19 D5
Kona Islander Inn.......................20 D5
Kona Reef................................21 D6
Kona Seaside Hotel....................22 B3
Royal Kona Resort.....................23 D6
Uncle Billy's Kona Bay Hotel.......24 C4

To Hawaiian Oasis B&B
(3mi); Kiwi Gardens (3mi);
Nancy's Hideaway (5mi);
Saddle Rd (36mi);
Waimea (42mi)

To La Bourgogne (3mi); Kona Yoga (4mi);
Kona Community Hospital (10mi); Kona Historical
Society Museum (10.5mi); Captain Cook (15mi)

To Old Kona
Airport State
Recreation Area (0.2mi)

Kamakahonu
Beach

Kailua Bay

To Holualoa
(5.5mi)

Onea Bay

To Ali'i Gardens
Farmers' Market (1mi);
Jameson's-by-the-Sea (3.2mi);
White Sands Beach Park (3.5mi)

EATING
Ba-Le Kona.............................(see 46)
Cassandra's Greek Taverna.........25 B4
Huggo's..................................26 D5
Kailua Village Farmers' Market....27 C4
Kona Farmers' Market................28 A2
Kona Inn................................(see 47)
KTA Super Store.....................(see 46)
Manna Korean BBQ................(see 43)
Ocean View Inn.........................29 B4
O's Bistro..............................(see 43)
Quinn's...................................30 B3
Royal Jade Garden.................(see 49)
Safeway................................(see 43)
Sibu Café.................................31 B4
Thai Rin................................(see 41)
Tres Hombres...........................32 D6

DRINKING
Durty Jake's...........................(see 42)
Hard Rock Café......................(see 42)
Kanaka Kava..........................(see 42)
LuLu's...................................(see 42)
Other Side...............................33 A2
Sam's Hideaway.....................(see 48)

ENTERTAINMENT
Beach Volleyball Court................34 D5
Blockbuster...........................(see 46)
Kona Henna Studio.................(see 48)
Stadium Cinemas......................35 B1
Windjammer Lounge...............(see 23)

SHOPPING
Crazy Shirts..........................(see 48)
Made on the Big Island Outlet...(see 18)
Mele Kai Music.........................36 A2
Pacific Vibrations......................37 C4

TRANSPORT
24-hour Gas Station..................38 B3
Gas Station..............................39 C4
Hawaiian Pedals.....................(see 47)
HP Bike Works.........................40 B2

OTHER
Ali'i Sunset Plaza......................41 D5
Coconut Grove Marketplace........42 D5
Crossroads Shopping Center........43 D3
Free Parking.............................44 C4
Kid's Play Corner.......................45 A2
Kona Coast Shopping Center.......46 B3
Kona Inn Shopping Village..........47 C4
Kona Marketplace.....................48 C4
Lanihau Center.........................49 C3
North Kona Shopping Center.......50 B3
Pay Parking..............................51 A4

Hale Halawai
Park

Depending on wind conditions and volcanic activity, Kona inhabitants might encounter lung-challenging vog (see p247). Also see p227 for information on tsunami, crime and drugs. For information on ocean safety, see p50.

SIGHTS

Kailua-Kona's downtown area, starting at the north end of Ali'i Dr, includes a handful of historic buildings and landmarks, and popular (often too popular) family beaches at both the north and south ends. Many historic sites are still standing in Kailua: the site of King Kamehameha's final heiau, the first Christian church in the Hawaiian Islands and a stone palace that Hawaiian royalty used as a vacation home.

Ahu'ena Heiau

Kamehameha the Great established his kingdom's royal court in Lahaina on Maui, but he returned to his Kamakahonu ('Eye of the Turtle') residence, on the north side of Kailua Bay, where he died in May 1819. His personal temple, **Ahu'ena Heiau** (admission free), lies just *makai* (seaward) of King Kamehameha's Kona Beach Hotel (p79). Hotel permission is not necessary to view the site.

Moku'aikaua Church

On April 4, 1820, the first Christian missionaries to the Hawaiian Islands sailed into Kailua Bay. When they landed, they were unaware that the traditional religion had been abolished on that very spot just a few months before. Their timing couldn't have been more auspicious. King Liholiho gave them this site, just a few minutes' walk from Kamehameha's Ahu'ena Heiau, to establish Hawai'i's first Christian church.

Completed in 1836, **Moku'aikaua Church** (☎ 329-1589; 75-5713 Ali'i Dr; admission free; ☿ services 8am & 10:30am Sun, 7pm Wed) is a handsome building with walls of lava rock held together by a mortar of sand and coral lime. The posts and beams, hewn with stone adzes, and smoothed down with chunks of coral, are made from resilient ohia, and the pews and pulpit are made of koa, the most prized native hardwood. The steeple tops out at 112ft, making the church the tallest structure in Kailua. The interior is cool and serene, and specially built to take advantage of tradewinds that blow through its length.

Hulihe'e Palace

Hawaii's second governor, 'John Adams' Kuakini, commissioned this simple but elegant two-story house in 1838 as his private residence. Used as a vacation getaway for Hawaiian monarchs, the house, originally built with lava rock in 1885, was plastered over inside and out by King Kalakaua, who preferred a more-polished style after his travels abroad.

Prince Kuhio, who inherited the palace from his uncle Kalakaua, auctioned off the furnishings and artifacts to raise money, but his wife and other female royalty meticulously numbered each piece and recorded the name of the bidder. Eventually the Daughters of Hawai'i, a group founded in 1903 by daughters of missionaries, tracked down the owners and persuaded many to donate the pieces for display in the **museum** (☎ 329-1877; 75-5718 Ali'i Dr; www.huliheepalace.org; adult/senior/child $6/4/1; ☿ 9am-4pm Mon-Fri, 10am-4pm Sat & Sun) they established at the palace.

The two-story palace contains both Western antiques, collected on royal jaunts to Europe, and Hawaiian artifacts, such as a table inlaid with 25 kinds of native Hawaiian wood, some now extinct, and a number of Kamehameha the Great's personal war spears.

Photography is prohibited in the museum to protect the pieces from light, and to keep people from duplicating the designs. Admission includes a 40-minute tour, which provides interesting anecdotes about past royal occupants. The walking tour (p77) offered by the Kona Historical Society also includes museum admission.

Kailua Pier

Kailua Bay, just across the street from Ahu'ena Heiau, was once a major cattle-shipping area. Cattle driven down from hillside ranches were stampeded into the water and forced to swim out to waiting steamers, where they were hoisted aboard by sling and shipped to Honolulu slaughterhouses.

Built in 1915, the pier was long the center of sportfishing, but it simply got too crowded to handle all the action. Now Kona's charter fishing boats use the larger Honokohau Harbor north of town. Kailua Pier is mainly used by dive boats and cruise ships, though its hoist and scales are still used for weigh-ins during billfish tournaments.

Kona Brewing Company

In the nondescript North Kona Shopping Center, the **Kona Brewing Company** (☎ 334-2739; www.konabrewingco.com; North Kona Shopping Center, 75-5629 Hwy 11; admission & tour free; ☒ 11am-10pm, to 11pm Fri & Sat, tours 10:30am & 3pm Mon-Fri) is a Kona icon and the Big Island's first microbrewery. Started in 1994 by Cameron Healy and his son Khalsa, this little family-run operation now serves its brews throughout the islands and in nine mainland states plus Japan. With nine beers on tap, including the original deep-copper Fire Rock Pale Ale, and six seasonal brews featuring ingredients from coffee to ginger to coconut, you'll surely find one that pleases your palate. Handcrafted ales can be sampled at the conclusion of the tour.

Old Kona Airport State Recreation Area

With an unglamorous name, this spacious **beach**, located on the site of the old Kona airport, is often bypassed. But it's worth visiting. You'll find solitude here, amid the sound of waves rather than traffic noise. To get there, take the Kuakini Hwy to its end, 1 mile north of downtown.

The old runway skirts along a long sandy beach, but lava rocks also run the length of the shore between the sand and the ocean. Swimming is relatively poor here but the beach is perfect for fishing and exploring the tide pools. At low tide, the rocks reveal countless aquarium-like pockets holding tiny sea urchins, crabs and bits of coral. A couple of breaks in the lava, including one in front of the first picnic area, allow entry into the water.

The **Garden Eel Cove**, which can be reached by a short walk from the north end of the beach, is a good area for scuba divers and confident snorkelers. The reef fish are large and plentiful, and a steep coral wall in deeper waters harbors big moray eels and a wide variety of other sea creatures, such as lionfish and cowries.

When the surf's up, local surfers flock to an offshore break at 'Shark Rocks.' In high surf, though, it's too rough for other water activities.

Facilities include restrooms, showers and covered picnic tables on a lawn dotted with beach heliotrope and short coconut palms. The Kailua-Kona end of the park contains a gym, soccer and softball fields, four night-lit tennis courts and a horseshoe-toss pit. Next to the old runway is a mile-long loop that locals use as a jogging track. Last, but surely not least, there's ample parking.

White Sands Beach Park

Just south of Kailua-Kona you'll find a popular county beach park called **White Sands**, **Magic Sands** or **Disappearing Sands**. All the same beach, it earned its moniker because the sand can disappear literally overnight during high surf in winter. The exposed rocks and coral make the beach too treacherous for average swimmers. Eventually, however, the sand magically returns, transforming the shore back into a white-sand beach. White Sands is known as an ideal boogie-boarding and bodysurfing spot. Facilities include restrooms, showers, picnic tables and a volleyball court; a lifeguard is on duty.

ACTIVITIES

Swimming

While small and few, Kailua-Kona beaches are convenient and popular with both locals and tourists. But they face the same fate of all city beaches: crowds and zooming highway traffic nearby.

The miniature beach out the front of King Kamehameha's Kona Beach Hotel (p79) is Kailua-Kona's only downtown swimming spot. The atmosphere amidst cars, buildings and passersby is nothing special, but the waters are calm and safe for children, and the hotel's beach hut rents snorkels, kayaks, beach chairs and umbrellas.

Just beyond Kailua, however, your options increase dramatically in North Kona (p106) and Keauhou (p86). Check out Old Kona Airport State Recreation Area (left) and White Sands Beach Park (above) if you need to stay close to Kailua-Kona.

Snorkeling

While you'll find snorkeling and diving outfits (for gear or tours) in Kailua-Kona, the actual ocean sites are located north or south of the town.

For snorkeling, most head to nearby Kealakekua Bay State Historical Park (p94) or Kahalu'u Beach Park (p86) to gawk at the thriving marine life. If you join a snorkeling cruise, gear is usually provided. But if you plan to snorkel frequently, rent your gear in Kailua for the best selection and prices.

A good bet is **Snorkel Bob's** (☎ 329-0770; www
.snorkelbob.com; 75-5831 Kahakai Rd; ⏰ 8am-5pm),
near the Royal Kona Resort, where you can
rent snorkel, mask and fins for $9 per week
(check the freebie tourist guides available
around town for coupons).

Diving

Near the shore, divers can see steep drop-
offs with lava tubes, caves and diverse
marine life. In deeper waters there are 40
popular boat-dive areas, including an air-
plane wreck off Keahole Point.

One well-known dive spot is Red Hill, an
underwater cinder cone about 10 miles south
of Kona. It has beautiful lava formations –
including ledges and lots of honeycombed
lava tubes nicely lit by streaks of sunlight – as
well as coral pinnacles and many brightly
colored nudibranchs (mollusks).

Most dive tours launch from Honokohau
Harbor (p103) but either do business from
Kailua-Kona or have no brick-and-mortar
location whatsover. The cost of a two-tank
dive ranges from $90 to $120, depending on
whether you need to rent gear. For a unique
underwater thrill, go night diving to see giant
manta rays, which will cost between $65 and
$120. The larger five-star PADI operations
offer certification courses for around $500.

Aloha Dive Company (☎ 325-5560, 800-708-5662;
www.alohadive.com) A personable small company run by
locals Mike and Buffy Nakachi and Earl Kam. Groups are
limited to six on the 28ft boat.

Big Island Divers (☎ 329-6068, 800-488-6068; www
.bigislanddivers.com; 74-5467 Kaiwi St; ⏰ 8am-6pm)
More-personable staff with expansive shop (it's the
number one Aqua Lung dealer on the island). Offers
manta-ray dives nightly either with six to eight divers
(with one guide) or 12 divers (two guides).

Dive Makai (☎ 329-2025; www.divemakai.com) A small,
friendly operation run by a husband-and-wife team with a
31ft boat. In business for nearly three decades, they provide
thorough predive briefings, limit groups to 12 people and
keep dives unstructured.

Jack's Diving Locker (☎ 329-7585, 800-345-4807;
www.jacksdivinglocker.com; Coconut Grove Marketplace,
75-5819 Ali'i Dr; ⏰ 8am-9pm) One of the best outfits for
introductory dives, as well as night dives to see the manta
rays. Housed at a 5000ft facility, with a store, classrooms,
a tank room and a 12ft-deep dive pool. There are also two
38ft boats and one 23ft craft, with up to 12 divers each.

Kona Coast Divers (☎ 329-8802; www.konacoastdivers
.com; 74-381 Kealakeha Parkway, Honokohau Harbor;
 ⏰ 8am-5pm) This outfit uses a boat custom-designed for
diving, and it offers manta-ray night dives.

Also see the long-standing dive outfit, Sea
Paradise (p96) based at Keauhou Harbor.

Snuba

In between scuba diving and snorkeling is
'snuba' diving. Join a **Snuba Big Island** (☎ 326-
7446; www.snubabigisland.com) tour and descend to
depths up to 25ft; a breathing hose is attached
to a small raft carrying your scuba tank. The
only other equipment: small weight-belt,
mask, and fins. Beach dives (1½-hour tour
$79, departures 9am, 11am, 1pm and 3pm)
leave from Kailua Pier and boat dives (three-
hour tour, one/two dives $120/145, depar-
tures 8:30am and 12:30pm) leave Honokohau
Harbor. Minimum age is eight, but kids as
young as four can go by wearing a floatation
device and staying at the surface.

Surfing

White Sands Beach Park (opposite) is a favorite spot for boogie boarding, while board
surfers like Banyans, near the banyan tree

FLYING CARPETS OF THE SEA

Of all the underwater wonders of Hawaii, perhaps the most awesome are the Pacific manta rays.
These living 'flying carpets' are gentle creatures, which is fortunate, considering their wingspan
can measure 12ft across! They feed on plankton, catching them with gaping mouths as they glide
and dive around. Since plankton are attracted to light, divers can shine spotlights to bring them
closer to shore, thus setting off a manta mealtime extravaganza.

The best locations for manta sightings can shift over time, so dive outfits will take you to the
most promising spots. Even if you're not a certified diver, you can snorkel at the surface and view
the mantas from above. As they cruise around in the surf with their white underbellies flashing
against the dark waters, it's hypnotic to watch and an unforgettable Hawaiian adventure.

It's important to remember that you're just an observer. Never approach or touch a manta
ray. Remember that mantas make their best showings when there's no moon.

KONA

north of White Sands Beach, and Pine Trees near Wawaloli (OTEC) Beach (p105).

For expert advice on surfing and Kona beaches, visit **Pacific Vibrations** (☎ 329-4140; pacvibe@hawaii.rr.com; 75-5702 Likana Ln, at Ali'i Dr; ☷ 10am-5:30pm Mon-Fri, to 3:30pm Sat), the first surf shop in west Hawai'i. Cavernous, jam-packed and still family-run, the staff includes professional surfers and an Ironman triathlete. You can also buy or rent boards ($10 to $20 per day).

Fishing

Kona has more than 100 charter fishing boats; many are listed in the *Fishing* freebie, which can be picked up at tourist offices and airports. The standard cost for joining an existing party starts at $60 per person for a half-day (four-hour) trip, and your buddies who don't fish can ride along for about $40 each. Otherwise, if you charter a whole boat, you can take up to six people for between $200 and $425 for a half-day, and $495 and $750 for a full day, depending upon the boat. Prices include fishing equipment but not food or drink.

You can also catch the boats coming in and ogle the fish weighed at Honokohau Harbor from 11am for the morning charters and around 3pm for the afternoon and full-day charters. Boats flying white flags scored *'ahi* (yellowfin tuna), blue flags indicate marlin, and inverted flags signify a catch-and-release excursion.

There are centers that book numerous boats each:

Charter Desk (☎ 329-5735, 888-566-2487; www.charter desk.com)

Charter Services Hawaii (☎ 334-1881, 800-567-2650; www.konazone.com)

Fins & Fairways (☎ 325-6171; www.fishkona.com)

Kona Charter Skippers Association (☎ 329-3600, 800-762-7546; www.konabiggamefishing.com)

Fitness Centers & Yoga

If Kailua's balmy weather and skimpy attire inspire you to work out, local gyms are easy to find.

Club In Kona (☎ 326-2582; www.theclubinkona.com; 75-5699 Kopiko St; per day/week $15/45; ☷ 5am-10pm Mon-Fri, 7am-7pm Sat & Sun) The most conveniently located gym is fully equipped and includes a pool. Pilates and yoga classes are offered.

Gold's Gym (☎ 334-1977; 74-5583 Luhia St; per day/week $20/50; ☷ 5am-10pm Mon-Fri, 7am-7pm Sat

& Sun) Kailua's best gym for serious athletes features free weights, resistance and aerobic machines, lockers, showers, sauna and juice bar.

Kona Yoga (☎ 331-1310; www.konayoga.com; Sunset Shopping Plaza, 77-6425 Hwy 11, D202; drop-in class $15) Smallish, slightly makeshift studio offers only a few classes, but founder Barbara Uechi is well trained in the Iyengar method, and she incorporates yoga philosophy in her teaching. Acupuncture and massage are available, too. Drive slowly along Kuakini Hwy, as the building is easy to miss.

KAILUA-KONA FOR CHILDREN

Children are likely to enjoy Kailua-Kona's colorful, carnival atmosphere (and to overlook any tourist tackiness!). The beaches are clearly the first-choice answer: snorkeling at Kahalu'u Beach Park (p86) or at the little beach at King Kamehameha's Kona Beach Hotel (p79), boogie boarding at White Sands Beach Park (p74) or tide-pool hunting at Old Kona Airport State Recreation Area (p74). For older kids interested in outer space, the Ellison S Onizuka Space Center (p106) might make for a fascinating stop along the highway. A Jacques Cousteau adventure on the Atlantis Submarine (opposite) would also probably intrigue all youngsters, but the cost might deter parents.

If you're seeking a local 'babysitter,' try the **Kid's Play Corner** (☎ 334-1800, 866-305-1800; www.kidsplayhawaii.com; Kaiwi Sq, 74-5565 Luhia St; per hr child 2-3/4-7/8-12 $5.75/4.75/4; ☷ 7:30am-8pm Mon-Thu, 7:30am-10pm Fri & Sat), a daycare center open to kids aged two to 12. Drop-in kids are welcome at the cheerful indoor facility, which includes plastic ball pits, games (electronic and board), arts and crafts, quiet reading loft and building-block area. A completed enrollment form and proof of immunization for tuberculosis is required. It's a handy option for rainy days or kid-free evenings.

Other kid-friendly attractions include the following:

Fun Factory (☎ 334-1578; Kona Inn Shopping Village, 75-5744 Ali'i Dr 102; token 25¢; ☷ 10am-10pm Sun-Thu, to midnight Fri & Sat) Mostly tourist kids jam this arcade in the thick of Ali'i Dr foot traffic.

Kona Bowl (☎ 326-2695; 75-5591 Palani Rd; per game adult/child $3.75/3.25, shoe rental $2.75; ☷ 9am-10pm Sun, Mon, Wed & Thu, 9am-11pm Tue, 9-12:30am Fri & Sat) Retro and slightly divey, the bowling alley features Friday- and Saturday-night 'Cosmic Bowling' (per game $4.25, per hour $26.50, shoes included), which means bowling to loud music in the dark (with black lights, glow-in-the-dark pins, chaser lights along the lanes and laser lights bouncing everywhere). If you're not into bowling, there are video games, karaoke and a sports lounge.

TOURS

Atlantis Submarines (☎ 329-6626, 800-548-6262; www.atlantisadventures.com; 45min ride adult/child $80/42; ☺ departures 10am, 11:30am & 1pm) Submarines dive down about 100ft in a coral crevice in front of the Royal Kona Resort. The sub has 26 portholes, carries 48 passengers and the outing lasts one hour, including the boat ride to the sub. Japanese-language narration is available. The subs depart from Kailua Pier and board offshore.

Kailua Bay Charter Company (☎ 324-1749; www .konaglassbottomboat.com; 50min tour adult/child $25/10; ☺ departures 10:30am, 11:30am & 12:30pm Mon-Sat) Ralph Jewell's 36ft glass-bottom-boat cruise shows off Kona's underwater reef in more vivid colors than you'd see down below. Because you're skimming the waters, you can also see the coastline and perhaps dolphins or whales. There's an onboard naturalist plus easy boarding for elderly or mobility-impaired travelers. It departs from Kailua Pier.

Kona Historical Society (☎ 323-3222; www.kona historical.org; 75min tour incl palace admission $15; ☺ 9:30am & 1:30pm Tue & Fri) Offers a walking tour that starts at King Kamehameha's Kona Beach Hotel and covers historical sites such as Hulihe'e Palace, Moku'aikaua Church and the Kona Inn.

FESTIVALS & EVENTS

Kailua's two main festivals highlight the region's specialty commodities: beer and coffee.

Kona Brewers Festival (2nd Sat in Mar; ☎ 334-2739; www.konabrewingco.com; admission $40) A food-and-beer event geared for 'just folks' rather than the connoisseur crowd, the Kona Brewers Festival feature 30 craft breweries annually. Beer tasters can also try gourmet samples from some two dozen local restaurants. The owners of the Kona Brewing Company (p74) established the festival in 1995, and funds go to local environmental and cultural organizations. Tickets are usually sold out the day before the festival, so order in advance.

Hawaiian International Billfish Tournament (early Aug; ☎ 329-6155; www.konabillfish.com) Of the numerous fishing tournaments held in Kona, this is the granddaddy of them all, accompanied by a week of festive entertainment.

Kona Coffee Cultural Festival (early Nov; ☎ 326-7820; www.konacoffeefest.com; admission $3, surcharges apply for some events) For 10 days during coffee harvest season, the community celebrates the Kona coffee pioneers and their gourmet brew. The dozens of events include a cupping competition (akin to wine tasting), art exhibits, farm tours, parades and a race to pick the most coffee beans in three minutes (a recent winner picked over 23lb!).

THE ULTIMATE ENDURANCE TEST

When thousands of athletes and fans swoop into Kailua each October, locals gripe about the traffic and crowds. But nobody can deny the awesome spectacle of the **Ironman Triathlon World Championship** (3rd Sat in Oct; ☎ 329-0063; www.ironmanlive.com; Suite 101, 75-5722 Hwy 11, Kailua-Kona, HI 96740). The granddaddy of races is a grueling, nonstop combination of a 2.4-mile ocean swim, 112-mile bike race and 26.2-mile run. Start time is 7am (6:45am for the pros) at the Kailua Pier, and top triathletes cross the finish line around 3pm; the finish line stays open to stragglers until midnight (kudos!). And it all has to be done in 17 hours, although the top athletes cross the finish line in about half that time. Luc Van Lierde of Belgium set the current men's record at eight hours and four minutes in 1996, while the women's record, set by Paula Newby-Fraser of the USA in 1992, is eight hours and 55 minutes.

Harsh *kona* (leeward) conditions make the event the ultimate endurance test, even by triathlon standards. Heat reflected off the lava landscape commonly exceeds 100°F, making dehydration and heat exhaustion major challenges. Many contenders arrive weeks before the race just to acclimatize themselves. On the day of the race, over 5500 volunteers line the 140-mile course to hand out 26,000 gallons of fluid to athletes pushed to the max.

Begun in 1978 with just 15 participants, the Ironman was labeled 'lunatic' by *Sports Illustrated* after the second race. By 1980, the Ironman had enough participants to receive TV coverage on ABC's *Wide World of Sports*, and the numbers continue to grow. Today the event draws up to 2000 athletes from each US state, each Canadian province and 50-plus other countries. Over 50,000 hopefuls compete in qualifying races to earn a coveted entry berth, while another 4000 gain entry through a race lottery for 200 participants.

For all this punishment, the top male and female winners can run home with $100,000 each. Altogether, a total of $480,000 is given to the top-10 males and females. In 2004, the event was marred by the positive drug test of female winner Nina Kraft of Germany.

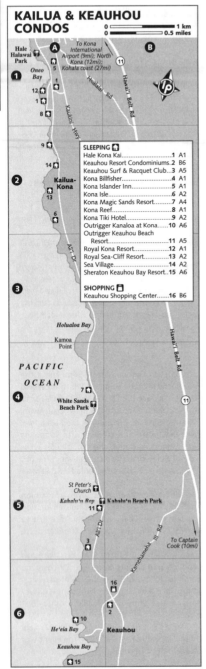

KAILUA & KEAUHOU CONDOS

0 ———— 1 km
0 ———— 0.5 miles

SLEEPING 🏠
Hale Kona Kai..............................1 A1
Keauhou Resort Condominiums..2 B6
Keauhou Surf & Racquet Club...3 A5
Kona Billfisher............................4 A1
Kona Islander Inn.......................5 A1
Kona Isle....................................6 A2
Kona Magic Sands Resort..........7 A4
Kona Reef..................................8 A2
Kona Tiki Hotel...........................9 A2
Outrigger Kanaloa at Kona......10 A6
Outrigger Keauhou Beach
    Resort..................................11 A5
Royal Kona Resort....................12 A1
Royal Sea-Cliff Resort..............13 A2
Sea Village................................14 A2
Sheraton Keauhou Bay Resort..15 A6

SHOPPING 🏠
Keauhou Shopping Center.......16 B6

SLEEPING

In the heart of Kailua, you'll find many hotels and condominiums along a lively oceanfront thoroughfare. Here, condos outnumber hotels many times over. Condos tend to be cheaper than hotels if you're staying a while, and most condo units have full kitchens. Reservations are recommended in the high season. The year-round heat in downtown Kailua-Kona can be brutal, so air-con is virtually indispensable wherever you stay – ask about it when making reservations.

Bookings in most of Kona's condominiums are managed by local agencies; the office manager on-site at the condo probably deals only with grounds maintenance. Check the agencies' websites for current availability. If you have your heart set on a particular condo, try doing a Google search of the condo name to find relevant management companies (which each might handle just a handful of units) and individual owners. Prices in the same condo might vary since units are separately owned. The following well-known agencies operate mainly by phone and Internet, rather than by running an actual walk-in business.

ATR Properties (☎ 329-6020, 888-311-6020; www.kona condo.com; Suite A-5, 75-5660 Kopiko St)

Hawaii Resort Management (☎ 329-9393, 800-622-5348; www.konahawaii.com; Suite 105C, 75-5776 Hwy 11)

Knutson & Associates (☎ 329-6311, 800-800-6202; www.konahawaiirentals.com; Suite 8, 75-6082 Ali'i Dr)

Property Network (☎ 329-7977, 800-358-7977; www.hawaii-kona.com; 75-5799 B-3 Ali'i Dr)

SunQuest Vacations & Property Management Hawaii (☎ 329-6438, 800-367-5168; www.sunquest -hawaii.com; 77-6435 Hwy 11)

West Hawaii Properties (☎ 322-6696, 800-799-5662; www.konarentals.com; Suite 234A, 78-6831 Ali'i Dr)

For additional information on condos, see p223. If you want to escape the marketplace atmosphere of Kailua, head to Keauhou (p87), just a few minutes' drive south.

Budget

Note that phone numbers are omitted for condos, as you must contact one of the local agencies (listed opposite).

Kona Tiki Hotel (Map p78; ☎ 329-1425; 75-5968 Ali'i Dr; r incl breakfast $61-75, with kitchenette $84; P 🏊) A sweet deal for a vintage three-story complex near the ocean, if you want a no-frills room (sans TV, phone and air-con). Most

KONA

KONA'S TOP FIVE SLEEPS

Hawaiian Oasis B&B (p80) A perfect blend of B&B intimacy and hotel amenities.

Outrigger Keauhou Beach Resort (p87) Affordable neighbor to a premier snorkeling beach.

Four Seasons Resort Hualalai (p107) Classy luxury and world-class golf.

Areca Palms Estate B&B (p92) Impeccable bedrooms and delicious breakfasts.

Kona Tiki Hotel (opposite) No-frills, oceanfront budget hunter's secret.

---

of the rooms have a queen-size and a twin bed, and all have a refrigerator and a breezy oceanfront lanai. It's perennially popular with return visitors. An advance deposit is required (full payment for three nights or less); no credit cards accepted.

Kona Islander Inn (Map p72; ☎ 329-9393, 800-622-5348; www.konahawaii.com; 75-5776 Hwy 11; studio condos $70-90; P ⊠ ⚲) You can't get any closer to the Ali'i Dr hub than the Islander, managed almost entirely by Hawaii Resort Management. Ground-floor rooms have a cavernous feel and furnishings are rather worn, but for the price, they're a bargain, with TV, kitchenette (the sink is shared with the bathroom) and phone with free local calls. The Islander draws a local crowd as well, and you might find a high-school band or club occupying whole wings. The cons: rampant mosquitoes in the garden lobby and a major lack of parking (roughly 50 spaces for 150 units!).

Kona Isle (Map p78; 75-6100 Ali'i Dr; 1-bedroom condos $60-115; P ⊠ ⚲) If the Kona Islander Inn is like the party dorm in college, this complex is the studious dorm, a reputation that gives the place plenty of repeat business and long-term residents. Units enjoy amenities including picnic tables, barbecue grills and chaise lounges overlooking the ocean. There's also a small saltwater pool near the beach.

Midrange

Hale Kona Kai (Map p72; ☎ 329-2155, 800-421-3696; hkk.kona@verizon.net; 75-5870 Kahakai Rd; 1-bedroom condos $125-135; P ⊠ ⚲) Just south of the Royal Kona Resort, Hale Kona Kai is a 22-unit gem right at the water's edge – ideal if you want to avoid the high-rise masses and enjoy the sound of the surf all night. The units aren't new, but they're comfortable,

often upgraded, and with a full kitchen and cable TV. All have waterfront lanai and the corner units enjoy a wraparound lanai. A $150 security deposit is required, and there's no holiday check-in.

Kona Magic Sands Resort (Map p78; ☎ 329-3333; 77-6452 Ali'i Dr; studio condos $95-125; P ⊠ ⚲) If it's true that location is everything, Magic Sands has it all, with White Sands Beach to the south and Pahoehoe Park to the north. Units in the all-concrete building (which keeps out noise and heat) are compact studios, but they have full kitchen, TV, phone, rattan furnishings and oceanfront lanai. It's great value for being right on the water.

King Kamehameha's Kona Beach Hotel (Map p72; ☎ 329-2911, 800-367-2111; www.konabeachhotel.com; 75-5660 Palani Rd; r $135-200; P $7 ⊠ ⚲) Located at the very north end of Ali'i Dr, this 460-room hotel is very convenient to restaurants and shops, but less so for beaches. Locals often stop here to browse at the shops and cool off, after driving to Kailua-Kona from other towns. The furnishings and fixtures are showing their age, but each room includes two double beds, private lanai, refrigerator, TV and phone. Hotel staff arrive quickly to solve any problems. The lobby is a well-used oasis with refreshingly chilly air-con blasting and a modest collection of showcases displaying traditional Hawaiian artifacts.

Sea Village (Map p78; ☎ 329-6438; 75-6002 Ali'i Dr; 1-bedroom condos $95-160; P ⊠ ⚲) One of the most popular Ali'i Dr condos, the Sea Village, about 2 miles outside town, features well-kept grounds that include a tennis court and pool. Call the front desk to fax a list of management agencies that handle bookings.

Kona Billfisher (Map p72; 75-5841 Ali'i Dr; 1-bedroom condos $90-105, 2-bedroom condos $115-135; P ⊠ ⚲) Although located on the *mauka* (inland) side of Ali'i Dr, the clean, low-key Billfisher feels more like an apartment complex than a tourist hotel with decor that's more consistent and better upkept than that at similarly priced complexes. The time-share units include a queen-size sofa bed, a king-size bed in the bedroom, both a ceiling fan and air-con, plus full kitchen and lanai. There's an extra charge for a telephone ($5 per week) and for air-con ($5 per day). All units close for maintenance monthly from 10am on the 13th to 3pm on the 15th.

Nancy's Hideaway (☎ 325-3132, 866-325-3132; www.nancyshideaway.com; 73-1530 Uanani Pl; studio/ 1-bedroom cottage $110/130; **P**) Driving 6 miles upland to Nancy's, you enter a whole different world, where the air is moist and cool, banana trees grow wild, and you can gaze upon Kailua town in the distance. Freestanding, immaculate cottages have private lanai, phone, TV, VCR and ample breakfast fixings. Perfect for visitors who want a home base far from the Ali'i Dr bustle. To maintain peace and quiet for all guests, Nancy prefers guests over age 12 and rates include breakfast.

Kiwi Gardens (☎ 326-1559; www.kiwigardens.com; 74-4920 Kiwi St; d/ste incl breakfast $85/95; **P**) Calling all '50s nostalgia buffs! Here you'll find a vintage soda fountain and juke box, along with the host's kitschy collection of Raggedy Ann dolls. If the decor is too cute for your taste, you can escape to clean, simple rooms, each with fridge. Breakfast includes seasonal fruits from the 80 trees in the yard, where guests may spot doves and quail.

If you want to cut costs, and don't mind joining the tourist herds, here are some good local standbys:

Kona Seaside Hotel (Map p72; ☎ 329-2455, 800-560-5558; www.konaseasidehotel.com; 75-5646 Palani Rd; r $120-140; **P** ⛱ ⛲) Attracts an older clientele or locals traveling for work (ask for the upgraded new wing).

Uncle Billy's Kona Bay Hotel (Map p72; ☎ 329-1393, 800-367-5102; www.unclebilly.com; 75-5744 Ali'i Dr; r $90-100; **P** ⛱ ⛲) A 133-room branch of the Uncle Billy family of hotels, it's popular with tour groups, offering rooms with TV, refrigerator and phone.

Top End

You can often avoid paying full rack rates with Internet specials, so check the websites first.

Royal Sea-Cliff Resort (Map p78; ☎ 329-8021, 800-688-7444; www.outrigger.com; 75-6040 Ali'i Dr; studio condos $185-235, 1-bedroom condos $215-320; **P** ⛱ ⛲) A condo complex that's operated just like a hotel by the ubiquitous Outrigger chain, the Royal Sea-Cliff feels like an upscale hotel, with an impressive atrium of giant sago palms and a gurgling (albeit artificial) stream. The modern units have stylish furnishings, full kitchen, washer and dryer. The complex offers tennis courts, freshwater and saltwater pools, a sauna and covered parking (once you arrive in Kona, you'll appreciate this benefit). No minimum stay. Check website for discount specials.

Kona Reef (Map p78; ☎ 329-2959, 800-367-5004; www.castleresorts.com; 75-5888 Ali'i Dr; 1-bedroom condos $180-260; **P** ⛱ ⛲) Most units at this condo are run by Castle Resorts, which offers all the services of a hotel. Though prices are slightly higher than other top-end places, the Reef is more modern and spacious, and Castle Resorts definitely takes care of its guests; if you lock yourself out or face a plumbing disaster, the on-site staff will come to your rescue. There's no guarantee that other management agencies' staff will arrive immediately, but it can be considerably cheaper to book through the agencies listed at the beginning of this section. Also check the website for the $130 Internet-booking specials.

Royal Kona Resort (Map p72; ☎ 329-3111, 800-774-5662; www.royalkona.com; 75-5852 Ali'i Dr; r $210-350; **P** ⛱ ⛲) The Royal Kona Resort is an oceanfront hotel with excellent, spacious rooms, all with a balcony; rooms are spread across three airy towers. At the south end, there's a charming saltwater lagoon, perfect for kids, and numerous tennis courts. The hotel is conveniently located next to Huggo's

---

AUTHOR'S CHOICE

Hawaiian Oasis B&B (☎ 327-1701; www.hawaiianoasis.com; 74-4958 Kiwi St; r $140-170, ste $160-190; **P** ⛲) If you can't decide between a B&B's intimacy and a hotel's amenities, this is the perfect combination. The suites are classily furnished and immaculate, complete with either kitchenette (microwave, refrigerator, toaster, tableware, coffee grinder and maker) or full kitchen. On the verdant two-acre estate, you'll find a 40ft lap pool, hot tub, bar and grill, tennis court, workout room and free wi-fi Internet access. No air-con is necessary since you're upland. Friendly hosts Mike and Carol Weaver can give you first-hand advice on local beaches and ocean sports, and they offer a range of activities such as snorkeling cruises, Harley-Davidson rides, gourmet cooking classes and personal fitness training. If you're into an active, healthy lifestyle (or want to be), Hawaiian Oasis lives up to its name. Rates include breakfast.

(p83) and Snorkel Bob's (p75). If you book online, you can find amazing deals ($105 for a garden view).

EATING

Kailua-Kona dining runs the gamut, from 'same old' tropical-theme restaurants to touristy hangouts that buzz with energy. If you want an ocean view, stay in the commercial strip along Ali'i Dr, where you can window shop and stroll (and perhaps get a dousing of sea spray) into the night.

You'll pass numerous open-air, balcony restaurants overlooking the water along Ali'i Dr but, in most cases, the setting will have to compensate for mediocre steak-and-seafood fare. If you want more options and a sample of locals' favorites, you might end up at a shopping mall with no view. Kailua is the major residential center of the Kona coast, so you'll find numerous malls just a few blocks from Ali'i Dr. This might not be the Hawaii you envisioned, but don't forget that great local cuisine might come in quite conventional settings.

Budget

All the places in this section are on the Kailua-Kona map.

Island Lava Java (☎ 327-2161; Ali'i Sunset Plaza, 75-5799 Ali'i Dr; meals $4-8; ☀ 6am-10pm) A popular hangout with both locals and tourists, who while away the hours at outdoor tables perfect for people-watching. The café scene hasn't quite hit the Big Island yet, but this comes close. Along with real Kona coffee, Lava Java offers the gamut of sandwiches and salads, plus enticing banana-nut pancakes and fresh-baked desserts.

Ocean View Inn (☎ 329-9998; 75-5683 Ali'i Dr; breakfast $3-6, lunch & dinner $5-11; ☀ 6:30am-2:45pm & 5:15-9pm Tue-Sun) Nothing fancy, but this fixture in the Ali'i Dr strip offers a comprehensive sampler of cheap local food. The endless menu is eclectic, and you'll find Chinese, Hawaiian, Japanese and American dishes side by side – usually a red flag – but Ocean View is good value.

Ba-Le Kona (☎ 327-1212; Kona Coast Shopping Center, 74-5588 Palani Rd; meals $3-7; ☀ 10am-9pm Mon-Sat, 11am-7pm Sun) A local Vietnamese chain, Ba-Le serves satisfying sandwiches made with freshly baked French bread or croissants, with interesting fillings like lemongrass chicken or tofu. Popular Vietnamese

fare includes green papaya salad topped with shrimp, rice-paper summer rolls and traditional *pho* noodle soups.

Manna Korean BBQ (☎ 334-0880; Crossroads Shopping Center, 75-1027 Henry St; mains $6-9; ☀ 10am-8:30pm Mon-Sat) A hole-in-the-wall that packs 'em in, despite the lack of ambience. Manna plates come with four 'veggies' and two scoops of rice. The most popular dish is charbroiled, marinated short ribs. No credit cards.

Cool off with shave ice from Scandinavian Shaved Ice Internet Café (p70), where 'small' ($2.50) seems like large and 'jumbo' ($3.50) borders on gargantuan. Surprise your tastebuds with island flavors such as guava and passionfruit.

GROCERIES

Kona farmers' market (Kaiwi St at Luhia St, old industrial area; ☀ 8am-5pm Sat, 8am-3pm Sun) This tiny, unassuming farmers' market is the best bet for fresh produce. Parking is easy and prices reasonable.

Kailua Village farmers' market (Ali'i Dr at Hualalai Rd, across Hale Halawai; ☀ 9am-5pm Thu-Sun) Carries a lot of cheesy tourist souvenirs and phony shell jewelry and 'Hawaiian' knickknacks, but it does include orchids, mac nuts, coffee and produce.

Ali'i Gardens farmers' market (Ali'i Dr, 2 miles south of Kailua Pier; ☀ 9am-5pm Thu-Sun) Run by the owners of Huggo's (see p83) and hardly resembles a farmers' market – with its 'permanent' kiosks selling mainly artsy-craftsy gift items.

If you want to eat on the run, **KTA Super Store** (☎ 329-1677; Kona Coast Shopping Center, 74-5594 Palani Rd; ☀ 5am-midnight), the Big Island's best grocery chain, has a full deli and bakery, and sells local edibles you won't find at Safeway. Try the *bento* boxes of sushi and grilled mackerel or salmon. Kona's biggest supermarket, **Safeway** (☎ 329-2207; Crossroads Shopping Center; 75-1027 Henry St; ☀ 24hr) has more standard fare. **Kona Natural Foods** (☎ 329-2296; Crossroads Shopping Center, 75-1027 Henry St; ☀ 8:30am-9pm Mon-Sat, to 7pm Sun), next to Safeway, stocks organic wines and produces a good selection of dairy and bulk items.

Midrange

Sibu Café (☎ 329-1112; Banyan Court, 78-5695 Ali'i Dr; meals $13-17; ☀ lunch & dinner) The chef can spice your dishes from mild to outrageously hot, using chili peppers grown on Mauna Kea.

For *pupu* (hors d'oeuvres), try the spring rolls with fresh *'ahi* or black tiger shrimp. Save room for the house specialty dessert: *ohelo* berries over *haupia* (coconut pudding) ice cream. The entire menu is available for take-out.

Quinn's (☎ 329-3822; 75-5864 Palani Rd; meals $9-20; ☉ 11am-11pm) Many locals are devoted fans of this seemingly conventional restaurant; they keep coming back for the consistently good seafood and steak dinners. And it's one of the few Kona restaurants that stays open late.

Kona Brewing Company (☎ 329-2739; 75-5629 Hwy 11; sandwiches & salads $8-11, small/large pizza $13/22; ☉ 11am-10pm Mon-Thu, to midnight Fri & Sat, 1-9pm Sun) Always a good bet, this restaurant-pub serves creative Greek, spinach and Caesar salads and thin-crust pizzas. Wash it all down with one of the fresh brews made on-site or opt for the four-beer sampler ($6.50).

Cassandra's Greek Taverna (☎ 334-1066; 75-5669 Ali'i Dr; lunch mains $7-9, dinner mains $15-30; ☉ 11am-10pm) Although the setting is rather touristy, Cassandra's serves authentic Greek fare, including an impressive souvlaki, moussaka, or gyros plate for $18; appetizers include calamari, pickled octopus and the ubiquitous Greek salad. If you just want to hang out, there's a bar, a pool table and a clear view of canoe paddlers in the bay.

Tres Hombres (☎ 329-2173; 75-5864 Walua Rd; mains $9-15; ☉ 11:30am-9pm) It beats Pancho & Lefty's (a busier Mexican joint on Ali'i Dr), with its fine margaritas and fresh chips. Menu items include steak fajitas, *chile relleno* (green peppers stuffed with cheese) and fish tacos. Service is inconsistent (some say it's attentive, others say slow).

Thai Rin (☎ 329-2929; Ali'i Sunset Plaza, 75-5799 Ali'i Dr; mains $9-14; ☉ lunch & dinner Mon-Sat) For an inexpensive, sit-down dinner, Thai Rin offers a range of traditional dishes, from red, green or yellow curries to whole fish steamed in ginger black-bean sauce. Most dishes offer choice of tofu, seafood or meat, so vegetarians will have a good selection.

Royal Jade Garden (☎ 326-7288; Lanihau Center, 75-5595 Palani Rd; mains $7-10; ☉ 10:30am-9pm) A family business that many locals consider their favorite Chinese restaurant in Kona. The vinyl-chair, formica-table setting is nondescript, but the food is tasty and servings ample. Ask the server for daily specials that don't appear on the menu. Kids are welcome at this casual, family-style restaurant.

> **KONA'S TOP FIVE EATS**
>
> **Hualalai Grille by Alan Wong** (p107)
> **Ke'ei Café** (p94)
> **Teshima Restaurant** (p91)
> **Kenichi Pacific** (p88)
> **O's Bistro** (below)

Top End

O's Bistro (☎ 327-6565; Crossroads Shopping Center, 75-1027 Henry St; dinner mains $25; ☉ 10am-9pm) Formerly known (and acclaimed) as Oodles of Noodles, the restaurant relaunched a new urban-chic look in July 2004. Still run by Amy Ferguson, the bistro has introduced an eclectic menu of island fish and meats prepared with an Asian-fusion flavor, along with her signature noodle dishes ($10 to $16). Veg eaters must stick to the appetizers and salads, such as savory grilled eggplant, Portabello mushroom, goat cheese and heirloom tomato stack ($10). The low-lit yuppie interior is incongruous to the shopping-mall setting, but such is the norm around here.

Kona Inn (☎ 329-4455; Kona Inn Shopping Village, 75-5744 Ali'i Dr; lunch mains $10, dinner mains $17-28; ☉ 11:30am-9:30pm) The namesake inn first opened in 1929 as the Big Island's first hotel. Nowadays it's a restaurant overlooking the water, surrounded by an outdoor pedestrian mall, but the interior is handsome, with koa furnishings and gleaming hardwood floors – and the view can't be beat. American steak and seafood dinners are livened up with island-style *pupu*, like seared *'ahi* dusted with rice paper and a salad of Maui onion, vine-ripened tomato and feta cheese.

La Bourgogne (☎ 329-6711; Kuakini Plaza, 77-6400 Nalani St, at Hwy 11; mains $24-32; ☉ dinner Tue-Sat) For many Kona residents, this intimate French restaurant is the hands-down choice for special occasions. Again, the location is a minimall (roughly 3 miles south of Kailua), with no ocean views. But the food is impeccable and unlike any other dining experience in Kona. Specialties include roast duck with raspberries and pine nuts, and lobster braised with shallots, tomato, brandy and cream. Staff can help you navigate the extensive wine list. Reservations are a must.

For a spectacular oceanfront view, there are other fine-dining options that serve decent steak and seafood – the draw is the location, not the cuisine. Both of the following restaurants are long-standing Kailua destinations:

Huggo's (☎ 329-1493; 75-5828 Kahakai Rd; mains $25-30; ☑ lunch Mon-Fri, dinner daily)

Jameson's-by-the-Sea (☎ 329-3195; 77-6452 Ali'i Dr; mains $20-25; ☑ lunch Mon-Fri, dinner daily)

DRINKING

There's no shortage of bars featuring happy hours and island *pupu* in a mixed bag of hangouts, from lonely-hearts dives to touristy spots that haul 'em in. Luckily Kailua is a compact town, and an easy stroll down Ali'i Dr lets you check out most of your options before stepping inside (though the two best options are off the main drag).

Kona Brewing Company (☎ 329-2739; 75-5629 Kuakini Hwy; ☑ 11am-10pm Mon-Thu, to midnight Fri & Sat, 1-9pm Sun) Here there's no view and mediocre service by young, flippant servers, but the Big Island's first microbrewery is considered by beer aficionados to be the island's (and perhaps the state's) best. Now an established commercial venture (with the requisite logo T-shirts and gear), Kona Brewing continues to produce flavors unique to the island (ask for seasonal brews not on the menu).

Other Side (☎ 329-7226; 74-5484 Kaiwi St; ☑ 1pm-2am) Away from the hubbub of Ali'i Dr, you'll finally find a bar with many more locals than tourists. You can request tunes from over 400 CDs (from rap to Steely Dan), and join a diverse, laid-back crowd for darts, foosball, pool and an insanely long happy hour that lasts from opening time until 6pm!

Huggo's (☎ 329-1493; 75-5828 Kahakai Rd; ☑ bar to midnight) A long-standing fixture on the Ali'i Dr circuit, Huggo's might strike you as a bit predictable, but the prime waterfront location and decent *pupu* menu appeal to those past the college-party crowd. There's live jazz music on Saturday nights.

LuLu's (☎ 331-2633; Coconut Grove Marketplace, 75-5819 Ali'i Dr; ☑ 11am-10pm) An outdoor sports bar with 13 TV screens and a lively (either touristy or young) crowd. But LuLu's is spacious (with a view) and ideal during play-off seasons.

Durty Jake's (☎ 329-7366; Coconut Grove Marketplace, 75-5819 Ali'i Dr; ☑ 11-1am, to 2am Fri & Sat) Right downstairs from LuLu's, Jakes offers eight TVs plus dancing to live music or karaoke on most nights. You'll find an older, less raucous clientele here. Jake's also serves full meals, but they're mediocre. Go to hang out, not eat.

Hard Rock Café (☎ 329-8866; Coconut Grove Marketplace, 75-5815 Ali'i Dr; ☑ 11am-11pm) Does anyone still get excited about this anymore? Apparently, recently legal 20-somethings still do. The Kailua branch, which draws mainly a tourist crowd, keeps up the Hard Rock tradition of blasting rock music and plastering the walls with memorabilia. The only draw is the splendid ocean view.

Sam's Hideaway (☎ 326-7267; Kona Marketplace, 75-5725 Ali'i Dr; ☑ 10-1:30am) Located in the back of an alley off Ali'i Dr, it's smoky, dimly lit and totally untouristy. The nightly karaoke is for diehard fans.

ENTERTAINMENT
Hula & Luau

Kailua-Kona's big hotels offer colorful, albeit hokey, evening luau. The Royal Kona Resort's Windjammer Lounge also puts on a pleasant sunset show at 6pm from Tuesday to Sunday.

AUTHOR'S CHOICE

Kanaka Kava (☎ 327-1660, 866-327-1660; Coconut Grove Marketplace, 75-5803 Ali'i Dr; ☑ 11am-10pm Sun-Wed, to 11pm Thu-Sat) You won't find any beer or wine at Kanaka Kava – instead, you drink the juice from *'awa* (kava), a native plant and mild relaxant used by ancient Hawaiians. The outdoor tables are always jammed, and the owner, Zachary Gibson, is constantly in motion as chef, host and kava server. He grows his own *'awa* in Waipi'o Valley, and patrons drink it either plain ($3) or fruit juice–flavored ($4) from coconut-shell cups (it's an acquired taste).

Locals know Gibson is also a marvelous chef and they repeatedly come for his satisfying salads ($10 to $14) – a choice of fish, shellfish, chicken, tofu or *poke* (chopped raw fish marinated in soy sauce, oil and chili pepper) over a bed of fresh organic greens and veggies, marinated seaweed and baby bamboo. His Hawaiian à la carte items, including *haupia*-sweet-potato pie ($4) and taro steamed with coconut milk ($3), rival the fare at any upscale place.

King Kamehameha's Kona Beach Hotel (☎ 326-4969; www.konabeachhotel.com; 75-5660 Palani Rd; adult/child $34.50/17.50, incl dinner $60/24; ☒ 5-8:30pm Tue-Thu & Sun) This beachfront luau starts with a shell-lei greeting, followed by a torch lighting, buffet dinner and Polynesian dance show. If you stop by around 10am on luau days, you can watch staff bury the pig in the *imu* (underground oven) right on the beach. Drinks are included with or without dinner.

Royal Kona Resort (☎ 329-3111, 800-774-5662; www.royalkona.com; 75-5852 Ali'i Dr; adult/child $32/22, incl dinner $59/27, 1 child admitted free per paying adult; ☒ 6pm Mon, Wed & Fri) This luau also includes an open bar, a buffet dinner and the whole cast of flamboyant dancers, musicians and fire performers.

It's hard to differentiate between the two – just choose the more convenient location.

Cinemas

For the most populated city along the Kona Coast, Kailua is surprisingly sedate at night. This is no mecca for film or theater, but you can find first-run movies on 10 screens at **Stadium Cinemas** (☎ 327-0444; Makalapua Shopping Center, 74-5475 Kamaka'eha Ave). If you want to hole up with a video or DVD (as most condos come equipped with players), try **Blockbuster** (☎ 326-7694; Kona Coast Shopping Center, 74-5588 Palani Rd; ☒ 10am-10pm, to midnight Fri & Sat).

Sports

If you're walking down Ali'i Dr at night, you can see beach-volleyball matches at the sand pit next to the Coconut Grove Marketplace. Watch locals of all shapes and sizes play pickup games, or join in yourself.

SHOPPING

Downtown Kailua-Kona is jammed with small shops selling souvenirs, aloha shirts,

surf gear, island crafts and beach accessories. Check carefully – you can find quality art and clothing sellers amid the tourist traps.

Pacific Vibrations (☎ 329-4140; pacvibe@hawaii.rr .com; 75-5702 Likana Ln, at Ali'i Dr; ☒ 10am-5:30pm Mon-Fri, to 3:30pm Sat) Surfers (and wannabe surfers) can find the latest in shorts, swimsuits, rash guards, boards and other gear here.

Made on the Big Island Outlet (☎ 326-4949; 75-5660 Palani Rd; ☒ 9am-5pm Mon, 9am-6pm Tue-Fri, 10am-6pm Sat & Sun) At King Kamehameha's Kona Beach Hotel, this store stocks a huge selection of top-notch island crafts, edibles, clothing and oddities, including take-home potted bonsai.

Mele Kai Music (☎ 329-1454; Ka'ahumanu Plaza, 74-5467 Kaiwi St; ☒ 10am-7pm Mon-Fri, to 6pm Sat) Though cramped and off the main drag, locals come here to find musical instruments, including guitars and ukulele, plus a decent selection of classic and contemporary Hawaiian CDs.

Crazy Shirts (☎ 329-2176; Kona Marketplace, 75-5719G Ali'i Dr; ☒ 9am-9pm) The iconic T-shirt company, founded in 1964, offers unique island designs on heavyweight cotton. A Kilauea motif is made from volcanic-ash dye and the Kona Brewing Company line features shirts colored tan using…beer!

If you're seeking the **Hula Heaven** (www .hulaheaven.net), a source for authentic Hawaiian collectibles since the 1970s, you'll have to shop online. The Kailua walk-in store is gone, and has been replaced by a website. However, you can still find top-quality vintage aloha shirts, plus antique maps and prints, on sale via the website.

GETTING THERE & AWAY
Air

Most visitors arrive on the Big Island at **Kona International Airport at Keahole** (KOA; ☎ 329-3423;

A SOUVENIR TO WEAR HOME

Along Ali'i Dr you'll find more tattoo parlors than you might expect. If you want to go home with a cool island design like a *honu* (turtle) on your arm, but don't want anything permanent, try a henna tattoo at **Kona Henna Studio** (☎ 329-2919; Kona Marketplace, 75-5725 Ali'i Dr; ☒ 11am-8pm Wed-Mon). Henna is a natural plant dye that marks the skin reddish-brown and designs last one to four weeks (those on hands and feet are the darkest and last longest). Shadow and Maria Diessner, the young husband-and-wife owners, will help you choose a design from literally hundreds, both contemporary and traditional *mehndi* (designs from India and the Middle East), or you can custom-design your own. Prices depend on size: a small design costs $5, but on average they cost between $15 and $20.

www.hawaii.gov/dot/airports/hawaii/koa), located on Hwy 19, 7 miles north of Kailua-Kona. Surrounded by miles of lava desert, the airport is small, and passengers walk right across the tarmac to get on and off planes. The main drawback is severe weekday traffic on Hwy 19 during commute hours. Try not to arrive mid-afternoon if you're headed to Kailua.

Bus

The **Hele-On Bus** (☎ 961-8744; www.co.hawaii.hi.us /mass_transit/heleonbus.html) runs weekday routes from Kailua to Captain Cook. Fares are 75¢ to $2.25 per ride. The southbound bus departs four times a day from 9:30am to 4:25pm at the Lanihau Center. The northbound bus runs three times a day (first departure 6am, last at 2:15pm).

The Hele-On Bus also offers a three-hour ride to Hilo from the Lanihau Center at 6:45am on the No 7 Downtown Hilo bus. If you're coming to Kailua-Kona from Hilo, take the No 16 Kailua-Kona bus. The one-way fare in either direction is $5.25.

Between Kailua and Keauhou, **Ali'i Shuttle** (☎ 938-1112) has one (yes, only one!) bus running daily except Sunday. The one-way fare anywhere along this 45-minute route is $2, or you can get a daily/weekly/monthly pass for $5/20/40. The bus leaves Keauhou Bay starting at 8:30am, then runs every 1½ hours thereafter, with the last run at 7pm. Stops include Keauhou Shopping Center, Kahalu'u Beach Park, Royal Kona Resort, Kona Inn Shopping Village, King Kamehameha's Kona Beach Hotel and the Lanihau Center. In the southbound direction, the bus leaves the Lanihau Center every 1½ hours from 9:10am to 6:10pm. (If you miss the bus, flag down the driver anywhere along the route.)

Car & Motorcycle

If you're driving to Kona from Hilo, the distance is 92 miles and the trip takes 2½ hours; for other driving times and distances, see p240. Note that Hwy 19 (Queen Ka'ahumanu Hwy) then becomes Hwy 11 (Hawai'i Belt Rd) at Palani Rd.

GETTING AROUND
To/From the Airport

Most tourists rent cars from rental booths right outside the baggage-claim area. Taxis can be found curbside; the approximate

fare from the airport to Kailua-Kona is $20, and to Waikoloa it's $40.

Shuttle-bus services typically cost nearly as much as taxis. **Speedi Shuttle** (☎ 329-5433; www.speedishuttle.com) charges $17/30 per person and $18/32 for two people to Kailua-Kona/Waikoloa (plus tax for all fares). Call 48 hours in advance. If you make a round-trip booking, the return fare is discounted by 10%.

Bicycle

Renting a bike to get around Kailua town will save you time and parking costs. A good outfit, **Hawaiian Pedals** (☎ 329-2294; Kona Inn Shopping Village, 75-5744 Ali'i Dr; per day $20; ☺ 9am-9pm) rents mountain and hybrid bikes. Go to affiliated **HP Bike Works** (☎ 326-2453; www.hpbike works.com; 74-5599 Luhia St; per day $35-40; ☺ 9am-6pm) for better-quality bikes.

Bus

The Hele-On Bus and Ali'i Shuttle make stops within Kailua, so they're an in-town option. However, service is so limited that you'd make better time walking!

Car & Motorcycle

The center of Kailua-Kona gets congested. Free public parking is available in the lot behind Kona Seaside Hotel, between Likana Lane and the Kuakini Hwy. The Kona Inn Shopping Village provides complimentary parking for patrons in the lot behind the Kona Bay Hotel. Patrons of Kona Marketplace can park for free at the rear of that center. The Coconut Grove Marketplace and Ali'i Sunset Plaza share an enormous free parking lot out back.

At the north end of Ali'i Dr, the big parking lot behind King Kamehameha's Kona Beach Hotel offers free parking for the first 15 minutes; it costs $1 per half-hour after that. If you patronize a hotel shop or restaurant, you can get a limited amount of free parking (from 30 minutes to two hours).

Taxi

New Yorkers and Londoners, be warned that locals never ride cabs. So, they're rather scarce. In town, you must telephone ahead for a pickup. There are a couple of reliable companies:

Aloha Taxi (☎ 329-7779; ☺ 5am-10pm)
D&E Taxi (☎ 329-4279; ☺ 6am-9pm)

AROUND KAILUA-KONA

Just south of Kailua, you'll find Keauhou, a tidy resort area that's generally ritzier than Kailua but not as extravagant as South Kohala. Upland toward the east, the tiny artists' community of Holualoa preserves the lazy pace of old-time Hawai'i in the heart of Kona coffee country.

Keauhou

pop 2400

Keauhou lies along the coast immediately south of Kailua, starting at Kahalu'u Bay and running south beyond Keauhou Bay and the Sheraton Keauhou Bay Resort & Spa. This stretch of prime real estate, which is owned by the state's biggest private landholder, Bishop Estate Kamehameha Schools, was once the site of a major Hawaiian settlement. Although several historical spots can still be explored, they now share their grounds with a planned community of three hotels, nine condo complexes, a shopping center and a 27-hole golf course.

INFORMATION

The following are at the **Keauhou Shopping Center** (☎ 322-3000; www.keauhou-resort.com/shopping .asp; 78-6831 Ali'i Dr (at Kamehameha III Rd):

Bank of Hawaii (☎ 888-643-3888; ⏰ 10am-7pm Mon-Fri, to 3pm Sat & Sun) Has a 24-hour ATM.

Keoki's Surfin' Ass Café (☎ 322-9792; per 5 min $3; ⏰ 6:30am-8pm Mon-Fri, to 6pm Sat & Sun) Internet access, plus 100% Kona coffee and the Donkey Balls line of chocolate and mac-nut treats.

KTA Super Store (☎ 322-2311; ⏰ 7am-10pm)

Longs Drugs (☎ 322-5122; ⏰ 8am-10pm Mon-Sat, to 6pm Sun)

Post office (☎ 322-7070; ⏰ 9am-4pm Mon-Fri, 10am-3pm Sat)

SIGHTS

St Peter's Church

The 'Little Blue Church' is one of Hawai'i's most photographed small churches and a favorite choice for weddings (despite the hefty $150 fee). Made of clapboard with a corrugated-tin roof, it practically sits right on the water; a beautiful etched-glass window casts soft light over the entire church, especially at sunset.

Built in the 1880s, it was moved from White Sands Beach to this site in 1912. The church now sits on an ancient Hawaiian religious site, Ku'emanu Heiau. Hawaiian royalty, who surfed the waters at the northern end of Kahalu'u Bay, paid their respects at this temple before hitting the waves. Several tidal waves and hurricanes have unsuccessfully attempted to relocate it.

The church is located on the *makai* side of Ali'i Dr, just to the north of the 5-mile marker.

Kahalu'u Beach Park

The Big Island's best easy-access snorkeling spot, **Kahalu'u Bay** is kind of like a giant natural aquarium, and loaded with colorful marine life. If you haven't tried snorkeling, this is a great place to learn. Rainbow parrotfish, silver needlefish, brilliant yellow tangs, Moorish idol and butterfly fish are among the numerous tropical fish often seen here. At high tide, green sea turtles often swim into the bay to feed.

An ancient breakwater called Paokamenehune, which according to legend was built by the *menehune* (little people), sits on the reef and protects the bay. Still, when the surf is high, Kahalu'u can harbor strong rip currents that pull in the northward direction of the rocks near St Peter's Church. Experienced local surfers challenge the waves offshore, but they're too much for beginners. It's easy to drift away without realizing it – check your bearings occasionally to make sure you're not being pulled by the current. Also check out water-condition reports posted on the weathered display board by the picnic pavilion.

Located right along Ali'i Dr, Kahalu'u's main drawbacks are traffic noise and throngs of tourists. The locals joke that 'if you forget sunscreen, take a dip in Kahalu'u Bay and you'll be covered with more than enough!'

The 'salt-and-pepper' beach (composed of lava and coral sand) is rather cramped and cannot match the vast blanket of white sand at South Kohala beaches. But once you're underwater, you won't care. Facilities include showers, restrooms, changing rooms, picnic tables and grills. A lifeguard is on duty.

Keauhou Bay

This bay, which has a launch ramp and space for two dozen small boats, is one of the most protected bays on the west coast. If you come by on weekdays in the late afternoon, you can watch the local outrigger canoe club practicing in the bay.

In a small clearing, just south of the harborside dive shacks, a stone marks the site where Kamehameha III was born in 1814. The young prince was said to have been stillborn and brought back to life by a visiting kahuna (priest).

To get to the bay, turn toward the ocean off Ali'i Dr onto Kamehameha III Rd. There are restrooms and showers.

At the harbor, you'll see snorkeling and diving catamarans such as the **Sea Paradise** (☎ 322-2500, 800-322-5662; www.seaparadise.com) and **Sea Quest** (☎ 329-7238; www.seaquesthawaii .com), which depart here for the Kealakekua Bay area. Also, **Ocean Safaris** (☎ 326-4699; www .oceansafariskayaks.com; end of Kamehameha III Rd) is headquartered here. This outfit specializes in tours that include **snorkeling and cliff jumping** (3½hr tour adult/child $59/29.50; ☼ departures 8:30am Mon-Sat, 9:30am Tue) or early-morning **dolphin sighting** (2hr tour $30; ☼ departures 7am Tue). They've turned even scaredy cats into daredevils!

Original Hawaiian Chocolate Factory

A tiny **chocolate factory** (☎ 322-2626; www.original hawaiianchocolatefactory.com; 78-6772 Makenawai St; ☼ tours by appointment only) on the slopes of Mt Hualalai, Bob and Pam Cooper's mom-and-pop company is unique in its exclusive use of Big Island cocoa beans, and offers free tours. You might find it hard to believe that the sinfully sweet bars of chocolate come from beans that smell like stinky socks. However, the chocolate pods are lovely shades of yellow, gold and fuchsia, and they're harvested by hand every two weeks year-round.

FESTIVALS & EVENTS

The **Kona Chocolate Festival** (typically 4th Sat in Mar; ☎ 937-7596; Outrigger Keauhou Beach Resort; admission advance/day of event $35/40) is a decadent dream come true for chocoholics. Accompanied by champagne, wine and live music, you can sample the creations of chefs, candy and ice-cream makers and chocolatiers in an evening-long gala.

SLEEPING

Before paying the rack rates here, check the websites for huge online discounts.

Outrigger Kanaloa at Kona (☎ 322-9625, 800-688-7444; www.outrigger.com; 78-261 Manukai St; 1-bedroom condos $240-380; P ☒ $10/day ☒) The tropical townhouse-style condominiums at the Outrigger Kanaloa are spacious, sitting on an oceanfront lava ledge. The gated complex, on a side road off Kamehameha III Rd, feels exclusive and safe. Full kitchens include tableware and cookware, and two-bedroom condos include two full baths. There are three pools (two for families, one for adults), two lighted tennis courts and free wi-fi access. The $180 'value rate' here is for the $240 unit, but online prices can drop to $150. Walkup only (no elevator access).

Keauhou Resort Condominiums (☎ 322-9122, 800-367-5286; 78-7039 Kamehameha III Rd; 1-bedroom

---

AUTHOR'S CHOICE

Outrigger Keauhou Beach Resort (☎ 322-3441, 800-462-6262; www.outrigger.com; 78-6740 Ali'i Dr; r $190-250; P per day $5 ☒ ☒) You can't get any closer to Kahalu'u Beach than this pleasantly low-key, 309-room resort, now run by Outrigger. In the open-air lobby area, you'll find two restaurants, a gym and a serene view of tidepools and *honu* (green sea turtles). Tastefully furnished rooms include a refrigerator, coffeemaker, TV and lanai. You'll probably lack an ocean view, however, as the hotel is built perpendicular to the shoreline. Throughout the year an outstanding $120 'value rate' applies to garden-view rooms.

The grounds of this resort also include historical sites along easily walkable paths. At the north end, there are the ruins of Kapuanoni, a fishing heiau, and the reconstructed summer beach house of King Kalakaua next to a spring-fed pond that was once used as a royal bath. Toward the south end there are other heiau sites, including the remains of the Ke'eku Heiau, a probable *luakini* (temple of human sacrifice).

The resort is airy and overlooks a *pahoehoe* (smooth lava) rock shelf containing scads of tide pools. You'll see not only sea urchins and small tropical fish but also *honu*. When the tide is at its very lowest, you can walk out onto a flat lava tongue carved with numerous petroglyphs about 25ft from the shore.

condos $85-125; (P) (X) (≋)) Although these units are three decades old, most are well maintained and come with full kitchens, washers and dryers. Besides, the property is the cheapest in Keauhou. Whack on another $25 for a two-bedroom unit for up to four people.

Keauhou Surf & Racquet Club (☎ 329-9393, 800-622-5348; 78-6800 Ali'i Dr; 2-bedroom condos $125-195; (P) (X) (≋)) A sprawling modern complex, the Keauhou Surf comes with three tennis courts, a grass volleyball court and a pool. Not all units have views, but each is spacious and comes equipped with lanai, full kitchen, washer, dryer, TV and VCR. The atmosphere is quiet and rather staid, and at midday you might find the pool occupied by a seniors' water-aerobics class. Rates do not include a $75 cleaning fee per stay.

Sheraton Keauhou Bay Resort & Spa (☎ 322-3411, 877-488-3535; www.starwood.com/hawaii; 78-128 Ehukai St; r $320-500, ste $800; (P) (X) (≋)) At the time of writing, the former Kona Surf had just reopened as the Sheraton. All spiffed up, with sleek white facades and a large pool with spiral slide, the resort seemed forlornly vacant. Too bad, because the oceanfront location is primo and who wouldn't appreciate brand-new facilities?

EATING

Edward's at Kanaloa (☎ 322-1434; Kanaloa at Kona, 78-261 Manukai St; dinner mains $30; 🕑 8am-3pm & 5-8:30pm) You'll find a truly spectacular sunset view and knowledgeable service.

Kama'aina Terrace (☎ 322-3441, 800-462-6262; www.outrigger.com; Outrigger Keauhou Beach Hotel, 78-6740 Ali'i Dr) This place offers an early-bird $18 three-course dinner (green salad, choice of fish, chicken or beef, dessert and coffee or tea) between 5:30pm and 6:30pm Sunday to Thursday.

Located at the **Keauhou Shopping Center** (☎ 322-3000; 78-6831 Ali'i Dr), **Kenichi Pacific** (☎ 322-6400; mains $20-30; 🕑 lunch Tue-Fri, dinner daily) is a standout, featuring Asian-fusion specialties including the subtly smoky-flavored bamboo salmon ($23) and miso-cured black cod appetizer ($14).

The other restaurants at the shopping center are just average mall-quality:

Drysdale's Two (☎ 322-0070; mains $7-16; 🕑 11am-midnight) Well-known sports bar and eatery with the requisite steaks, burgers and buffalo wings, specializing in sandwiches and burgers.

Royal Thai Café (☎ 322-8424; mains $6-10; 🕑 11am-10pm) Dominated by Asian statuary and a large aquarium, but the food holds its own.

ENTERTAINMENT

Verandah Lounge (☎ 322-3441, Ohana Keauhou Beach Resort; 🕑 3-10:30pm) Sedate venue featuring jazz on Tuesday night and mellow Hawaiian music Wednesday to Saturday. Drink prices are reasonable, considering the primo oceanfront location. You can almost always spot *honu* from the balcony.

Keauhou Cinema (☎ 324-7200; Keauhou Shopping Center, 78-6831 Ali'i Dr) Multiscreen, shows first-run movies.

Keauhou Shopping Center (☎ 322-3000; 78-6831 Ali'i Dr) Every Friday there are free ukulele lessons from 10am to 11am for intermediate players and 11am to noon for beginners. From 6pm to 8pm, there's a free hula show.

GETTING AROUND

Keauhou has a free on-call **shuttle service** (☎ 322-3500) that runs around the resort environs between 9am and 4pm.

Holualoa

pop 6000

Holualoa is a sleepy village perched in the hills, 1400ft above Kailua-Kona. The slopes catch afternoon showers, so it's lusher and cooler than on the coast. It's an enviable location, with a fine view of Kailua Bay's sparkling turquoise waters below. This tiny, upland village might be Kona's best-kept secret, though relentless west Hawai'i development is making inroads. Simple, old homes, half hidden by jungle-like gardens, now stand side by side with sprawling new ones. Worse, Holualoa Rd, the sole thoroughfare, has become an informal bypass road for Kailua-bound traffic along the jammed Queen Ka'ahumanu Hwy. A long-standing artists' community supports craft shops, galleries and a nonprofit art center. Avoid visiting Holualoa on Sunday or Monday, as most galleries will be closed.

ORIENTATION & INFORMATION

This is pretty much a one-road village, with everything lined up along Hwy 180. There's a general store, a Japanese cemetery, an elementary school, a couple of churches and a library. From Kailua-Kona, it's a winding but very scenic 4 miles up Hualalai Rd to

Holualoa, passing poinsettia flowers, coffee bushes and a variety of fruit trees.

SIGHTS
Kona Blue Sky Coffee Company
The Twigg-Smith Estate's Kona Blue Sky Coffee farm covers more than 400 acres on Mt Hualalai's slopes. As other large farms have done, Kona Blue Sky established a small **visitors center** (☎ 322-1700, 877-322-1700; www.konablueskycoffee.com; 76-973A Hualalai Rd; ◷ 9am-3:30pm Mon-Sat) offering free guided walking tours and sampling. Visitors watch a short video before learning more about the meticulous handpicking, sun-drying and roasting of the precious beans. Free samples of coffee and chocolate-covered beans are offered.

Kimura Lauhala Shop
Don't be fooled by the cheap *lauhala* (pandana plant) impostors, whose products are probably made in Southeast Asia of low-grade leaves. For the real deal, visit the Kimura family's **shop** (☎ 324-0053; cnr Hualalai Rd & Hwy 180; ◷ 9am-5pm Mon-Fri, 9am-4pm Sat) for top-quality, handmade *lauhala* crafts (see p37).

Originally the family ran an old plantation store that sold salt and codfish. Then in the 1930s, during the Great Depression, Mrs Kimura started weaving *lauhala* hats and coffee baskets and selling them at the plantations.

Today, three generations of Kimuras still weave *lauhala* here, assisted by the wives of local coffee farmers, who do piecework

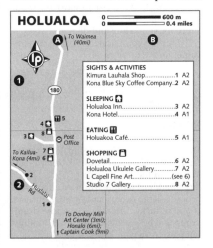

HOLUALOA

0 ————— 600 m
0 ————— 0.4 miles

To Waimea (40mi)

SIGHTS & ACTIVITIES
Kimura Lauhala Shop.................1 A2
Kona Blue Sky Coffee Company.2 A2

SLEEPING
Holualoa Inn.............................3 A2
Kona Hotel................................4 A1

EATING
Holuakoa Café..........................5 A1

SHOPPING
Dovetail....................................6 A2
Holualoa Ukulele Gallery............7 A2
L Capell Fine Art.....................(see 6)
Studio 7 Gallery........................8 A2

To Kailua-Kona (4mi)

Post Office

Hualalai Rd

To Donkey Mill Art Center (3mi); Honalo (6mi); Captain Cook (9mi)

---

at home when it's not coffee season. The most common items are placemats, open baskets and hats of a finer weave. One of the Kimuras' signature pieces is their tote – an elegant, sturdy bag with bamboo handles and a cotton lining. They've had to fend off buyers who want to mass-distribute their creations, for they have no intention of filling bulk orders or even selling online – a refreshing attitude in this corporate age.

Donkey Mill Art Center
Rustic and unpretentious, this **art center** (☎ 322-3362; www.donkeymillartcenter.org; 78-6670 Hwy 180; admission free; ◷ 10am-4pm Tue-Sat) displays impressive collections and offers workshops ($80 to $255) taught by recognized artists in painting, woodblock printing, sculpture, bamboo weaving, raku clay work and papermaking. Check the website for a schedule. Sponsored by the Holualoa Foundation for Arts & Culture, the Donkey Mill is located 3 miles south of Holualoa village.

If you're baffled by the name, the building is an historic coffee mill that was built in 1954 and with a donkey painted on the roof. The 'Donkey Mill' has been a landmark since then.

SLEEPING & EATING
In Holualoa, you have two lodging options. One's luxurious and one's just the opposite, but both represent authentic Hawai'i.

Kona Hotel (☎ 324-1155; Hwy 180; s/d with shared bathroom $25/30) You can't miss the Inaba family's Kona Hotel, a bright pink wooden building in Holualoa village. Built in 1926, it's an old-time, family-run hostelry with a lobby that resembles a living room, cluttered with photos and memorabilia from a bygone era. Rooms are spartan with just a bed and a dresser, but they're clean. A window in the men's rest-room upstairs (perfectly positioned above the urinal) is an underground legend for its panoramic ocean view. With only 11 rooms, the place is often full so book ahead.

Holualoa Inn (☎ 324-1121, 800-392-1812; www .holualoainn.com; 76-5932 Mamalahoa Hwy; r incl breakfast $175-225; 🖳) Perched atop 40 acres of sloping meadows, with grand views of the coast, this is a spectacular inn. The exterior of the 6000-sq-ft contemporary house is all western red cedar and the interior floors are red eucalyptus from Maui. If you're traveling with more than two people, go for the Bali suite, which presents absolutely unbeatable views. Guest amenities include a tiled swimming pool, a Jacuzzi, a billiard table, a rooftop gazebo, a living room with fireplace, a TV lounge, and facilities for preparing light meals.

Holuakoa Café (☎ 322-2233; Hwy 180; lunch mains $6.50-8; 🕒 6:30am-3pm Mon-Fri) At this laid-back, mildly claustrophobic café-and-gift-shop combo, you'll find tasty sandwiches, soup, quiche, salads, espresso and herbal teas. If you ask, the servers will gladly offer their Kona coffee recommendations. This café is the only eatery in town (a restaurant is planned for the lot next door, but it's been standing half-built for ages).

SHOPPING

Thanks to Holualoa's long-standing community of artists, here you'll find galleries displaying unique, sophisticated (although expensive) art that's a cut above the stereotypical 'tropical' motifs. Most galleries are open from around 10am to 4pm, Tuesday to Saturday, or by appointment.

Studio 7 Gallery (☎ 324-1335; Hwy 180) showcases the work of prominent artist and owner Hiroki Morinoue, whose media include watercolor, oil, woodblock and sculpture. Setsuko, his wife, is an accomplished potter herself and also the gallery director. Like a little museum, the gallery is serene, showcasing pieces that blend Hawaiian and Japanese influences, with wooden walkways over lava stones.

In the historic Holualoa post-office building, the **Holualoa Ukulele Gallery** (☎ 324-1688; www.holualoaukulelegallery.com; Hwy 180) sells ukulele crafted by the owner, Sam Rosen (who's also a longtime goldsmith), as well as other island artisans. The average cost of a handmade ukulele is between $450 and $950. The signed portraits of local ukulele legends Jake Shimabukuro and 'Ohta-san' give the gallery a professional seal of approval.

Adjacent to the ukulele gallery, **Dovetail** (☎ 322-4046; Hwy 180) displays the elegant work of local artist and custom furniture designer Gerald Ben, and **L Capell Fine Art** (☎ 937-8893; Hwy 180) features abstract paintings.

SOUTH KONA

Beyond Kailua-Kona, the Kuakini Hwy (Hwy 11) meanders south through a line of upland villages: Honalo, Kainaliu, Captain Cook and Honaunau. At a higher elevation, the foliage is verdant, with towering palms and fruit trees growing wild. Here lies the acclaimed 22-mile 'Kona Coffee Belt,' where you'll see coffee farms and macadamia-nut groves along the highway. The area is cooled by frequent afternoon showers, which you'll find refreshing after the lowland heat.

Keep your eyes peeled as you drive along the highway, as you might miss the sights. The tiny, one-stop towns rush by, and it's easy to miss a turn (backtracking is a pain on a two-lane road!). If there's no traffic, you can drive from Kailua to Kealakekua Bay in just over half an hour, but during rush hour you'll need at least an hour. The South Kona Coast is short on sandy beaches, but there are excellent spots offshore for snorkeling and diving.

To further complicate the highway name game: note that when Hwy 11 meets Hwy 180, its common name switches from Kuakini Hwy to Mamalahoa Hwy. So you'll hear Hwy 11 called the Mamalahoa when driving in South Kona.

HONALO
pop 2000

Don't blink or you'll miss Honalo, at the intersection of Hwys 11 and 180. **Daifukuji Soto Mission**, on the *mauka* side of Hwy 11, is a large Buddhist temple with two altars, gold brocade, large drums and incense burners. If you're lucky, the *taiko* (Japanese drum) group will be practicing. As in all Buddhist temples, leave your shoes at the door.

Teshima Restaurant (☎ 322-9140; 79-7251 Hwy 11; mains $9-12; ☺ 6:30am-1:45pm & 5-9pm) is a homey, family-run place that's been serving delicious Japanese food since the 1940s. A good sampler is the *teishoku* (set meal) of miso soup, sashimi, fried fish, sukiyaki, *tsukemono* (pickled vegetables) and rice. If you're lucky, 'Grandma' Teshima, the almost-100-year-old family matriarch, will stop at your table and refill your rice bowl. No credit cards are accepted. The place is jammed with locals during dinner, so eat either early or late. Extra parking is available in the Daifukuji Soto Mission lot next door.

KAINALIU

Kainaliu is another barely-there town that you can't help liking. Shops along Hwy 11, such as the long-standing **Kimura Store** (☎ 322-3771; ☺ 9am-6pm Mon-Sat, 10:30am-4:30pm Sun) – which carries the breadth of fine island fabrics – mingle with 'new' antique shops and art galleries. **Island Books** (☎ 322-2006; 79-7360 Mamalahoa Hwy) is a well-stocked second-hand bookstore with plenty of titles on travel and Hawaii.

The town's focal point is the **Aloha Theatre** (☎ 322-2323; www.alohatheatre.com), home of the Aloha Community Players. Check the bulletin board for current performances, which range from indie film screenings to live music and dance.

Undoubtedly the best eatery in town, **Aloha Angel Café** (☎ 322-3383; Hwy 11; breakfast & lunch $6-13, dinner $14-22; ☺ 8am-2:30pm daily, 5-9pm Wed-Sun) has a distant ocean view from its skinny terrace outside. Choose among vegetarian dishes and fresh fish tacos, hearty salads and sandwiches, fruit smoothies, fresh-squeezed juices, espresso and heavenly cookies.

Another healthy choice is **Evie's Natural Foods** (☎ 322-0739; Hwy 11; snacks $3-8; ☺ 9am-9pm Mon-Fri, to 5pm Sat & Sun) located on the *makai* side of Hwy 11. Evie's sells organic produce, fruit juices, smoothies, salads and sandwiches.

KEALAKEKUA

pop 1650

Kealakekua means 'Path of the Gods,' to recognize a chain of 40 heiau that once ran from Kealakekua Bay all the way to Kailua-Kona. Today the town is a tropical jungle of

plumeria, banana, lychee and papaya trees growing wild. Lush and balmy, with stunning views of the ocean, this is the Hawai'i of people's fantasies. It's still small and very laid-back and not built up like the South Kohala coast, and you cannot find a better snorkeling and kayaking spot anywhere on the island.

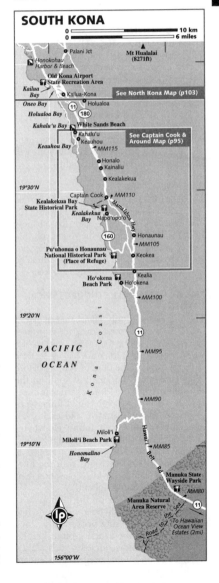

SOUTH KONA

KONA

Orientation & Information

Although tiny, Kealakekua is the commercial center of Kona's upland towns with a **post office** (☎ 322-1656; cnr Hwy 11 & Haleki'i Rd; ☾ 9am-4:30pm Mon-Fri, 9:30am-12:30pm Sat) and **First Hawaiian Bank** (☎ 322-3484; 81-6626 Hwy 11). The main hospital serving the entire Kona Coast, **Kona Community Hospital** (☎ 322-9311; www.kch.hhsc.org; 79-1019 Haukapila St), is here.

Sights & Activities

KONA HISTORICAL SOCIETY MUSEUM

While modest in size, the Kona Historical Society's one-room **museum** (☎ 323-3222; 81-6551 Hwy 11; suggested donation $2; ☾ 9am-3pm Mon-Fri) contains interesting displays of period photos and other memorabilia, plus a good selection of Hawaii-themed books, from history to children's literature. The stone-and-mortar building (1875) was once a general merchandise store and post office. Helpful staff will answer questions on nearby sights.

GREENWELL FARMS

This **farm** (☎ 323-2275; 81-6581 Hwy 11; ☾ 8am-5pm Mon-Fri, 8am-4pm Sat), between the 111- and 112-mile markers, has been open for business since the 1850s. Aided by the young volcanic soil of Kona, handpicked coffee trees can yield a million pounds of beans annually. Coffee samples and short tours are free.

AMY BH GREENWELL ETHNOBOTANICAL GARDEN

The Big Island's only **ethnobotanical garden** (☎ 323-3318; www.bishopmuseum.org/exhibits/greenwell/greenwell.html; suggested donation $4; ☾ 8:30am-5pm Mon-Fri, free guided tours 1pm Wed & Fri, 10am 2nd Sat of the month) displays the flora of Hawai'i before Western contact. Located just south of the 110-mile marker, the 15-acre garden features landscaped walking paths amid three types of plants: endemic (native and exclusive), indigenous (native but found elsewhere) and Polynesian (introduced by the islands' original settlers). The garden is arranged as an *ahupua'a* (land division) with the lowland species planted at a lower elevation than those naturally found upland.

Though sponsored by the Bishop Museum, this is a small operation with few staff. This is a blessing because your tour guide might be the actual groundskeeper, who gives a minidiscourse on each plant's habitat and traditional usage. The islanders made the most of their limited resources, and plants provided raw material not only for food but for medicine, canoes and dye. Beware of voracious mosquitoes.

KONA COFFEE LIVING HISTORY FARM

Another Kona Historical Society project, the former D Uchida **farm** (☎ 323-2006; adult/child $15/7.50; ☾ tours on the hr 9am-2pm Mon-Fri) gives a close look at rural immigrant life on the Big Island from the early 20th century to 1945. The tour price is rather steep, but the docents are knowledgeable locals who walk you through the historic 1913 homestead of Daisaku and Shima Uchida, with its processing mill, drying roofs and traditional Japanese bathhouse. Free coffee samples (and mosquito repellent) are provided.

BIG ISLAND YOGA CENTER

The **Big Island Yoga Center** (☎ 329-9642; www.bigislandyoga.com; 81-6623 Hwy 11, across First Hawaiian Bank; drop-in class $12-14) was established in 1989. This airy studio offers Iyengar-method classes, which focus on alignment and use props (all available to borrow free of charge). During work hours, you must park your car across the street, which can be jammed during rush hours.

Sleeping

Areca Palms Estate B&B (☎ 323-2276, 800-545-4390; www.konabedandbreakfast.com; Hwy 11; r incl breakfast $90-125) The owners, who hail from Oregon, prove you need not be local-born to epitomize the aloha spirit. Outgoing and clued into their adopted community, the hosts go out of their way to help guests enjoy Hawai'i. Their immaculate house resembles an airy cedar lodge, with lots of natural wood, country-style furnishings and exposed-beam ceilings. All rooms have private bathroom, cable TV and big closets stocked with luxurious robes. Guests have free use of the common living room, with a guest phone and an outdoor Jacuzzi amid the sprawling lawn and – you guessed it – giant areca palms. The full breakfasts, which might include homemade pancakes, eggs and fresh papaya and pineapple, get rave reviews. It's between the 110- and 111-mile markers.

Rainbow Plantation B&B (☎ 323-2393, 800-494-2829; www.rainbowplantation.com; 81-6327B Hwy 11; r $75-95) City slickers, here's your chance to experience life on a tropical farm. Macadamia and coffee trees thrive, as do a couple of pigs, fowl and peacocks, mini Shetland ponies and *koi* (Japanese carp) in an outdoor pond. Rooms aren't fancy, and the worn furnishings could be cleaner (mildew seen on shower curtain), but all have refrigerator, TV and private entrance. The back-to-nature setting is ideal for kids, and the hosts (who speak German and French) are

welcoming. You're guaranteed to remember this B&B (and the scrumptious banana pancakes!). Rates include breakfast, except on Sundays.

Banana Patch (☎ 322-8888, 800-988-2246; www.bananabanana.com; Mamao St; r $55; 1-/2-bedroom cottage $145/165) Here you'll find two comfortable vacation cottages secluded amid thick, unruly foliage (watch out for spiderwebs) for guests who consider clothing optional. Tastefully

---

CHECK THE LABEL

On the slopes of Hualalai and Mauna Loa sit roughly 650 coffee farms on a strip of land just 2 miles wide and 22 miles long. Most farms are modest 3-acre, independent farms. But from this unassuming region comes the world-renowned Kona coffee.

Missionaries introduced the coffee tree to Hawaii in 1828. By the turn of the century, coffee was an important cash crop throughout the state. However, the instability of coffee prices eventually drove island farmers out of business – except on the Big Island, where Kona coffee was extraordinarily enough to sell at a profit during gluts in world markets.

Why is Kona coffee so special? First, *Coffea arabica* flourishes with a climate of sunny mornings and rainy afternoons, which is typical in Kona at elevations between 500ft and 2800ft. Second, coffee thrives in rich volcanic soil and mild, frost-free temperatures. Third, only a select variety of *arabica* called 'Kona Typica' (and never the inferior *robusta*) qualifies to produce the superior beans. Finally, Kona farmers use exceptionally meticulous methods to cultivate their crops, with all planting and picking done by hand.

The fruit of the coffee plant starts as green berries, turning yellow, orange, and then deep red (called 'cherry') when ripe. The cherries don't ripen all at once, so they must be picked several times from August to late January. It takes 8lb of cherry (about 4000 beans) to produce 1lb of roasted coffee.

Unassuming visitors are sometimes fooled by cheap coffee labeled 'Kona Coffee' in giant lettering, followed by the miniscule word 'blend' – which means it is probably only 10% Kona coffee. Quality depends not only on the label, but factors such as roasting, grade of the beans, and whether the beans are 'estate' (all from one farm) or a blend of Kona beans from different farms. You might also care about whether beans are organically grown or not. Genuine Kona coffee can be found in several ways:

■ Look for the **Kona Coffee Council** (www.kona-coffee-council.com) seal of approval on the bag.

■ Expect to pay around $20 per pound.

■ Check for a 'purge valve' on the bag (another sign it's the real deal), which allows air and heat to escape from freshly roasted beans (the bag should be well inflated).

There are over 100 private labels for 100% Kona coffee. From Holualoa to Honaunau, tiny 'backyard' growers abound, and every mom-and-pop outfit has a side business selling its family-farm beans. The pioneering coffee farmers of the early 20th century were mostly entrepreneurial Japanese families, who wanted to escape the yoke of sugarcane-plantation life by leasing the coffee lands then being abandoned. They kept the industry alive, but today most of those family farms are gone – the next generations of Japanese Americans had no desire to continue as farmers.

In recent years there has been an explosion of 'gentleman farms' run by mainland transplants. Coffee estates, it seems, have developed a cachet similar to that of Napa Valley vineyards. This might be good news for the Big Island: while Kona coffee production had dropped to a low point by 1980, the gourmet-coffee craze during the past two decades has spurred sales of the highly aromatic Kona beans. Today Kona coffee is the most commercially successful coffee grown in the USA. Coffee fans, don't miss the annual **Kona Coffee Cultural Festival** (p77).

decorated, both cottages have a full kitchen and a Jacuzzi. Grounds can get muddy during the rainy season.

Pineapple Park (☎ 323-2224, 877-865-2266; www .pineapple-park.com; Hwy 11; dm $20, r without/with bathroom $45/85) Pineapple Park is a popular hostel (with another branch in Puna, p190) run by Annie Park and Doc Holliday. Not surprisingly, the hostel primarily draws hang-loose European or younger travelers. The hostel has a guest kitchen, laundry facilities and a large common lounge. You can't miss the hostel, located between the 110- and 111-mile markers, because dozens of rentable kayaks (single/double $20/40) front the building.

Eating

Ke'ei Café (☎ 322-9992; mains $11-19; ⊙ dinner Tue-Sat) One of the best restaurants around, the Ke'ei Café is a touch more elegant than most others in South Kona. You can't go wrong with the fresh catch prepared in your choice of three creative ways, including sautéed on miso salad with green papaya slivers. It's located just south of the 113-mile marker.

Chris' Bakery (☎ 323-2444; Hwy 11; snacks $1-5; ⊙ 6am-1pm) Sweetly irresistible offerings great for on-the-road snacking.

Philly Sophical Deli (☎ 322-6607; Hwy 11; mains $5-8; ⊙ 7am-6pm Mon-Fri, 7:30am-4pm Sat) Inside a warehouse, this East Coast–style deli caters to carnivores, with liverwurst and pastrami and Philly cheese steak, though veg sandwiches are also available. Generous eggs, pancakes and other breakfasts, too.

CAPTAIN COOK

pop 3200

This little town, named after the ill-fated British navigator, commands grand views verdant greenery stretching for miles toward the ocean and the brilliant bay beyond. The town itself is small and unpretentious, with modest government offices and a shopping center, a hotel, a gas station and a handful of restaurants. As you continue south, you'll pass numerous roadside coffee-tasting rooms that sell locally grown beans and offer free freshly brewed samples.

Sights

KEALAKEKUA BAY STATE HISTORICAL PARK

Kealakekua Bay is one of the Big Island's (and the state's) premier snorkeling spots.

In the pristine waters, a spectacular diversity of marine life thrives. The bay is both a state park and a marine-life conservation district. Among the protected species are spinner dolphins that swim into the bay. Note that it's illegal to remove or damage coral, sand and rock, and fishing is restricted.

To reach the park, take Napo'opo'o Rd, off Hwy 11, for 4.5 miles. At the end of the road you'll see **Napo'opo'o Beach**. While the beach is a poor swimming and snorkeling spot, the **Napo'opo'o Wharf** is the best place to launch a kayak to reach outstanding snorkeling waters. You can't miss it, as kayakers arrive en masse every morning.

From Napo'opo'o Beach, the **Captain Cook Monument** is visible at the far north end of the bay. The area near the monument is **Ka'awaloa Cove**, a decent diving and excellent snorkeling spot that's accessible only by sea or by a dirt trail beginning inland near the town of Captain Cook.

Captain Cook died in Ka'awaloa Cove, at the hands of the Hawaiians during a 1779 skirmish. In 1878 Cook's countrymen erected a 27ft monument in Cook's honor near the site of his death. The ruins of the ancient village of Ka'awaloa sit on the land behind the monument.

If you turn right at the end of Napo'opo'o Rd, you'll see **Hiki'au Heiau**, a large platform temple above the beach. Nearby facilities include bathrooms and showers. It's forbidden to launch kayaks around the heiau.

South of Kealakekua Bay, there are two mediocre beaches: **Manini Beach** is a small, remote beach that lacks a safe entry point. The shoreline is rocky and exposed to regular northwest swells, so swimming and snorkeling conditions are poor. When the surf's up, you can catch waves off the point just south of Manini Beach. The best point of entry is to your right, just after entering the beach. There are no facilities except a portable toilet.

Further south is **Ke'ei Bay**, which isn't really worth visiting (especially with Ka'awaloa Cove just north). To get there, you must take a rough dirt road, just past Manini Beach (if you reach Ke'ei Transfer Station, you've gone too far). At the bay, you'll find a beach and a small canoe launch, a few shacks, but no facilities – and residents who prefer not to be disturbed. Surfers and paddlers test the waters, but swimming is poor.

KONA

Finally, if you keep following Napo'opo'o Rd to the end and turn left, you can go 4 miles south through scrub brush to Pu'uhonua o Honaunau (p100). But beware: the road is barely one lane and roadside grasses conceal trenches.

Activities
SNORKELING
The best place to snorkel is Ka'awaloa Cove, along the 200yd adjacent to the Captain Cook Monument. The water is protected from ocean swells and thus exceptionally clear. You can see coral gardens, a stunning underwater cliff dropping off 70ft to 100ft, abundant tropical fish and perhaps sea turtles.

A big draw is the chance (about 30% on any given day) to see spinner dolphins. Some believe that human contact with dolphins harms their sleep habits and health; thus do keep a distance and be passive (absolutely do not chase them). The more humans push the limits, the more local, state and federal officials will crack down on access to see such species in the wild. So it's wise to show some restraint.

If you reach the Ka'awaloa Cove by land, you can slip into the ocean from the rocks on the left side of the cement dock fronting the monument. The water starts out at 5ft deep and gradually deepens to 30ft.

If you don't want to paddle or hike to the cove, you can catch a snorkeling cruise.

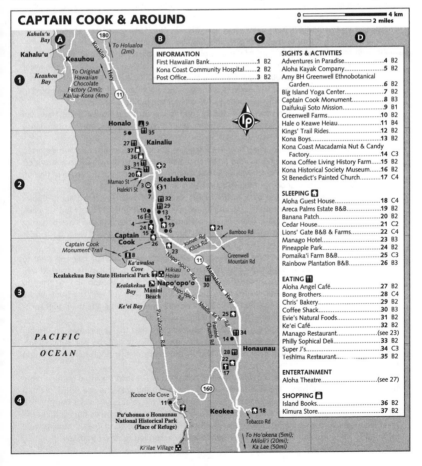

CAPTAIN COOK & AROUND

0 — 4 km
0 — 2 miles

INFORMATION	
First Hawaiian Bank	1 B2
Kona Coast Community Hospital	2 B2
Post Office	3 B2

SIGHTS & ACTIVITIES	
Adventures in Paradise	4 B2
Aloha Kayak Company	5 B2
Amy BH Greenwell Ethnobotanical Garden	6 B2
Big Island Yoga Center	7 B2
Captain Cook Monument	8 B3
Daifukuji Soto Mission	9 B1
Greenwell Farms	10 B2
Hale o Keawe Heiau	11 B4
Kings' Trail Rides	12 B2
Kona Boys	13 B2
Kona Coast Macadamia Nut & Candy Factory	14 C3
Kona Coffee Living History Farm	15 B2
Kona Historical Society Museum	16 B2
St Benedict's Painted Church	17 C4

SLEEPING	
Aloha Guest House	18 C4
Areca Palms Estate B&B	19 B2
Banana Patch	20 B2
Cedar House	21 C2
Lions' Gate B&B & Farms	22 C4
Manago Hotel	23 B3
Pineapple Park	24 B2
Pomaika'i Farm B&B	25 C3
Rainbow Plantation B&B	26 B3

EATING	
Aloha Angel Café	27 B2
Bong Brothers	28 C4
Chris' Bakery	29 B2
Coffee Shack	30 B3
Evie's Natural Foods	31 B2
Ke'ei Café	32 B2
Manago Restaurant	(see 23)
Philly Sophical Deli	33 B2
Super J's	34 C3
Teshima Restaurant	35 B2

ENTERTAINMENT	
Aloha Theatre	(see 27)

SHOPPING	
Island Books	36 B2
Kimura Store	37 B2

KONA

The most popular destination is Kealakekua Bay, but cruises might head to less trafficked surrounding coves. Most cruises arrive in the morning when waters are calmer, leave around noon, and generally stay offshore. They depart from various harbors along the Kona coast, so remember to find out exactly where to meet. Prices for the following tours include snorkeling gear, beverages and food.

Catamarans

Sea Paradise (☎ 322-2500, 800-322-5662; www.seaparadise.com; 78-7128 Kaleiopapa Rd, Keauhou Harbor; adult/child 4hr tour $95/79; ☼ departures 9:30am, office open 7:30am-4:30pm), with its friendly, experienced crew, sails you to secluded coves near Kealakekua Bay in a sleek sailing catamaran. It's also a scuba dive outfit offering manta-ray night dives and instruction for beginners. Private charters can be arranged.

THE FINAL DAYS OF CAPTAIN COOK *Nanette Napoleon*

After first landing in what he called the 'Sandwich Islands' (see p23) Captain Cook's expedition continued its journey into the North Pacific. Failing to find the fabled passage through the Artic, Cook sailed back to Hawaii, landing at Kealakekua Bay on January 17, 1779, one year after his first sighting of O'ahu, and once again at the time of the annual *makahiki* festival.

Cook's initial arrival at Waimea Bay on Kaua'i had coincided with the *makahiki*, a period when all heavy work and warfare was suspended in order to pay homage to Lono (the god of agriculture and peace) and to participate in games and festivities. To the Hawaiians, Cook appeared to be the *kinolau* (earthly form) of the great god, and was thus revered.

Since word of Captain Cook's arrival the previous year had spread to all the other islands, his welcome at Kealakekua Bay was even more spectacular, with more than 1000 canoes in the water surrounding his ships and 9000 people on shore to greet him. Cook later wrote in his journal, 'I had nowhere in the course of my voyages seen so numerous a body of people assembled in one place,' quite unaware that he was seen as the second coming of Lono.

Once landed, Cook and his men were greeted by Chief Kalaniopu'u and feted in grand Hawaiian style, with a big luau accompanied by hula dancing, boxing demonstrations and an abundance of the local brew, 'awa.

After two weeks of R and R, including sexual indulgences, Cook restocked his ships and departed the Kealakekua on February 4 and headed north once again. En route they ran into a storm off the northwest coast of the Big Island, where the *Resolution* broke a foremast. Uncertain of finding a safe harbor in the area, Cook returned to Kealakekua Bay on February 11.

Although Cook was welcomed back to the island, Kalaniopu'u was concerned about Cook's reappearance because it meant that he would again need to provide the crew's food supplies. This time mutual respect and admiration turned to animosity as parties on both sides began to go beyond the bounds of diplomacy and goodwill. Thievery and insult issued from both sides and tensions escalated.

After a cutter (rowboat) was stolen, Cook ordered a blockade of Kealakekua Bay and went to shore to take Kalaniopu'u as a hostage until the boat was returned, a tactic that had worked well for him in other island groups. As a ruse, Cook told Kalaniopu'u that he wanted him to return to the *Resolution* with him to talk about the recent disputes. This plan sat well with the chief, whose culture dictated that disputes be settled by *ho'oponopono*, where everyone airs their grievances and does not leave until a mutual resolution to the dispute is found.

En route to the shore with Cook, Kalaniopu'u received word that the Englishmen on the big ships had shot and killed a lower chief, who had been attempting to exit the bay in his canoe. A brutal battle ensued along the shore, resulting in the death of five Englishmen, including Captain Cook, and 17 Hawaiians.

The death of Cook stunned both sides into ending the battle. The sailors wanted nothing more than to leave, but the Hawaiians had taken Cook's body from the area and the British wanted to retrieve it. Over the next two weeks both sides negotiated the release of Cook's body, which had been dismembered in the fashion accorded high chiefs. Several skirmishes during that time resulted in the death of about 50 indigenous Hawaiians. Some, but not all, of Cook's remains were returned to his ship, after which they were buried at sea according to naval tradition.

KONA

Fair Wind (☎ 322-2788, 800-677-9461; www.fair -wind.com; 4½hr morning tour adult/child $99/59, 3½hr afternoon tour $65/39; ⏲ departures 9am & 2pm) sails into Kealakekua Bay aboard a comfortable 100-passenger, 60ft catamaran fully equipped with showers, restroom, bar and fully covered cabin. The trips leave from Keauhou Bay, which allows for more snorkeling time than other boats.

Rafts

Captain Zodiac (☎ 329-3199, 800-422-7824; www.cap tainzodiac.com; 4hr tour adult/child $80/65; ⏲ departures 8am & 12:45pm) has tours aboard bouncy, zippy 16-passenger, 24ft Zodiac rubber rafts departing from Honokohau Harbor, with pickups possible at Kailua and Keauhou piers. Tours include about an hour of snorkeling time at Kealakekua Bay followed by visits to sea caves and lava tubes.

Sea Quest (☎ 329-7238; www.seaquesthawaii.com; 4hr morning tour $80, 3hr afternoon tour $60; ⏲ departures 8am & 1pm) offers a real personal touch and takes a maximum of six people out in rigid-hull inflatable boats, departing from Keauhou Bay. Check website for Internet discounts.

DIVING

Within the bay, the Napo'opo'o area is shallow with little coral, but diving conditions improve if you swim further out. Between the Napo'opo'o landing and the southern

---

AUTHOR'S CHOICE

Adventures in Paradise (☎ 323-3005, 866-824-2337; www.bigislandkayak.com; 81-6367 Hwy 11, at Keopuka Rd; 1-person kayak $25, 2-person kayak $45-50; ⏲ 7:30am-5pm) Friendly, professional and remarkably thorough, the owner goes the extra mile in sharing his first-hand familiarity with Big Island waters. Novice kayakers get detailed instructions on technique and safety, which practically guarantees a successful voyage. He's also mindful of the backlash against snorkelers seeking to swim with dolphins and thus advises visitors to respect wildlife and not to disturb their habitat. He also offers kayaking-and-snorkeling cruises, manta ray night dives and hiking expeditions to Kealakekua or Kiholo bays, Mauna Kea or Kilauea Volcano.

---

tip of Manini Beach, marine life abounds amid coral, caves, crevices and ledges in waters up to about 30ft deep. But the bay's best diving spot is Ka'awaloa Cove, where depths range from about 5ft to 120ft – the diversity of coral and fish is exceptional.

The aptly named Long Lava Tube, just north of Kealakekua Bay, is an intermediate dive site. Lava 'skylights' allow light to penetrate through the ceiling, yet nocturnal species may still be active during the day, and you may see crustaceans, morays and even Spanish dancers. Outside are countless lava formations sheltering critters such as conger eels, triton's trumpet shells and schooling squirrelfish. Bring your dive light!

See p75 for a list of recommended dive shops in Kailua-Kona. Also check the snorkeling companies above, as many also take divers out.

KAYAKING

Most snorkelers travel to Ka'awaloa Cove by a 30- to 45-minute kayak jaunt from Napo'opo'o Wharf. At the landing, a bunch of locals have established a 'business' of helping tourists launch their kayaks. They expect a $5 tip. Depending on the tides and your paddling strength, they might be quite helpful. But remember that if a different person helps you when your return, you'll be expected to pay again. Also, while most such locals are decent folks trying to snag a few bucks, be on guard for vagrants, ice addicts, alcoholics and all-around no-good *buggahs*!

No kayak hire outfits are available at the beach, but you'll see countless kayaks for rent along Hwy 11, especially between the 110- and 111-mile markers. Guided kayaking tours are prohibited in Kealakekua Bay, but you can join a tour to other, similarly spectacular coves along the coast. Also see p87 for Ocean Safaris kayaking tours departing from Keauhou Bay.

Aloha Kayak Company (☎ 322-2868; www.aloha kayak.com; Hwy 11; 1 /2-person kayak $25/40; ⏲ 8am-5pm) Opposite Teshima Restaurant in Honalo, this popular Hawaiian-owned outfit also conducts adventure tours to go cliff-jumping and paddling in sea caves. It tries to include a mini Hawaiian-history lesson in its tours.

Kona Boys (☎ 323-1234; www.konaboys.com; 79-7491 Hwy 11; 1-/2-person kayak $27/47; ⏲ 7:30am-5pm) A decent outfit half a mile south of Kealakekua town, run by laid-back guys who give surfing and diving lessons.

HIKING

If you're up for a long, sweaty hike, the Captain Cook Monument Trail is a steep trek (with no plateaus) down to the north end of Kealakekua Bay. The trail is poorly maintained, and you're likely to find it overrun with tall grasses and loose gravel. Only diehard hikers would prefer hiking over kayaking to the monument area.

To get to the trailhead, turn *makai* off Hwy 11, onto Napo'opo'o Rd, and drive past two telephone poles. On the third pole, you'll see an orange arrow pointing toward a dirt road toward the sea. Start walking down the dirt road (not the chained asphalt road) and after 200yd it will fork – stay to the left, which is essentially a continuation of the road you've been walking on. The route is fairly simple, and in most places runs between two rock fences on an old jeep road. When in doubt, stay to the left.

Eventually the coast becomes visible and the trail veers to the left along a broad ledge, goes down the hill and then swings left to the beach. An obelisk monument a few minutes' walk to the left marks the spot where Captain Cook was killed at the water's edge.

Queen's Bath, a little lava pool with brackish spring-fed water, lies at the edge of the cove, a few minutes' walk from the monument toward the cliffs. The water is cool and refreshing, and this age-old equivalent of a beach shower is a great way to wash off the salt before hiking back – although the mosquitoes can get a bit testy here.

A few minutes beyond Queen's Bath, the path ends at Pali Kapu o Keoua, the 'sacred cliffs of Keoua,' a chief and rival of Kamehameha. Numerous caves in the cliffs were the burial places of Hawaiian royalty, and it's speculated that some of Captain Cook's bones were placed here as well. A few lower caves are accessible, but they contain nothing more than beer cans. Those higher up are hard to access and probably still contain bones. These caves are sacred sites and should be left undisturbed.

Going down is a relatively easy hour-long hike, while the trek back can take anywhere from 1¼ hours for strong hikers and up to three hours for the average person. Go early in the morning, as it's hot and largely unshaded. Don't miss the trail's right-hand turn back up onto the lava ledge, as another 4WD road continues straight from the intersection north along the coast – for miles. Note there are no facilities at the bottom of the trail. Bring snorkeling gear and lots of water.

Adventures in Paradise (p97) offers guided hikes on this trail.

HORSEBACK RIDING

Kings' Trail Rides (☎ 323-2388; www.konacowboy.com; 81-6420 Hwy 11; weekday/weekend rides $135/150) takes horseback riders down the Captain Cook Trail to Kealakekua Bay for lunch and snorkeling. Prior riding experience is preferable for this steep, rocky trail. Look for the 'trail rides' sign, *mauka* of Hwy 11 near the 111-mile marker.

Sleeping

Manago Hotel (☎ 323-2642; Hwy 11; s $46-51, d $49-54, tatami r $68, s/d with shared bathroom $27/30) Now run by the family's third generation, the Manago Hotel is ideal for no-frills lodging: spartan but clean rooms (no TV) in an unpretentious wooden building. The hotel started in 1917 as a restaurant, serving bowls of *udon* (thick Japanese noodles) to salesmen on the then-lengthy journey between Hilo and Kona. The *tatami* (Japanese woven mat) rooms include a *furo* (Japanese bathtub) and traditional woven floor mats. On the grounds, the koi pond and collection of potted cacti, succulents and ornamentals resemble a well-tended backyard garden. It's between the 109- and 110-mile markers.

Cedar House (☎ 328-8829, 866-328-8829; www.cedarhouse-hawaii.com; Bamboo Rd; r $85-95, 2-bedroom ste $110, r with shared bathroom $70-75) If you're into coffee, you'll appreciate the vista of coffee trees practically right outside your window. The gracious hosts are actual coffee growers (guests can sample their farm's brew), with intriguing first-hand information about Kona's prized commodity. The aptly named cedar-and-redwood house is handsome and airy, with lots of windows and an ocean-view deck. To reach Cedar House, you must drive 1 mile on a winding road (but what else is new in upland Kona?). It's off Hwy 11 between the 109- and 110-mile markers.

Pomaika'i Farm B&B (☎ 328-2112, 800-325-6427; www.luckyfarm.com; Hwy 11; r $60-75) Also known as Lucky Farm (*pomaika'i* means lucky), this longtime B&B is surrounded by dense foliage that brings the outdoors...in. You'll find a degree of homey, 'lived-in' disarray in the common kitchen area, with a refrigerator, a microwave and a barbecue grill. The two duplex units behind the house are the best deal, but for a more rustic experience, try the converted coffee barn with simple outdoor shower. Watch out for the extremely steep driveway. It's between the 106- and 107-mile markers.

Eating

Manago Restaurant (☎ 323-2642; Manago Hotel, Hwy 11; mains $7.50-13.50; ⏰ breakfast, lunch & dinner Tue-Sun) Just like the hotel, Manago Restaurant is nothing fancy; rather it's the island's Japanese version of a meat-and-potatoes eatery. You won't be disappointed by its famous pork chops ($9) or fried whole *opelu* (scad mackerel; $8.75). Mains come with self-serve sides, including pickled *ogo* (seaweed), potato salad, white rice, and quite forgettable caféteria-style peas and carrots.

Coffee Shack (☎ 328-9555; 83-5799 Hwy 11; meals $6.25-7.25; ⏰ 7am-sunset) A local favorite for its generous Caesar, Greek and Cobb salads, as well as take-out sandwiches from smoked Alaskan salmon to hot pastrami and Swiss. Don't miss it. The Shack is located between the 108- and 109-mile markers.

Super J's (Hwy 11; mains $6; ⏰ 10am-6pm Mon-Sat) If you're craving Hawaiian take-out, Super J's, south of the 107-mile marker, is your best bet for *kalua* pig (pig cooked traditionally in an underground oven) with cabbage.

HONAUNAU

pop 2400

The main attraction around Honaunau is Pu'uhonua o Honaunau National Historical Park, commonly called the 'Place of Refuge.' Many residents in the Honaunau and Napo'opo'o area are small coffee and macadamia-nut growers.

Sights

ST BENEDICT'S PAINTED CHURCH

John Berchmans Velghe, a Catholic priest who came to Hawai'i from Belgium in 1899, is responsible for the unusual painted interior of this **church** (☎ 328-2227; Painted Church Rd; admission free; ⏰ mass at 4pm Sat, 7:15am Sun). When Father John arrived, the church was on the coast near the Place of Refuge. One of his first decisions was to move the church 2 miles up the slopes to its present location. It's not clear whether he did this as protection from tsunami, or just as an attempt to rise above – both literally and symbolically – the Place of Refuge and the old gods of 'pagan Hawai'i.'

Father John then painted the walls with a series of Biblical scenes as an aid in teaching the Bible to natives who couldn't read. He designed the wall behind the altar to resemble the Gothic cathedral in Burgos, Spain. In true Hawaiian style, painted palm leaves look like an extension of the slender columns that support the roof of the church.

KONA COAST MACADAMIA NUT & CANDY FACTORY

Most coffee and macadamia-nut 'visitors centers' are covers for gift stores. The Kamigaki family's Kona Coast **factory** (☎ 328-8141; www.konaoftheworld.com; Middle Ke'ei Rd; admission free; ⏰ 8am-4:30pm Mon-Fri, to 4pm Sat, 11am-3pm Sun) is no exception. The main attraction is a modest historical display with a husking machine and nutcracker. You can try it out, one macadamia nut at a time. The showroom overlooks the real operation out back, where nuts by the bagful are husked and sorted. That said, the mac nuts here are delicious and, at under $8 a pound, a real bargain!

Sleeping & Eating

Lions' Gate B&B & Farms (☎ 328-2335, 800-955-2332; www.konabnb.com; Hwy 11; incl breakfast r $110, ste $175-180) Located on a family-run, 10-acre working macadamia-nut and coffee farm, Lions' Gate is a secluded getaway. The two rooms have a private entrance and lanai, TV, DVD and a refrigerator; an adjoining bedroom can be added to form suites. Guests also have access to wi-fi or Ethernet access, microwave, snorkeling gear, barbecue grill, Jacuzzi and a gazebo. There are excellent ocean views from every room, and for breakfast you'll sample the hosts' own coffee and nuts. It's at the 105-mile marker.

Aloha Guest House (☎ 328-8955, 800-897-3188; www.alohaguesthouse.com; 84-4780 Hwy 11; r $110-190, ste $250; 💻) The only word for the commanding views of the coast from this upscale B&B: unforgettable. Each of the five units is classily appointed (a step above the typical B&B) and include custom-designed glass shower, refrigerator and access to an outdoor Jacuzzi and microwave. Free use of computer, printer, photocopier and fax.

Youthful, personable hosts speak German and serve full breakfasts. The access road is unpaved, however, so it takes 10 minutes to drive up from the highway. Rates include breakfast.

Bong Brothers (☎ 328-9289; www.bongbrothers.com; Hwy 11; snacks less than $5; ☒ 9am-6pm Mon-Fri, 10am-6pm Sun) Restaurants are scarce in Honaunau proper, and your best bet is take-out from this place, located in an historic 1929 building. Bong Brothers is the name of both a small market and a coffee mill next door. The market displays good, farmers' market produce outside, where you can find deals on local favorites like fresh lychee. Inside, you can buy organic produce, smoothies and deli dishes; a vegetarian chef cooks up homemade soups and healthy specials (around $5) for lunch.

PU'UHONUA O HONAUNAU NATIONAL HISTORICAL PARK

In ancient Hawaii, the *kapu* system regulated all daily life. A common person could not look at the *Ali'i* (chief) or walk in his footsteps. Women could not prepare food for men or eat with them. One could not fish, hunt or gather timber except during certain seasons.

If one broke the *kapu,* the penalty was always death. After all, they believed, the violation had angered the gods, who might retaliate with volcanic eruptions, tidal waves, famine or earthquakes. Thus, to appease the gods, they hunted down and killed the violator.

However, there was one way to escape. Commoners who broke a *kapu* could get a second chance, if they reached the sacred ground of a *pu'uhonua* (place of refuge). Similarly, a *pu'uhonua* also gave sanctuary to defeated warriors and wartime 'noncombatants' (men who were too old, young, or unable to fight).

To reach the *pu'uhonua* was more challenging than it might seem. Since royals and their warriors lived on the grounds immediately surrounding the refuge, *kapu* breakers had to swim through open ocean, braving currents and sharks, to reach safety. Once inside the sanctuary, priests performed ceremonies of absolution that apparently placated the gods. *Kapu* breakers could then return home for a brand new beginning.

Information

Nowadays the *pu'uhonua* is an impressive **national park** (☎ 328-2288; www.nps.gov/puho; 1-week pass adult/family $3/5; ☒ 6am-8pm Mon-Thu, to 11pm Fri-Sun) fronting Honaunau Bay. The park's tongue twister of a name simply means 'place of refuge at Honaunau.' The rangers here seem especially numerous and helpful; get a brochure from the entrance station.

Early morning or late afternoon is the optimum time to visit the park to avoid the midday heat. Or visit the park on a full-moon night for an especially powerful (if slightly eerie) atmosphere. Twenty-minute orientation talks are given at 10am, 10:30am, 11am, 2:30pm, 3pm and 3:30pm. Every summer, on the weekend closest to July 1, a **cultural festival** gives visitors a chance to taste traditional food and to see hula, coconut and lauhala weaving, a *hukilau* (net fishing) and a 'royal court.'

Sights

The half-mile **walking tour** is easy to navigate using the brochure map. While most of the sandy trail is accessible by wheelchair, the sights near the water traverse rough lava rock and require walking.

Pu'uhonua o Honaunau comprises two sections: the royal grounds, where Kona *ali'i* lived, and the place of refuge, separated by a massive stone wall. **Hale o Keawe Heiau**, the temple on the point of the cove, was built around 1650. Buried there are the bones of 23 chiefs. It was believed that the *mana* (spiritual power) of the chiefs remained in their bones and bestowed sanctity on those who entered the grounds.

The reconstructed heiau appears authentic, with a carved wooden *ki'i* (statue), the embodiment of the gods, standing almost 15ft high beside it. Leading up to the heiau is the **Great Wall** separating the *pu'uhonua* to the west, and the royal grounds to the east. Built around 1550, this stone wall is more than 1000ft long and 10ft high. You'll also pass two older heiau, a petroglyph, legendary stones, a fishpond, lava tree molds, a hand-carved koa canoe and a few thatched huts and shelters.

At the southern end of the park, **tide pools** in *pahoehoe* (smooth-flowing) lava rock contain tiny black *pipipi* (tiny black mollusks). Near the picnic area at the southern end, tide pools contain coral, black-shelled crabs, small fish and eels, sea hares, and sea urchins with rose-colored spines.

Activities

Near the park are two popular snorkeling areas and an easy trail.

SWIMMING & SNORKELING

Swimming is allowed at shallow Keone'ele Cove inside the Place of Refuge. The cove was once the royal canoe landing. Snorkeling is best when the tide is rising, as the water is deeper and the tide brings in fish. Sunbathing is discouraged, and visitors cannot leave towels or mats on the ground.

Just north of the Place of Refuge is Two-Step, a terrific place to snorkel, with a variety of reef fish and coral close to shore. It's also popular with kayakers and canoe paddlers. From the park's parking lot, take the narrow one-way road marked with a 15mph sign (to the left as you exit the park).

Snorkelers step off a lava ledge immediately north of the boat ramp into about 10ft of water. It then drops off fairly quickly to about 25ft. Some naturally formed lava steps make it fairly easy to get in and out of the water, but there's no beach here. In winter, high surf can create rough waters.

Visibility is excellent, especially if you come at noon when the sun is directly overhead. The predatory 'crown of thorns' starfish can be seen here feasting on live coral polyps. Divers can investigate a ledge a little way out that drops off about 100ft.

HIKING

Hiking the 1871 Trail to Ki'ilae Village is a 2-mile round trip starting at the park. Ask a ranger to direct you to the nearby trailhead (off the road toward the picnic grounds) and to lend you a booklet describing the marked sights along the way.

On the way to the abandoned village you'll pass a collapsed lava tube and temple ruins before reaching the steep Alahaka Ramp, which once allowed riders on horseback to travel between villages. Halfway up the ramp is Waiu-O-Hina lava tube, which opens to the sea; bring a flashlight, if you want to explore it, because the floor is rough and jagged rocks jut from overhead.

At the top of the ramp, incredible vistas spread out below. Keep going to the spot where Ki'ilae Village once stood, heading back where the trail ends at a fence. The trail is tree-lined but not shaded, so a morning or late-afternoon excursion is advised.

HO'OKENA

If you have the time to explore South Kona, Ho'okena is a worthwhile detour. The locals are friendlier than their neighbors in Miloli'i, but they often view over-eager tourists with a touch of wariness. The village is just over 2 miles down a narrow road that turns off Hwy 11 between the 101- and 102-mile markers.

Ho'okena was once a bustling village with two churches, a school, courthouse and post office. King Kalakaua sent his friend Robert Louis Stevenson here in 1889 to show him a typical Hawaiian village. Stevenson stayed a week with the town's judge and wrote about Ho'okena in *Travels in Hawaii*.

In the 1890s, Chinese immigrants began to move into Ho'okena, setting up shops and restaurants. A tavern and a hotel opened, and the town got rougher and rowdier. In those days, Big Island cattle were shipped from the Ho'okena landing to market in Honolulu. When the circle-island road was built, the steamers stopped coming and people moved away. By the 1920s, the town was all but deserted.

Today Ho'okena is a tiny fishing community with an attractive **beach** that's been designated a county park. With soft, black sand and calm waters for snorkeling, you can escape the tourist hordes here. The beach does have a reputation for drug activity, however. When the winter surf is up, local kids hit the waves here. When it's calm, kayakers paddle around, and you can snorkel straight out from the landing. It drops off pretty quickly, and there's lots of coral, but don't go too far out or you may encounter strong currents. There are picnic tables, but no drinking water. Camping is allowed with a county permit (p223).

MILOLI'I

Miloli'i means 'fine twist.' Historically, the old fishing village was known for its skilled sennit twisters, who used bark from the *olona* (a native shrub) to make fine cord and highly valued fishnets. Villagers still live close to the sea, and many continue to make a living from it. But today Miloli'i seems rather isolated, and as you drive toward the coastal village, the rows of makeshift homes on stilts seem incongruous to the surrounding lava terrain. Miloli'i residents generally prefer their seclusion and don't welcome tourists poking around. Be on guard, as 'ice' (crystal methamphetamine) problems are common here.

The village sits at the edge of an expansive 1926 lava flow that covered the nearby fishing village of Ho'opuloa. The turnoff is just south of the 89-mile marker on Hwy 11, 5 miles down a steep, winding paved single-lane road that cuts across the long-ago flow. At the end of the road, you'll reach a peaceful, deserted beach park with an expanse of tide pools. Camping is allowed with a county permit (p223), but while there are picnic tables, the restrooms are locked.

NORTH KONA

Hot, arid country lies along the Queen Ka'ahumanu Hwy (Hwy 19), running north 33 miles from Kailua-Kona up the Kona Coast to Kawaihae in the South Kohala district. On the route you'll notice the Big Island's sanitized version of graffiti – sweet messages spelled out in stones of white coral against the black lava background. From much of this coast, you can look inland and see Mauna Kea, and to the south of it, Mauna Loa, which are often snowcapped in winter.

Heading north from Kailua-Kona, you'll first pass Honokohau Harbor and Kaloko-Honokohau National Historical Park, just a couple of miles from town. A big open lava tube lies on the inland side of Hwy 19, north of the 91-mile marker and just before a speed limit sign. It seems rather tame if you've been to Hawai'i Volcanoes National Park but interesting if you haven't. The tube and the expansive lava flow surrounding the airport are both from the last eruption of Mt Hualalai, in 1801.

Farther north is Kekaha Kai State Park, which provides vehicle access to a nice undeveloped section of the coast. Many more beautiful secluded beaches and coves lie along this sparsely populated coastline, but they're hidden from the road and accessible only by foot. Once you hike in, you'll find white-sand beaches tucked between a sea of hardened lava and a turquoise ocean.

Continuing up the highway, you'll pass the 87-mile marker and the turnoff to the Kona Village Resort, built on the site of a former fishing village. The shoreline between Kailua-Kona and Waikoloa was once dotted with tiny fishing villages, but most were wiped out by the tsunami of 1946.

The flat, straight highway is part of the Ironman Triathlon (p77) route and has wide, smooth bike lanes bordering both sides of the road. Cyclists take heed: When the air temperature is above 85°F, reflected heat from asphalt and lava can edge the actual temperature above 100°F, and no drinking water or services are available along the road.

HONOKOHAU HARBOR

In 1970, this harbor was built 2 miles north of Kailua-Kona to alleviate traffic off Kailua Pier. These days, almost all of Kona's catch comes in here. To reach the harbor, turn *makai* on Kealakehe Rd just north of the 98-mile marker. You'll pass dozens of boat launches.

Sights
HONOKOHAU BEACH

Just north of the harbor, **Honokohau Beach** used to be a favorite of nudists. But now, under control of the park, swimsuits are de rigueur.

This beautiful hook-shaped beach has large-grained sand and a mix of black lava, white coral and rounded shell fragments. The water is acceptable for swimming and snorkeling, although the bottom is a bit rocky. This is an excellent spot to see green sea turtles taking in some sun. It is the site of an ancient heiau and has a replica of an old Hawaiian dwelling. The only facilities are pit toilets at the end of the trail. Bring mosquito repellent in case they're biting.

Take Honokohau Harbor Rd from Hwy 19, turning right in front of the marina complex. Follow the road for about 400yd, until the dry dock boatyard; pull off to the right and look for the trailhead at a break in the lava wall on the right, near the end of the road. A well-beaten, five-minute-walk path leads to the beach.

Activities
SNORKELING

The area between Honokohau Harbor and Kailua Bay is a marine-life conservation district. **Kamanu Sail & Snorkel** (☎ 329-2021; adult/

child $55/35; ⓒ departures 9am & 1:30pm) sails a 36ft catamaran out of Honokohau Harbor for snorkeling at Pawai Bay, just north of the Old Kona Airport State Recreation Area. The boat, which motors down and sails back, takes a maximum of 24 people.

DIVING

Accessible by boat, off the coast of Honokohau Harbor, Turtle Pinnacle is a premier dive site for spotting turtles, which congregate here to clean their shells (small fish feed off the algae and parasites on the turtles' shells). The turtles are accustomed to divers, so they don't shy away from photo opportunities. Other frequent sightings in the water include frogfish, octopi and pipefish.

Another good spot is off Kaiwi Point, south of Honokohau Harbor, where sea turtles, large fish and huge eagle rays swim around some respectable drop-offs. Nearby is Suck 'Em Up, a couple of lava tubes you can swim into and let the swell pull you through; like an amusement-park ride.

For a list of recommended diving operators, see p75.

FISHING

If you chartered a fishing excursion, many companies leave from Honokohau Harbor; for information on bookings see p76). If it's just the spectacle you want to see, catch the boats as they pull up and weigh their haul of marlin and 'ahi. Drive straight in, park near the gas station and walk to the dock behind the adjacent building. The best times to catch the weigh-ins are around 11:30am and 3:30pm.

Tours

Although the best whale watching is found off Maui, the Big Island is another prime spot. The season for humpback whales usually starts around January and runs to March or April. However sperm, false killer, dolphin and melon-headed whales, plus five dolphin species, can be seen in Kona waters year-round. Some snorkeling or fishing cruises also offer whale-watching tours during humpback season, but marine-mammal biologist Dan McSweeney of **Whale Watch** (☎ 322-0028; www.ilovewhales.com; adult/child $60/40; ⓒ seasonal departures 7:10am & 1:30pm) specializes in

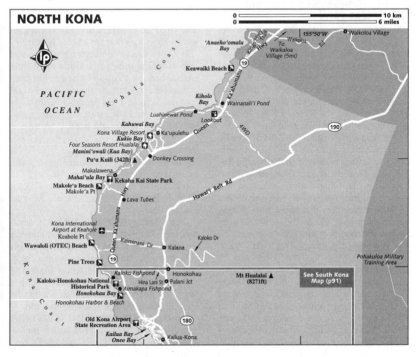

NORTH KONA

0 _____ 10 km
0 _____ 6 miles

PACIFIC OCEAN

Kohala Coast

'Anaeho'omalu Bay
To Waikoloa Village (5mi)
Waikoloa Village
Keawaiki Beach
155°50'W
Waikoloa Village
Waikoloa Rd

Kiholo Bay
Wainanali'i Pond
Luahinewai Pond
Kahuwai Bay
Lookout
Kona Village Resort
Ka'upulehu
Kukio Bay
Four Seasons Resort Hualalai
Manini'owali (Kua Bay)
Pu'u Kuili (342ft)
Donkey Crossing
Queen Ka'ahumanu Hwy

Makalawena
Mahai'ula Bay
Kekaha Kai State Park
Makole'a Beach
Makole'a Pt
Lava Tubes

Kona International Airport at Keahole
Keahole Pt
Wawaloli (OTEC) Beach
Kaiminani Dr
Kalaoa
Kaloko Dr

Pine Trees
Kaloko Fishpond
Honokohau
Kaloko-Honokohau National Historical Park
Hina Lani St
Palani Jct
Aimakapa Fishpond
Honokohau Bay
Honokohau Harbor & Beach
Mt Hualalai (8271ft)

Old Kona Airport State Recreation Area
Kailua Bay
Oneo Bay
Kailua-Kona

Hawai'i Belt Rd
4WD
190
19

Pohakuloa Military Training Area
See South Kona Map (p91)

whales. He leads three-hour whale-watching cruises leaving from Honokohau Harbor between the 97- and 98-mile markers. Hydrophones allow passengers to hear whale songs. The tours have a 24-hour nonrefundable cancellation policy.

Eating

Harbor House Restaurant (☎ 326-4166; harbor complex; mains $5-14; ☉ 11am-7pm Mon-Sat, 11am-5:30pm Sun) Serves frosted mugs of beer ($2 during happy hour), shrimp and chips ($7.50) and chicken, turkey and beef burgers ($5.75 to $7). There's also a fish market that sells fresh fish and smoked marlin by the piece.

Mac Pie (☎ 329-7437; www.macpie.com; Suite 2B, 74-5053 Hwy 19; ☉ 10am-6pm Mon-Fri, noon-5pm Sat) Across from Honokohau Harbor on the *mauka* side of Queen Ka'ahumanu Hwy, behind the Chevron, offers delectable pies from locally grown Macadamia nuts and Maui cane sugar. You can pick up one for the road or ship overseas as gifts. Flavors include: maple mac, vanilla, choc o nilla, Kona coffee, Kona mocha, and butterscotch.

KALOKO-HONOKOHAU NATIONAL HISTORICAL PARK

This **national historical park** (☎ 329-6881; www.nps .gov/kaho; ☉ 7:30am-3:30pm) covers around 1160 acres of fishponds, ancient heiau and house sites, burial caves, petroglyphs, *holua* (sled course), a restored 1-mile segment of the ancient King's Trail footpath, and the entire oceanfront between Kaloko and Honokohau Harbor. It is said the bones of Kamehameha were buried in secret near Kaloko.

Yet the park is virtually unknown, even by locals, who recognize the Kaloko name only because Costco is located in the nearby Kaloko Light Industrial Area. The park is worth exploring, but it might seem desolate at first glance: a seemingly endless expanse of lava rock. Temperatures are unbearable during the midday heat. Go in the early morning or late afternoon (or when it's overcast), so you can enjoy the interpretive trails.

Information

The entrance is between the 96- and 97-mile markers, down a newly paved road leading to a small visitor center that was built in 2003 (having been 'in development' since 1978). A ranger and information brochures are available.

Sights & Activities

On the northern end of the coast is **Kaloko Fishpond**. Before the park took over the land from Hu'ehu'e Ranch, mangrove had invaded the fishpond and proliferated, causing native birds to abandon the habitat. The park service eradicated the mangrove in a labor-intensive process that involved cutting and torching the trees, then tearing the new shoots up and burning the roots.

Aimakapa Fishpond, slightly inland from Honokohau Beach on the park's southern end, is the largest pond on the Kona Coast and a habitat for endangered water birds. Like Kaloko, a mangrove invasion required intensive eradication efforts. If you visit this brackish pond, you're likely to see the *ae'o* (Hawaiian black-necked stilt) and *'alae ke'oke'o* (Hawaiian coot), both endangered native water birds that have thrived since the pond was cleared.

Kahinihiniula (Queen's Bath) is a brackish spring-fed pool in the middle of a lava flow. Although inland, the water level changes with the tide; at high tide, saltwater seeps in and the water in the pool rises. To get there, walk inland from the northern end of Honokohau Beach. The pool is marked by *ahu* (stone cairns) and Christmas berries, always a good sign that freshwater is nearby.

If you're interested in birds, wetlands and archaeological sites, you'll enjoy wandering around here for a couple of hours. But keep in mind that amenities are scarce in the vast park, aside from a few portable bathrooms. Come equipped with water, sunscreen and anything else you might need.

Eating

North Kona is a region rather than a town, so restaurants and shops are scarce. But you'll find a few options at the Kaloko Light Industrial Area on the *mauka* side of Hwy 19.

Costco (☎ 334-0770; 73-5600 Maiau St; annual membership $45; ☉ 11am-8:30pm Mon-Fri, 9:30am-6pm Sat, 10am-6pm Sun) If you're a member of this bulk discount retailer and you want a cheap meal, the snack bar here serves pizza and concession fare. If you're traveling with a group for over a week, you'll save a bundle on bulk groceries and discount gas, too.

Sam Choy's Kaloko (☎ 326-1545; 73-5576 Kauhola St; meals under $10; ☉ 6am-2pm Mon-Sat, 7am-2pm Sun) This is the famous Big Island chef's first

ANN CECIL

Kona coffee (p93)

Jellyfish, off the Kona Coast

CASEY & ASTRID WITTE MAHANEY

Drying coffee beans (p93)

ANN CECIL

LAWRENCE WORCESTER
Kayaking (p55) is a popular activity

Hitting the waves (p55), Kailua-Kona
HOLGER LEUE

Hapuna Beach Prince Hotel Golf Course (p117), Mauna Kea Resort Area
HOL

restaurant. The setting is surprisingly casual, with Formica tables, 1950s-style diner chairs and a cement floor. Try the Hawaiian interpretation of 'comfort food': tomato beef, teriyaki steak, chicken stir-fry, fried fish, *laulau* (bundles of pork or beef, with salted fish, that are wrapped in leaves and steamed) and *lomilomi* salmon (raw diced salmon marinated with tomato and onion). Still family-run, you might even see Sam here when he's in town.

Kailua Candy Company (☎ 329-2522, 800-622-2462; www.kailua-candy.com; 73-5512 Kauhola St; ☺ gift shop 8am-6pm Mon-Sat, 8am-4pm Sun) An establishment since 1977 and ranked by *Bon Appetit* magazine as one of the 'top 10 chocolate shops in America.' Specialties include handmade tropical truffles (try the guava-rum in dark chocolate or the coffee-cinnamon in milk chocolate) and macadamia nut *honu*, made of buttery caramel over dry-roasted macs, covered by luscious chocolate. The company president, Cathy Smoot Barrett, who took over her parents' company almost two decades ago, is a lively fountain of information on all things chocolate.

Kona Coffee & Tea Company (☎ 888-873-2035; www.konacoffeeandtea.com; Suite 5A, 73-5053 Hwy 19; ☺ 8am-5pm Mon-Fri, 9am-5pm Sat) It has a great selection of locally grown, world-class coffees, including a winner from the 2003 Kona Coffee Cultural Festival. There are specific tours, informational videos about the history of Kona coffee and its plantation, plus plenty of gifts for the coffee and tea connoisseur.

Rainbow Café (☎ 329-8839; 73-5612 Kauhola St; meals under $8.50; ☺ 8:30am-8pm Mon-Fri, 10am-6pm Sat, 10am-3pm Sun) For a quick and inexpensive meal try the offering of tasty local or Chinese plates, plus American-style breakfasts.

KEAHOLE POINT

At Keahole Point, the seafloor drops steeply just offshore, providing a continuous supply of both cold water from 2000ft depths and warm surface water. These are ideal conditions for – you'll never guess it – ocean thermal-energy conversion (OTEC).

Sights & Activities

NATURAL ENERGY LABORATORY OF HAWAII AUTHORITY

In 1974 the Hawaii State Legislature created the Natural Energy Laboratory of Hawaii Authority (Nelha) to provide a support facility for OTEC research and related technologies. Electricity has been successfully generated at the site, and research continues into ways to make this an economically viable energy resource. **Public lectures** (☎ 329-7341; www.nelha .org; adult/children $5/free; ☺ 10-11:30am Wed & Thu) are held here and require reservations.

Today Nelha also sponsors a variety of commercial ventures, including aquaculture production of ogo, algae, abalone, lobster and black pearls. One of Nelha's tenants is a Japanese company that desalinates pristine Hawaiian seawater from 2000ft and sells it as a tonic, Ma Ha Lo Hawaii Deep-Sea Water, in Japan.

The turnoff is 1 mile south of Kona airport, between the 94- and 95-mile markers.

WAWALOLI (OTEC) BEACH

The Nelha access road also leads to Wawaloli Beach, a great spot for exploring tide pools covering the rocky lava coastline. Swimming conditions are poor, except among the protected tide pools. Swimming is best here at high tide and it's a nice place for families with kids. The beach is pleasantly uncrowded and just right for watching the horizon or eating outdoors. Picnic tables, rest rooms and showers are available. The only drawback: planes occasionally drone overhead.

PINE TREES

To see one of the best **surfing** breaks in west Hawai'i, drive about 2 miles further south to Pine Trees. When the access road to Nelha veers to the right, look leftward for a well-worn 4WD road leading south.

On weekends, local surfers flock to Pine Trees in a continuous procession of SUVs (sports utility vehicles). There is surf at a number of points along this stretch depending on the tide and swell. The final bay gets the most consistent yet more-forgiving waves. An incoming mid-tide is favorable in general, but as the swell picks up in the winter these breaks often close out. To score at this point, you'll have to *talk story with da locals to find da powah surf, brah!* While appreciated by surfers, swimmers will find the shoreline too rocky and inaccessible, but many go for the show. You'll need a 4WD; walking is possible, if you can stand the heat. Gates are closed between 8pm and 6am.

Why Pine Trees? Early surfers spotted mangrove trees near the break, which they thought were pines. No mangroves (or pines) are immediately visible today but the name has stuck.

ONIZUKA SPACE CENTER

The **Astronaut Ellison S Onizuka Space Center** (☎ 329-3441; adult/child $3/1; ☯ 8:30am-4:30pm), opposite the car rental booths at the Kona Airport, pays tribute to the Big Island native who perished in the 1986 *Challenger* space shuttle disaster.

The little museum features exhibits and educational films about space and astronauts. Items on display include a moon rock, a NASA space suit and scale models of spacecraft. There's also a small space-themed gift shop.

KEKAHA KAI STATE PARK

Formerly known as Kona Coast State Park, **Kehaka Kai** (☯ 9am-7pm Thu-Tue) is a 1600-acre park comprising pristine beaches that remain relatively secluded, mostly due to rough access. Shaded picnic tables, barbecue grills and portable toilets are available on the main site but most of the park is completely undeveloped.

Sights & Activities
MAHAI'ULA BEACH
The largest and easiest to reach, Mahai'ula Beach has salt-and-pepper sand, along with coral rubble. The inshore waters are shallow, and the bottom is gently sloping. Snorkeling and swimming are usually good, but during periods of high surf, which are frequent in winter, surfing is the sport of choice on the bay's north side.

To reach Mahai'ula Beach, take the *makai* access road off Hwy 19, about 2.5 miles north of Kona airport, between the 90- and 91-mile markers. The unpaved road (barely passable in a 2WD) runs for 1.5 miles across a vast lava flow that's totally devoid of trees and greenery. From the first parking area, take a five-minute walk north.

Remember, walking even 15 minutes can be punishing at high noon. Be prepared for the heat, or plan your trek in the morning.

MANINI'OWALI (KUA BAY)
Manini'owali, also called Kua Bay, is what many consider to be a perfect, crescent-shaped beach, with turquoise waters and deep white sand. Most of the year, the surf is suited to swimmers, and in winter, the waves kick up for boogie boarders and bodysurfers. But winter storms can generate currents in the bay that temporarily strip the beach of its sand.

Officials plan to complete a $2.5 million paved access road (just south of the 88-mile marker) and facilities all by spring 2005 – a controversial decision because Mahai'ula is the larger beach and can accommodate more visitors.

Currently there are no trees or awnings to provide shade, very little vegetation and no facilities. Prior to 2005, people accessed Manini'owali by taking the turnoff just north of both the 88-mile marker and **Pu'u Ku'ili**, the 342ft grassy cinder cone *makai* of the highway. The road, marked by a stop sign and gate, is 1 mile to the beach. Even a 4WD can't make it the whole way.

MAKALAWENA & MAKOLE'A BEACHES
These beaches require either a 4WD or a hike. Occasionally campers have been harassed or assaulted by hostile locals at these deserted beaches, so be alert to trouble.

To the north lies Makalawena Beach, a pristine, white-sand beach owned by the Kamehameha Schools Bishop Estate. To reach this beach, you must hike in about 1.25 miles, which takes roughly half an hour. To start the trek, park by the service road that's cabled off, and walk toward the old house on the beach. Find the coastal trail further *makai* and hike north.

You'll be walking on lava rock, and the relentless Kona sun will get your blood pumping en route. But the payoff will be a dip in clear waters ideal for swimming and snorkeling and especially for boogie boarding. At the southern end, behind the dunes, a brackish pond lets you rinse off before hiking back. There are no facilities and almost no crowds during the week.

Another hidden treasure, Makole'a Beach, south of Kekaha Kai, is a small black-sand beach, where you probably won't encounter another soul. If you're walking down the park, find the easy-to-navigate 'path' along the lava fields; follow the coastline and you can't lose your way (an easier walk than to Makalawena). With a 4WD, turn left at the first parking lot in the park; drive for

KONA

about 1000yd until you reach a path, which is marked by coral and goes to the ocean; from here it's probably wise to walk rather than drive to the beach.

This beach might be less breathtakingly impressive than the others within park grounds, but black sand near Kona is rare. There's no shade and the lava rock and black sand add to the heat, so bring plenty of water. Again, there are no facilities.

KA'UPULEHU

After the 1946 tsunami, this fishing village, accessible only by boat, was abandoned until the early 1960s, when a wealthy yachter, who had anchored offshore, concluded Ka'upulehu would be the perfect place for a hideaway hotel.

The Kona Village Resort opened in 1965. It was so isolated it had to build its own airstrip to shuttle in guests – the highway that now parallels the Kona Coast wasn't built for another decade. In 1996, a second upscale hotel, the Four Seasons Resort, opened at Ka'upulehu Beach, about a 10-minute walk south of Kona Village Resort.

The new hotel opened up the shoreline, making the white-sand beach at **Kukio Bay**, and a string of pristine little coves further south, easily accessible. There are showers, rest rooms, drinking water and parking. A 1-mile-long coastal footpath through the lava connects Kukio Bay with the Four Sea-

---

DONKEY CROSSING

In the evenings, donkeys come down from the hills to drink at spring-fed watering holes and to eat seedpods from the *kiawe* (mesquite-like trees) along the coast between Kua and Kiholo Bays. The donkeys are descendants of the pack animals that were used on coffee farms until the 1950s, when Jeeps replaced them.

Growers, who had become fond of these 'Kona nightingales,' as the braying donkeys were nicknamed, released many of the creatures into the wild rather than turn them into glue. The donkeys were largely forgotten until Hwy 19 went through in 1974.

Keep an eye out for the donkeys at night. They need to cross the road for their evening feed, and often ignore the 'Donkey Crossing' signs on the highway!

---

sons via an area of reddish lava and brackish water, where turtles can be seen.

The PGA-tour **Four Seasons Hualalai Course** (☎ 325-8000), designed by golfing legend Jack Nicklaus, is open only to members and resort guests of the Four Seasons.

Sleeping

Kona Village Resort (☎ 325-5555, 800-367-5290; www .konavillage.com; 1 Kahuwai Bay Dr; 1-bedroom hale $515-910, 2-bedroom hale $850-1125; 🏊) If you want to escape the modern-day world, but still enjoy fine dining and gorgeous settings, one-of-a-kind Kona Village fits the bill. Here, you'll escape phones, clocks, radios, TVs and air-con. And you'll sleep in a 'village' of thatched-roof *hale* (houses) standing on stilts around an ancient fishpond or along a sandy beach. However, the interiors are modern and comfortable, with a high ceiling, a fan, rattan furnishings, a refrigerator and probably a Jacuzzi. Excellent restaurants are a stroll away, as are a spa, a fitness center, two swimming pools and a glass-bottom boat. Daily accommodation rates include meals and activities.

Kona Village is a favorite of some wealthy CEOs, movie stars, and others who normally live at just the opposite pace of this place. The staff keeps the 82-acre grounds off limits to nonguests except during guided tours at 11am daily.

If you simply can't get over the irony of paying big bucks to 'go native,' you can drop in for the spectacular Friday-evening luau.

Four Seasons Resort Hualalai (☎ 325-8000, 800-332-3442; www.fourseasons.com; 100 Ka'upulehu Dr; r $540-780, 1-bedroom ste $935-3450; 🖥 🏊) Known for its impeccable service and classy luxury, the newest resort on the Gold Coast is also the only five-diamond resort on the Big Island. If you're here, go for the full treatment at the world-class spa. The adjacent beach isn't great for swimming; an underwater reef drops off steeply, causing currents that can carry you far out to sea. Hollywood stars, such as Denzel Washington and Heather Locklear, have been spied here. Resort guests can enjoy the Jack Nicklaus–designed golf course. The course is not open to nonguests.

Eating

Hualalai Grille by Alan Wong (☎ 325-8525; Golf Clubhouse, Four Seasons Resort Hualalai, 100 Ka'upulehu Dr; mains $30-38; ☯ lunch & dinner) Nicknamed the '19th Hole,' the Hualalai Grille reopened under the direction of celebrity chef Alan Wong in early 2004, with signature dishes like the 'New Wave' Opihi Shooter appetizer – a tall glass of local limpets in spicy tomato water, fennel basil and *ume shiso* (Japanese plum) essences. Creative fish entrées and intriguing Hawaii-style versions of American classics, like the 'soup and sandwich' appetizer with chilled red-and-yellow tomato soup, fois gras, and a grilled cheese sandwich with kalua pig.

Also at the Four Seasons Resort Hualalai is the more formal **Pahuia** (☎ 325-8000; mains $25-48; ☾ 6:30-11:30am & 6pm-9:30pm), an elegant oceanfront restaurant featuring consistent regional Hawaiian cuisine.

Entertainment

Kona Village Resort (☎ 325-5555; 1 Kahuwai Bay Dr; per person $78; ☾ 5:30pm Fri) The best commercial luau on the Big Island. The old-world Polynesian setting makes the show feel

---

DETOUR: KONA COAST BACKCOUNTRY

Layers of angular lava dominate the landscape, where jagged *'a'a* (rough lava) criss-crosses frozen tongues of *pahoehoe* (quick flowing, smooth ropy lava). The searing leeward heat is compounded by the dark volcanic rock. Centuries of flows from Mauna Loa and Hualalai have etched this section of the Kona Coast. Pele allows no easy access, but those who are willing to be humbled by the heat and harshness shall find that gold, turquoise and onyx gems await, where the fingers of lava meet the sea.

The North Kona section of the Queen Ka'ahumanu Hwy has slowly been developed since the 1970s because of its stark yet beautiful contrasts of white sandy coves tucked among black lava. World-renowned destination hotels and golf courses have encroached on many of these once pristine natural beaches. Due to historic significance some of the coast has been protected from development in the form of state and national parks, but as private real-estate prices soar, former owners are selling their coastal property for big money.

One redeeming section of the coast that is highly worth the extra effort is the coastal trail from 'Anaeho'omalu Bay south to **Keawaiki Beach**. Hugging the coastline, the trail is relatively well marked, crossing varying beaches and lava fields. Start by heading south from the beach at the Waikaloa Beach Marriott. Adding continued solitude with each forward step, the protected coves and outer reefs at **Kapalaoa Beach** provide good possibilities for swimming, snorkeling and surfing.

Rounding the first point you will come upon Pu'uanahulu Homesteads, a swath of vacant private homes. Continue along white coral and black boulder beaches alternating with *'a'a* lava flows for another slow mile. Here you will stumble upon a lone palm at Akahu Kaimu. Tucked just behind the beach here is probably the most pristine **brackish pool** on the island. The water along the coast here is a bit rough for snorkeling, but the pond provides cool, clear tranquility with a myriad of colors among the volcanic rocks. A few fish, eels and other sea life have made their way in through subsurface caves, so enjoy a snorkel in this large pool when the tide is high. Stop here for a break to swim and enjoy complete solitude.

Another half mile of similar terrain brings you to another private homestead (usually vacant). Continue from here for another 1.5 miles over rugged *'a'a* flows, and past swimming holes and hidden snorkeling gems when the water is calm. The trail is marked by an occasional white coral, but mainly follows the coast until the beach at Keawaiki. You will know you are there when you reach the former estate of Francis I'I Brown, an influential and loved 20th-century Hawaiian businessman. Fenced in by barbed wire it is now protected as a historical site. Passing the house you will find a lava trail through a grove of mesquite trees. This leads for 1.5 miles over *'a'a* back to the highway. A mile back towards the road is the Kiholo-Pukako Trail, a restored part of the ancient kings' trail system that circumnavigates the entire island. Hike the 1.5 miles back to 'Anaeho'omalu or hitch back from the small dirt turn out *makai* side of the road between 78- and 79-mile markers.

Bring at least 2L of water per person and plenty of food for this long day hike. The sun is intense from reflection off the lava and sea and there is almost no shade so make sure to bring a wide-brimmed hat, sunglasses and a few applications of sunscreen.

authentic, and the fire eaters, dancers and singers certainly earn their pay. Reservations are required.

Beach Tree Bar & Grill (☎ 325-8000; Four Seasons Resort Hualalai, 100 Ka'upulehu Dr) Sitting at a bar, watching the sunset: this is the perfect setting for it. There's live music from Tuesday to Saturday.

KIHOLO BAY

Halfway up the coast, just south of the 82-mile marker, you'll come to a lookout that commands a great view of Kiholo Bay. With its pristine turquoise waters and shoreline fringed with coconut trees, the bay is an oasis in the midst of the lava.

An inconspicuous trail down to the bay starts about 100yd south of the 81-mile marker (see the cars parked along the highway). Walk straight in about 10ft, then veer left and follow a 4WD road, the beginning of which has been blocked off by boulders to keep vehicles out. Near the end of the trail, look for a faint footpath toward the left. Allow 20 to 30 minutes in total to get there.

Kiholo Bay, almost 2 miles wide, has a lovely, large spring-fed pond called Luahinewai at the southern end of the bay. It's refreshingly cold and fronted by a black-sand beach, which is great for swimming when it's calm. As you walk to the freshwater pond, check out the **Queen's Bath**, a freshwater swimming hole that appears deceptively small but actually extends back into the rock for about 40ft. Look for a *makai* opening in the trees after you pass the gargantuan yellow estate and tennis courts.

On the northern end, follow a primitive trail that leads to a lovely cove of black sand great for sunbathing and a bit of solitude. You can actually walk across a shallow channel to a small island with boulders and white sand. The water is okay for swimming when it is clear, but expect a mix of warm and cool water and it is often a bit cloudy depending on the tide. For snorkeling, you're better off at the beaches of Kekaha Kai State Park (p106). However, exploring the area is interesting and there is a good chance you'll see *honu*.

South Kohala

From Waikoloa to Kawaihae, the endless vista of lava rock might strike you as barren and otherworldly. But the South Kohala desert is significant in Hawaiian history, and ancient trails, heiau, fishponds and petroglyphs still remain along the coast.

In the midst of the stark terrain, you'll see an incongruous string of unbelievably green oases. These are the swanky resorts and pro golf courses that have sprung up since the 1960s, when Laurence Rockefeller built the pioneering Mauna Kea Beach Hotel.

Today the stretch from Kohala down to Kona is known as Big Island's Gold Coast: Some attribute the nickname to the abundant yellow tang in coastal waters. But most point to the big bucks generated by upscale tourism here. The resorts are located on the island's prime beaches, which are legally accessible to all (though access is given only grudgingly at some resorts). Public beach parks, such as world-famous Hapuna Beach, are also numerous and first-rate.

The only real residential community is Waikoloa Village, located on the *mauka* (inland) side of the highway, just north of the 75-mile marker. Originally an inexpensive neighborhood intended for resort employees, the village is now financially out of reach for most locals and comprises many mainland and retiree transplants.

The constant sunshine here is ideal beach weather. But driving along the Queen Ka'ahumanu Highway can be brutally hot, especially if you're stuck in the rush-hour crawl. South Kohala exemplifies both old and new Hawai'i in more ways than one.

HIGHLIGHTS

- Reveling in perfect, crescent-shaped **Kauna'oa Bay** (p117)
- Admiring King Kamehameha the Great's **Pu'ukohola Heiau** (p118)
- Sunning, swimming and people watching at **Hapuna Beach State Recreation Area** (p117)
- Contemplating the mysteries of the **Puako Petroglyph Preserve** (p115)
- Exploring the historical sites and beaches at **Mauna Lani Bay Hotel & Bungalows** (p114)
- Enjoying the sun (and spectacular sunset) at **'Anaeho'omalu Beach Park** (opposite)

Orientation

It's impossible to get lost in South Kohala: only the Queen Ka'ahumanu Hwy cuts through the endless lava terrain, letting you access paved roads to coastal resorts or to Waikoloa Village (and rough paths to once-secret beaches). This two-lane highway might seem modest compared to the multi-lane thoroughfares on the mainland, but don't be fooled. Many highway deaths occur on this stretch due to speeding. Since only one lane goes in either direction, idiots sometimes use the bike-lane 'shoulder' to pass slower traffic, adding to the danger.

Without wheels, you have few options to explore South Kohala. There are three **Hele-On** (☎ 961-8744; www.co.hawaii.hi.us/mass_transit/heleon bus.html) bus routes to the Waikoloa Resort Area but they cater to local commuters who work at the resorts, hence the departure times from Hilo: 3:30am to 5:30am!

WAIKOLOA RESORT AREA

Heading north, a turnoff just south of the 76-mile marker leads to the Waikoloa Beach Marriott and Hilton Waikoloa Village hotels. You'll first pass Kings' Shops, a shopping mall where you'll find the Kohala branch of the **Big Island Visitors Bureau** (☎ 886-1655, 800-648-2441; www.gohawaii.com /bigisland; Suite B15, Kings' Shops, 250 Waikoloa Beach Dr; ☺ 8am-4:30pm Mon-Fri) upstairs. Take note that they're a marketing agency for local businesses: all they provide are brochures on island attractions, and they can neither recommend one over another nor can they book tours for you. It's not worth the stop unless you're in the mood to shop. Downstairs, among all the shops, you'll find a couple of Hilton Grand Vacations Club booths, which provide similar brochures. But their objective is to find timeshare buyers, so the impressive discounts they offer apply only to those people who sign up for one of their sales presentations.

For general services, head to the residential community of Waikoloa Village (population 4800); turn *mauka* onto Waikoloa Rd just north of the 75-mile marker. In the village, there's a **post office** (☎ 883-9245; 69-1895 Pua Melia St; ☺ 9am-4:30pm Mon-Fri, 10am-2pm Sat) to the right (if you're driving east) and a grocery store, **Waikoloa Village Market** (☎ 883-1088; 68-3916 Paniolo Ave; ☺ 6:30am-9pm), to the left.

Sights & Activities

'ANAEHO'OMALU BEACH PARK

Dubbed 'A Bay' by the linguistically challenged, **'Anaeho'omalu Beach** (☺ 6am-8pm) is long and sandy, and curves along an attractive bay. Popular with families, swimmers and picnickers, this is perhaps the only beach suited to windsurfing. Winter weather can produce rip currents, but the water is usually quite calm.

Both ends of the bay are composed of prehistoric lava flows from Mauna Kea, with *'a'a* (rough, jagged lava) to the north and *pahoehoe* (smooth-flowing lava) to the south. The southern end of the beach has public facilities, with showers, toilets, changing areas, drinking water and parking.

The northern end of the beach, which fronts the Waikoloa Beach Marriott, has a small fitness area with swing ropes, chin-up bars and a volleyball net. The **Ocean Sports beach hut** (☎ 886-6666, ext 2; www.hawaiioceansports .com) announces the latest water conditions, and hires out windsurfing equipment and kayaks (at rip-off prices of $15 per hour for a single and $22 per hour for a double). Ocean Sports also offers standard-priced windsurfing and scuba-diving lessons, boat dives, catamaran and glass-bottom-boat cruises.

For snorkeling, there's a decent spot at the north end, directly in front of the sluice gate. Here you'll find coral formations, a fair variety of tropical fish and, if you're lucky, *honu* (turtles).

'Anaeho'omalu was once the site of royal fishponds, and archaeologists representing the Bishop Museum have found evidence of human habitation here dating back more than a thousand years. Two large fishponds lie just beyond the line of coconut trees on the beach. A short footpath starts near the showers and bypasses fishponds, caves, ancient house platforms and a shrine. Check the interpretive plaques along the way.

To get there, drive along Waikoloa Beach Dr toward the resorts and make a left turn opposite the entrance to the Kings' Shops.

WAIKOLOA PETROGLYPH PRESERVE

On Waikoloa Beach Dr, a lava field etched with impressive petroglyphs is off to the right, immediately before the Kings' Shops complex. If you park at the shopping complex, it's a five-minute walk along a signposted path to the first of the etchings.

Stay on the path at all times. Do not walk on the petroglyphs and cause irreparable damage, as careless tourists do. Many date back to the 16th century; some are graphic (humans, birds, canoes) and others, cryptic (dots, lines). Western influences appear in the form of horses and English initials. For a larger collection, head to the Puako Petroglyph Preserve (p115).

HILTON WAIKOLOA VILLAGE

When it opened in 1988, at a cost of $360 million, this hotel (formerly a Hyatt) billed itself as the world's most expensive resort. Aptly nicknamed 'Disneyland,' the ostentatious 62-acre Hilton Waikoloa Village is, if nothing else, eye candy.

Most of the hotel's glamour lies in its constructed enormity. Even the beach is artificial, with a saltwater lagoon stocked with tropical fish and fantasy swimming pools with a 175ft twisting waterslide (kids adore it). You'll see lots of families riding kayaks or paddling pedal boats in the 'lake,' oblivious to the natural wonders nearby.

Perhaps the biggest draw is the dolphin pool, where guests can get thrillingly close to one of them. **DolphinQuest** (☎ 800-248-3316; www.dolphinquest.org; adult/child $150/125, family up to 5 $700) even sponsors a 'dolphin training adventure' for $295. The dozen or so cetaceans seem healthy as they leap and swim in large tanks, and are carefully supervised during guest programs.

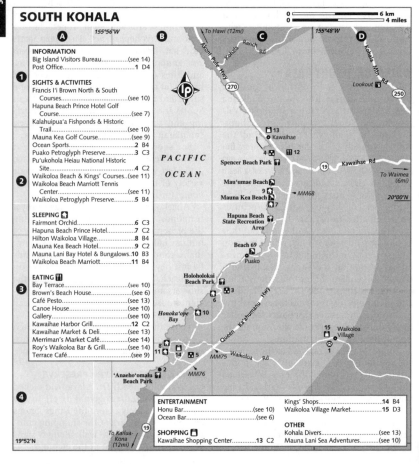

SOUTH KOHALA

0 _____ 6 km
0 _____ 4 miles

INFORMATION
Big Island Visitors Bureau..............(see 14)
Post Office..**1** D4

SIGHTS & ACTIVITIES
Francis I'i Brown North & South
    Courses.....................................(see 10)
Hapuna Beach Prince Hotel Golf
    Course..(see 7)
Kalahuipua'a Fishponds & Historic
    Trail...(see 10)
Mauna Kea Golf Course...................(see 9)
Ocean Sports.....................................**2** B4
Puako Petroglyph Preserve.............**3** C3
Pu'ukohola Heiau National Historic
    Site..**4** C2
Waikoloa Beach & Kings' Courses..(see 11)
Waikoloa Beach Marriott Tennis
    Center...(see 11)
Waikoloa Petroglyph Preserve..........**5** B4

SLEEPING 🏠
Fairmont Orchid................................**6** C3
Hapuna Beach Prince Hotel..............**7** C2
Hilton Waikoloa Village....................**8** B4
Mauna Kea Beach Hotel....................**9** C2
Mauna Lani Bay Hotel & Bungalows.**10** B3
Waikoloa Beach Marriott..................**11** B4

EATING 🍴
Bay Terrace.....................................(see 10)
Brown's Beach House.......................(see 6)
Café Pesto.......................................(see 13)
Canoe House....................................(see 10)
Gallery...(see 10)
Kawaihae Harbor Grill.....................**12** C2
Kawaihae Market & Deli..................(see 13)
Merriman's Market Café...................(see 14)
Roy's Waikoloa Bar & Grill..............(see 14)
Terrace Café.....................................(see 9)

ENTERTAINMENT
Honu Bar...(see 10)
Ocean Bar..(see 6)

SHOPPING 🛍
Kawaihae Shopping Center..............**13** C2

Kings' Shops....................................**14** B4
Waikoloa Village Market...................**15** D3

OTHER
Kohala Divers...................................(see 13)
Mauna Lani Sea Adventures...........(see 10)

To Hawi (12mi)
Ranch Rd
Kohala Mtn Rd
Lookout
Kawaihae
Spencer Beach Park
Kawaihae Rd
To Waimea (6mi)
Mau'umae Beach
Mauna Kea Beach
Hapuna Beach State Recreation Area
Beach 69
Puako
Holoholokai Beach Park
Honoka'ope Bay
Waikoloa Village
Waikoloa Rd
'Anaeho'omalu Beach Park
To Kailua-Kona (12mi)

PACIFIC OCEAN

Akoni Pule Hwy
Kohala Rd
Queen Ka'ahumanu Hwy

155°56'W   155°48'W
20°00'N
19°52'N

If you don't feel like walking, you can navigate the sprawling grounds in canopied boats that cruise artificial canals, or on a modernistic tram like the Monorail. The lobby showcases a multimillion-dollar art collection of museum-quality pieces from Melanesia, Polynesia and Asia. It's particularly big on Papua New Guinea, along with replicas, such as a giant Buddha sculpture.

GOLF & TENNIS

Golfers can head straight for the **Waikoloa Beach & Kings' Courses** (☎ 886-7778, 877-924-5656), both at the Waikoloa Beach Marriott. Nonguests are charged green fees of $150, but at all the premier South Kohala courses you can beat the nonguest prices by waiting until mid-afternoon to tee off for a 50% discount. Carts are mandatory.

Tennis courts are available at the **Waikoloa Beach Marriott Tennis Center** (☎ 886-6789; per court 1st hr $10, per subsequent hr $5). Six courts rent for a surprisingly reasonable cost. Nonguests are welcome, too.

Festivals & Events

Great Waikoloa Food, Wine & Music Festival (☎ 886-1234; www.dolphindays.com; Hilton Waikoloa Village; admission $100; ☺ 3rd weekend Jun) combines over 30 of the state's best chefs with an array of fine wines and boutique brews, plus world-class jazz artists. This festival is part of the three-day **Dolphin Days Summer Fest**, established in 1994 to celebrate the first birthday of the first dolphin born at the resort.

Sleeping

Waikoloa Beach Marriott (☎ 886-6789, 888-924-5656; www.waikoloabeachmarriott.com; 69-275 Waikoloa Beach Dr; garden-/ocean-view r $240/310; ☒ ☙) Formerly the Royal Waikoloan, the 545-room Marriott is an older resort, but the best choice in the Waikoloa resort area. Its beachside location is far superior to the Hilton's, and each room has either two double beds or one king bed, cable TV, phone, air-con and private lanai. The Kings' Shops are within walking distance, so you're not captive to resort fare for all your meals. The hotel is slated to undergo major renovations throughout 2005, but only a section at a time.

Hilton Waikoloa Village (☎ 886-1234, 800-221-2424; www.hiltonwaikoloavillage.com; 425 Waikoloa Beach Dr; garden-view r $200-470, ocean-view r $240-690; ☒ ☙) This megaresort might be over the top, but the sheer magnitude can make an impression – and it's more affordable than the other resorts. Kids seem to enjoy the 'rides' and parents might appreciate the safe, waveless waters. Grounds are plush, with all the usual Hilton amenities and two 18-hole golf courses.

Parents can enroll their kids (ages five to 12) in Camp Menehune, day or night camps offering crafts, games and water activities geared toward daily themes. Kids will be entertained and parents can relax and enjoy grown-up adventures. Reservations must be made at least 24 hours in advance (by Internet or by calling ☎ 886-1234, ext 1202).

Eating

If you want to avoid the decent but overpriced fare at the resorts, head to **Kings' Shops** (☎ 886-8811; 250 Waikoloa Beach Dr), where you'll find a typical mall food court, plus the two famous island chefs' outposts:

Merriman's Market Café (☎ 886-1700; www .merrimanshawaii.com; dinner mains $15-25; ☺ 11am-9pm) The second location of the well-known Merriman's in Waimea (p135), the Market Café serves tasty Mediterranean-influenced dishes featuring organic island-grown produce, fresh fish caught locally, and the finest artisan breads, cheeses and wines. The al fresco café setting is casual, and lunch mains stay under $16.

Roy's Waikoloa Bar & Grill (☎ 886-4321; www .roysrestaurant.com; mains $22-25; ☺ lunch & dinner) This branch of the world-famous Roy's restaurants serves excellent regional Hawaii cuisine. At dinner, expect creative main courses such as rack of lamb in a *liliko'i* (passionfruit) cabernet sauce or blackened *'ahi* (yellowfin tuna) with pickled ginger.

Entertainment

If you can afford the Kona Village luau (p108), go for it. Otherwise, you can expect the standard colorful luau show at two Waikoloa resorts:

Hilton Waikoloa Village (☎ 886-1234; adult/child $72/36; ☺ 6pm Fri) Presented by 'Legends of the Pacific,' this luau show includes a dinner buffet and one cocktail.

Waikoloa Beach Marriott (☎ 886-6789, 888-924-5656; www.waikoloabeachmarriott.com; 69-275 Waikoloa Beach Dr; adult/child $67/33; ☺ 5:30pm Sun & Wed) This poolside luau is the typical commercial show with Hawaiian-style dinner buffet, open bar and Polynesian dances.

The Kings' Shops shows an **outdoor movie** (admission $5; 🕑 7pm Tue) on a 17ft by 10ft digital screen located on the lawn on the shopping center's *mauka* side. Bring blankets and lawn chairs. Shows change monthly.

Shopping

Kings' Shops (☎ 886-8811; 250 Waikoloa Beach Dr) is a relaxed, open-air mall geared for tourists. Single counters selling Bulgari, Burberry and Louis Vuitton sit beside Macy's, a food court and a few finer restaurants. If you're sleeping nearby, stop by for a change of scenery from resort grounds. If not, don't bother.

MAUNA LANI RESORT AREA

Constructed in 1983 by a Japanese company, the Mauna Lani Resort truly resembles an oasis. Once you turn off the highway onto Mauna Lani Dr (at the splash of coconut palms and bougainvillea), you pass a long stretch of lava with virtually no vegetation. Halfway along there's a strikingly green golf course sculpted in the black lava. Drive to the end to reach Mauna Lani Bay; the Fairmont Orchid and Holoholokai Beach Park are to the north (veer right).

Sights & Activities

Built on an historic site, the Mauna Lani Bay Hotel & Bungalows is refreshingly accessible to nonguests who wish to explore

---

GOLD COAST RESORT REPORT

Four Seasons Resort Hualalai (p107) For impeccable service and a touch of exclusivity.

Hapuna Beach Prince Hotel (p118) For virtually the same features as the Mauna Kea (they're 'sister' hotels).

Hilton Waikoloa Village (p112) For an extravagant, larger-than-life amusement park.

Kona Village Resort (p107) For privacy and a taste of old Hawai'i.

Mauna Kea Beach Hotel (p117) For the island's premier golf course and a postcard-perfect beach.

Mauna Lani Bay Hotel & Bungalows (opposite) For the prettiest architecture amid ancient Hawaiian sites.

Remember, while rack rates typically range from $350 to $1000, you can almost always find special deals on the resorts' websites.

---

the trails, fishponds and even beaches. Commonly called 'Mauna Lani Beach,' the beach fronting the hotel is protected, but the water is rather shallow; snorkelers might prefer exploring a coral reef beyond the inlet. A less frequented cove is down by the Beach Club restaurant, a 15-minute walk towards the south.

HONOKA'OPE BAY

One mile south of the hotel is this bay, which is protected at the southern end and is good for swimming and snorkeling when the seas are calm. You can reach the bay either on foot, by an old coastal trail that passes an historic fishing and village site, or by taking a new access road.

PAUOA BAY

A calm lagoon, Pauoa Bay is a little-known jewel located at the Fairmont Orchid (see p116). Natural freshwater springs flow into the warm bay, creating amusing gushes of chilly water from the ocean floor. Marine life abounds, making the bay perfect for snorkeling. Caveat: nonguest access is frowned upon by the Fairmont Orchid.

KALAHUIPUA'A FISHPONDS

These ancient fishponds lie along the beach just south of the hotel, partly under a shady grove of coconut palms and milo (native hardwood) trees. They are among the few still-working fishponds in Hawai'i, and are stocked, as in ancient times, with *awa* (Hawaiian milkfish). Water circulates from the ocean through traditional *makaha* (sluice gates), which allow small fish to enter but keep mature, fattened catch from leaving. You might notice fish sporadically jumping into the air and slapping down on the water, an exercise that knocks off parasites.

KALAHUIPUA'A HISTORIC TRAIL

This trail begins on the inland side of the Mauna Lani Bay Hotel, at a marked parking lot, opposite the resort's little grocery store. Pick up a free, self-guided trail map from the concierge desk.

The first part of the historic trail meanders through a former Hawaiian settlement that dates from the 16th century, passing lava tubes once used as cave shelters and a few other archaeological and geological sites marked by interpretive plaques. Keep

MYSTERIES CARVED IN STONE

Ki'i pohaku (images in stone), or petroglyphs, are found throughout the Hawaiian islands. They are most common on the Big Island, perhaps because it is the youngest island and has the most extensive fields of smooth pahoehoe lava, on which the images are made. Ki'i pohaku are pecked into lava using a very dense rock. The images include various styles of human figures, as well as items significant in the lives of ancient Hawaiians, such as turtles, canoes and sails.

Other markings such as concentric circles and other geometric shapes are enigmatic. The 'why' of ki'i pohaku, as well as the locations of specific fields is the subject of much debate, and the intentions of the makers have, of course, long been lost. Many petroglyph fields are found along major trails or on the boundaries of ahupua'a (land divisions). Other examples of petroglyphs can be found at the Waikoloa Petroglyph Preserve (p111) and the Pu'u Loa Petroglyphs (p202).

Stepping on, or making rubbings of, petroglyphs, will damage them. Please obey posted signs and respect barriers. Take as many photographs as you like. Early morning or late afternoon light is best, because even fainter images reveal themselves when the angle of the light is low.

a watchful eye out for quail, northern and red-crested cardinals, saffron finches and Japanese white-eyes.

The trail then skirts fishponds lined with coconut palms and continues out to the beach, where you'll find a thatched shelter with an outrigger canoe and an historic cottage with a few Hawaiian artifacts on display. If you continue southwest past the cottage, you can loop around the fishpond and back to your starting point – a round trip of about 1.5 miles.

Take a break en route, at the cove near the southern tip of the fishpond, where the swimming is good and a restaurant offers simple lunches.

HOLOHOLOKAI BEACH PARK

North of the Fairmont Orchid, this beach has a rocky shoreline composed of coral chunks and lava. While not great for swimming, the waters are fine for snorkeling during calm surf. Facilities include showers, drinking water, restrooms, picnic tables and grills.

To get there, take Mauna Lani Dr and turn right at the rotary, then right again on the beach road immediately before the Fairmont Orchid. The park also leads to the Puuako petroglyphs.

PUAKO PETROGLYPH PRESERVE

Containing more than 3000 petroglyphs, this petroglyph preserve is one of the largest collections of ancient lava carvings in Hawaii and definitely worth a visit.

To see the petroglyphs, you'll take a pleasant 750yd walk from Holoholokai Beach Park. From the mauka end of the Holo-

holokai Beach parking lot, a well-marked trail leads to the preserve. The walk is easy, but don't wear rubbah slippah because the thorny foliage on the way can pierce your feet and the ground is rocky. The path is only partly shaded so the heat can be stifling.

GOLF

The **Francis I'i Brown North & South Courses** (☎ 885-6655; Mauna Lani Bay Hotel & Bungalows) are widely considered among the Big Island's top world-class golf courses. Nonguests pay green fees of $185 to play either course. The South Course is more scenic and popular, with its signature 15th-hole featuring a tee shot over crashing surf. The North Course is more challenging and interesting, however, with a par-three 17th hole within an amphitheater of black lava rock.

Sleeping

Mauna Lani Bay Hotel & Bungalows (☎ 885-6622, 800-367-2323; www.maunalani.com; 68-1400 Mauna Lani Dr; mountain-/ocean-view r $390/575; ☒ ☒) Although over two decades old, the ritzy yet classily low-key Mauna Lani remains one of Hawaii's finest resorts. The modern, open-air building is centered around a spacious atrium that has sleek water sculptures, colorful orchid sprays and towering coconut trees. Outside, historic ponds and trails are meticulously maintained; a saltwater stream and ponds around the hotel hold colorful reef fish, small black-tipped sharks and a few turtles. Staff at this 350-room hotel are welcoming, and guests and nonguests alike are invited to tour the grounds and enjoy the beaches. Check the website for promotional packages.

Fairmont Orchid (☎ 885-2000, 800-845-9905; www
.fairmont.com/orchid; 1 N Kaniku Dr; garden-/ocean-view r
$435/605) Just north of the Mauna Lani Bay
Hotel, the 539-room Orchid has an elegant,
continental atmosphere. You'll feel totally
pampered here, with marble bathrooms and
truly luxurious furnishings, although you
might have to use your imagination to feel
you're in Hawaii. Service is always impeccable and the large swimming pool is a hit
with kids.

Eating

Brown's Beach House (☎ 885-2000; Fairmont Orchid;
mains $24-37; ☽ lunch & dinner) Brown's, a long-
time favorite, serves flavorful island dishes
like seared foie gras, *unagi* sushi, sautéed
grilled *moi* (Pacific threadfin, which in ancient Hawaii was reserved only for royalty),
and soft-shell crab. (The chef de cuisine, Et-
suji Umezu, moved to head the Four Seasons
Hualalai Grille, p107, in spring 2004, but the
quality seems to be holding.)

Canoe House (☎ 885-6622; mains $27-50; Mauna
Lani Bay Hotel & Bungalows; ☽ dinner) Mauna
Lani Bay Hotel's most upscale restaurant has a
romantic, oceanfront setting and a menu
that blends Asian and Hawaiian influences,
with an emphasis on seafood. Dishes include grilled lemon-pepper scallops or
pancetta-wrapped mahimahi with coconut-
and-spinach risotto.

Gallery (☎ 885-7777; Mauna Lani Bay Hotel & Bungalows; lunch $8-15, dinner $25-30; ☽ lunch daily, dinner Tue-Sat) At the Mauna Lani Bay Hotel's
golf clubhouse (Francis I'i Brown North &
South Courses), the Gallery serves continental and Pacific Rim dishes. The fresh
fish is a specialty; try the *onaga* (red snapper) encrusted with macadamia nuts.

KONA COAST'S TOP FIVE BEACHES

'Anaeho'omalu Beach Park (p111) The only
windsurfing waves on the island.
Hapuna Beach State Recreation Area
(opposite) A party beach where you can see and be
seen (if you can find parking).
Kahalu'u Beach Park (p86) Convenient city
beach and novice snorkeler's heaven.
Kauna'oa Bay (opposite) Classically perfect
crescent-shaped beach.
Makalawena Beach (p106) Pristine surf at a
white-sand gem 'off the beaten track' (4WD only).

Bay Terrace (☎ 885-6622; Mauna Lani Bay Hotel &
Bungalows; breakfast mains $8-20, breakfast buffet $24;
☽ breakfast) Delicious breakfasts and a generous buffet, if you're hungry.

Entertainment

The resorts offer the expected level of nighttime amusement, but a couple of places are
recommended.

Honu Bar (☎ 885-6622; Mauna Lani Bay Hotel; ☽ 6pm-
midnight) Billiards, cigars, and occasional live
entertainment accompany premium wines,
cocktails and liqueurs. The hotel **atrium** also
has live Hawaiian music and hula dancing
nightly from 6pm to 9pm.

Ocean Bar (☎ 885-2000; Fairmont Orchid; ☽ 11:30am-
10pm) Here you'll find live music nightly,
and awesome sunset views from the chaise
lounges.

PUAKO

pop 450

Puako is a one-road beach town that's lucky
to remain off the beaten tourist track. The
town is simply a mile-long row of houses,
with many marked 'shoreline access' points.
To get here, take either the marked turnoff
from Hwy 19, or a bumpy side road from
Hapuna Beach State Recreation Area.

The main attraction at Puako is giant tide
pools, set in the swirls and dips of *pahoehoe*
coastline. Some pools are deep enough to
shelter live coral and other marine life. A
narrow beach of pulverized coral and lava
lines much of the shore. Snorkeling can be
excellent off Puako but the surf is usually
too rough in winter.

For the easiest beach access, go to the
south end of the village, stopping just before
the 'Road Closed 500 Feet' sign. Take the
short dirt road toward the water. There is
no beach per se, but there is a small cove
that's used for snorkeling and shore diving;
be careful of the undertow. A couple of minutes' walk north brings you to a few petroglyphs, a board for *konane* (a game similar
to checkers) chinked into the lava, and tide
pools deep enough to cool off in.

Nearby, beautiful **Beach 69** has easy access
and gentle waves. There's plenty of shade,
and boundary trees make it feel like each
group of sunbathers has a private little plot.
No facilities are available. Turn down Puako
Rd between the 70- and 71-mile markers;
take the first right turn (the road quickly

becomes one lane). Look for telephone pole No 71 to the left and park. Follow the 'road' to its end, and then tramp along the footpath that runs parallel to a wooden fence. In case you're wondering, telephone pole No 71 was once numbered No 69, which gave the beach its nickname.

HAPUNA BEACH STATE RECREATION AREA

Already legendary as the Big Island's most popular and accessible beach, Hapuna is also ranked among the world's best beaches by *Condé Nast Traveler*. The clear waters and deep, white sand that gently slopes into the ocean won't disappoint you. But be warned that Hapuna gets jammed on weekends, and if you wait till noon, you'll be stuck in the parking lot forever.

When it's calm, Hapuna affords good swimming, snorkeling and diving. When the surf's up in winter, the bodysurfers and boogie boarders get their turn. High winter surf can produce strong currents close to the shore and a pounding shorebreak, and waves over 3ft should be left for the experts. Hapuna has had numerous drownings, and many of the victims have been tourists who were unfamiliar with the water conditions.

A tiny cove with a small sandy beach lies about five minutes' walk north of the park. The water is a bit calmer there and, in winter, less sand is kicked up by the waves. The park has a landscaped picnic area, showers, pay phones, drinking water and pitiable restrooms. Lifeguards are on duty. Be sure to lock your car.

Just up from the beach are six state-owned A-frame **cabins** (per night $20) with milliondollar views. Each sleeps four people on two platforms (you sleep head to head) and has lights and electricity. They are also surprisingly bug-free. Amenities include shared bathrooms with showers and a cooking pavilion with a stove and fridge. See p223 for reservation information.

MAUNA KEA RESORT AREA

In the early 1960s, the late Laurence Rockefeller obtained a 99-year lease on the land around Kauna'oa Bay from his friend Richard Smart, owner of Parker Ranch (p131). Five years later, Rockefeller opened Mauna Kea Beach Hotel, the first luxury hotel on the Neighbor Islands.

The hotel, located just north of the 68-mile marker, remains a first-class act – perhaps not the newest or flashiest, but the respected granddaddy of them all. The lobby and grounds have displays of Asian and Pacific artwork, including bronze statues, temple toys and Hawaiian quilts. The north garden holds the prized possession: a 7th-century pink granite Buddha from a temple in southern India. Free public **tours** (☎ 882-7222, call to confirm) are given at 10:30am.

The **Mauna Kea Golf Course** (☎ 882-5400) consistently ranks among the top 10 courses in the world. Nonguests pay green fees of $195, while guests pay $130 and also have privileges at **Hapuna Beach Prince Hotel Golf Course** (☎ 880-3000).

But the prize of the Mauna Kea Beach Hotel is a gift from nature: **Kauna'oa Bay** (nicknamed 'Mauna Kea Beach') might be the most visually stunning beach on the Big Island. The crescent-shaped cove has fine white sand and a gradual slope that fosters excellent swimming conditions most of the year. On the north end, snorkeling conditions are good during calm waters.

The beach is open to the public, but only 30 parking spaces are set aside daily for nonguests. By noon, you'll probably be too late. If you're having a drink or lunch at the hotel, you can handily bypass the issue of obtaining a parking pass.

Just to the north of Mauna Kea Beach is a delightful gem, **Mau'umae Beach**, with soft white sand, shady trees and protected waters. Locals are proprietary about this beach (for good reason) so don't overstep your welcome. To get here, go toward the Mauna Kea Beach Hotel, turn right on Kamahoi and cross two wooden bridges. Look for telephone pole No 22 on the left and park (you'll probably see a bunch of cars parked). Walk down the trail to the Ala Kahakai sign and turn left toward the beach. You can also get here from nearby Spencer Beach, by walking 10 minutes on the Ala Kahakai Trail, a shady coastal path.

Sleeping & Eating

Mauna Kea Beach Hotel (☎ 882-7222, 800-882-6060; www.maunakeabeachhotel.com; 62-100 Mauna Kea Beach Dr; mountain-/ocean-view r $360/565) After 40 years, this icon is showing signs of age, but for the island's premier beach and golf course, you can't top the Mauna Kea Beach Hotel.

Kauna'oa Bay is guaranteed to satisfy any tropical fantasy, and pro golfers almost unanimously cite the Mauna Kea course as the island's best. That said, the rooms here are small and simple, and if you're forking over a few hundred a night, you might be let down. Check the website for hot deals (eg mountain-view room for $250).

If you're spending an evening here, don't miss the luminous manta ray 'show' at the lookout point near the lobby between 7pm and 10pm, when lights are shone to attract the sea creatures into the bay. Also try to catch the decadent Sunday brunch at the **Terrace Café** (☎ 882-7222; brunch buffet $38; ✆ lunch Sun), where you can feast on sushi, dim sum, prime rib, lobster bisque, domestic and imported cheeses, and Belgian waffles (from the waffle station), plus the usual array of bacon, eggs, made-to-order omelettes and fresh fruit.

Hapuna Beach Prince Hotel (☎ 880-1111; 866-774-6236; www.princeresortshawaii.com; terrace-/oceanview r $360/460) The Mauna Kea Beach Hotel's 'sister' resort, open since 1994, tends to be overshadowed and lacks as much oceanfront access, but the two share the same amenities and buses transport guests between the two. Also, it's located next to Hapuna Beach to the south. With 350 rooms, it largely gears its services to Japanese tourists and even has a bilingual concierge desk. Despite its manicured lawns, golf course and restaurants, however, it still lacks the charm of the Mauna Kea Beach Hotel and the energy of the Waikoloa resorts.

SPENCER BEACH PARK

Spencer Beach Park, off Hwy 270 south of Kawaihae, is a low-key place for visitors with children, with a shallow, sandy beach that's protected by a reef and the jetty to the north. The waters are calm but they tend to be silty. The rocky south end of the beach past the pavilion is better for snorkeling, although entry is not as easy; kayaking is prohibited.

The park has a lifeguard station, picnic tables, barbecue grills, restrooms, showers, drinking water and both basketball and volleyball courts. A footpath leads south to Mau'umae Beach near the Mauna Kea Beach Resort.

Camping is allowed, and though the campsites are exposed and crowded together, it's still the best beach north of Kona to sleep under the stars. See p223 for information on obtaining a county permit.

PU'UKOHOLA HEIAU NATIONAL HISTORIC SITE

By 1790 Kamehameha the Great had conquered Maui, Lana'i and Moloka'i. However, power over his home island of Hawai'i proved to be a challenge. When told by a prophet that if he built a heiau dedicated to his war god Kuka'ilimoku atop Pu'ukohola (Whale Hill) in Kawaihae he'd rule all the islands, Kamehameha built **Pu'ukohola Heiau**, a structure that's 224ft by 100ft, with 16ft to 20ft walls.

It is believed that men formed a human chain 20 miles long, transporting rocks hand to hand from Pololu Valley in North Kohala – and with Kamehameha laboring alongside his men. After finishing the heiau by summer 1791, Kamehameha held a dedication ceremony and invited his rival and cousin, Keoua, the chief of Ka'u. When Keoua came ashore, he was killed and taken

---

AUTHOR'S CHOICE: A POKE SMORGASBORD

The Hawaiian word *poke* (*poh*-keh) means to slice or cut. But today it's chiefly known by its other definition: a savory dish made from bite-sized pieces of raw, fresh fish mixed with *ogo* (seaweed), *inamona* (kukui nut relish), salt, soy sauce and vinegar. *Poke* is ubiquitous 'soul food,' served at restaurants, sold in plastic tubs at groceries and made at home. (On the mainland, chic restaurants now offer diced, marinated sashimi, which is just an overpriced, copycat version of *poke*!)

Locals flock to the Hapuna Beach Prince Hotel for the annual **Poke Festival** (☎ 880-3424; www.pokecontest.com; admission $5 with Aloha Festivals ribbon, also $5; ✆ Sep), which is the signature event of the Aloha Festival (see p229) in September. Founded by Waimea resident Gene Erger in 1992, the contest now attracts over 55 professional chefs and amateurs, who concoct *poke* with ingredients such as soy sauce, tofu or macadamia nuts! Each contestant makes 5lb of their entry and provide 2oz tasting cups for post-judging sampling. The festival ends with a craft fair and celebrity golf tournament for charity.

DETOUR: EXPLORING KOHALA'S WATERS

Most visitors head to Kona for diving and snorkeling. But the waters off the Kohala coast are just as pristine and teeming with marine life. If you're staying in North or South Kohala (or in nearby Waimea) explore the waters from Kawaihae Harbor instead of fighting gridlock all the way to Kona.

The North Kohala Coast drops off more gradually than the Kona Coast, so you'll probably see reef sharks, spinner dolphins and rays, but not large schools of tuna and other deepwater fish. Kohala is the oldest area of the Big Island, so coral growth is lush, with lots of lava tubes, arches and pinnacles. The area's yet to be 'discovered' so divers can enjoy healthy reef ecosystems and uncrowded sites.

Snorkelers can also find excellent conditions, and by tagging along on a dive boat, can glimpse larger marine life, including turtles, spinner dolphins and whales in winter. Even along the coast, protected reefs, eg at Puako, are a good place to snorkel.

In Kohala, the best dive and snorkel outfit, **Kohala Divers** (☎ 882-7774; www.kohaladivers.com; Kawaihae Shopping Center, Hwy 270; 2-tank morning dive $109, 1-tank night dive $89; ☼ departures 7:45am & sunset), is conveniently located near Kawaihae Harbor and also offers intro to advanced diving courses, snorkeling and whale watching. Staff is knowledgeable and friendly and keep dive groups small (maximum of six). If you'd like to explore on your own, you can rent gear at the shop.

Other options for water sports include **Ocean Sports** (☎ 886-6666, ext 2; www.hawaiioceansports .com) in the Waikoloa resort area and **Mauna Lani Sea Adventures** (☎ 885-7883; www.hawaiisea adventures.com; 68-1400 Mauna Lani Dr).

---

to the *luakini* (temple of human sacrifice) as the first offering to the gods. With Keoua's death, Kamehameha took sole control of the Big Island, eventually ruling all the islands by 1810.

Back then Pu'ukohola Heiau was adorned with wooden *ki'i* (statues) and thatched structures, including an oracle tower, altar, drum house and shelter for the high priest. After Kamehameha's death in 1819, his son Liholiho and powerful widow Ka'ahumanu destroyed the deity images and the heiau was abandoned.

Today, only the basic rock foundation remains, but it's still impressive and has been designated a **national historic site** (☎ 882-7218; admission free; ☼ 7:30am-4pm). There's a two-minute trail to the heiau starting at the visitors center, which has a few displays and pamphlets. If you arrive after hours, park at Spencer Beach Park and walk to the heiau along an old entrance road closed to vehicle traffic.

KAWAIHAE

Kawaihae is a nondescript port town (though it does boast the island's second-largest deepwater commercial harbor), just a stopping point between North Kohala and the Kona Coast. There's little more than the harbor, fuel tanks, cattle pens and a tiny beach park. The good news is you won't starve, though.

At the Kawaihae Shopping Center just across from the harbor, you'll find a handful of eateries: **Café Pesto** (☎ 882-1071; Kawaihae Shopping Center, Hwy 270; lunch/dinner mains $11/20, large/small pizza $11/18; ☼ 11am-9pm, to 10pm Fri & Sat) is sure to please with gourmet thin-crust pizza and inspired seafood salads and pastas. If you're looking for sundries or deli take-out, the **Kawaihae Market & Deli** (☎ 880-1611; Kawaihae Shopping Center, Hwy 270; ☼ 4:30am-9pm Mon-Fri, 5:30am-8pm Sat & Sun) offers standard convenience items plus pasta and tofu salads that are a bit better than you might expect.

About 400yd south of Café Pesto (off Hwy 270), **Kawaihae Harbor Grill** (☎ 882-1368; dinner mains $18; ☼ lunch & dinner) attracts a huge local following (especially Waimea residents) due to the reliable seafood, kid-friendly service and lively upstairs seafood bar.

North Kohala

If you bypass North Kohala, as do too many visitors, you'll miss one of the most untouched, striking areas of the Big Island. So do stop to catch a glimpse of old Hawai'i in a place even locals rarely visit, and explore significant historical sites, quaint towns and a breathtaking valley at the end of the road.

The Kohala Mountains form a central ridge on this northernmost tip of the island: the leeward side is dry desert, while the windward side features coastal cliffs and spectacular valleys. A winding highway cuts through the rolling pastureland blanketing the mountains, making for perhaps the island's most scenic drive. When the road peaks at 3564ft, Maui rises out of the mist, while Mauna Kea and Mauna Loa loom inland. Stop at the scenic lookout near the 8-mile marker, where the expanse below – from endless grassy fields to distant coastal towns – displays the vastness of the Big Island.

Along the coast, there are two highly sacred places, Lapakahi State Historical Park and Mo'okini Luakini Heiau. Geologically the oldest part of Big Island, North Kohala is also the site of King Kamehameha I's birth. Remember, ancient Hawaiian sites are seldom ornate, and you might need to take a second glance to appreciate their significance. Don't expect an elaborate constructed chapel or towering pillars of marble. Rather, try to observe the setting, which is carefully chosen, and the power of the *'aina* (land) might reveal itself.

NORTH KOHALA

HIGHLIGHTS

- Trekking down to misty, rugged **Pololu Valley** (p126)

- Stretching your body and mind in **Kapa'au** (p125)

- Living a childhood water adventure by **Flumin' da Ditch** (p124)

- Visiting an ancient *piko* (navel) of spiritual power at **Mo'okini Luakini Heiau** (p123)

- Feasting on creative sushi and the island's best ice cream in **Hawi** (p124)

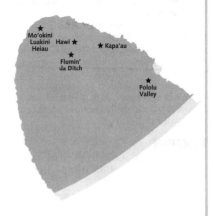

Orientation

There are two fully paved routes into the district: an inland road (Kohala Mountain Rd, Hwy 250) and a coastal road (Akoni Pule Hwy, Hwy 270), which intersect in Hawi. The Akoni Pule Hwy starts in Kawaihae and ends at a lookout above Pololu Valley, where a trail descends to the valley floor. Kohala Mountain Rd runs for 20 miles between Hawi and Waimea.

AKONI PULE HIGHWAY

The land along the Akoni Pule Hwy (Hwy 270) remains largely undeveloped, making it quite easy to imagine the Hawai'i of old. The view of the horizon is spectacular, stretching straight and uninterrupted, as far as the eye can see.

Lapakahi State Historical Park

Strolling the grounds of this **park** (☎ 882-6207; admission free; ☷ 8am-4pm, closed most holidays) transports you back to the remote fishing village it was 600 years ago. The terrain was rocky and dry, so the ancient villagers turned to the sea for their food. Fish were plentiful, and the cove fronting the village provided a safe year-round canoe landing. Eventually some of the villagers moved to the wetter uplands and began to farm, trading their crops for fish with those who had stayed on the coast. In the process, Lapakahi grew into an *ahupua'a,* a wedge-shaped division of land radiating from the mountainous interior out to the sea. When the freshwater table dropped in the 19th century, the village was abandoned.

Within the 262-acre park, you can walk a 1-mile **loop trail** that leads to the remains of stone walls, house sites, canoe sheds and fishing shrines. Displays show how fishers used lift nets to catch *opelu,* a technique still practiced today, and how the salt used to preserve the fish was dried in stone salt pans. Visitors can try their hands at Hawaiian games, with game pieces and instructions laid out for *'o'o ihe* (spear throwing), *konane* (Hawaiian checkers) and *'ulu maika* (stone bowling).

As part of a marine-life conservation district, Lapakahi cove is full of yellow tangs and other colorful fish. Snorkeling is strongly discouraged. If pressed, staff say it's allowed within a limited area of the cove: toward the north, the waves are angerous; toward the south, the waters are sacred and off-limits, as kahuna once gathered medicines here. But donning a swimsuit and splashing around in Lapakahi cove is like skateboarding at the Vatican – it will raise eyebrows.

Further, guides sternly warn that if you venture off-trail, you are trespassing and perhaps offending the spirits of the ancients. Once you hear the accounts of tourists who trampled on hidden gravesites, returned to their hotels and subsequently heard bizarre screams all night long…you'll probably want to stick to the straight and narrow.

The park, which is largely unshaded, is just south of the 14-mile marker. Brochures are available at the trailhead. Guided tours are offered but you must call in advance.

Mahukona Beach Park

One mile north of Lapakahi, this beach park is a low-key fishing and swimming spot used mainly by locals. Once a key port for the Kohala Sugar Company, you can

---

NORTH KOHALA UPCOUNTRY RIDES

The upcountry drive along the Kohala Mountain Rd, between Waimea and Hawi, crosses acres of rolling ranchland that's easy to appreciate from the car. To take a closer look, a horseback ride is a bit pricey but kids enjoy it. Companies typically don't allow those under 4ft tall, children under eight, or those who weigh more than 230lb.

Paniolo Riding Adventures (☎ 889-5354; www.panioloadventures.com; Hwy 250; rides $75-125) offers a variety of horseback rides over the 11,000-acre Ponoholo Ranch, a working cattle ranch. Horses are selected according to the rider's experience, but they're all riding horses, not trail horses, and you can canter with the lead wrangler. Dress up like a *paniolo* (cowboy) with the boots, hats, chaps and Australian dusters provided free of charge.

Kohala Na'alapa Stables (☎ 889-0022; www.naalapastables.com; Kohala Ranch Rd; rides $55-75) has tour guides that allow open-range rather than head-to-tail riding so they don't feel like kiddie rides. Rides cross the pastures of Kahua Ranch, which spans 8500 acres, and affords fine views of the coast.

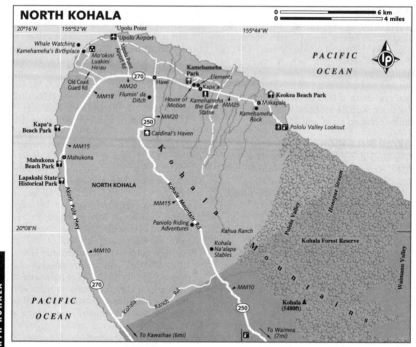

NORTH KOHALA

still see the abandoned landing, which connected to the sugar mills by rail.

Beyond the landing, you can find interesting snorkeling and diving spots, although
they're usually too rough in winter. Entry,
via a ladder, is in about 5ft of water. Heading
north, it's possible to follow an anchor chain
out to a submerged boiler and the remains
of a ship submerged 25ft deep. You'll find a
shower near the ladder, where you can rinse
off. There is no sandy beach, however.

To reach the small, ratty county park,
veer left (south) as you drive in. There are
restrooms, but they won't win any prizes
in cleanliness. Those planning on camping
in the unkempt grassy area should bring
their own drinking water and plenty of insect repellent. For information on camping
permits, see p223.

Kapa'a Beach Park

On the plus side, the waters at this beach
park are clear and quite good for snorkeling, if you venture past the rocks close to
shore. The view of Maui can be spectacular,
and there's never a crowd here.

But on the negative side, the beach park is
rather unkempt, with neither a sandy beach
nor great facilities. There is a barbecue grill,
port-a-potties and a few picnic tables, but
no showers or decent restrooms. Don't be
surprised to find the path to the water littered with cigarette butts and trash. Camping is allowed; see p223 for information on
obtaining a permit.

This county park is 1.25 miles north of
Mahukona, just above the 16-mile marker
on Hwy 270.

HAWI

pop 940

Less than a thousand people live in Hawi
(hah-*vee*), but they certainly enjoy a variety of charming shops and eateries. Today
there's a mixture of old-timers and newcomers drawn by the low-key village flavor
and cheaper real estate. North Kohala used
to be sugar country, and Hawi was the biggest of half a dozen sugar towns. Kohala
Sugar Company, which had incorporated
all of the mills, closed down its operations
in 1975. You can still see an occasional strip

of feral cane among the pastures outside of town.

Entering town via the Akoni Pule Hwy, you'll pass the small **visitors center** (Hwy 270; ☾ 9am-5pm Mon-Fri), post office, grocery store and gas station. The park on Kohala Mountain Rd (Hwy 250), in front of the post office, is cool and shady with giant banyan trees. Behind the park is the old sugar-mill tower, a remnant of the town's former mainstay.

Sleeping

Kohala Village Inn (☎ 889-0404; www.kohalavillage inn.com; 55-514 Hawi Rd; d $60, ste $90-95) In a motel-style building located right off the highway, you'll find rooms that are plain and clean but have no fan, air-con or phone. The attached restaurant is decent but the others just down the street are better.

Cardinals' Haven (winter ☎ 884-5550, summer ☎ 425-822-3120; r $60; ☾ mid-Nov–mid-May) Open

---

DETOUR: MO'OKINI LUAKINI HEIAU

One of the oldest and most historically significant temples in the Hawaiian islands, **Mo'okini Luakini Heiau** (☎ 373-8000; admission free but advance notice required; ☾ dawn-dusk) sits on a grassy knoll near 'Upolu Point at the northern tip of the Big Island. The massive structure, which measures about 250ft by 125ft, with walls 6ft high, was a 'closed' heiau, reserved for *ali'i nui* (kings and ruling chiefs) for fasting, praying and offering of human sacrifices to their gods.

The heiau was built from 'sunrise to first light' by up to 18,000 'little people' passing water-worn basalt stones by hand in complete silence from Pololu Valley to the site – a distance of 14 miles – under the supervision of Kuamo'o Mo'okini, who dedicated it to the god Ku. According to the Mo'okini genealogical chants, the heiau was built around AD 480.

Five hundred years later, Pa'ao, a priest from Samoa raised the walls to 30ft and changed the altar to a scalloped shape as his *ho'okupu* (offering) to the gods. He was the first to introduce human sacrifices in an effort to stem dilution of the royal bloodlines and to enforce stricter codes of moral conduct among the people.

In 1963, the National Park Service under the US Department of the Interior designated Mo'okini Luakini Heiau as Hawaii's first registered National Historic Landmark. Fifteen years later, then-landowners Oceanic Properties and Bishop Estate deeded the site to the state with two stipulations: no excavations could ever occur at the site, and the heiau's *kahuna nui* must be consulted on all matter regarding the site.

The current *kahuna nui*, Leimomi Mo'okini Lum, is the seventh high priestess of the Mo'okini bloodline serving the temple. In 1978, she lifted the only *kapu* (taboo) that restricted entrance to and exit from the temple, so people could safely visit the site. But all other *kapu* remain in effect to protect the sacred heiau grounds.

In 1979 Mrs Lum established Na Mamo O Hawai'i Nei (Children's Day), an annual event during *makahiki* (ancient festival from mid-October to mid-February, with sports, religious celebration and taboo on war) season, when thousands of schoolchildren visit the heiau and learn Hawaiian history from the singular perspective of a *kahuna nui* in the bloodline.

To get there, turn *makai* off the Akoni Pule Hwy onto the Old Coast Guard Station Rd, between the 18- and 19-mile markers. Follow the one-lane paved road for about a mile. Turn right onto a red-cinder road. Two locked cattle gates block this road along the way; you must call ahead to arrange for someone to open them. Restrooms are not available and the site is not wheelchair-accessible. An alternate route, which doesn't require advance notice, is to drive toward 'Upolu Airport then turn south on the coastal dirt road. But it's less accessible because the road gets muddy and impassable after rains. Of course, you can walk in from either route if necessary. From the heiau site, you'll have a clear view of Maui across the channel and, during winter, humpback whales.

About 1000yd down a dirt road below the heiau, you'll find the legendary site of Kamehameha's birth (p22). According to legend, when Kamehameha was born on a stormy winter night in 1758, his mother was told by a kahuna that her son would be a powerful ruler and conquer all the islands. The ruling high chief of Hawai'i ordered all male newborns killed. Thus, after he was taken to the Mo'okini Luakini Heiau for his birth rituals, he was spirited away by a faithful retainer into hiding in the mountains.

during winter only, you can join the owners in their lovely rural home 3 miles from central Hawi. From the yard, you can look across cattle pastures clear out to Maui. The guest unit comes with a TV, a kitchenette and a sofa bed. Originally from Switzerland, the owners speak fluent German and French as well as English.

Eating

Sushi Rock (☎ 889-5900; Hwy 270; nigiri $4-5, sushi rolls $7-10; ☿ lunch & dinner) In a small but charming space (shared with the gift shop, Without Boundaries), Sushi Rock offers impressive, island-influenced sushi. The setting is personal and the youthful owner-chef Rio Miceli, a Hawi native, serves creative rolls such as the Kohala, with *'ahi poke*, fresh papaya and cucumber, rolled in macadamia nuts – plus all the traditional *nigiri* sushi.

Bamboo (☎ 889-5555; Hwy 270; lunch/dinner $8/10; ☿ lunch & dinner Tue-Sat, lunch Sun) A long-time favorite, and the only fine-dining option in North Kohala, Bamboo serves excellent island food amid tourist-tropical but pleasant decor. Savor the coconut grilled chicken or sesame-nori-crusted tiger shrimp, and save room for the homemade desserts. There's live music on Friday and Saturday nights. Reservations are recommended.

Aunty's Place (☎ 889-0899; Hwy 270; meals $10; ☿ lunch & dinner Mon-Sat, noon-9pm Sun) Gerda 'Aunty' Medeiros makes pizzas all day, and

traditional German dinners at night, served in a casual diner setting. While the owner doesn't like to compare her 'housewife cooking' to Waimea's Edelweiss (p136) restaurant's 'hotel cooking,' she shouldn't be so modest. Hawi's main nightlife attraction happens here on Friday evening, when the karaoke mikes are open 9:30pm to 2am.

Hula La's Mexican Kitchen & Salsa Factory (☎ 889-5668; Hwy 270; meals $5-10; ☿ 10am-8pm) Tasty Mexican fare, including filling burritos and homemade tropical salsa, are on offer, but there's only a smattering of tables in close quarters or on the lanai. Credit cards aren't accepted.

If you want to pick up food to go, try the **farmers' market** (☿ 7:30am-1pm Sat) held at the park on Hwy 250. **Kohala Health Food** (☎ 889-0277; Hwy 270; ☿ 10am-5pm Mon-Fri, to 4pm Sat) sells tea, organic juices and packaged natural-food items. **Kohala Coffee Mill** (☎ 889-5577; Hwy 270; snacks $3-5; ☿ 6:30am-6pm) is a comfy place to hang out and treat yourself to muffins, fresh-brewed Kona coffee and heavenly Tropical Dreams ice cream.

Shopping

Without Boundaries (☎ 889-5900; Hwy 270; ☿ 11am-5pm) is a find for unusual artsy gifts.

Getting There & Away

A car is indispensable in North Kohala, and the scenery is worth the drive. You can take

---

GONE FLUMIN'

Kohala Ditch is an intricate series of ditches, tunnels and flumes once used to irrigate sugar cane fields. The ditch runs 22.5 miles and was built by Japanese immigrant laborers, who were paid about $1 a day for very hazardous work that killed over a dozen during construction. The water, which originates from Waikoloa Stream, midway between the Pololu and Waipi'o Valleys, was a necessity in the drier Hawi area.

Much of the ditch runs through 19,000 acres of Kohala land, which the agricultural giant Castle & Cooke sold a few years back to a developer. The last Kohala cane was cut in the 1970s, but the ditch continues to be a source of water for Kohala ranches and farms. No development has yet occurred, but the owners allow Kamuela Kayak Corporation to lead guided kayak rides through scenic, remote lands. **Flumin' da Ditch** (☎ 889-6922, 877-449-6922; www.flumindaditch.com; 3hr tour adult/child & senior $85/65; ☿ departures 8:15am & 12:15pm) rides hark back to childhood adventures during plantation days, when daring kids would trespass onto the plantation and 'go fluming,' drifting down the canals on inner tubes or anything that floated.

The Flumin' da Ditch kayaks sit four or five people (depending on passenger girth). Don't expect rapids or whitewater on the journey, but be prepared to get soaked! The same company offers Hummer tours, driving military Humvees into the otherwise inaccessible Kohala rain forest. While you might indeed see an enchanted forest sans noise and people, however, why ruin the tranquility in a monster vehicle?

either the coastal Akoni Pule Hwy (Hwy 270) or the curving, upland Kohala Mountain Rd (Hwy 250), both of which pass through the main towns of Hawi and Kapa'au.

The **Hele-On Bus** (☎ 961-8744; www.co.hawaii .hi.us/mass_transit/heleonbus.html) operates solely between the South Kohala resorts and the towns of Hawi and Kapa'au. The route is meant to serve resort workers, with only one departure and one arrival on weekdays. The southbound bus (to the resorts) departs from Hawi at 6:35am; the northbound bus leaves the Hilton Waikoloa Village at 4:15pm and arrives in Hawi at 5:20pm.

KAPA'AU
pop 1160
The largest town in North Kohala, Kapa'au has a courthouse, police station, library and bank. During the King Kamehameha Day festivities on June 11 (a state-wide holiday), the park hosts a parade and Hawaiian dancing, music and food.

Sights & Activities
Kamehameha Park, located on Kamehameha Park Rd off the Akoni Pule Hwy on the *makai* (seaward) side, boasts a large, modern gymnasium, including everything from a ballpark to a swimming pool, all free and open to the public.

KAMEHAMEHA THE GREAT STATUE
This statue on the front lawn of the North Kohala Civic Center may look familiar. Its lei-draped and much-photographed twin stands opposite Honolulu's Iolani Palace. The statue was constructed in 1880 in Florence, Italy, by American sculptor Thomas Gould. When the ship delivering it sank off the Falkland Islands, a second statue was then cast from the original mold. The duplicate statue arrived at the islands in 1883 and took its place in downtown Honolulu. Later the sunken statue was recovered from the ocean floor and completed its trip to Hawaii.

This original statue was then sent here, to Kamehameha's childhood home, where it now stands.

KALAHIKIOLA CHURCH
Protestant missionaries Elias and Ellen Bond, who arrived in Kohala in 1841, built Kalahikiola Church in 1855. The church

itself is usually locked, but the detour through lush foliage with its chirping birds is pleasant. The land and buildings on the drive in are part of the vast Bond estate (proving that missionary life wasn't one of total deprivation).

If you want to look, turn inland off the Akoni Pule Hwy onto a narrow road 900yd east of the Kamehameha statue, between the 23- and 24-mile markers. The church is another 900yd up from the highway.

KAMEHAMEHA ROCK
Kamehameha Rock is on the inland side of the road, about 2 miles east of Kapa'au, on a curve just over a small bridge. According to legend, Kamehameha carried this rock uphill, from the beach below, to demonstrate his strength.

When a road crew attempted to move the rock to a different location, the workers managed to get it up onto a wagon, but the rock stubbornly fell off – a sign that it wanted to stay put. Not wanting to upset Kamehameha's mana, the workers left it in place.

YOGA
In a peaceful space in the historic Sakamoto Building, **House of Motion** (☎ 884-5700; houseof motion@aol.com; 54-3877 Hwy 270; drop-in class $13) offers Ashtanga yoga, tai chi and other movement classes. Classes are small and rigorous (and during the noon hour, classmates might be the town's firefighters). An adjoining **boutique** (☒ 10am-5pm) has the hip yoga clothing, mats and irresistible, eye-catching bags.

Sleeping
Kohala Country Adventures Guest House (☎ 889-5663, 866-892-2484; www.kcadventures.com; off Hwy 270; d $85-110, ste $160) Get away from it all on a 10-acre property with tropical gardens, avocado trees, livestock and a clear view of Maui. Rates include breakfast.

Eating
Kohala Rainbow Café (☎ 889-0099; Hwy 270; sandwiches & salads $8; ☒ 11am-5pm) Just opposite the Kamehameha statue, this really is *the* place to eat in town. Jen's has tasty chicken Caesar salads, good chili and a recommendable Greek wrap sandwich with organic greens. Also on the menu are fresh fruit smoothies, deli sandwiches and soups.

Takata Store (☎ 889-5413; Hwy 270; ☺ 8am-7pm Mon-Sat, to 1pm Sun) The largest market in North Kohala is stocked with produce, meat and all kinds of other edibles.

Shopping

In the historic **Nambu Hotel Building**, a handful of shops and galleries makes for pleasant browsing. **Kohala Book Shop** (☎ 889-6400; Hwy 270; ☺ 11am-5pm Mon-Sat) is not only the biggest and best used bookstore on the island, but also a gathering place for local authors and literary luminaries from abroad. **Elements** (☎ 889-0760; Hwy 270; ☺ 10am-6pm Mon-Fri, to 5pm Sat) showcases a sophisticated collection of fine jewelry designed by owner John Flynn, plus ceramics and other artwork made by local artists. Drool over Flynn's stunning multi-sapphire 18-carat-gold earrings and other unique pieces.

Getting There & Away

Like Hawi, Kapa'au is easily accessible by car on either the Akoni Pule Hwy or Kohala Mountain Rd. Hele-On Bus service is minimal, only between North Kohala and the South Kohala resorts on weekdays. A single southbound bus departs from Kapa'au at 6:20am; a single northbound bus leaves the Hilton Waikoloa Village at 4:15pm and arrives in Kapa'au at 5:25pm.

THE BIG ISLAND FOR KIDS

- Picnic at **Lili'uokalani Park** (p167)

- Go **horseback riding** in Waimea (p132) or North Kohala (p121)

- Hike with walking sticks in **Pololu Valley** (right)

- Meet a **dolphin** up close (p117)

- Scream on carnival rides at Hilo's annual **county fair** (p172)

- See the moon and planets from atop **Mauna Kea** (p141)

- Walk through a **lava tube** (p200)

- Get lost in a maze at **World Botanical Gardens** (p156)

- Get wet kayaking the **Kohala ditch** (p124)

- Learn to snorkel at **Kahalu'u Beach Park** (p86)

MAKAPALA

Makapala has only a few hundred residents. If you're hiking down to Pololu Valley, the town's little store is the final place to get a drink or snack – if it's open.

While located along a scenic rocky coast, **Keokea Beach Park** isn't a big draw because there's no sandy beach. Signs warn about dangerous shorebreaks and strong currents, though a protected cove allows for decent swimming. The park has restrooms, showers, drinking water, picnic pavilions and barbecue grills, but no camping.

The park is about 1 mile in from the highway; take the marked turnoff about 1.5 miles before Pololu Valley Lookout. On the way down to the beach, you'll pass an old **Japanese cemetery**. Most of the gravestones are in *kanji* (Japanese script), and in front of a few, there are filled sake cups.

POLOLU VALLEY

The Akoni Pule Hwy ends at a viewpoint that overlooks secluded Pololu Valley, with its scenic backdrop of steeply scalloped coastal cliffs spreading out to the east. The lookout has the kind of strikingly beautiful angle that's rarely experienced without a helicopter tour – and it's just as stunning as the more famous Waipi'o Valley Lookout.

Pololu was once thickly planted with wetland taro. Pololu Stream fed the valley, carrying water from the remote, rainy interior to the valley floor. When the Kohala Ditch was built, it siphoned off much of the water and put an end to the taro production. The last islanders left the valley in the 1940s, and the valley slopes are now forest-reserve land.

Sights & Activities

The **Pololu Valley Trail**, from the lookout down to Pololu Valley, takes less than 30 minutes to walk. It's steep, but not overly strenuous, and you'll be rewarded with lovely vistas throughout. Be cautious with your footing – much of the trail is rocky or packed clay, which gets slippery when wet. The uphill climb might actually be easier than the trek downhill because of the loose rocks. At the trailhead, Good Samaritans leave walking sticks for your assistance. Cool breezes and a canopy of trees keep the walk comfortable.

The black-sand beach fronting the valley stretches for about 900yd and can make an enjoyable stroll. Driftwood collects in great quantities and, on rare occasions, glass fishing floats get washed up as well. Cattle and horses roam the valley; a gate at the bottom of the trail keeps them in. The surf is usually intimidating in winter, and there can be rip currents year-round. This is not a swimming beach: much of the shoreline is rocky and there are no facilities.

Intrepid hikers can go all the way to the next valley, **Honokane Nui**, but the trail is treacherously slippery and traverses private property, and it's relatively easy to get lost. It takes about two hours each way from the lookout. Follow the vague trail on the eastern side of Pololu Valley, going up the 600ft mountain and over the ridge before dropping into Honokane Nui Valley. Don't hike too close to the ocean, as waves can be strong enough to sweep you away. You might encounter wild cattle along the way.

Tours

Another way to explore Pololu Valley is by mule. **Hawaii Forest & Trail** (☎ 331-8505, 800-464-1993; www.hawaii-forest.com) offers morning **mule rides** (adult/child $95/75; ☻ departures 8am & noon Mon-Sat), which cross streams and pastureland toward waterfalls and valley lookouts, though not into the valley itself. The company runs these excursions on private land with permission from landowners, so you're led to places you cannot otherwise access. Mules are used because the sure-footed creatures are steadier than horses and can handle heavier loads. In the early 20th century they helped Japanese laborers build the Kohala Ditch, which you'll also see on the tour. It's best to book in advance.

NORTH KOHALA

Waimea & Mauna Kea

Resting on the saddle between the Kohala Mountains and the north flank of Mauna Kea, the expansive plains of Waimea are on the cusp of opposing coasts. Alternating clouds and sun create the ideal pastureland on which the famous Parker Ranch was born. The ranch eventually grew to encompass the majority of the land descending the flanks of Mauna Kea.

In both historic and modern times, the ranch has been a pillar of the community. Today Waimea is also connected to Mauna Kea through the astronomical research that takes place on the summit. Both the Keck and Canada-France-Hawaii telescopes have their monitor stations located in Waimea, tying the community further to the mountain that frames the town.

Waimea town (also called Kamuela) is known for its abundance of excellent restaurants and country pace of living. Despite the absence of beaches and tropical weather, it's a destination for art galleries, shopping and entertainment. The Kahilu Theatre plays host to an impressive collection of international live music acts and, staying true to its cowboy roots, there are various annual rodeos around town.

WAIMEA & MAUNA KEA

HIGHLIGHTS

- Dining at one of Waimea's top-rated **restaurants** (p134)
- Learning the history of **Parker Ranch** (p131) and its legendary *paniolo*
- Hiking the **Kohala Forest Reserve Trail** (p136) to breathtaking views from the back of Waipi'o Valley
- Stargazing on **Mauna Kea** (p141), Hawai'i's highest summit
- Testing your will by hiking the **Mauna Loa Observatory Trail** (p144)

WAIMEA (KAMUELA)
pop 7000

Amid rolling pastureland and cool mist, Waimea shows off another face of the Big Island. This is former cowboy country and Hawai'i's largest cattle ranch, Parker Ranch (p131), is stationed here. It spreads across about 7% of the Big Island, and almost everything in Waimea is owned, run or leased by Parker Ranch.

Waimea certainly has its *paniolo* (cowboy) influences, but it's also rapidly growing in size and sophistication. Wealthy mainlanders have moved in and the town serves the upscale subdivisions emerging on former ranches in the Kohala Mountains. Waimea's relative proximity to the Mauna

Kea summit means a growing number of astronomers and engineers settle here.

Situated midway between the east and west coasts of Hawai'i on the north slope of Mauna Kea, Waimea boasts easy access to much of the Big Island's varied climates. At 2670ft the town becomes the tipping point for weather between the windward and leeward sides of the island. At times brisk winds bring towering thunderheads sweeping across the range that slowly dissipate on their passage to the desert of the Kona Coast. This diversity epitomizes Hawai'i's fickle nature, and you can certainly catch a glimpse here of why they call Hawaii the 'Rainbow State.'

For most visitors, Waimea is a stopover between Kailua-Kona and Hilo, but the town

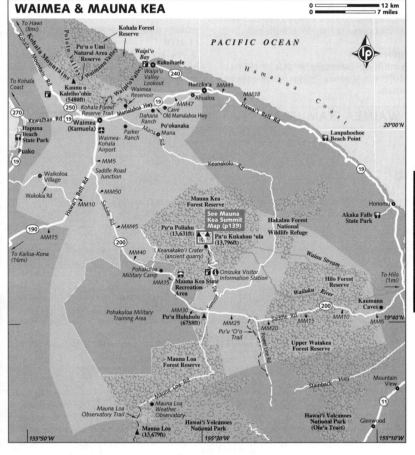

WAIMEA & MAUNA KEA

has first-rate art galleries and some of the island's best restaurants and B&Bs. There is also plentiful high-end shopping to suit many tastes. Don't be caught off-guard by Waimea's chilly weather, which includes daily fog and brisk winds.

Orientation

Highways around Waimea pass a mix of lava flows and dry, grassy rangeland studded with prickly pear cacti. You'll see distant coastal views, wide-open spaces, awe-inspiring cloud formations and tall roadside grasses that have an incredible golden hue in the morning light.

Note that Hwy 190 is usually called Mamalahoa Hwy. From Hilo, Hwy 19 is also called Mamalahoa Hwy, but once it intersects with Hwy 190, it is called Kawaihae Rd. Further east, there's Old Mamalahoa Hwy, which intersects Hwy 19 at both ends.

Information

North Hawaii Community Hospital (☎ 885-4444; 67-1125 Mamalahoa Hwy; ☻ 24hr) Emergency services available.

Post office (☎ 885-6239; 67-1197 Mamalahoa Hwy) Located southwest of Parker Ranch Center. Be sure to address all Waimea mail to Kamuela.
Waimea Visitor Center (☎ 885-6707; 65-1291 Kawaihae Rd; ☻ 8:30am-3:30pm Mon-Fri) Amiable staff and located in the Lindsey House, which was built in 1909 by Parker Ranch for a five-star employee.

Sights

Most of Waimea's sights are along the Mamalahoa Hwy around three consecutive stoplights. Prominently located in Waimea's center, near a grove of cherry-blossom trees, is the **WM Keck Observatory office** (☎ 885-7887; 65-1120 Mamalahoa Hwy; ☻ 8am-4:30pm Mon-Fri). It's a working office, so there's little for visitors to see besides a short video and simple displays about the Mauna Kea telescopes. For more on the observatory, see p140.

PARKER RANCH MUSEUM & VISITOR CENTER

If you know little about the Big Island's history, this small **museum** (☎ 885-7655; www .parkerranch.com; Parker Ranch Center, 67-1185 Mamalahoa Hwy; adult/senior/child $6.50/5.50/5; ☻ 9am-5pm

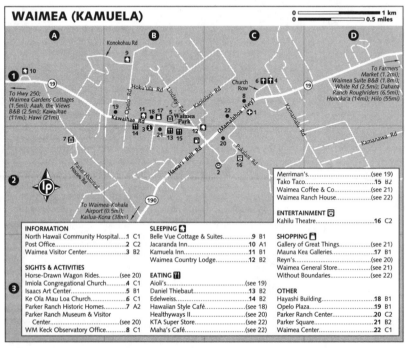

HOME ON DA RANGE

Until recently the Parker Ranch was the nation's largest privately owned ranch, peaking at 225,000 acres. It is currently the fifth largest in the USA with approximately 35,000 cattle on 175,000 acres, contained by 850 miles of fence. The ranch produces more than 10 million pounds of beef annually while holding almost 7% of the island's total land area.

In 1793 King Kamehameha the Great received a herd of long-horned cattle as a gift from British Captain George Vancouver. Showing great foresight, Kamehameha made the herd *kapu* (taboo) to let them grow in numbers. Yet by 1815 the wild herd became a nuisance to the land and a threat to the Hawaiian people.

In 1809, at the age of 19, John Palmer Parker arrived on the Big Island from New England aboard a whaler. Parker gained the favor of Kamehameha through his skill with a rifle and was commissioned to bring the cattle under control.

No easy task, the wily Parker selected elite specimens as payment, while butchering and cutting the herds down to size. For his successful efforts Parker was allowed the hand of one of Kamehameha's granddaughters, forever tying his name to Hawaiian royalty. In the process he landed himself a tidy bit of land eventually gaining control of the entire Waikoloa *ahupua'a,* a traditional land division that runs from the mountains clear down to the sea. With the cattle he managed to domesticate, he ultimately created the Parker Ranch legacy.

As Parker's enterprise grew, three Mexican-Spanish cowboys were brought over from Mexico to help round up the herd and train the locals in the time-tested traditions of cattle ranching. The Hawaiian word for cowboy, *paniolo*, is a corruption of the Spanish word *españoles*. The *paniolo* way has since become a rich part of the Hawaiian tradition in Waimea. Descendants still work the ranches today and indeed the local pride in their heritage is evident in the multiple rodeos held each year. These technicians show their skill and are some of the best in the world, winning international rodeos consistently.

Mon-Sat, last entry 4pm) provides a manageable introduction to the Parker legacy.

With just a few displays, you'll learn about the ranch's history through Parker-family memorabilia, such as portraits, lineage charts, traditional Hawaiian quilts and cowboy gear, including saddles and branding irons. Also displayed are Hawaiian artifacts such as stone adzes, poi (fermented taro) pounders and *kapa* (bark cloth) bedcovers.

If you plan to visit other Big Island museums, the admission fee might seem a bit steep for the size of the collection. A worthwhile feature is the 25-minute movie on the Parker Ranch then and now. A highlight is footage of the early methods of exporting cattle, where *paniolo* rush cattle into the sea, then lift them by slings onto the decks of waiting steamers.

PARKER RANCH HISTORIC HOMES

See how wealthy landowners lived in these two re-creations of fine 19th-century **homes** (☎ 885-5433; www.parkerranch.com; Mamalahoa Hwy; adult/senior/child $8.50/8/6.50; 🕙 10am-5pm, last entry 4pm), less than 1 mile south of the intersection of Hwys 190 and 19.

Built in 1962, **Pu'uopelu** is the estate's sprawling 8000-sq-ft grand manor, which showcases the collection of European and Chinese art owned by the last Parker Ranch owner, Richard Smart. One room is French provincial, with chandeliers, skylights and master Impressionist paintings. Another room is covered with playbills and photos of Smart, who studied theater and performed on Broadway and in Europe. The local scoop is that this theatrical eccentric greeted tourists in his bathrobe on more than one occasion before his death in 1992.

Next door is modest **Mana Hale**, a re-creation of the original 1840s home built by John Parker in the hills outside Waimea. Parker constructed his home in the same saltbox style that was popular in his native Massachusetts, except he used Hawaiian koa wood. The original interior was dismantled board by board and rebuilt here. It's now decorated with period furnishings and old photos of the hardy-looking Parker clan.

ISAACS ART CENTER

Appreciation for the arts is the direct result of the cultural growth of Waimea. George

WAIMEA & MAUNA KEA

and Shirley Isaacs, other patrons and the Hawaiian Preparatory Academy (HPA) have successfully started a new tradition while preserving an old one. They have restored a 1915 schoolhouse and eloquently transformed it into an **art center** (☎ 881-4056; bnouges@hpa.edu; 61-1268 Kawaihae Rd; ✆ 10am-5pm Tue-Sat, or by appointment). Functioning as a gallery and museum, the center offers an excellent collection of both local and international artwork.

On entering the elongated plantation-style schoolhouse one is greeted by a Big Island classic: Herb Kawainui Kane's *The Arrival of Captain Cook at Kealakekua Bay in January 1779*, a studied visual account of the famous initial contact between Hawaiians and Europeans. As one stares down the building, there are six connecting classrooms visible. Originally separated by sliding doors equipped with chalkboards, the layout keeps the doors open to provide an ideal exhibition setting. At the far end of the hall, Hawaiian artist Madge Tennent's *Lei Queen Fantasia* is stunning in its impressionistic style and grand scale, emphasizing the color and beauty of Hawaiian culture. Other highlights in the collection include engravings by 16th-century German artist Albrecht Dürer and an etching by Rembrandt.

'Art brings a dimension to community that is very special,' says curator Bernard Nougés. Opened in August 2003, the center offers opportunities for HPA middle school faculty and gives students access to the work for analysis and copying. Nougés also runs an auction, which raises student scholarship money. The arrival of the center in Waimea provided one of the only venues on the Big Island exhibiting significant works of art while also showcasing one of Hawaii's most prominent collections of fine art outside of the Honolulu Academy of Arts. Located across the street from Parker Sq, the Isaacs Art Center is not to be missed.

CHURCH ROW

Waimea's first Christian church was a grass hut built in 1830. It was replaced in 1838 by a wooden structure that was also built using coral stones carved out of the reef. They named it Imiola, which means 'seeking salvation.'

The current **Imiola Congregational Church** (admission free; ✆ services 8:30am & 10:15am) was constructed in 1857, and restored in 1976. The interior is simple and beautiful; it's built entirely of koa, most of it dating back to the original construction. In the churchyard is the grave of missionary Lorenzo Lyons, who arrived in 1832 and spent 54 years in Waimea. Lyons wrote many of the hymns, including the popular 'Hawai'i Aloha,' that are still sung in Hawaiian here each Sunday. Also in the garden is the church bell, which is too heavy for the church roof to support.

The green-steepled church next door is the all-Hawaiian **Ke Ola Mau Loa Church**. Buddhists, Baptists and Mormons also have places of worship in this row.

Activities

Waimea is the place for horseback riding, and the island's best outfit is near town. **Dahana Ranch Roughriders** (☎ 885-0057, 888-399-0057; www.dahanaranch.com; ride per 1/2 hr $55/100; ✆ 9am, 11am, 1pm & 3pm) is owned and operated by a native Hawaiian family – and it's both a working ranch and the most-established horseback tour company on the Big Island. They breed, raise, train and use only their own American Quarter Horses for their tours. Horses cross the open range of a working cattle ranch rather than follow trails, and you can trot, canter and gallop. Rides are by appointment only. For a special 'city slicker' adventure ($130 per person, minimum four people), you can help drive a 100-head herd of cattle. Dahana is also the only outfit on the island that lets very young children (aged three and up) join in. The ranch is located 7.5 miles east of Waimea, off Old Mamalahoa Hwy.

Courses

In early November the annual **Waimea Ukulele & Slack Key Guitar Institute** (☎ 885-6017; www.kahiluthetre.org) brings prominent local

---

NAME DROPPING

Waimea is also referred to as Kamuela, which is the Hawaiian spelling of Samuel. Although some say the name comes from an early postmaster named Samuel Spencer, most claim it's for Samuel Parker of Parker Ranch fame. Regardless, the result is the same: confusion. The post office made the official change to Kamuela to avoid confusion with Waimeas on the other islands.

musicians together for a concert at the Kahilu Theatre (p135) and a series of workshops ($40 to $60 each) ranging from beginner to master classes, including songwriting and improv. Such greats as Led Ka'apana and Dennis Kamakahi have taught at the institute. Evening *kanikapila* (open-mike jam sessions) charge just $5 admission.

Waimea for Children

Kids typically enjoy the novelty of a **horse-drawn wagon ride** (☎ 885-7655; www.parkerranch .com; Parker Ranch Center, 67-1185 Mamalahoa Hwy; adult/child $15/12; ☿ hourly departures 10am-2pm Tue-Sat). The guides put on a lively show and tell stories of life on the range, as you see acres of cattle country. Rain is no problem because the wagon is covered.

Festivals & Events

Small rodeo events occur year-round. The major events include:

Fourth of July Rodeo (Jul 4) A uniquely Waimea event (with cattle roping, bull riding and other hoopla), which celebrated its 42nd anniversary in 2004.

Round-Up Rodeo (1st Mon in Sep) Another whip-cracking event after Labor Day weekend.

Aloha Festivals Ho'olaule'a During the statewide Aloha Festivals in August and September, with food, games, art and crafts, and entertainment; the Aloha Festival Paniolo Parade honors local cowboys with marching bands, elaborately decorated floats and equestrian units.

Christmas parade In early December, the town gets into the Kalikimaka spirit with a block party.

Sleeping

Waimea's well-priced accommodations and central location makes it a good alternative for travelers who prefer upcountry scenery, cooler weather and open spaces.

MIDRANGE & TOP END

If you're seeking comfort, charm and insider information, a plethora of B&Bs fit the bill.

Waimea Suite B&B (☎ 937-2833; cookshi@aol.com; Lokua St; ste $145) If you stay at this immaculate, spacious suite, you'll have the added benefit of meeting your host, who knows almost everything about Waimea and the Big Island. Located 2 miles east of town off Hwy 19, the suite has a private entrance and sleeps up to four people. Amenities include a huge kitchen stocked with local snacks and condiments, dining lanai, cable, TV, VCR, telephone and stereo. Two-night minimum

stay required (three during holidays). Rates include breakfast.

Aaah, The Views B&B (☎ 885-3455; www.aaah theviews.com; 66-1773 Alaneo St; s $65-75, d $75-85, ste $115-125, all incl breakfast) A longtime B&B that's been under new ownership since 2004, this place has a playful air, like a tree house. Guests are welcome to use the common kitchen, yoga and meditation rooms, and hammocks on the porch overlooking a stream. The Dream Room is a loft-style suite with multiple windows and a skylight, a Jacuzzi tub and an outdoor shower on a private deck. The Treetop Suite, also with a private deck and entrance, can accommodate up to six people. All rooms have cable TV, VCR, phone, fridge, microwave and coffee maker. Rates include breakfast.

Waimea Gardens Cottages (☎ 885-8550; www .waimeagardens.com; studio $140, cottage d $150-160) Just 2 miles west of town (near the intersection of Kawaihae Rd and Hwy 250), two charming cottages offer more-upscale lodging, with polished hardwood floors, antique furnishings, patio French doors and a deck. One has a fireplace, the other has a Japanese-style soaking tub adjacent to a private garden. There's also a spacious studio unit near the lawn, where a seasonal stream flows. There's a three-day minimum stay. All rates include breakfast.

Belle Vue Cottage & Suites (☎ 885-7732; www .hawaii-bellevue.com; Konokohau Rd; d $95-175, per extra person $25) Run by Vivian and Gayland Baker, this B&B boasts views of Mauna Loa, Mauna Kea, Haleakala and the 'Gold Coast.' Sitting atop Knob Hill and framed by the Kohala Mountains, it is located within walking distance of shops and restaurants: at the west end of town take Opelu Rd just behind Merriman's Restaurant. There are three suites, one in the main house and two in the adjacent two-story cottage. The penthouse suite has a king-size bed, plus queen sofa bed, a kitchenette, private bathroom, living room, TV, lanai, and private entrance. The other suites offer similar amenities in a studio size apartment with queen beds. The hosts speak French and German as well as English, creating a cozy atmosphere with a nice European feel, and there is a fresh island continental breakfast (included in the price) and cut flowers. Families with children are catered for as rooms are equipped with cribs.

Jacaranda Inn (☎ 885-8813; www.jacarandainn.com; 65-1444 Kawaihae Rd; ste $159/225, cottage $450; 🖳) More than a B&B, this luxurious guesthouse was originally the ranchland's bunkhouse for the Parker Ranch. Accommodating up to ?? people, there are eight unique suites, plus an additional three-room cottage. The styles range from Hawaiian Plantation to Victorian, Western, Asian and contemporary. All suites include grand private bathrooms, sitting room and lanai. Most suites also include bathtubs with double Jacuzzi jets and TV. Located 1 mile west of town on Hwy 19, the inn sits on 12 acres of former ranchland. No details are spared in this country getaway. The main house, built in 1897, serves daily breakfast in the historic garden room and has phone and Internet access. Nonrefundable reservations are required one month in advance and rates include breakfast.

Waimea's two hotels are reasonably priced, no-frills lodging options.

Kamuela Inn (☎ 885-4243, 800-555-8968; www .kamuelainn.com; 1600 Kawaihae Rd; r $60-85, ste $90-185) Clean and simple, the Kamuela Inn is a deal. All rooms have TV and private bathroom, but only 'new wing' rooms have phones. Suites sleep up to four people and resemble a modest apartment unit, with a refrigerator, stove and cooking equipment. Free pastries and coffee are on offer in the morning.

Waimea Country Lodge (☎ 885-4100, 800-367-5004; www.castleresorts.com; 65-1210 Lindsey Rd; r $100-105, with kitchenette $115) Rooms at this small motel have private bathroom, phone, TV and a view of the Kohala hills. Standard rooms have two double beds; superior rooms have two kings or queens, plus a fridge. There can be early-morning noise from trucks unloading at the nearby shopping center.

Eating
BUDGET
Despite its high standard of living, Waimea has its fair share of tasty cheap eats, too.

Maha's Café (☎ 885-0693; Waimea Center, 65-1158 Mamalahoa Hwy; breakfast $3-5, lunch under $10; 🕑 8am-4:30pm Thu-Mon) Stepping into Maha's is like going home – if your mom is a former resort chef who whips up delicious island-style fare. Guaranteed to please are the poi pancakes with coconut syrup, and grilled fish with taro and greens. It has a cozy setting inside Waimea's first frame house, which was built in 1852.

Tako Taco (☎ 887-1717; Kawaihae Rd; meals $3.25-8.50; 🕑 11am-8pm) Stop in here for some fresh Waimea-style Mexican food that would make any *paniolo* proud! It serves fresh vegetarian, fish and meat burritos, tacos, quesadillas, nachos, tostadas and organic salads and offers an excellent side bar of homemade salsas to complement your order. Eat in the eclectic shack or take out for a picnic with the kids across the road at Waimea Park. The service is fast and portions are adequate.

Hawaiian Style Café (☎ 885-4295; Hayashi Bldg; meals $5-10; 🕑 6am-12:45pm Mon-Fri, 7:30am-noon Sun, 4-7:30pm Tue-Fri) Work up your appetite with a surf or nice hike before stuffing yourself on some greasy local grinds at this classic establishment. The restaurant is in a funky old building with a dinner-style counter and booths in the front and back rooms. Grand portions include: egg dishes ($6), French toast ($4.50), beef stew ($6.50) and chicken-fried steak ($7.50). Almost all of the lunch and dinner plates come with two scoops of rice. The Friday special luau plate comes with *kalua* pig, *lomilomi* salmon (minced, salted salmon, diced tomato and green onion), pickled vegetables and poi ($10). The *loco moco* (dish of rice, fried egg and hamburger patty topped with gravy or other condiments) here is a must, by far the biggest and best on the island, brah! Be sure to finish your plate otherwise you may get *da stink eye* from the chef. It's closed the last Saturday, Sunday and Monday of every month, and often closes for a few weeks in October.

Waimea Coffee & Co (☎ 885-4472; Parker Sq; 🕑 6:30am-5pm Mon-Fri, 9am-4pm Sat, 10am-3pm Sun) Specializing in sweet snacks, ice cream, teas, espresso and 100% pure Kona coffee. New ownership brings some nice additions, like homemade chai tea and a newly introduced lunch menu including wraps, salads and personal pizzas.

The Parker Ranch Center and the adjacent Waimea Center have a local deli, bakery and ice-cream shop. Both shopping centers offer

---

TOP FIVE WAIMEA EATS

Daniel Thiebaut (opposite)
Hawaiian Style Café (above)
Maha's Café (left)
Merriman's (opposite)
Tako Taco (above)

good and reasonably priced Korean, Thai, Chinese and Japanese restaurants.

Groceries

For the freshest organic produce, cheeses, flowers and lei, island-made jams and homemade goods, check out the **farmers' market** (☎ 7am-noon Sat) at the Hawaiian Home Lands office, near the 55-mile marker on Hwy 19. The best supermarket is **KTA Super Store** (☎ 885-8866; 65-1158 Mamalahoa Hwy; ☎ 9am-7pm Mon-Fri, 9am-5pm Sat & Sun) in the Waimea Center. **Healthyways II** (☎ 885-6775; Parker Ranch Center; ☎ 9am-7pm Mon-Sat, 9am-5pm Sun) is an ample natural food store with a choice of hot and cold deli for meals to take on the road.

MIDRANGE

With such varied dining options, visitors can eat well without draining the wallet.

Aioli's (☎ 885-6325; Opelo Plaza, 65-1227 Opelo Rd; dinner mains $13-21; ☎ 11am-8pm Tue-Thu, 11am-9pm Fri & Sat) Frequented by locals, Aioli's bakes its own breads, cakes and pastries, and at lunch serves well-made sandwiches, salads and soups. Dinners vary from goat-cheese enchiladas to fresh seafood and steaks. There's no liquor license, but you can bring your own beer or wine (no corkage fee). Take-out is also available.

Waimea Ranch House (☎ 885-2088; Waimea Center; lunch $7-11, dinner $13-31; ☎ lunch Wed-Sun, dinner Wed-Mon) It's a popular family spot serving classic Italian fare. Two rooms make up this restaurant: one houses the bar, where smoking is allowed; the nicer dining area, complete with fireplace, provides the cozy ranch house atmosphere.

TOP END

Several award-winning restaurants make Waimea a terrific stopover for 'foodies.'

Merriman's (☎ 885-6822; Opelo Plaza, 65-1227 Opelo Rd; lunch $7-12, dinner $17-33; ☎ lunch Mon-Fri, dinner daily) A pioneer of fine dining in Waimea, Merriman's still ranks among the Big Island's best. Chef and owner Peter Merriman pioneered the use of fresh, organically grown and chemical-free products from Big Island farmers and fishers. A specialty is the delicious wok-charred 'ahi, blackened on the outside and sashimi-like inside. At dinner, there are a few vegetarian meals ($17 to $19) and seafood and meat dishes ($24 to $36). At lunch, there are various salads,

soups, sandwiches and a few hot grilled dishes, including a tasty coconut chicken with peanut sauce ($10) and beef kebab with Waimea tomatoes ($11.50).

Edelweiss (☎ 885-6800; Kawaihae Rd; lunch $8-12, dinner $25-35; ☎ lunch Tue-Sat, dinner Tue-Sat) Also on Waimea's 'restaurant row,' this restaurant with its rich German fare fits well in the cool Waimea climate. There is a well chosen, albeit simple, selection of wines, and of course German beers on tap. Starters include a cup of Manhattan chowder and a simple salad with tarragon dressing, or opt for a salad with Waimea tomatoes, Maui onions and English Stilton cheese. Complete dinners include both the soup of the day and a salad, a vegetable and coffee or tea. Weiner schnitzel ($22.50) comes with creamed spinach and a buttery, mustard-based potato salad. The busy wait staff typically spews out a laundry list of daily specials to a packed house.

AUTHOR'S CHOICE

Daniel Thiebaut (☎ 887-2200; www.daniel thiebaut.com; 65-1259 Kawaihae Rd; lunch mains $9-15, dinner mains $20-30; ☎ lunch & dinner) Topping the list of gourmet establishments, Thiebaut's features French-Asian cuisine and a pleasing plantation-style setting in the historic Chock In Store building. The menu features local produce, fish and meat. For lunch vegetarians will enjoy mac-nut tofu with stir-fried veggies and tahini sauce ($9.50). With other highlights like cream of butternut squash soup ($6.50) and seared 'ahi (yellowfin tuna) on a bed of wilted spinach ($30) it is hard to make a wrong choice. Top it all off with chocolate decadence and your choice of more than 30 wines available by the glass. You'll have to get there early just to decide. If there's a wait, pull up a rattan chair in the bar/lounge area; reservations definitely recommended, especially at dinner.

Entertainment

Waimea isn't exactly hopping with nightlife.

Kahilu Theatre (☎ 885-6017, box office 885-6868; www.kahilutheatre.org; Parker Ranch Center, 67-1185 Mamalahoa Hwy; admission $15-45; ☎ showtimes vary) This venue headlines quite an impressive list of performances, including classic and contemporary music, dance and theater, featuring performers from George Winston to the Paul Taylor Dance Company to the Harlem Gospel Choir. A big draw is the annual Waimea Ukulele & Slack Key Guitar Institute (p132).

Shopping

The shopping, like the dining, in Waimea appeals to locals and tourists. This is a good sign as you know that you're getting quality local arts, crafts and apparel as opposed to some common souvenir found on parts of the island with more tourist traffic.

Gallery of Great Things (☎ 885-7706; Parker Sq, 65-1279 Kawaihae Rd) A standout among Waimea's antiques, art and collectibles galleries. Browse for Hawaiian, Polynesian and Asian art, furnishings and photographs.

Without Boundaries (☎ 885-1959; Waimea Center) Part gift store and part travel agency, selling merchandise that's mostly nouveau, not Hawaiian. Notables include soaps, teas, candles, Hawaiian-style bags and local-made longboard skateboards. Also look for Hawaiian hand-painted silk scarves and historic note cards featuring Kailua-Kona (c 1895) and JFK's presidential visit to Waikiki in 1963.

Waimea General Store (☎ 885-4479; Parker Sq, 65-1279 Kawaihae Rd) Don't let the name fool you: this store sells everything from Hawaiian cookbooks to toys to locally made jams and candy. The kitchen department is especially popular and carries items that are hard to find elsewhere.

Mauna Kea Galleries (☎ 887-2244; www.mauna keagalleries.com; 65-1298 Kawaihae Rd) This gallery/store has all things Hawaiian and Polynesian. It is a collector's heaven, with vintage furniture, posters, paintings, photographs, prints and paraphernalia. There is a lot of attention to detail as each piece is a classic in the collection.

Reyn's (☎ 885-4493; Parker Ranch Center, 67-1185 Mamalahoa Hwy) At this local version of Brooks Brothers you'll find the understated aloha shirts that islanders wear in lieu of suits. The classic Reyn's look uses Hawaiian fabrics in reverse.

Getting There & Around

While there's Waimea-Kohala Airport south of Waimea, flights are rare and inconsistent. Check with **Pacific Wings** (☎ 888-575-4546; www

.pacificwings.com) for possible flights from Honolulu and Kahului, Maui. The **Hele-On Bus** (☎ 961-8744; www.co.hawaii.hi.us/mass_transit /heleonbus.html) goes from Waimea to Kailua-Kona on its No 16 Kailua-Kona route ($3, one hour), and to Hilo on its No 7 Downtown Hilo route ($4.50, 1¾ hours). The bus stops at the Parker Ranch Center.

The drive from Kailua-Kona is 40 miles along Hwy 190, which becomes Old Mamalahoa Hwy in town. From Hilo the drive is 55 miles along Hwy 19 around the Hamakua Coast.

A car is indispensable in Waimea, though it's a compact, three-stoplight town. There is ample free parking here. For information on car hire, see p241.

AROUND WAIMEA
Kohala Forest Reserve

Heading east on Hwy 19 approximately 3 miles out of town towards Honoka'a, there is an excellent hike along the **Kohala Forest Reserve Trail** leading to unparalleled views of the back of Waipi'o Valley. Turn left on White Rd (also called Lindsey Subdivision Rd) and go up 1 mile to the end of the road and park before the gate. Entering through the gate (close it behind you!) walk 1.5 miles past Waimea Reservoir to another gate signaling the entrance to the Kohala Forest Reserve.

The difference in scenery around here is immediate, as you'll enter a forest of large ohia trees, giving a taste of what these hills felt like before the arrival of the ranches. Enjoy the peaceful songs of the birds as you meander up the wide gravel path following the Upper Hamakua Ditch. Within 500yd into the reserve, the trail narrows and you'll find yourself passing a massive bamboo forest on your right. About 2 miles into the hike the bamboo fades and you enter groves of ginger, which provide a sweet fragrance. The trail here is a bit rocky and weaves another 500yd, converging and leaving the ditch at various points.

You will certainly know when you've reached the first viewpoint. Just below are the upper streams of Waipi'o Valley drainage, and the view out to the ocean is magnificent. If you arrive just after rain, the waterfalls will be surging, adding to the splendor of the moment. The trail continues along the contours of the gulches below for another 2 miles and is very pleasant, offering different

HOLGER LEUE

Pololu Valley lookout (p126), North Kohala

ANN CECIL

'Anaeho'omalu Beach (p111), Waikaloa Resort Area

Coral 'graffiti' (p199) on lava, Kohala Coast

HOLGER LEUE

Horses grazing, Parker Ranch (p131)

Rugged landscape, near Waimea

Telescope observatories (p140), Mauna Kea

views of the valley with each turn. The trail is narrow and follows the ditch the whole way; if it is wet, watch your step, as the drop off is abrupt. It is a nice hike regardless of the weather, but if you can catch a clear day you'll get the peaceful forest setting and the breathtaking views, making this one of the finest short hikes on the Big Island.

Waimea to Honoka'a

Hwy 19 goes east from Waimea to Honoka'a through rolling hills and cattle pastures, with views of Mauna Kea to the south.

For a peaceful, scented back road, turn right off Hwy 19 onto the Old Mamalahoa Hwy just west of the 52-mile marker. (If coming from Hilo, turn left at the 43-mile marker opposite Tex Drive In and then take the next immediate right.) This 10-mile detour winds through hill country, with small roadside ranches, old wooden fences and grazing horses. This is a part of Hawaii that tourists have yet to discover. Nobody's in a hurry on this road, if they're on it at all. It can make an interesting alternate route for cyclists, although you'll need to be cautious as the road is narrow and winding.

Drop into the old miner's quarry cave along the roadside 4 miles from the turnoff coming from Waimea. The entrance is on the inside of a prominent bow in the road. Overgrown with ferns, it feels like you are entering a hobbit home. There is a labyrinth of interesting tunnels dug by early miners. Bring a good flashlight and decent shoes.

MAUNA KEA

Mauna Kea ('White Mountain,' or 'Mountain of Wakea') is Hawai'i's highest peak, and its 13,796ft summit now houses 13 astronomical observatories, considered the greatest collection of major astronomical telescopes in the world. To the Hawaiians, Mauna Kea is the abode of the gods where the islands were created. With direct roots to their creation myth, Mauna Kea is probably the most sacred site in all of Hawaii. Considering this and the resurgence of Hawaiian culture since the '70s, you can imagine the controversy over the activities on the summit.

The access road to Mauna Kea starts off passing through open range with grazing cattle, where you'll probably see Eurasian skylarks in the grass. If you're lucky you might see an 'io (Hawaiian hawk) soaring overhead. The grassy mountain slopes are the habitat of many birds, including the nene and the *palila*, a small yellow honeycreeper that lives nowhere else in the world. Mouflon (mountain sheep) and feral goats roam freely. Silversword, a distant relative of the sunflower, is also found at this high elevation. For more information about wildlife in Hawaii see p41.

SADDLE UP BRAH!

As the name states, Saddle Rd (Hwy 200) is the road that runs along a saddle-shaped valley between the island's two highest points, Mauna Kea to the north and Mauna Loa to the south. At sunrise and sunset there's a gentle glow on the mountains and a light show on the clouds. In the early morning, it's crisp enough to see your breath, and if you take the spur road up to Mauna Kea, you'll reach permafrost.

Although the 50-mile, two-lane road is paved, it is narrow, winding and hilly, with blind turns, no lights and frequent thick fog. Most car-rental contracts prohibit travel on this road; **Harper Car & Truck Rentals** (☎ 969-1478, 800-852-9993; www.harpershawaii.com; 456 Kalaniana'ole Ave, Hilo) is the only company with no restrictions on Saddle Rd. On this remote route, accidents are quite frequent and often fatal, especially from dusk until just after dawn. There are no gas stations or facilities along the way.

If you're coming from Kona, the road starts off in cattle ranchland with rolling grassy hills and eucalyptus groves. The pastures and fences soon become fewer among fields of lava and the military takes over where the cows leave off. You'll eventually come to the Quonset huts of the Pohakuloa Military Training Area. Most vehicles here are military-owned, although in hunting season you'll come across a fair number of pickup trucks.

From Hilo, the terrain of Saddle Rd is ohia-fern forest, shrubby near the mountain but thicker and taller toward Hilo. This section of road has been upgraded, but it's winding; beware of oncoming drivers who hog the center of the road to cut curves.

DETOUR: HAKALAU FOREST NATIONAL WILDLIFE REFUGE

To go off the beaten path and see real Big Island wilderness, drive Mana/Keanakolu Rd to the Hakalau Forest National Wildlife Refuge – a place few locals have ever ventured. This extremely remote wildlife refuge protects a portion of the state's largest koa and ohia forest, which provides habitat for endangered bird species, including the native hoary bat and 'io (Hawaiian hawk). About 7000 acres are open to public access, but only on weekends and state holidays.

The drive takes two hours from either Waimea or Hilo; 4WD is absolutely necessary and the road might be closed after rains. You'll be roughin' it, as there are no facilities, signage or trails. The only folks who typically come here are ranchers and hunters, and you're far from anywhere if you get stuck en route.

To get here from Waimea, drive east on Hwy 19 until you reach the 55-mile marker; turn onto Mana Rd, which leads around the eastern flank of Mauna Kea. After 15 miles, the road becomes Keanakolu Rd and continues about 25 miles to Summit Rd (the access road to Mauna Kea summit) and then connects with Saddle Rd (which is another starting point, if you're coming from Hilo). Along the way, you'll pass through private ranches, and numerous cattle gates must be opened and closed.

About halfway between Waimea and Saddle Rd, you'll pass a stone monument to David Douglas, the famed Scottish botanist for whom the Douglas fir tree is named. Douglas planted trees here and in 1834 died under mysterious circumstances: his gored body was found trapped with an angry bull in a pit, on the slopes of Mauna Kea. Hunters commonly dug and camouflaged pits to trap feral cattle, but the probability of both Douglas and a bull falling in together seemed unlikely. A key suspect was an Australian convict named Ned Gurney, who had been hiding out nearby, and was the last person to see Douglas alive.

You need a permit, which you can obtain by calling or writing to the **refuge manager** (☎ 933-6915; 32 Kino'ole St, Hilo, HI 96720; ☽ 8am-4pm Mon-Fri). An ideal time to visit is during the second week in October, which is National Wildlife Refuge Week, when Hawaiian ornithological experts and rangers are on hand. Another possibility is to do volunteer tree planting on weekends, but you'd have to arrange this beforehand. Staff is very limited, and the first priorities are birds and plants, not tourists, but they do welcome interested visitors. **Hawaii Forest & Trail** (☎ 331-8505, 800-464-1993; www.hawaii-forest.com; tours $145) offers a birding adventure tour in the Hakalau refuge.

Environmental protection is paramount here because the mountain is the exclusive home of numerous plants, birds and insects – and the introduction of non-native species upsets the existing ecology. A predominant invasive plant here is mullein, which has soft woolly leaves and shoots up a tall stalk. In spring, the stalks get so loaded down with flowers that they bend over from the weight of big yellow 'helmets.' Ranchers inadvertently introduced mullein as a freeloading weed in grass seed.

Orientation & Information

To reach the summit and the Onizuka Visitor Information Station, first take the Mauna Kea Access Rd, which begins heading east off Saddle Rd, just past the 28-mile marker opposite a hunters' check station. Bear in mind that the Mauna Kea summit is not a national, state or county park. There are no facilities, restaurants, gas stations or

emergency services anywhere on Mauna Kea. It's strongly recommended that 4WD vehicles are used beyond the Onizuka Visitor Information Station. For more information see p144.

Weather conditions can change rapidly, and daytime temperatures range from the 50s (°F) to below freezing. The summit can be windy, and temperatures are just as low in observatory viewing rooms as outside. Bring warm clothing, sunglasses and sunscreen. Call the **recorded hotline** (☎ 935-6268) for info on weather and road conditions.

Dangers & Annoyances

At altitudes above the Onizuka Visitor Information Station's 9200ft level, your body might not adjust properly to the low atmospheric pressure (roughly half the pressure at sea level). Altitude sickness (see p245) and respiratory conditions (see p247) are common, and the symptoms include nausea, headaches, drowsiness, impaired reason, loss of balance, shortness of breath and dehydration. If you feel ill at the summit, the only way to recover is to descend. Kids under 16, pregnant women, and those with high blood pressure or circulatory conditions should not go to the summit.

Absolutely all travelers to the summit should stop first at the Onizuka center for at least 30 minutes to acclimatize before continuing up the mountain.

Sights

ONIZUKA VISITOR INFORMATION STATION

Officially the **Onizuka Center for International Astronomy** (☎ 961-2180; www.ifa.hawaii.edu/info/vis; ☯ 9am-10pm), the center was named for Ellison Onizuka, a Big Island native, and one of the astronauts who perished in the 1986 *Challenger* space-shuttle disaster.

The center is approximately one hour's drive from Hilo, Waimea or Waikoloa, and two hours from Kailua-Kona. The drive to the Onizuka Visitor Information Station from the Saddle Rd intersection is just over 6 miles, plus 2500ft in elevation. On the way you'll see

majestic clouds spread out like a soft feather bed below you. Mauna Kea doesn't appear as a single main peak but rather a jumble of lava-rock peaks, some black, some red-brown, some seasonally snowcapped.

More than 100,000 tourists visit Mauna Kea annually, and most pass through the Onizuka Visitor Information Station. Stopping here is a must to acclimatize for at least a half-hour for the journey to the summit. The rangers, interpretive guides and volunteers are extremely knowledgeable on all aspects of Mauna Kea, including hiking, historical and cultural significance, road access and astronomy.

The center is modest: a room with photo displays of the observatories, information on discoveries made from the summit, computer-driven astronomy programs and exhibits on the mountain's history, ecology and geology. You can watch a video about Mauna Kea's observatories or pick another of many astronomy videos to watch while you acclimatize, perhaps with a cup of coffee, hot chocolate, instant noodles or freeze-dried astronaut food, which are all sold here.

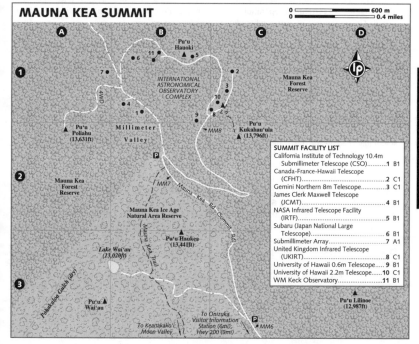

MAUNA KEA SUMMIT

SUMMIT FACILITY LIST

California Institute of Technology 10.4m Submillimeter Telescope (CSO)	**1** B1
Canada-France-Hawaii Telescope (CFHT)	**2** C1
Gemini Northern 8m Telescope	**3** C1
James Clerk Maxwell Telescope (JCMT)	**4** B1
NASA Infrared Telescope Facility (IRTF)	**5** B1
Subaru (Japan National Large Telescope)	**6** B1
Submillimeter Array	**7** A1
United Kingdom Infrared Telescope (UKIRT)	**8** C1
University of Hawaii 0.6m Telescope	**9** B1
University of Hawaii 2.2m Telescope	**10** C1
WM Keck Observatory	**11** B1

Across from the visitor center, a 10-minute uphill hike on a well-trodden trail crests **Pu'u Keonehehe'e**, a cinder cone, and offers glorious sunset views.

SUMMIT RD

Visitors are allowed to travel up to the summit during the daytime, because vehicle headlights are not allowed between sunset and sunrise because they interfere with astronomical observation. Driving on the summit after sunset is strongly discouraged. See p144 for important information on driving to the summit.

About 4.5 miles up from the visitor information station, on the east side of the road, is an area dubbed 'moon valley,' because it's where the Apollo astronauts rehearsed with their lunar rover before their journey to the real moonscape.

If you drive to the summit instead of attempting the grueling hike, you'll miss a few important Mauna Kea sights. But nonhikers have another option to see the adze quarry at Keanakakoi and Lake Waiau (opposite). As you get near the summit, you can park at the hairpin turn just before the final ascent to the observatories (look for the 10mph sign and you'll see the trailhead signs), then walk down and over to see the lake (turn right at the trail junction) or to the quarry (keep heading straight downhill). It'll take an hour or so to see both, depending on your level of fitness and acclimatization.

SUMMIT OBSERVATORIES

At the summit, massive dome-shaped observatories rise up from the vast, stark terrain. The juxtaposition is striking: you'll feel as

---

ON THE SUMMIT

The University of Hawai'i (UH) holds the lease on the 'Mauna Kea Science Reserve,' which comprises approximately 11,216 acres above the 12,000ft level – essentially the entire summit. The university built the summit's first telescope in 1968 with a 24-inch mirror, and now leases property to others. Under one of the lease provisions UH receives observing time at each telescope. Of the 13 telescopes currently in operation, all have base stations in Hilo, except WM Keck and the Canada-France-Hawaii Telescope, which have bases in Waimea.

The **WM Keck Observatory** (www2.keck.hawaii.edu), a joint project of the California Institute of Technology (Caltech), the University of California and NASA, houses the world's largest and most-powerful optical-infrared telescope. Keck featured a breakthrough in telescope design. Previously, the sheer weight of the glass mirrors was a limiting factor in telescope construction. The Keck telescope has a unique honeycomb design with 36 hexagonal mirror segments (each 6ft across) that function as a single piece of glass.

In January 1996, the 390in Keck I telescope discovered the most-distant galaxy ever observed, at 14 billion light-years away. The discovery of this 'new galaxy,' in the constellation Virgo, has brought into question the very age of the universe itself, because the stars making up the galaxy seemingly predate the 'big bang' that is thought to have created the universe.

A replica of the first telescope, Keck II became operational in October 1996. The two interchangeable telescopes can function as one – 'like a pair of binoculars searching the sky' – allowing them to study the cores of elliptical galaxies. The cost for the twin Keck observatories, each weighing 300 tons and reaching a height of eight stories, is approximately $200 million.

Just 150yd west is Japan's **Subaru Telescope** (www.naoj.org), which opened in 1999 after a decade of construction. Its $300-million price tag makes this the most-expensive observatory yet constructed, and its 22-ton mirror, reaching 27ft in diameter, is the largest optical mirror in existence. In case you're wondering, Subaru is the Japanese word for the Pleiades constellation (and the telescope has nothing to do with the automaker!). The Subaru Telescope offers free tours (see p143).

Recently completed is the Submillimeter Array, sponsored by the Smithsonian Astrophysical Observatory and a Taiwanese institute, and UH is envisioning future projects to maintain Mauna Kea's status as the premier site for astronomical research. In coming years, some existing telescopes might become obsolete and lose funding, resulting in fewer but superior telescopes. Learn more about all the observatories at www.ifa.hawaii.edu.

if you've found a futuristic human colony on another planet. These observatories constitute the greatest collection of state-of-the-art optical, infrared and millimeter-submillimeter telescopes on earth. Viewing conditions on Mauna Kea are optimal with clear, dry and stable air that is also relatively free of dust and smog. At almost 14,000ft, the summit is above 40% of the earth's atmosphere, and over 90% of its water vapor. Only the Andes match Mauna Kea for cloudless nights, but air turbulence in the Andes makes viewing more difficult there.

You won't see a lot inside the observatories. Currently only two have visitor galleries but they're unstaffed and minimal: the **WM Keck Observatory visitor gallery** (www2.keck.Hawaii .edu; admission free; 🕙 10am-4pm Mon-Fri) includes a display, 12-minute video screening, public bathrooms, a viewing area inside the Keck I dome, and the **University of Hawai'i 2.2m Telescope** (admission free; 🕙 10am-4pm Mon-Thu). The Subaru Telescope and visitors information station offer guided summit tours (p143).

At the summit, sunsets and moonrises are breathtaking. If you look toward the east at sunset, you can see 'the shadow,' which is a gigantic silhouette of Mauna Kea looming over Hilo. Moonrises at such a high altitude cause unusual sights, depending on the clouds and weather: the moon might appear squashed and misshapen, or it might resemble a brushfire.

Activities

STARGAZING

The Onizuka Visitor Information Station (p139) offers a free star-gazing program from 6pm to 10pm nightly, weather permitting (but bad weather prevents stargazing only two to three nights per month). Visitors generally need not call ahead, but if you'd like to confirm that the program is on, call the Visitor Information Station. There is no pre-recorded message about the status. At 9200ft the skies are among the clearest, driest and darkest on the planet. In fact, at the station you're above the elevation of most major telescopes worldwide. This is the only place you can use telescopes on Mauna Kea; there are no public telescopes on the summit. Remember that stargazing is hit-or-miss depending on cloud cover and moon phase. The busiest nights are Friday and Saturday.

Two worthwhile programs are offered the first and third Saturdays of each month. The first is called 'The Universe Tonight,' where a special speaker from one of the observatories will present to the public their recent discoveries. On the third Saturday of the month the 'Malalo I Ka Lani Po' program features a speaker from the community covering a cultural aspect of Mauna Kea. Both programs begin at 6pm and are followed by the regular evening stargazing.

HIKING

The daunting 6-mile **Mauna Kea Summit Trail** starts at an altitude of 9200ft and climbs almost 4600ft. High altitude, steep grades and brisk weather make the hike very strenuous. Don't attempt it in inclement weather. Get a very early start if you're braving this climb, and give yourself the maximum number of daylight hours; most people need at least five to reach the summit, slightly less for the return trip (10 hours total). Before you start, go to the Onizuka Visitor Information Station to get a hiking map and sign the hiker registration form; rangers are available to answer questions.

The hike starts near the end of the paved road above the Onizuka Visitor Information Station. Park at the center and walk up the road about 200yd. Before it curves to the right and becomes gravel, an old track leads off to the left. Follow the 'Humu'ula Trail' signs and climb uphill, taking a right at the next fork. After 100yd you'll see another trail sign pointing uphill. From here the trail continues doggedly upward, while numerous false spur trails only lead back to the access road. The first mile is marked with signs, and starts out roughly parallel to the summit road, then diverges around cinder cones.

DIMMING THE LIGHTS

You might notice, as you tour around the Big Island, that the streetlights have an unusual orange glow. In order to provide Mauna Kea astronomers with the best viewing conditions possible, streetlights on the island have been converted to low-impact sodium. Rather than using the full iridescent spectrum, these orange lights use only a few wavelengths, which the telescopes can be adjusted to remove.

After around 45 minutes to an hour, the summit road comes back into full view, about 100yd to your right. Remember to take time to acclimatize as you go, with frequent rest breaks if necessary. Vegetation begins to disappear and the path is marked intermittently with red painted poles, and sometimes with reflectors. The trail continues upward through ash-and-cinder terrain. Past the two-hour point, the trail starts to ascend more gradually as it weaves among giant cinder cones. After a level traverse over some basalt flows and glacial till, the trail rises through white boulders and the summit of Mauna Kea looms far ahead.

Along the way you'll pass the **Mauna Kea Ice Age Natural Area Reserve**. A Pleistocene glacier once moved down this slope, carrying earth and stones that carved grooves, which are still visible in the rocks. Entering a broad valley after about three hours, the battering winds die down temporarily. A sharp, short ascent on crumbly soil takes you over a rise. **Keanakako'i**, an ancient adze quarry, comes into view off to the right; look for large piles of bluish-black chips. From this spot, extremely dense and hard basalt was quarried by ancient Hawaiians to make tools and weapons that were traded throughout the islands. As this is a protected area, nothing should be removed. The quarry is about two-thirds of the way up the trail.

After a steep mile-long ascent, the trail meets another jeep road from the right. Continue straight past the intersection until you reach a four-way junction, where a 10-minute detour to the left brings you to **Lake Waiau**. This unique alpine lake, sitting inside Pu'u Waiau at 13,020ft, is the third-highest lake in the USA. Set on porous cinder, in desert conditions of less than 15in of rainfall annually, the lake is only 10ft deep, yet it's never dry. It's fed by permafrost (leftover from the last Ice Age) and meltwater from winter snows, which, elsewhere on Mauna Kea, quickly evaporate. Hawaiians used to place umbilical stumps in the lake to give their babies the strength of the mountain.

Back at the four-way junction, make your way north (uphill) and make a final push upward to meet the Mauna Kea Access Rd at an impromptu parking lot. Suddenly the observatories are visible up on the summit, and straight ahead is Millimeter Valley,

nicknamed for the three submillimeter observatories on the summit. The trail ends here at the 7-mile marker of the access road, just below the hairpin turn, but the top of the mountain is still snickering at you another 1.5 miles further up the road.

A few hikers will want to turn back before reaching the summit. If you're in that category, you have a choice of either backtracking along the same 5-mile trail you just came up (only if the weather and visibility are good) or walking down along the shoulders of the road, which is faster and easier even though it's 2 miles longer. Below the 5-mile marker, the road leaves the pavement and returns to gravel on its final leg back to the Onizuka Visitor Information Station.

To reach the summit from the hairpin turn described previously, follow the main road up to the right (not the spur road into Millimeter Valley) for over 1 mile. Past the 8-mile marker, where the road forks, veer right and look for an unofficial trail that starts opposite the University of Hawai'i's 2.2m telescope observatory. This 200yd trail-of-use descends steeply east, crosses a saddle, and scrambles up Pu'u Wekiu to Mauna Kea's true summit, which is marked by a USGS summit benchmark sticking out of the ground. Given the biting winds, high altitude and extreme cold, most people don't linger long before retracing their steps back down.

The trail's steep grade and crumbling cinders make for a most unnerving walk down, especially as daylight fades and afternoon clouds roll in. If you walk back down along the paved road instead of the trail, you'll not only save time but you'll increase your chances of getting a lift. If, however, you're tempted to hitch a ride up from the Onizuka Center…then don't! Unless you have spent the previous night on the mountain, you won't be properly acclimatized.

SKIING

Skiing in Hawai'i is a curiosity event. Snow does fall on the upper slopes of Mauna Kea each winter and, while there's no guarantee, the ski season usually starts between early January and late February, and can continue for around two months. After major snowstorms, locals (who are generally nonskiers) sometimes attempt to slide down the mountain on surfboards, boogie boards and inner tubes!

Skiing Mauna Kea is a notch on your novelty belt. The altitude is tough, and the slopes can harbor exposed rocks and ice sheets. Don't expect any ski lodges, lifts, trails, patrols, equipment or grooming on the mountain. The slopes can be very steep, and there are vertical drops of 5000ft. Commercial ski tours on Mauna Kea are prohibited.

Tours

The Onizuka Visitor Information Station offers free Mauna Kea **summit tours** (☺ 1pm Sat & Sun). You must provide your own 4WD transportation to the summit. To join the tour, arrive at the visitor center by 1pm; the first hour is spent watching videos about astronomy on Mauna Kea as you acclimatize. After the orientation, you caravan up to the summit, where you hear a talk on the summit telescopes, including their history, ownership, mirror size and the type of work they do. The tours visit one or two of the summit telescopes, most commonly the University of Hawai'i's 2.2m telescope and WM Keck's 10m telescope. Tours depart from the summit at about 4:30pm and are subject to cancellation at any time depending on the weather, so call ahead.

Subaru Telescope (www.naoj.org/Information/Tour /Summit; ☺ tours at 10:30am, 11:30am & 1:30pm) offers 30-minute summit tours up to 15 days per month, in English and in Japanese. You must make advance reservations (by Internet only) and you need your own transportation to the summit.

If you prefer not to drive, a handful of companies offer sunset tours of the summit. **Hawaii Forest & Trail** (☎ 331-8505, 800-464-1993; www .hawaii-forest.com; tours $155) hosts an enjoyable hot picnic dinner at a Parker Ranch outpost before its sunset 'Mauna Kea Summit and Stars Adventure.' With gloves and a hooded parka provided, you'll have ample opportunity to acclimatize and get bundled up before heading to the summit. There are pickups in Kailua-Kona and Waikoloa.

Mauna Kea Summit Adventures (☎ 322-2366, 888-322-2366; www.maunakea.com; tours $165) has been leading tours to the summit for two decades. Serving soup, sandwiches and hot beverages, it also includes gloves and parkas. There are pickups in Kailua-Kona, Waikoloa and Waimea. You get a 15% discount for Internet bookings made two weeks in advance.

For active types, **Arnott's Lodge** (☎ 969-7097; www.arnottslodge.com; 98 Apanane Rd, Hilo; tours guests /nonguests $60/90) offers a similar tour with the option to hike around Onizuka Center and even the last few hundred feet to the summit.

A SACRED SITE

Astronomers marvel at Mauna Kea's extraordinary viewing conditions and local businesses appreciate the economic boom from the observatories. But native Hawaiians see Mauna Kea – a sacred temple – being desecrated by science and development.

Traditionally, Mauna Kea is translated not only as White Mountain but also as Wakea's Mountain. Wakea is the sky-father of the islands and the Big Island is considered his first-born child. Lake Waiau is the *piko* (umbilicus) connecting the islands to the heavens.

Mauna Kea is also associated with the goddess Poliahu, the embodiment of snow, whose home is Pu'u Poliahu, a hill near the summit. According to legend, Poliahu is more beautiful than her sister Pele. During catfights over men, Pele would erupt Mauna Kea, then Poliahu would pack it over with ice and snow. Then an angry Pele would erupt again. Back and forth they would go. Interestingly, the legend is metaphorically correct. As recently as 10,000 years ago, there were volcanic eruptions up through glacial ice caps here. Because of its spiritual significance, Pu'u Poliahu is off-limits to astronomical domes.

Native Hawaiians have allied with some environmentalists to oppose development on Mauna Kea, asserting that observatories dump tens of thousands of gallons of human waste at the summit. Further, some observatories use mercury to float mirrors used in telescope operations, and spills have occurred. Reputedly neither the EPA nor the State Department of Health keeps records or follows any baseline standards. The Office of Hawaiian Affairs is currently challenging the approval of a $50 million Keck project for lacking an environmental impact statement.

Tours depart from the Hilo Bay Hostel (p172), with an extra pickup stop at the nearby Hilo Hawaiian Hotel (p173), between noon and 3pm (depending on the season) and return between 9pm and 11pm.

Festivals & Events

For two days, the Waiki'i Ranch hosts visitors from all over as Hawaii's best performers showcase talents at the **Annual Waiki'i Music Festival** (☎ 883 2077; mid-Jun), a big two-day concert and festival at Waiki'i Ranch, off Saddle Rd on the slopes of Mauna Kea, on the Waimea side. Artists set up booths, and local food is plentiful at concessions. The event benefits North Hawaii Community Hospital and North Hawaii Hospice.

Sleeping

At the 35-mile marker you'll find a campground and cabins at Mauna Kea State Recreation Area. The site has temporary closure during periods of drought so be sure to get an update by calling the **Division of State Parks** (☎ 974-6200; www.hawaii.gov/dlnr/dsp; PO Box 936, Hilo, HI 96721; ⏰ 8am-noon Mon-Fri). Facilities include picnic tables and rest rooms, but there's no water and the site is used mainly as a waystation for local hunters. The cabins contain basic kitchens and bathrooms, and bed space for up to six people. Nearby military maneuvers can be noisy.

The closest hotels and B&Bs are located in Waimea (p133) and Hilo (p172).

With an elevation of 6500ft, the area commonly experiences cool days and cold nights and is a good base for those planning to hike Mauna Kea or Mauna Loa.

Getting There & Around

From Kona, Saddle Rd (Hwy 200) starts just south of the 6-mile marker on Hwy 190. From Hilo, drive *mauka* (inland) on Kaumana Dr, which becomes Saddle Rd (Hwy 200). All drivers should start with a full tank of gas, as there are no gas stations on Saddle Rd. Look for the turnoff to the mountain around the 28-mile marker heading east.

Driving to the summit is suitable only for 4WD vehicles. Once you pass Hale Pohaku, the residential complex for scientists just above the Onizuka center, the 8 miles to the summit are unpaved gravel for the first 5 miles, followed by pavement for the last 3 miles. The drive takes about 25 minutes.

You should drive in low gear and loosen the gas cap to prevent vapor lock. The upper road can be covered with ice, and loose cinder is always a problem. Be particularly careful on the way down, especially if you develop any signs of altitude sickness at the top. Driving when the angle of the sun is low – in the hour after sunrise or before sunset – can create extremely hazardous blinding conditions.

AROUND MAUNA KEA
Mauna Loa's Northern Flank

The road to Mauna Loa starts near the 28-mile marker, roughly 200yd east of the Mauna Kea Access Rd. Turn south onto the red asphalt road and proceed 17.5 miles up the northern flank of Mauna Loa to a weather observatory at 11,150ft. There are no visitor facilities or bathrooms at the weather observatory.

The narrow road is gently sloping and passable in a standard car, but it's a winding, nearly single-lane drive, with blind spots, so leave 45 minutes to drive up. To avoid vapor-lock problems, loosen your gas cap before starting. Park in the lot below the weather station; the equipment used to measure atmospheric conditions is highly sensitive to vehicle exhaust.

The summit and domes of Mauna Kea are visible from here. When conditions are just right you can glimpse the 'Mauna Kea shadow' at sunset – it's a curious phenomenon in which Mauna Kea sometimes casts a blue-purple shadow behind itself in the sky.

The **Mauna Loa Weather Observatory** is the trailhead for the very steep and difficult **Observatory Trail**. Access to the trailhead is a 19-mile paved spur off the Saddle Rd. As the trail gains 2620ft in just 6.4 miles, top physical condition is a pre-requisite and altitude sickness (p245) is very likely for anyone who has not properly acclimatized. Sleeping overnight near the observatory to become adjusted may evade symptoms. There is lava tube that can be used as a shelter 1.5 miles along the trail. Other suggestions for avoiding altitude sickness include taking frequent stops while driving up from Saddle Rd, and camping on one of the 4WD roads along the way. Overnight hikers need to register in advance with the **Kilauea Visitor Center** (☎ 985-6017; ⏰ 7:45am-5pm) in Hawai'i Volcanoes National Park, and having the right equipment is also a priority (see p206). Note the Observatory Access Rd may be closed during winter months.

The actual trailhead is about 500yd below the observatory, down a 4WD road. Set out early – either before or with the rising sun. The trail crisscrosses a series of 'a'a (a rough, jagged type of lava) and *pahoehoe* (smooth-flowing) lava flows as well as the old 4WD road. Signs mark the major trail changes. After about 4 miles, the trail connects up with the Mauna Loa Summit Trail (p205), which starts down in the main section of the national park. From the trail junction, it's just over 2.5 miles around the caldera's western side to Mauna Loa summit at 13,677ft, or about 2 miles along the caldera's eastern side to Mauna Loa cabin at 13,250ft. All told, the hike to the cabin will take at least four to six hours.

Mauna Loa to Hilo
The section of Saddle Rd between Mauna Loa and Hilo is sprinkled with interesting short hikes.

Near the turnoff to Mauna Kea, just past the 28-mile marker heading west, is a 20-minute hiking trail up a cinder cone called Pu'u Huluhulu (Shaggy Hill), an ancient *kipuka* (oasis) created by Mauna Kea more than 10,000 years ago. The hike is easy and you'll be rewarded with panoramic views of Mauna Loa, Mauna Kea and Hualalai. More recent *pahoehoe* and 'a'a flows from Mauna Kea between 1500 and 3000 years old surround this raised slice of local life.

An interesting taste of the 6000ft climate on Mauna Loa can be explored on the **old Pu'u 'O'o Trail** (note this is not the same trail to the active Pu'u 'O'o cinder cone in Hawai'i Volcanoes National Park). Coming from Hilo between Mile marker 22 and 23 the turnoff for the trailhead is on the left side. This 4-mile trail, marked by *ahu* (cairns), wends through several *kipuka* and boasts interesting leeward flora and fauna (p41) crisscrossed by lava flows. Return on the trail if it becomes vague or continue following it until you meet up with a 4WD road to make a loop back to the highway. This so-called Power Line road (marked with a PLR sign) is closed with a gate at the highway but is hikeable. The junction is about 3 miles in from Saddle Rd. Allow three to four hours round trip and bring clothing for cool, damp weather.

Hamakua Coast

The Hamakua Coast winds along the island's verdant northern shoreline, from the dramatic cliffs of Waipi'o Valley down toward the Laupahoehoe area. In the heart of a now defunct landscape from the Hawaiian sugar industry, wild cane stalks up to 8ft tall blow in the trade winds. Alongside the highway, the expanse of ocean alternates between deep aquamarine on sunny days and stormy green during showers. Brilliant green monkey pod crowns and orange African tulip tree blossoms envelop the streams and waterfalls that pulse down Mauna Kea's eastern flank.

All along its length the Hawai'i Belt Rd (Hwy 19) is an impressive feat of engineering, spanning lush ravines that locals call gulches – Maulua Gulch, Laupahoehoe Gulch and Ka'awali'i Gulch – from east to west. The setting is certainly picturesque, with inviting back roads if you have time to dawdle.

The Hawai'i Belt Rd passes small towns and unmarked roads that will reward the curious with unfrequented black-sand beaches and genuine aloha. If you're just passing through on the Kona-to-Hilo circuit, at least make time for Waipi'o Valley Lookout, majestic Akaka Falls and the Pepe'ekeo 4-Mile Scenic Drive. There are many lovely B&Bs along this stretch of coast, but only a few budget places worth recommending. There are, however, campsites at several public beach parks.

HIGHLIGHTS

- Backcountry hiking in **Waimanu Valley** (p153)
- Getting lost around the back roads of the **Old Mamalahoa Highway** (p157)
- Gazing 2000ft down into historic **Waipi'o Valley** (p151)
- Losing yourself in the mist of majestic **Akaka Falls** (p158)
- Sunning, swimming or surfing at one of the coast's dramatic **black-sand beaches** (p154)

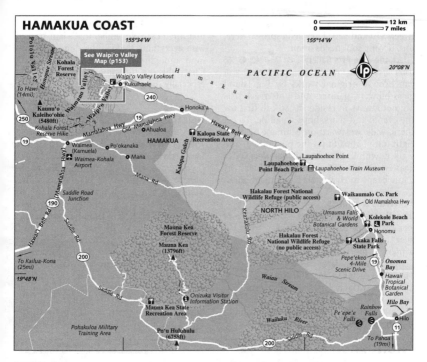

HAMAKUA COAST

HONOKA'A

pop 2200

The town of Honoka'a has had to reinvent itself over and over, and it's gone from cattle to sugar to tourism. However, it's a survivor, and makes for a relaxing stop along the Hawai'i Belt Rd. Most of the people living here are descendants of sugar-cane plantation workers, from the first Scottish and English immigrants to the later Chinese, Portuguese, Japanese, Puerto Rican and Filipino arrivals. The Honoka'a Sugar Company mill, dating from 1873, processed its last harvest in 1993.

Honoka'a's main street, Mamane St, runs just a block or two, but it's worth a trip to see traditional Western plantation-style architecture. There are also a number of antique shops chock-full of vintage plantation-era paraphernalia. If nothing else, Honoka'a will transport you back to late-19th- and early-20th-century Hawai'i. The town remains the largest on the Hamakua Coast, and residents of Waipi'o Valley (often driving muddy trucks with hounds scrambling around in the back) come 'topside' to stock

up on supplies here, although for major shopping they head to Waimea or Hilo.

Information

In town you'll find all the basics: a bank with an ATM and a gas station (though you'll pay around 20¢ more per gallon up here), a grocery store, a coin laundry and a **post office** (☎ 800-275-8777; 45-490 Lehua Rd; ⏰ 9am-4pm Mon-Fri, 8:15-9:45am Sat). For Internet access, the **Virtual Lounge** (☎ 775-9355; www.vlhawaii.com; Mamane St; per 30min $3, unlimited wi-fi $5; ⏰ 9am-6pm Mon-Sat) is simple but roomy. There are visitor information brochures at Tex Drive In (p149), just off of the Hawai'i Belt Rd above town.

Sights

Beside the library is the **Katsu Goto Memorial**. A Japanese cane-field worker, Goto was hanged by Honoka'a sugar bosses and accomplices in 1889 for his attempts to improve labor conditions on Hamakua plantations. He's considered one of the first union activists.

Do you possess the coveted purple aura? You can find out at **Starseed Beads & Gems** (☎ 775-9344; 45-3551A2 Mamane St; ⏰ 10am-5pm

Mon-Sat), where aura photographs cost between $10 and $20. They sell espresso here, too, if your soul needs a jolt.

At the **Live Arts Gallery** (☎ 775-1240; 45-368 Lehua St; admission free; ☼ 10am-5pm Mon-Sat) you can browse original works by Big Island glass blowers, painters and potters. Artists are not always in residence, so call first for the events-and-workshops schedule. To get there, walk westward on Mamane St, turn right onto Lehua St (at the post office) and walk downhill. Also here is **Hamakua Coffee Roasters** (☎ 936-4359), roasting up local organic beans to rival their Kona neighbors.

Festivals & Events

The **Hamakua Music Festival** (☎ 775-3378; www .hamakuamusicfestival.org; Honoka'a People's Theater, Mamane St; admission $20-30; ☼ mid-May & early Oct) is a premier music event bringing world-class Hawaiian music, jazz, classical and more to Hamakua each October and November. The festival awards scholarships to music students Island-wide, presents student workshops with visiting celebrities and provides the only funding for music teachers in public schools.

The **Annual Taro Festival** is a one-day annual affair each November that's jam-packed with everything that can be done with taro (and some things that probably shouldn't!). Check this out for some homegrown fun – especially the poi-eating contest.

Sleeping

Near Honoka'a you'll find a handful of B&B gems that let you escape it all.

Waipi'o Wayside B&B (☎ 775-0275, 800-833-8849; www.waipiowayside.com; Hwy 240; r incl breakfast $95-175) If you appreciate fine furnishings and attention to detail, this 1932 plantation house, nestled in a mac-nut orchard, couldn't be more perfect. There are five elegant and cozy rooms, each with genuine antique furnishings, sprays of tropical flowers, plush linens and a library of literary titles. Relax on the sprawling lanai or in the garden gazebo (a picturesque site for weddings and parties). Full homemade breakfasts include organic coffee, 30 types of tea, seasonal fruit, scrumptious homemade muffins and the host's unique egg dishes. It's between the 3- and 4-mile markers on Hwy 240.

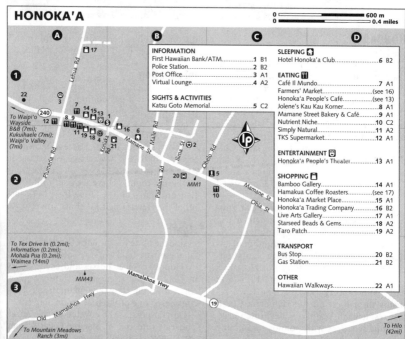

HONOKA'A

0 ____ 600 m
0 ____ 0.4 miles

INFORMATION
First Hawaiian Bank/ATM................1 B1
Police Station....................................2 B2
Post Office..3 A1
Virtual Lounge...................................4 A2

SIGHTS & ACTIVITIES
Katsu Goto Memorial.........................5 C2

SLEEPING 🛏
Hotel Honoka'a Club.........................6 B2

EATING 🍴
Café Il Mundo....................................7 A1
Farmers' Market...........................(see 16)
Honoka'a People's Café................(see 13)
Jolene's Kau Kau Korner....................8 A1
Mamane Street Bakery & Café..........9 A1
Nutrient Niche.................................10 C2
Simply Natural.................................11 A2
TKS Supermarket............................12 A1

ENTERTAINMENT 🎭
Honoka'a People's Theater.............13 A1

SHOPPING 🛍
Bamboo Gallery...............................14 A1
Hamakua Coffee Roasters..........(see 17)
Honoka'a Market Place....................15 A1
Honoka'a Trading Company............16 B2
Live Arts Gallery..............................17 A1
Starseed Beads & Gems..................18 A2
Taro Patch.......................................19 A2

TRANSPORT
Bus Stop...20 B2
Gas Station.....................................21 B2

OTHER
Hawaiian Walkways.........................22 A1

To Waipi'o Wayside B&B (7mi); Kukuihaele (7mi); Waipi'o Valley (7mi)

To Tex Drive In (0.2mi); Information (0.2mi); Mohala Pua (0.2mi); Waimea (14mi)

To Mountain Meadows Ranch (3mi)

To Hilo (42mi)

Mamalahoa Hwy

Old Mamalahoa Hwy

MM43

MM1

Waianuhea B&B (☎ 775-1118, 888-775-2577; www.waianuhea.com; 45-3503 Kahana Dr, Ahualoa; r $170-350) For classy luxury, Waianuhea makes a huge impression. Located in the Hamakua Coast's secluded upcountry, the house is spacious and classily appointed, with gleaming hardwood floors and skylights – but there's also a touch of whimsy, with funky plastic Philippe Starck chairs here and there. Though swanky, the atmosphere is unpretentious, kids are welcome and you'll feel right at home. All electricity for the B&B is solar generated.

Hotel Honoka'a Club (☎ 775-0678, 800-808-0678; www.hotelhonokaa.com; Mamane St; dm/s/d with shared bathroom $15/25/35, r $45-65, ste $80) This place is on the tattered side, but it's the only game right in town. Cheaper rooms with a shared bathroom are at the quieter end of the hotel. There are also nicer rooms with private bathrooms and a bit of a view; the more expensive room has a queen bed and a TV. The manager speaks German and Japanese.

Eating

Tex Drive In (☎ 775-0598; Hwy 19; sandwiches & plate lunches $4-7; ☺ 6am-8:30pm) For many, Tex is reason enough to drive between Hilo and Kona. Its famous *malasada* costs 85¢ plain. For a quarter extra you can get a delicious filling of flavor – perhaps papaya-pineapple or classic Bavarian Crème. Island-style sandwiches, fresh fish burgers and plate lunches are also served. The Dutch owner has turned Tex into a little empire, with a gift shop, a garden shop and a garden on the property.

Simply Natural (☎ 775-0119; Mamane St; dishes $3.50-8; ☺ 9am-3:30pm Mon-Sat) Enjoy a taste of the taro tradition from Waipi'o Valley with Elizabeth's special banana taro pancakes. Other breakfast specials include omelettes and smoothies that make a meal. The place also serves fresh fish sandwiches, salads and homemade ice cream.

Café il Mondo (☎ 775-7711; 45-3626A Mamane St; sandwiches $5.50, pizza $9-18; ☺ 11am-8pm Tue-Sat) This casual Italian restaurant serves tasty sandwiches, soups, salads and pizza (available by the slice before 5pm). A house specialty is fresh-squeezed lemonade. Outdoor seating lets you sit and watch the world amble by.

Mamane Street Bakery Café (☎ 775-9478; Mamane St; baked goods $2; ☺ 6am-noon Mon-Fri) If you walk in, the aroma will compel you to try all the delectable cookies, cinnamon rolls, cakes and breads. The pastries sold at all the Starbucks cafés on the Big Island come from this bakery.

Jolene's Kau Kau Korner (☎ 775-9498; 45-3625 Mamane St; lunch dishes $4.50-8; ☺ 10am-8pm Mon, Wed & Fri, 10am-3pm Tue & Thu) This local-style eatery represents the local beef industry very generously on its menu. The burgers are exceptional, regular or mushroom.

Honoka'a People's Café (☎ 775-0000; Mamane St; breakfast $3.30-5.50, dinner $5.50-9; ☺ 8am-noon Tue, Wed & Fri-Sun, 5:30-9pm Fri-Sun) Located in the Honoka'a People's Theater, this vegetarian café serves coffee and espresso drinks, delicious breakfast burritos, and chili and enchiladas on movie nights.

GROCERIES

Nutrient Niche (☎ 775-9477; Mamane St; ☺ 10am-6:30pm Mon-Fri, 10am-5pm Sat) This is Honoka'a's resident health-food store and café. Friendly and packed only with good things, head here for picnic fixings or a healthy homemade meal. Guest chefs provide a variety of fresh fusion lunches.

Farmers' market (Mamane St; ☺ 10am-2pm Sat) A visit to the farmers' market, in front of Honoka'a Trading Company, is also a good option before you head to Waipi'o Valley.

TKS Supermarket (cnr Mamane & Lehua Sts) The TKS is another option for stocking up on the basics.

Entertainment

In a historic building dating from 1930, the **Honoka'a People's Theater** (☎ 775-0000; Mamane St; adult/child/senior $6/3/4) shows movies each weekend. It also hosts jazz, classical and Hawaiian performing artists during the Hamakua Music Festival (p148).

Shopping

Bamboo Gallery (☎ 775-0433; 45-3490 Mamane St; 🕙 10am-5pm Mon-Sat) Photographer Nick Kato shows off a wide selection of island art and crafts, from Japanese antiques to Hawaiian collectibles. Kato, who grew up in Japan, also publishes attractive Japanese-language travel books.

Taro Patch (☎ 775-7228; Mamane St; 🕙 9am-5pm) One of the best Hawaiian gifts shops on the island, Taro Patch has a nice selection of silkscreen T-shirts from island woodblock prints. Find service with aloha as you browse the other quality apparel, books, art and crafts.

Honoka'a Market Place (☎ 775-8255; Mamane St; 🕙 9:30am-5pm) If it's traditionally sewn island quilts that you want, be sure to stop in here for a full selection of local designs, as well as hand-painted quilts and pillows. You'll also find Hawaiian woods and apparel.

Mohala Pua (☎ 775-7800; Tex Drive In, Hwy 19; 🕙 9am-6pm) Well kept and very well stocked with its namesake 'blossoming flowers,' this garden shop will ship orchids, bromeliads, hibiscus and other plants to your home.

THE AUTHOR'S CHOICE

Honoka'a Trading Company (☎ 775-0808; Mamane St; 🕙 10am-5pm) Open since 1986, this is the island's best antique store. It's jam-packed with vintage aloha wear, antiques, used books, rattan and koa furniture, and hand-selected Hawaiian artifacts. Near the ceiling, the display of genuine old-time business signs is a history lesson in itself.

Getting There & Away

The Hele-On Bus (p239) arrives in Honoka'a from Kona on the No 7 Downtown Hilo route, then continues on to Hilo ($3.75); from Hilo you can reach Honoka'a either by the No 31 Honoka'a route or the No 16 Kailua–Kona route, which continues to Kona. Fares run $3.75 to $4.50. It takes 1½ hours from either direction.

KUKUIHAELE

pop 300

Outside Honoka'a, about 7 miles toward Waipi'o Valley, a loop road off Hwy 240 leads right down to the tiny village of Kukuihaele. Its name means 'traveling light' in Hawaiian, referring to the 'night marchers,' ghosts of Hawaiian warriors carrying torches, passing through on their way to Waipi'o. Night marchers are believed to walk through ancient battlefields on the night of Huaka'ipo (27th phase of the moon). According to legend, if you look directly at them or if you're in their way, you'll die. It's possible to survive if one of your ancestors is a marcher – or if you lie face down on the ground.

There's not much to see in Kukuihaele. Its 'commercial center' consists of the Last Chance Store and Waipi'o Valley Artworks gallery and bookshop. Kukuihaele is also the jumping-off point for tour operators into Waipi'o Valley.

Sleeping

Cliff House Hawaii (☎ 775-0005, 800-492-4746; www .cliffhousehawaii.com; Hwy 240; house $195) Gorgeously set on 40 private acres, the aptly named Cliff House is perched above the stunning cliffs of Waipi'o Valley. With sweeping windows and a wraparound lanai, you'll have unforgettable views of the verdant valley and endless Pacific. The Cliff House has two bedrooms with queen-size beds, a living-dining room and a full bathroom and kitchen. It's near the end of Hwy 240.

Hale Kukui Orchard Retreat (☎ 775-7130; 800-444-7130; www.halekukui.com; 48-5460 Kukuihaele Rd; studios $125, 2-bedroom cottage d $160-175) Tranquil and secluded in a thriving orchard, all units (even the spacious 400-sq-ft studio) include a full kitchen and a dining area, plus a private jet tub on the deck. Here you'll have enough space and privacy to feel as if you own the place (if only!). For $5, guests can pick as much fruit as they can eat: there are 26 varieties to choose from, including litchi, pomelo, papaya, banana and star fruit.

Waipi'o Lookout (☎ 775-1306; www.waipiohi.net; PO Box 5022, Kukuihaele, HI 96727; 1-bedroom apt per day/week/month $85/510/1600) This cute apartment is on the 1st floor of a contemporary two-story house on the ridge about 200yd before the Waipi'o Valley Lookout. There's a futon, a queen bed, a full kitchen, a phone, a TV and a lanai with sweeping valley views.

A HARD NUT TO CRACK

William Purvis, a sugar-plantation manager who brought seedlings from Australia, planted Hawaii's first macadamia trees in Honoka'a in 1881. For 40 years the trees were grown in Hawaii, as in Australia, mainly for ornamental purposes, because the nutshells were once considered too hard to crack.

Hawaii's first large-scale commercial macadamia orchard was planted in Honoka'a in 1924. Macadamia nuts have proven to be one of the most commercially viable agricultural crops in Hawaii. They are high in fat *(da good kine)*, protein and carbohydrates and are an excellent source of several essential vitamins and minerals.

Waipi'o Ridge Vacation Rental (☎ 775-0603; rlasko3343@aol.com; Hwy 240; trailers $75, 1-bedroom cottage d $85) Located right at the Waipi'o Valley trailhead (at the end of Hwy 240), these units offer the view of a lifetime. The cottage has a casual feel, with island-style decor and wooden furnishings made by the owner, queen-size bed and sofa bed, full kitchen, TV and VCR. If you want to 'rough it,' you might try the funky, scruffy 24ft Airstream-trailer-turned-vacation-shelter, which has a kitchenette and an outdoor shower.

Eating

In the village, the **Last Chance Store** (☎ 775-9222; ⏰ 9am-3:30pm Mon-Sat) is just that – no food or supplies are available in Waipi'o Valley. This small grocery store has snacks, canned chili, beer, water and wine. **Waipi'o Valley Artworks** (☎ 775-0958, 800-492-4746; ⏰ 8am-5pm) sells Tropical Dreams ice cream, muffins, inexpensive sandwiches and coffee (plus fine koa wood bowls and ceramic art). Overnight parking for campers in Waipi'o or Waimanu is available here (car/van per day $7.50/15; call first in July and August).

WAIPI'O VALLEY

Hwy 240 ends abruptly at the edge of cliffs overlooking Waipi'o Valley, the largest of seven spectacular amphitheater-headed valleys on the windward side of the Kohala Mountains. Down in the Waipi'o (Curving Water) grows a fertile jungle, flowering plants, and *lo'i* (taro patches). Extending 6 miles deep, numerous waterfalls feed – and, during heavy rains, can sometimes flood – the stream dividing the valley. Where the stream meets the ocean it cleaves a black-sand beach a mile wide. Some of the near-vertical *pali* (cliffs) wrapping around the valley reach heights of 2000ft. The whole place pulsates with mana, and on clear days

the dark outline of Maui is visible in the distance.

Many of the valley's 50 or so residents have *lo'i*, and you may see farmers knee-deep in the muddy ponds. Other Waipi'o crops include lotus root, avocados, breadfruit, oranges, limes and *pakalolo* (marijuana). You'll also find *kukui* (candlenut) trees and Turk's cap hibiscus.

History

Known as the Valley of the Kings, Waipi'o was the most fertile and productive valley on the Big Island. In ancient times, Waipi'o Valley was the political and religious center of Hawai'i and home to the highest *ali'i* (chiefs or royalty). Umi, the Big Island's ruling chief in the early 16th century, was a respected spiritual leader and propagated many of Waipi'o's *lo'i*. Of these original *lo'i*, some are still in production today. Waipi'o is also the site where Kamehameha the Great received the statue of his fearsome war god, Kukailimoku.

According to oral histories, several thousand people lived in this fertile valley before the arrival of Westerners. The site of a number of important *heiau* (sacred temple) testifies to Waipi'o's sacred status. The most sacred, Paka'alana, was also the site of one of the island's two major *pu'uhonua* (places of refuge; the other is now a national historic park, see p100), but today its exact location is unknown.

In 1823 William Ellis, the first missionary to visit Waipi'o Valley, guessed the population to be about 1300. Later in that century, immigrants, mainly Chinese, began to settle in Waipi'o. At one time the valley had schools, restaurants and churches, as well as a hotel, a post office and a jail.

Towards the end of the 19th century and in the early 20th century many valley farmers

HAMAKUA COAST

TARO'S ROOTS

According to legend the first-born son of Wakea (the sky father and creator of life) was of premature birth and died soon afterwards. At his burial a taro plant sprouted from the child's body. The leaf was named *lau-kapa-lili* (quivering leaf), but the stem was named Haloa. Wakea soon had another son, who was to become the progenitor of all the peoples of the earth. He was named Haloa after the stalk of the taro plant.

switched to rice cultivation, following traditions brought by Chinese migrants. Ideally suited to the climate, rice production surpassed taro during this time, but never eliminated the Hawaiian staple. The region eventually became uncompetitive as a rice producing area, as the viable land in the valley was no match for the lower prices and mass production happening in mainland California. Taro eventually made a comeback in Waipi'o, with factories producing the labor-intensive poi. This tradition has lasted through resurgence in the '60s and '70s as younger generations have tried to hold on to their cultural roots. Today the cultivation of taro and production of poi is an important part of the identity of the Hamakua Coast and the people of the Big Island. Fittingly, the Hawaiian proverb says, *aia ke ola i ka hana* (labor produces what is needed). By maintaining the original process the farmers are better able to understand their heritage and tap back into the roots of Hawaiian culture.

In 1946 Hawai'i's most devastating tsunami slammed great waves far back into the valley. Coincidentally or not, no one in this sacred place perished (and every valley resident was spared during the great 1979 flood). But afterwards most people resettled 'topside,' and Waipi'o has been sparsely populated ever since.

Dangers & Annoyances

Avoid hiking during the winter rainy season, when streams in the Waipi'o and Waimanu Valleys can swell, usually for just a few hours, to impassable. It's dangerous to attempt crossing swollen streams if the water reaches above your knees. Such rising waters should be considered life-threatening

obstacles, as flash floods are possible. Just be patient and wait for the water to subside.

If you decide it's essential to cross (eg if it's near sundown), look for a wide, relatively shallow stretch of stream rather than a bend. Before stepping off the bank, unclip your backpack's chest strap and belt buckle. This lets you easily slip out and swim to safety if you lose your balance and get swept away. Use a walking pole, grasped in both hands, on the upstream side (as a third leg), or go arm in arm with a companion, clasping at the wrist, and cross side-on to the flow, taking short steps.

Don't drink from *any* creeks or streams without first boiling or treating the water. Feral animals roam the area, making leptospirosis a real threat (see p244).

Sights & Activities

For a challenging two-day hike, the 9.5-mile Muliwai Trail leads you from the Waipi'o Valley Lookout down to Waipi'o Beach, and then all the way to the adjacent Waimanu Valley. Most people do just part of the Muliwai Trail, hiking down to Waipi'o Beach and back up, which is roughly 1½ hours round trip.

If you plan to hike the whole Muliwai Trail, bear in mind that it can take seven or eight hours one way – and hoofing it all the way to Waimanu Valley and back in a day is unrealistic, even for hard-core hikers. The last mile or so of the trail is precipitous and irregularly maintained, making this one of the most technically challenging hikes on the island. The final switchbacks are especially tough because hikers will probably be carrying a heavy backpack with camping gear.

Most people hike all the way into Waimanu Valley on the first day, camp for two nights and then walk back on the third day. You can get a head start by camping at Waipi'o Beach the night before. Theft can be a problem if you leave your rental car overnight. For greater security, overnight campers should park at Waipi'o Valley Artworks (p151).

WAIPI'O VALLEY HIKE

From beside the lookout, a 1-mile paved road leads down into Waipi'o Valley. It's so steep (25% grade) that only hikers and 4WD vehicles are allowed. The hike takes roughly 30 minutes down and 45 minutes back up. Only the bottom of the valley is shaded, and you'll definitely work up a sweat trekking uphill, so carry plenty of water.

If you detour five or 10 minutes to the left at the bottom of the hill, you may see wild horses grazing along the stream – a beautiful Hawaiian tableau with precipitous cliffs as a backdrop. Walk until you get a distant view of **Hi'ilawe Falls**, which at over 1200ft make up Hawai'i's highest free-fall waterfall. Hiking to the falls is possible but challenging. There's no trail and it's mainly a lot of bushwhacking. Only goats will make it to the falls in the heart of the rainy season.

Keep in mind that, while many valley residents tolerate visitors trekking down to visit the beach, they aren't keen on them exploring the valley interior. A lot of 'Private Property' and '*Kapu* – No Trespassing' signs are posted, and the further back in the valley you go the scarier the dogs become.

If you turn right at the bottom of the hill, **Waipi'o Beach** is only 10 minutes away (but tack on an extra 10 minutes, and a pound of mud, if it's rained recently). The beach is lined with graceful ironwood trees, which serve as a bar-rier against the winds that sometimes whip through here. Surfers catch wave action at Waipi'o, but mind the rip currents, rogue waves and treacherous undertow. When it's calm Waipi'o Beach is sublime, and you might encounter spinner dolphins.

Walk toward the stream mouth for a good view of **Kaluahine Falls**, which cascade down the cliffs to the east. Getting to the falls is more challenging than it looks, as the intervening coast is made up of loose, ankle-twisting lava. High surf breaking over the uppermost rocks can be dangerous. Local lore holds that night marchers (see p150) periodically come down from the upper valley to the beach and march to Lua o Milu, a hidden entrance to the netherworld.

MULIWAI TRAIL TO WAIMANU VALLEY

To continue on, cross the stream and walk toward the far end of the beach; there's a shaded path just inland of the rocks that passes by fishing boats and grazing land. The path turns left before reaching the cliffs, then veers right and ascends under thick forest cover.

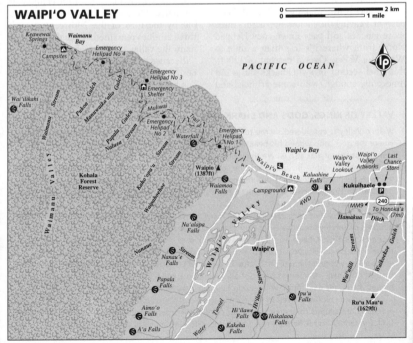

WAIPI'O VALLEY

The Muliwai Trail then rises over 1200ft in a mile of hard laboring up steep switchbacks on the northwest cliff face. This is an ancient Hawaiian footpath, known as the Z-trail by locals. The trail is used today by hikers and hunters who search for wild boar. The hike is exposed and hot, so cover this stretch in the early morning. Eventually the trail moves into ironwood and Norfolk pine forest, and tops a little knoll before gently descending and becoming muddy and frequented by mosquitoes. You lose sight of the ocean and instead you hear a rushing stream.

The trail crosses a gulch and ascends past a trail sign for Emergency Helipad No 1 on the *mauka* (inland) side of the trail. For the next few hours the trail finds a steady rhythm of wet and dry gulch crossings and forest ascents. A waterfall at the third gulch is a source of fresh water, but remember to treat the water before drinking. Mostly the trail is covered in squashed guava, lush ferns, buzzing gnats and the odd bee. For a landmark, look for Emergency Helipad No 2 at about the halfway point from Waipi'o Beach. Then look for an open-sided trail shelter with pit toilets that might be littered with trash.

Rest here before making the final difficult descent. Leaving the shelter, hop across three more gulches and pass Emergency Helipad No 4, from where it's less than a mile to Waimanu Valley. Over a descent of 1200ft, this final section of switchbacks starts out innocently enough, with some artificial and natural stone steps set in the mud, but the trail is poorly maintained and extremely hazardous later. A glimpse of **Wai'ilikahi Falls** on the far side of the valley wall might inspire hikers to press onward. The trail is narrow and washed out in parts, with sheer dropoffs into the ocean, and nothing to hold onto apart from mossy rocks and spiny plants. Dense leaves underfoot hide centipedes and slippery *kukui*. If the descent is impossible, head back to the trail shelter for the night instead, stopping at a stream gulch for water.

If you make it, Waimanu Valley is a mini-Waipi'o, minus the tourists. Most visitors only glimpse this valley in postcards or from a helicopter. On any given day you'll bask alone amid a stunning deep valley framed by cliffs, waterfalls and a black-sand beach. From the bottom of the switchbacks, the boulder-strewn beach is 10 minutes past the camping regulations signboard. When safe, ford the stream to reach the campsites on its western side.

Waimanu Valley once had a sizable settlement and contains many ruins, including house and heiau terraces, stone enclosures and old *lo'i*. In the early 19th century an estimated 200 people inhabited Waimanu, but by the turn of the 20th century only three families remained. Since the 1946 tsunami the valley has been abandoned.

Because it represents an unaltered Hawaiian freshwater ecosystem, Waimanu Valley has been set aside as a National Estuarine

---

VALLEY OF KINGS, GODS AND SHARK-MEN

Waipi'o Valley is considered sacred for many supernatural and regal reasons. Not only was this where the god Lono wooed his beautiful maiden Kaikilani and King Kamehameha I received the war god Ku, but it was also where the progenitor gods Kane and Kanaloa debauched themselves on the land's bounty – including *'awa*. According to legend, Kanaloa ('the *'awa*-drinker') and his followers revolted following a prohibition upon the narcotic beverage and were consequently banished to the underworld. The portal to this land of the dead is said to be carved into the steep cliffs above Waipi'o.

Other powers that once called Waipi'o Valley home – and perhaps still do – include Uli, the goddess of sorcery, and the legendary shark-man Nanaue. The Waipi'o version of this popular legend holds that Nanaue was fed meat as a youth to make him a strong and accomplished warrior. He quickly developed a taste for richer flesh, however, and started eating humans. He lured residents by warning them of shark attacks, but as folks started disappearing Nanaue topped the suspect list. Shark-men always have a shark's mouth marked on their back, and Nanaue's exposed him as the homicidal culprit, whereupon he hauled tail to Maui to feast there.

Liloa was a chief who lived in Waipi'o Valley, near the sacred heiau of Paka'alana. Liloa made several contributions to ancient Hawaiian culture: he brought homosexual practices and sired Umi, the farmer and fisherman responsible for laying out much of the *lo'i* in Waipi'o.

Sanctuary, and the removal of any plant or aquatic life (except for freshwater prawns and ocean fish) is forbidden.

On the return trip, be careful to take the correct trail. Walking inland from Waimanu Beach, do not veer left on a false trail-of-use that attempts to climb a rocky streambed. Instead keep heading straight inland past the camping regulations sign to find the trail to the switchbacks. It takes about two hours to get to the trail shelter, and about two more hours to reach the waterfall gulch: refill your water here. Exiting the ironwood forest soon after, the trail descends back to the floor of Waipi'o Valley.

Tours

If you're up for a hiking adventure, **Hawaiian Walkways** (☎ 775-0372, 800-457-7759; http://hawaiian walkways.com; guided hikes $95), located in Hokoka'a, will lead you to waterfalls and pools where you can swim.

If you opt out of hiking into the valley yourself, there are other options:

Waipi'o Na'alapa (☎ 775-0419; www.naalapastables .com; rides $75; ☾ departures 9:30am & 1pm) This outfit also offers a 2½-hour horseback ride, but children must be at least eight years old.

Waipi'o Ridge Stables (☎ 775-1007, 877-757-1414; www.waipioridgestables.com; rides $75-145; ☾ departures 9:30am) For horseback-riding tours, this follows a two-hour valley-floor route, or a five-hour trot out to Hi'ilawe Falls that ends with a picnic and a swim at a hidden waterfall.

Waipi'o Valley Shuttle (☎ 775-7121; www.waipio valleytour.com; adult/child $45/20; ☾ departures 9am, 11am, 1pm & 3pm Mon-Sat) Runs two-hour 4WD taxi tours, although the driver does point out waterfalls, identify plants and throw in a bit of history.

Waipi'o Valley Wagon Tours (☎ 775-9518; www .waipiovalleywagontours.com; adult/child $45/22.50; ☾ departures 9:30am, 11:30am, 1:30pm & 3:30pm Mon-Sat) For a quaint experience, this one-hour jaunt in an open mule-drawn wagon carts visitors over rutted roads and rocky streams.

Sleeping

Kamehameha Schools Bishop Estate, which owns most of Waipi'o Valley, allows camping at four primitive sites in a wooded area near Waipi'o Beach. There are no amenities: no drinking water, no showers and no toilets (campers are required to bring chemical toilets). The maximum stay is four days, and you must apply for a permit at least two weeks in advance – even earlier for weekends

and in summer. Each camper is required to sign a liability waiver, but the permits are free. Contact the **Kamehameha Schools Bishop Estate** (☎ 776-1104; PO Box 495, Pa'auilo, HI 96776).

Backcountry camping in Waimanu Valley, which is managed by the state, is allowed by free permit for up to six nights. Facilities include fire pits and a couple of composting outhouses. Reservations are taken no more than 30 days in advance by the **Division of Forestry & Wildlife** (☎ 974-4221; 19 E Kawili St, PO Box 4849, Hilo, HI 96720; ☾ 7:45am-4:30pm Mon-Fri). With two weeks' notice the permit can be mailed to you.

There is no overnight parking at the Waipi'o Lookout, so if you intend to camp overnight or in the back country the best place to leave your car is at Waipi'o Valley Artworks (p151) in Kukuihaele. There is a daily fee, but it's more secure than parking on the street.

KALOPA STATE RECREATION AREA

This 100-acre state park is a native forest, containing mainly the trees, shrubs and ferns that were already present when the Polynesians arrived. Hawaii's native plants are extremely precious because almost 90% are endemic, meaning they're found nowhere else on earth. At an elevation of 2000ft, the Kalopa forest is cooler and wetter than the coast, and normal precipitation is 100in per year. To get there, turn *mauka* off the Hawai'i Belt Rd at the Kalopa Dr sign and drive in 3 miles. You could have the park to yourself.

A nature trail beginning near the cabins loops for three-quarters of a mile through old ohia forest, where some of the trees measure more than 3ft in diameter. The woods are inhabited by the *'elepaio*, an easily spotted brown-and-white native forest bird with a loud whistle. It's about the size of a sparrow.

A longer hiking trail leads into the adjoining forest reserve. Begin trekking along Robusta Lane, on the left between the caretaker's house and the campground. It's about 600yd to the edge of Kalopa Gulch, through a thick eucalyptus forest. The gulch was formed eons ago by the erosive movement of melting glaciers that originated at Mauna Kea. The trail continues along the rim of the gulch for another mile, while a number of side trails along the way branch off and head west back into the recreation area.

HAMAKUA COAST

Tent camping is available in a grassy area surrounded by tall trees. There are rest rooms and covered picnic pavilions with electricity, running water and barbecue grills – the works! Simple group cabins have bunk beds, linens and blankets, plus hot showers and a fully equipped kitchen. Permits are required for the cabins and technically for the campsites, too. For details, see p223.

LAUPAHOEHOE
pop 470

The word Laupahoehoe means 'leaf of *pahoehoe* (smooth-flowing lava),' an apt name for the landmark **Laupahoehoe Point**, a flat peninsula formed by a late-stage Mauna Kea eruption. It's located midway between Honoka'a and Hilo; a highway sign points to the steep winding road that leads 1.5 miles to the coast. It's a scenic drive, with spectacular cliffs in the distance and dense foliage all around.

On April 1, 1946, tragedy hit the small plantation town when a tsunami up to 30ft high wiped out the schoolhouse on the point, killing 20 children and four adults. Today a monument listing the names and ages of the victims stands at Laupahoehoe Point. After the tsunami the whole town moved uphill. Along the way to the point, however, you can see the giant banyan tree that once stood at the school's center. Every April there's a community festival with food, music and old-timers who *talk story*.

Laupahoehoe is a rugged coastal area that's not suitable for swimming. The surf is usually rough, and sometimes crashes up over the rocks and onto the lower parking lot (roll up those windows!). Interisland boats once landed here, and many of the immigrant plantation laborers first set foot on the Big Island at Laupahoehoe.

The county beach park on the point has rest rooms, showers, drinking water, picnic pavilions and electricity. Both local and tourist families often camp here. For permit information, see p223. Watch out for strong gusts of wind when pitching your tent!

Beside the highway, the **Laupahoehoe Train Museum** (☎ 962-6300; adult/child $3/2; ☺ 9am-4:30pm Mon-Fri & 10am-2pm Sat & Sun) has all the ephemera, knickknacks and nostalgia of the bygone Hawaiian railroad era. Knowledgeable docents burst with pride when speaking of the restored length of track, ol' Rusty the switch engine, and other pieces of rail history that keep

turning up. The museum is visible from the Hawai'i Belt Rd between the 25- and 26-mile markers. Call first, as opening hours vary.

People interested in visiting the Hakalau Forest National Wildlife Refuge should see p138, as there is no *makai* (seaward) access to this pristine chunk of green. Birders will be particularly interested in this area, which protects at least eight endangered species.

UMAUMA FALLS & WORLD BOTANICAL GARDENS

At the 16-mile marker are the **World Botanical Gardens** (☎ 963-5427; www.wbgi.com; adult/teen/child/child under 5 $8/4.50/2/free; ☺ 9am-5:30pm). The Rainbow and Rainforest walks are on concrete paths and provide views of exotic and native Hawaiian plants. With 5000 species and growing, the gardens could use a couple of years to mature. There are many theme gardens, including the Native Hawaiian garden and the Children's Maze, while others are in the works, like a Japanese and Herbal garden. The big draw is the unadulterated view of **Umauma Falls**, which make up a tripartite waterfall cascading to the river below. Bring a coupon for free fruit and flowers with paid entrance. Take the left road across from the garden entrance and drive 6 miles, or follow the road past the garden entrance to the little stone wall on the left (it's about 250yd).

KOLEKOLE BEACH PARK

Beneath a highway bridge, this park sits at the side of Kolekole Stream, which flows down from Akaka Falls. It has small waterfalls, picnic tables, barbecue pits, rest rooms and showers. Locals go surfing and boogie boarding at the river-mouth break, but ocean swimming is dangerous.

Tent camping is allowed with a county permit, but be aware that the park is crowded with picnicking local families on weekends and in summer. For permit information, see p223.

To get there, turn inland off the Hawai'i Belt Rd at the southern end of the Kolekole Bridge, about 1300yd south of the 15-mile marker.

HONOMU
pop 540

Honomu is an old sugar town that might be forgotten today if it weren't for its proximity to Akaka Falls. Life here remains rural and

---

HIDDEN HAMAKUA COAST

Battered by windward rain, the streams and waterfalls of the Hamakua Coast rarely cease to flow. This history of erosion has forged some of the most spectacular sites on the island. Some sites are clearly marked tourist destinations, but it's only by ducking off the Hawai'i Belt Rd and exploring sections of the **Old Mamalahoa Hwy** that you can really get a taste of timeless Hawai'i. So if you're not in a hurry to get from Kona to Hilo, take the back roads through rainforest, deserted sugarcane fields, one-building towns and waterfalls that are bypassed by modern bridges over gulches that deliver the land back to the sea.

If you exit the Hawai'i Belt Rd between mile markers 20 and 19 heading south you'll come across the quaint and little-visited **Waikaumalo Co. Park**. Here you can picnic in the tranquil stream setting. Winding further south you'll drop in and out of various gulches as light trickles through the drooping flora that is slowly reclaiming the road. Stop at some of the classic old bridges to glimpse rarely seen streams.

The most noteworthy stop-off on this section of the old highway is just a half mile north of the entrance to the World Botanical Gardens. If you want to bypass paying to see the falls, try hiking down the steep trail on the southern *makai* side of the road along the narrow bridge. Hardy (some would say foolhardy) visitors can try to hike up Umauma Stream to the falls. It's less than a mile to the falls, but plan on a 1½- to two-hour hike. Count on getting wet, wear the stickiest shoes you can find and beware: it's a neck-risking, ankle-wrenching, boulder-hopping trial.

For more instant gratification, enjoy the falls and rocky gorge just below the bridge. If you're the adventurous type, swimming is possible in the lower pools and you'll find a local rope swing at the large open pool 100yd downstream.

If the water is high, just watch from a distance as the flow can be treacherous. The Hamakua Coast is infamous for flash floods, so beware the weather and turn back if it begins to rain. Hiking along the crude streamside trails is awkward; use discretion as they are often muddy and precariously located above cliff faces. Always bring water and be sure to hike with a friend. Famished mosquitoes add to the fun.

---

slow paced. Among the village's old wooden buildings you'll find a shop selling vintage glass bottles, a few worthy restaurants and galleries, an Internet café and a bakery.

Sleeping & Eating

The three lodgings in the area offer quite different options, and your choice will depend on your creature-comfort needs. As for food, there is only one worthwhile option, but it is one of the best on the whole coast.

Akiko's Buddhist Bed & Breakfast (☎ 963-6422; www.alternative-hawaii.com/akiko; s/d with shared bathroom $40/55, per week $265/355, studio per 2 weeks s/d $420/590) Nothing fancy, just basic, well-worn rooms suited to the spiritually inclined (but you need not be Buddhist). You can sleep on either Japanese monastery-style folding futons in the main house or regular beds in the house next door. A self-contained studio on the grounds requires a two-week minimum stay. Silence is observed between 6:30pm and 6am in the main house, and guests are welcome to join in Zen meditation at 5am on Monday, Wednesday and Friday.

Adjacent to Akiko is the Montanaga Garage Gallery. This funky, grand gallery and performance space is in a converted mechanic's garage. Past events include photography and sculpture exhibitions and gigs by ukulele masters. The calendar is varied; visit the website for the latest details. Yoga classes are also on offer in Akiko's beautiful studio out back; classes run on a drop-in basis and are open to the public on Sunday at 8:30am ($8).

Palms Cliff House Inn (☎ 963-6076; www.palms cliffhouse.com; 28-3514 Mamalahoa Hwy; r $175-375) Clearly one of the Big Island's most lavish B&Bs, Palms Cliff House has upscale rooms, all with plush linens, marble baths and private lanai overlooking Pohakumanu Bay and the vast horizon beyond; corner suites have indoor Jacuzzis. A gourmet breakfast is served on the lanai, and thoughtful amenities (from room safe to yoga mat) are tucked away in each room. This B&B has garnered rave reviews from national and local magazines. Some say it's rather pretentious, but no one can deny the luxury.

DETOUR: PEPE'EKEO 4-MILE SCENIC DRIVE

Between Honomu and Hilo, this 4-mile scenic loop off the Hawai'i Belt Rd between the 7- and 8-mile markers makes for a majestic tropical cruise. At the north end of the drive, **What's Shakin'** (🕑 10am-5pm) serves luscious smoothies.

The road crosses a string of one-lane bridges over little streams and through lush jungle. In places you'll be almost canopied by *liliko'i*, guava and tall mango trees as well as African tulip trees, which drop their orange flowers on the road. The fruit can be picked up along the roadside in season. There are also many small paths leading to babbling rivers or the coast. Look for one of these on the right, about 2.5 miles along, just after a one-lane wooden bridge.

If you crave more scenery, stop by **Hawaii Tropical Botanical Garden** (☎ 964-5233; www.hawaii garden.com; adult/child $15/5; 🕑 9am-4pm), a nature preserve with 2000 species of tropical plants situated amid streams and waterfalls. Buy your ticket at the yellow building on the *mauka* side of the road. The half-mile, self-guided walk should take a couple of hours. Bear in mind that the vibrant flowers and exotic ornamentals are all non-native, so the original Hawaiians saw a whole different landscape. For an example of pre-Captain Cook vegetation, visit the Amy BH Greenwell Ethnobotanical Garden (p92).

For a quick, pretty hike down to Onomea Bay, find the Na Ala Hele trailhead on the *makai* side of the road, just north of the botanical garden. After a 10-minute hike down a slippery jungle path, you'll come to a finger of lava jutting into the sea. A spur to the right leads to a couple of small waterfalls and a cove. Continuing straight on brings you to the diminutive bluffs overlooking the batik blues of Onomea Bay. Look for a rope tied to an almond tree for low-tide beach access. Beware of voracious mosquitoes.

Akaka Falls House (☎ 557-1025; www.akakafalls house.com; Hwy 220; r ind breakfast the 1st morning $225) This spacious guesthouse is the only option right in Honomu and it combines the unique feel of old Hawaii with modern amenities. A remodeled plantation house that sleeps up to 12, this is an excellent option for large groups or families. The two stories provide ocean and mountain views, a lanai with Jacuzzi, a massive, well-equipped kitchen, and a ping-pong table. Quiet and convenience are the fortes of this getaway, only a block from town and adjacent to Honomu Park, with its large grassy area and children's playground.

Woodshop Gallery & Café (☎ 963-6363; Hwy 220; lunch dishes $5.50-7.50; 🕑 10:30am-6pm) Woodshop offers one of the island's finest collections of handcrafted wooden bowls along with the best food between Hilo and Honoka'a. Try one of the superb burgers, including Fresh Ahi, Taro, Garden or regular ($5.80), or the curry fish plate ($7.50). If there's room for dessert, don't pass up the home-made ice cream – the ginger is divine.

Shopping

Hawaii's Artist Ohana (☎ 963-5467; Hwy 220; 🕑 10:30am-5:30pm Tue-Sat) Just up the road from the Woodshop Gallery & Café, this is another worthwhile gallery with a broad collection of fine Big Island art and handiwork, including fiber baskets, wooden bowls, pottery, jewelry and paintings.

Akaka Falls Aloha Fashion (☎ 963-6336; www .alohafashion.net; 🕑 10am-5pm Mon-Sat) Stop in at Aloha Fashion for an original boutique of handmade local aloha shirts and dresses. Owner Mieko Maetake uses her original designs to create unique island-style wear.

AKAKA FALLS STATE PARK

No one should miss a visit to the Big Island's most impressive 'drive-up' waterfall. Along a half-mile rain-forest loop, an unevenly paved trail passes through dense and varied foliage, including massive philodendrons, fragrant ginger, dangling heliconia, delicate orchids and gigantic bamboo groves.

If you start by going to the right you'll come to the 100ft **Kahuna Falls**, which, while attractive, are a bit wimpy when compared to what's further on. Up ahead, **Akaka Falls** drop a sheer 420ft down a fern-draped cliff. Their mood depends on the weather – sometimes they rush with a mighty roar, while at other times they gently cascade. With a little luck, you'll catch a rainbow winking in the spray.

To get there, turn onto Hwy 220 between the 13- and 14-mile markers.

Hilo

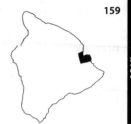

With a crescent-shaped bay and vibrant foliage growing wild, Hilo (population 41,000) is the Big Island's undeniably scenic capital and commercial center. But it has by and large remained 'old Hilo town.' Here, you'll find relatively few tourists among the longtime locals – probably because measurable rain falls on 278 days per year. Heavy rains have deterred both developers and tourists, and resorts have never really caught on anywhere in east Hawai'i.

Hilo (*hee*-low) is a well-kept secret. The population has remained stable over the years, and ethnic groups, including Caucasian, Hawaiian, Japanese, Filipino, Portuguese and Chinese, live together quite harmoniously. Town residents enjoy easy access to Hawai'i Volcanoes National Park, relatively affordable housing and a diverse cultural scene. The copious rainfall only means gushing waterfalls, lush valley gardens and tropical fruits aplenty.

Recently, however, Hilo has been discovered, and the influx of newcomers from the mainland has somewhat changed its boondocks reputation and unpretentious vibe. For better or worse, upscale restaurants, chic yoga studios and high-end art galleries are springing up downtown, and 'new money' is pouring in from mainland transplants.

Natural forces have long been a threat to the town – lava from one side, tidal waves from the other. In 1984 a lava flow from Mauna Loa volcano stopped short just 8 miles above town, and during the post-WWII era, two devastating tsunami flattened the coastal town. Hilo is a survivor, however, and the historic buildings that remain have been beautifully restored. Hilo's downtown is a pedestrian heaven, with manageable distances, courteous drivers and inviting backstreets for strolling.

HIGHLIGHTS

- Picnicking at idyllic **Lili'uokalani Park** (p167)
- Foraging at the downtown **farmers' market** (p166)
- Catching waves with local *surfahs* at **Honoli'i Beach Park** (p168)
- Watching authentic hula at the **Merrie Monarch Festival** (p171)
- Strolling and shopping in **old Hilo town** (p169)
- Cooling off with **'ice shave'** (p175)

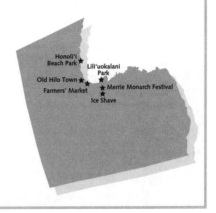

HISTORY

Hilo has long been a harbor town, starting with the first Polynesian settlers who farmed, fished and traded goods along the Wailuku River. By the 20th century, numerous wharves dotted the bay, a railroad connected Hilo with the Hamakua Coast, and the breakwater was being built. Hilo has been the island's center of commerce since then, though the departure of the sugar industry shifted the balance of economic and political power between east and west Hawai'i.

ORIENTATION

Hilo's charming and rather compact 'downtown' area is situated between Kamehameha Ave and Kino'ole St (both parallel to the bay) and also between Waianuenue Ave and Mamo St (both perpendicular to the bay).

Toward the east, on Banyan Dr, lies Hilo's modest hotel row, but most B&Bs are located in residential neighborhoods closer to the downtown area.

For the most-scenic drive from the airport to downtown Hilo, head north along Kanoelehua Ave and then turn left on to Kamehameha Ave. South of the airport, the shopping malls located along Kanoelehua Ave resemble typical mainland suburban sprawl, but this is Hilo's main retail district, complete with a constantly jampacked Wal-Mart and several other big-box stores.

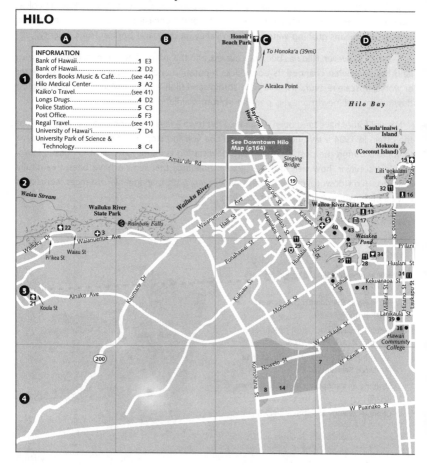

HILO

INFORMATION	
Bank of Hawaii	1 E3
Bank of Hawaii	2 D2
Borders Books Music & Café	(see 44)
Hilo Medical Center	3 A2
Kaiko'o Travel	(see 41)
Longs Drugs	4 D2
Police Station	5 C3
Post Office	6 F3
Regal Travel	(see 41)
University of Hawai'i	7 D4
University Park of Science & Technology	8 C4

You might wonder why Hilo sprawls like a suburb, with most homes located far from schools, shops and downtown. One reason is the history of tsunami devastating the bayfront area twice, which convinced locals to build on higher ground. Another is the ease of driving here. There's little traffic and people simply prefer houses with backyards and views of the Pacific from afar.

INFORMATION
Bookstores
Basically Books (Map pp164-5; ☎ 961-0144, 800-903-6277; 160 Kamehameha Ave; ☯ 9am-5pm Mon-Thu & Sat, to 6pm Fri, 11am-4pm Sun) Longtime indie bookseller that specializes in maps, travel guides and Hawaiian and out-of-print titles.

Book Gallery (Map pp164-5; ☎ 935-4943; 259 Keawe St; ☯ 9am-5pm Mon-Fri, 9am-3pm Sat) A Hilo favorite since 1968, with a wide selection of books by respected Hawaii publishers, including history, cookbook and children's titles. Knowledgeable, longtime staff.
Borders Books Music & Café (Map pp160-1; ☎ 933-1410; Waiakea Center, 301 Maka'ala St; ☯ 9am-9pm Sun-Thu, to 10pm Fri & Sat) Full-service chain where you can hang out for hours. Best choice for sheer volume of books, CDs and a range of newspapers and magazines.

Emergency
Police (Map pp160-1; ☎ 961-2213; 349 Kapiolani St) For nonemergencies.
Police, Fire & Ambulance (☎ 911) For emergencies.
Sexual Assault Hotline (☎ 935-0677)
Suicide Prevention Hotline (☎ 800-784-2433)

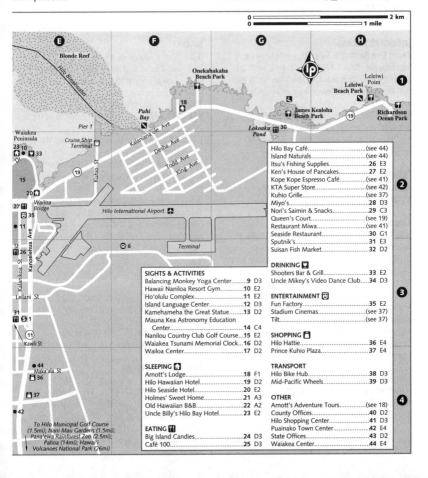

HILO IN...

One Day

Start by leisurely strolling around Hilo's historic **downtown** (opposite), bustling with shops and restaurants along the scenic bayfront. See local art exhibits at the **East Hawaii Cultural Center** (p165) and learn about Hawaiian history at the **Lyman House Memorial Museum** (p164). If you're lucky, it's Sunday or Wednesday and the **farmers' market** (p166) will be in full swing. Picnic at **Lili'uokalani Park** (p167) and stroll to **Mokuola** (p167). On a sunny afternoon, visit **Rainbow Falls** (p179) and **Pe'epe'e Falls & Boiling Pots** (p179), then hang out at a **beach** (p167). If it's raining, watch a $1 movie at **Kress Cinemas** (p177).

Two Days

Wake up to your favorite activity on day two, like golf at the **Hilo Municipal Golf Course** (p168), **yoga** (p169) or a power **walk** (p169). Then cruise north to explore the nearby Hamakua Coast (p146). The **Pepe'ekeo 4-mile scenic drive** (p158) is worth the detour. Stop at **Akaka Falls State Park** (p158), then grab a *malasada* (Portuguese doughnut) at **Tex Drive Inn** (p149) before hiking down **Waipi'o Valley** (p151).

Internet Access

Beach Dog Rentals & Sales (Map pp164-5; www .beachdog.net; ☎ 961-5207; 62 Kino'ole St; per 20 min $2.50; ⏱ 8am-10pm Mon-Fri, 10am-10pm Sat, to 6pm Sun) Airy space near the federal building, post office and Kalakaua Park.

Bytes & Bites (Map pp164-5; ☎ 935-3520; www .bytesandbites.net; 223 Kilauea Ave; per 15 min $2.50; ⏱ 10am-10pm) The largest Internet spot with 14 computers, in the midst of downtown.

Internet Resources

KonaWeb (www.konaweb.com) Although based in Kona, it's the best islandwide website. See p70 for details.

Library

Hilo Public Library (Map pp164-5; ☎ 933-8888; 300 Waianuenue Ave; ⏱ 11am-7pm Tue & Wed, 9am-5pm Thu & Sat, 10am-5pm Fri) If you buy a three-month library card for visitors ($10), you can sign up for free Internet use. The five high-speed terminals are popular, so you're limited to a 50-minute session per day, and you can make only one reservation per week (though you can 'walk on' if one is available). With the library card, you can also borrow any materials available to all cardholders, including an impressive selection of Hawaiian volumes, CDs and movies. Valid form of ID is required.

Media

NEWSPAPERS & MAGAZINES

Hawaii Tribune-Herald (www.hilohawaiitribune.com) Hilo's daily, published Sunday through Friday.

See the Directory (p223) for other publication listings.

RADIO

The lion's share of radio stations is based in Hilo. These stations can be heard only in east Hawai'i, due to the island's geography. Check out www.hawaiiradiotv.com/BigIsle Radio for a complete listing.

KAPA 100.3 FM Island hits on the station voted the best station in *Hawaii Island Journal*.

KANO 91.1 FM (www.hawaiipublicradio.org) Hawaii Public Radio featuring classical music and news.

KHBC 1060AM (www.khbcradio.com) Great variety, including Hawaiian and country, a Japanese language and music hour, and lots of 'talk story.' Don't miss longtime DJ Mel 'Mynah Bird' Medeiros from 6am to 10am Monday to Friday (to noon on Saturday) and his 'Trading Post,' a buy-sell-trade segment that'll give you a sense of local folks. Revel in the nostalgia when Mynah Bird plays the oldies (you'll surely hear Kenny Rogers' 'The Gambler' and 'Lucille').

KHLO 850AM Songs from yesteryear (simulcast with Kona's KKON /90AM).

KKBG 97.9 FM (kbigfm.com) Hawai'i's big hits.

KPUA 670AM (www.kpua.net) News, sports and talk radio (including…Rush Limbaugh).

KPVS 95.9 FM 'Kiss FM' contemporary pop.

KWXX 94.7 FM (www.kwxx.com) Island and pop hits.

Medical Services

Hilo Medical Center (Map pp160-1; ☎ 974-4700, emergency room ☎ 974-6800; 1190 Waianuenue Ave; ⏱ 24hr emergency) Located near Rainbow Falls.

Longs Drugs (Map pp160-1; ☎ 935-3357, prescriptions ☎ 935-9075; 555 Kilauea Ave; ⏱ 7am-7pm Mon-Fri, to 6pm Sat, 8am-5pm Sun) For prescriptions; located downtown.

KTA Super Store (Map pp160-1; ☎ 959-8700; Puainako Town Center, 50 E Puainako St; ☻ 5:30am-midnight) For prescriptions; south of the airport.

Money
All banks in Hilo have 24-hour ATMs.
Bank of Hawaii (Map pp160-1) Kawili St (☎ 961-0681; 417 E Kawili St); Pauahi St (☎ 935-9701; 120 Pauahi St)
First Hawaiian Bank (Map pp164-5; ☎ 969-2222; 120 Waianuenue Ave)

Post
Both post offices hold general delivery mail, but require completing an application in person. See p232 for details.
Main post office (Map pp160-1; ☎ 933-3019; 1299 Kekuanaoa St; ☻ 8am-4:30pm Mon-Fri, 8:30am-12:30pm Sat) Located near Hilo airport.
Downtown post office (Map pp164-5; ☎ 961-2976; 154 Waianuenue Ave; ☻ 8am-4pm Mon-Fri, 12:30-2pm Sat) Located in the Federal Building downtown.

Tourist Information
Big Island Visitors Bureau (Map pp164-5; ☎ 961-5797, 800-648-2441; www.gohawaii.com/bigisland; 250 Keawe St; ☻ 8am-4:30pm Mon-Fri) Provides little more than a brochure rack, since the marketing-agency staff can neither recommend one business over another nor book tours. But do check the website for a detailed events calendar.

Travel Agencies
To find the best deals, you'll probably do best by checking all the travel websites.
Kaiko'o Travel (Map pp160-1; ☎ 935-4456; www .pandaonline.com; Hilo Shopping Center, Suite 310, 1263 Kilauea Ave; ☻ 8am-5pm Mon-Fri) Call this excellent agency and check the website for cheap interisland tickets.
Regal Travel (Map pp160-1; ☎ 935-5796; 800-507-8370; www.regaltravel.com; Hilo Shopping Center, Suite 190C, 1251 Kilauea Ave; ☻ 9am-4:30pm) Another decent agency, which also has a Kailua-Kona office.

Universities
The **University of Hawai'i at Hilo** (Map pp160-1; ☎ 974-7311; www.hilo.hawaii.edu; 200 W Kawili St) has bachelor's and master's degrees. Enrollment is 3000, and at the time of writing, a **Mauna Kea Astronomy Education Center** (Map pp160–1) was to open in late 2005 at the University of Hawai'i at Hilo's **University Park of Science & Technology** (Map pp160-1; N Aohoku Pl), off Komohana Dr, where most astronomical observatories are. This $28 million project will include a planetarium, exhibit hall, classrooms, restaurant and gift shop.

SIGHTS
In downtown Hilo, charming early-20th-century architecture remains, and many buildings on the National Register of Historic

---

LITTLE TOKYO & BIG TSUNAMI

On April 1, 1946, Hilo Bay was inundated by a tsunami that had raced across the Pacific from an earthquake epicenter in the Aleutian Islands. It struck at 6:54am without warning.

Fifty-foot waves jumped the seawall and swept over the city. They ripped the first line of buildings from their foundations, carrying them inland and smashing them into the rows behind. As the waves pulled back, they sucked splintered debris and a number of people out to sea.

By 7am the town was littered with shattered buildings. The ground was not visible through the pile of rubble. Throughout Hawaii the tsunami killed 159 people and caused $25 million in property damage. The hardest hit was Hilo, with 96 fatalities.

Hilo's bayfront 'Little Tokyo' bore the brunt of the storm. Shinmachi, which means 'new town' in Japanese, was rebuilt on the same spot.

Fourteen years later, on May 23, 1960, an earthquake off the coast of Chile triggered a tsunami that sped toward Hilo at 440mph. A series of three waves washed up in succession, each one sweeping further into the city.

Although the tsunami warning speakers roared this time, many people didn't take them seriously. The tiny tsunami incidents of the 1950s had been relatively harmless, and some people actually went down to the beach to watch the waves.

Those along the shore were swept inland, while others further up were dragged out into the bay. A few lucky people, who managed to grab hold of floating debris, were rescued at sea. In the end, this tsunami caused 61 deaths and property damage of over $20 million.

Once more the Shinmachi area was leveled, but this time, instead of being redeveloped, the low-lying bayfront property was turned into parks, and survivors relocated to higher ground.

HILO

Places now house restaurants, stores and galleries. Wander down back alleys to see aging wooden storefronts, old pool halls and barbershops still using hand-pumped chairs. Locals refer to the coastal stretch along Hilo bay as 'bayfront.' Outside the downtown area, the main sights are on Banyan Dr, which starts at Hilo's landmark dock, Suisan

Fish Market (p174), where fisherfolk haul in their catches by 7am, although there's no action on Sundays.

Lyman House Memorial Museum

A great place to spend a rainy afternoon, this **museum** (Map pp164-5; ☎ 935-5021; www.lyman museum.org; 276 Haili St; adult/child $10/3; ☟ 9:30am-

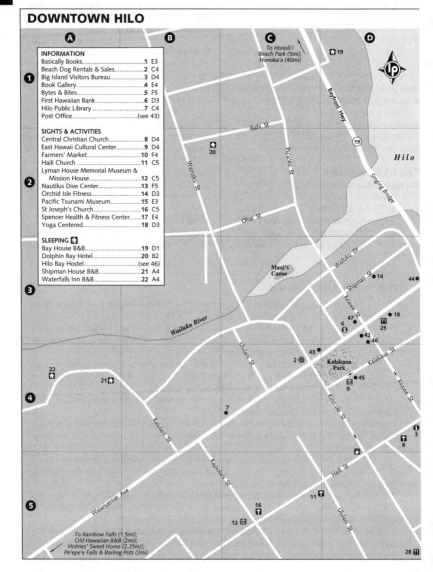

DOWNTOWN HILO

INFORMATION
Basically Books.....................................1 E3
Beach Dog Rentals & Sales.................2 C4
Big Island Visitors Bureau...................3 D4
Book Gallery...4 E4
Bytes & Bites..5 F5
First Hawaiian Bank..............................6 D3
Hilo Public Library...............................7 C4
Post Office.......................................(see 43)

SIGHTS & ACTIVITIES
Central Christian Church.....................8 D4
East Hawaii Cultural Center................9 D4
Farmers' Market.................................10 F4
Haili Church 11 C5
Lyman House Memorial Museum &
    Mission House................................12 C5
Nautilus Dive Center..........................13 F5
Orchid Isle Fitness.............................14 D3
Pacific Tsunami Museum....................15 E3
St Joseph's Church.............................16 C5
Spencer Health & Fitness Center.......17 E4
Yoga Centered....................................18 D3

SLEEPING
Bay House B&B...................................19 D1
Dolphin Bay Hotel..............................20 B2
Hilo Bay Hostel.............................(see 46)
Shipman House B&B..........................21 A4
Waterfalls Inn B&B.............................22 A4

To Honoli'i
Beach Park (5mi);
Honaka'a (40mi)

Hilo

Iliahi St

Wainaku St

Ohai St

Pu'u'eo St

Bayfront Hwy

Singing Bridge

Wailuku Dr

Wailuku River

Maui's
Canoe

Shipman St

Keawe St

Kalakaua St

Keawe St

Ululani St

Kalaniana'ole St

Kapiolani St

Kino'ole St

Haili St

Kalakaua
Park

Ululani St

Waianuenue Ave

To Rainbow Falls (1.5mi);
Old Hawaiian B&B (2mi);
Holmes' Sweet Home (2.25mi);
Pe'epe'e Falls & Boiling Pots (3mi)

HILO

4:30pm Mon-Sat) will teach you all about ancient Hawaiian life, such as the making of adzes from rare types of volcanic rock, and candles by skewering *kukui* nuts on coconut-frond spines. You can wander past displays of feather lei, *kapa* (cloth made by pounding the bark of the paper mulberry tree), and the framework of a traditional thatched house, as the mysteries of mana, kahuna and 'awa (kava) are revealed.

You pass through a lava tube, escorted by the sights and sounds of volcanic eruptions, curtains of fire, and molten lava. Science exhibits take you through Hawai'i's geological history, from the first volcanic cone that broke the sea's surface to modern-day Lo'ihi Seamount, with artifacts of spatter, olivine and Pele's tears (solidified drops of volcanic glass) and Pele's hair (fine strands of volcanic glass), both named after the Hawaiian goddess of the volcano.

Adjacent to the museum is the **Mission House**, built by the Reverend David Lyman and his wife, Sarah, in 1839. The two missionaries had seven children of their own, and, in the attic, they boarded a number of island boys who attended their church school. The house has many of the original furnishings, including Sarah Lyman's melodeon, rocking chair, china and quilts. Docent-led tours leave hourly throughout the day.

Pacific Tsunami Museum

This modern multimedia **museum** (Map pp164-5; ☎ 935-0926; www.tsunami.org; 130 Kamehameha Ave; adult/student $7/2; ☷ 9am-4pm Mon-Sat) captures the destructive horror and triumphant survival left in the wake of Pacific Ocean tsunami. The docents are well informed, probably because some are tsunami survivors themselves.

Tsunami have killed more Hawaiians than all other natural disasters combined, and this museum covers the entire Pacific region. Videos of oral histories and documentary pieces are projected on screens inside a minitheater, built in an old bank vault. Computers are available for those who want to know more about these gigantic waves.

The building itself, completed in 1930 and designed by CW Dickey, is a survivor. Both the 1946 and 1960 tsunami failed to wash it away. Look up at the tsunami-cam on the roof of the building, which projects live surf images online every day of the year.

East Hawaii Cultural Center

This **cultural center** (Map pp164-5; ☎ 961-5711; www.ehcc.org; 141 Kalakaua St; suggested donation $2; ☷ 10am-4pm Mon-Sat) showcases the work of local artists, most of whom are professionals, but local schoolkids' masterpieces also appear.

Map:

```
0 ───────── 200 m
0 ───────── 0.1 miles
```

Ⓔ   **Ⓕ**

EATING 🍴
Abundant Life Natural Foods..........23 E4
Café Pesto................................24 E4
Hilo Homemade Ice Cream............25 D3
KTA Super Store........................26 E5
Ocean Sushi Deli.......................27 E4
O'Keefe & Sons Bread Bakers........28 D5
Restaurant Kaikodo..................(see 47)
Reuben's................................29 F4
Tropical Dreams......................(see 32)
Tsunami Grill & Tempura..............30 E4

DRINKING 🍷
Cronies Bar & Grill.....................31 E3

ENTERTAINMENT 🎭
Kress Cinemas..........................32 E4
Palace Theater.........................33 E4

SHOPPING 🛍️
Alan's Art & Collectibles...............34 E4
Chase Gallery..........................35 E3
Fabric Impressions....................36 E4
Most Irresistible Shop.................37 E4
Orchidland Surfboards................38 E4
Sig Zane Designs......................39 E3

TRANSPORT
Da Kine Bike Shop.....................40 E4
Mo'oheau Bus Terminal...............41 F4

OTHER
Burns Building.........................42 D3
Federal Building.......................43 C4
FW Koehnen Building..................44 D3
Hawaiian Telephone Company
  Building...............................45 D3
Naha & Pinao Stones..................(see 7)
Pacific Building.........................46 D3
Toyama Building.......................47 D3

Bay

Bayfront Hwy

Kamehameha Av

Kamehameha Av

Mamo St

Kilauea Ave

Furneaux La

Punahoa St

Mo'oheau County Park

Wailoa River State Park

To Hilo International Airport (2mi)

To Two Ladies Kitchen (0.2mi)

Ongoing workshops and classes on a range of creative forms (including painting, drawing, ukulele and glasswork) are also held here. The building is a registered historic landmark that served as the Hilo police station until 1975. The hipped roof, which resembles a Hawaiian *hale* (house), covered lanai and other distinct features were common in 19th-century island homes.

Farmers' Market

One of the pioneering farmers' market in Hawaii, the Hilo **market** (Map pp164-5; cnr Mamo St & Kamehameha Ave; 7am-noon Wed & Sat) is a sight to behold. Dozens of local farmers, mostly Filipino immigrants, sell the gamut of island produce. Try both the solo (traditional yellow) and sunrise (strawberry pink) papayas, tart-flavored apple bananas, sweet Ka'u oranges, and lychee and mango in season. Here you'll see the real locals, for whom the market is a 'town square' of sorts. On the east side of Mamo St, T-shirt and craft sellers have set up shop; beware of fake 'Hawaiian' woven baskets, wood carvings and shell jewelry (though the real stuff can be found, too!). Flowers are an especially amazing deal, where $2 can buy you a huge protea bloom, or a bunch of vibrant anthuriums.

Wailoa River State Park

The arc-shaped bridges at this **state park** (Map pp160-1) are ideal for a quiet stroll. The Wailoa River flows through the park, ending at **Waiakea Pond**, a spring-fed estuarine pond with saltwater and brackish-water fish species (mostly mullet). There's a boat launch ramp, near the mouth of the river, for motorless boats. The park features two **memorials**: a tsunami memorial dedicated to the 1946 and 1960 victims; and a Vietnam War memorial – an eternal flame dedicated to the war casualties.

The **Wailoa Center** (Map pp160-1; 933-0416; admission free; 8:30am-4:30pm Mon, Tue, Thu & Fri, noon-4:30pm Wed) is an eclectic state-run gallery with striking photographs of tsunami damage displayed downstairs. Multicultural exhibits change monthly and might include woodwork, bonsai, Chinese watercolors or *oshibana* (Japanese dried-flower art), all done by locals who are both novices and professionals. It's best to arrive early, as the gallery staff sometimes lock up by 4pm.

Churches

Haili St was once called Church St after the churches lined up beside it. Catholic **St Joseph's Church** (Map pp164-5; cnr Haili & Kapiolani Sts) is a pink paean of Spanish-mission design, echoing that found in Southern California. Built in 1919, it has stained-glass windows and some trumpeting angels. **Haili Church** (Map pp164-5; 935-4847; 211 Haili St) was built in 1859 and looks as if it were airlifted straight out of the New England countryside. Services are held in Hawaiian and English. Downhill toward the bay, the Victorian-style **Central Christian Church** (Map pp164-5; 935-8025; 109 Haili St) was built by Portuguese immigrants in the early 20th century.

Banyan Drive

Hilo's short but scenic 'hotel row,' **Banyan Dr** (Map pp160-1), is best known for the enormous banyan trees lining the road. Royalty and celebrities planted the trees in the 1930s, and, if you look closely, you'll find plaques beneath the trees identifying Babe Ruth, Amelia Earhart and Cecil B DeMille, among them. The road wraps around the edge of Waiakea Peninsula, which juts into Hilo Bay. The road skirts the nine-hole Naniloa Golf Course (p168).

Not far away, on Kamehameha Ave, near Manono St, time stands still at the **Waiakea Tsunami Memorial Clock**. The clock is stuck

---

COUNT THE KING KAMEHAMEHA STATUES

On the bayfront side of Wailoa River State Park, a 14ft, Italian-made bronze **statue** (Map pp160-1) of Kamehameha the Great was erected in 1997. This statue, which underwent a $30,000 gold-leaf restoration in 2004, is not a copy of the 'identical' statues in Honolulu and Kapa'au (p125) – it's larger and the face is different (one Kamehameha Schools alumnus quipped that it looks like President Clinton!). The other two statues have an interesting history, and the Honolulu statue is gilded, while the Kapa'au statue is painted. And don't forget the fourth Kamehameha statue, another replica of the original, which stands at the US Capitol in Washington, DC.

ROCKS OF AGES

On the front lawn of the Hilo Public Library (Map pp164–5) are the Naha and Pinao Stones. The **Pinao Stone** was an entrance pillar to an old heiau. The **Naha Stone**, from the same temple grounds, is estimated at 3.5 tons. According to Hawaiian legend, anyone who had the strength to budge the stone would also have the strength to conquer and unite all the Hawaiian Islands. Kamehameha the Great reputedly met the challenge, overturning the stone in his youth.

From the Pu'ueo St Bridge, at the north end of Keawe St just beyond Wailuku Dr, you can see the current swirling around **Maui's Canoe** (Map pp164–5) a large rock in the upstream Wailuku River. Legend has it that the demigod Maui paddled his canoe with such speed across the ocean that he crash-landed here and the canoe turned to stone. Ever the devoted son, Maui was rushing to save his mother, Hina, from a water monster that was trying to drown her by damming the river and flooding her cave beneath Rainbow Falls.

---

at 1:05, the exact moment, in the predawn hours of May 23, 1960, when Hilo's last major tsunami swept ashore.

Lili'uokalani Park

With a picnic lunch and *goza* (roll-up straw mat), head to Hilo's 30-acre Lili'uokalani Park (Map pp160–1) and feel your stress melt away. Named for Hawaii's last queen, the Japanese-style park is a spacious green oasis with ponds, patches of bamboo, quaint arched bridges and a teahouse. Many of the lanterns and pagoda were donated by Japanese regional governments and sister cities in honor of the 100th anniversary of Japanese immigration to Hawaii. The 2 miles of paths here are perfect for a sunset stroll or an early-morning jog.

Mokuola (Coconut Island)

A tiny island connected to land by a footbridge, Mokuola (Map pp160–1), which means 'Island of Life,' is just opposite Lili'uokalani. The site is a county park with picnic tables and swimming, but it's most popular as a recreational fishing spot.

In ancient times, Mokuola was known as a *pu'uhonua* (place of refuge), and a powerful healing stone on the island was used by kahuna to cure the sick. Mokuola also had pure spring water, which was said to bring good health, and a birthing stone that instilled mana in the children born on the island.

Beaches   Map pp160–1

Make no mistake: Hilo is not a beach town. Though there are some decent pockets for snorkeling, catching a wave or watching the sunrise along **Kalaniana'ole Ave**, a 4-mile coastal road on the eastern side of Hilo. But all of these beaches can get fairly rough with rip currents and surf, so assess conditions carefully before venturing out.

About 1.5 miles east of the intersection of Kalaniana'ole Ave and Kanoelehua Ave, **Puhi Bay** is a good beginner dive site. If you enter from the grassy outcropping on the eastern side, you'll come to an interesting reef, 'Tetsu's Ledge,' at 30ft. The teeth-rattling waters are too cold for swimming, however.

A bit further east, **Onekahakaha Beach Park**, around 450yd north of Kalaniana'ole Ave, has restrooms, showers and a picnic area. A broad sandy-bottomed pool here is formed by a large boulder enclosure. As the water is just 1ft or 2ft deep in most places, it's popular with families with young children. On the Hilo side, an unprotected cove attracts snorkelers on calm days, but mind the seaward current. Swimmers and snorkelers are cautioned never to venture beyond the breakwater.

James Kealoha Beach Park is a county park that's known locally as 'Four Miles' because of the distance between the park and the downtown post office. There are showers and restrooms here. For swimming and snorkeling, most people head for the eastern side of the park, which is sheltered by an island and a breakwater. It's generally calm there, with clean, clear water and nice pockets of white sand. The west side of the park is open ocean and much rougher. Locals sometimes net fish here and it's a popular winter surfing spot, although there are strong rip currents.

Almost another mile eastward, **Leleiwi Beach Park** is the best shore-dive site in Hilo, but the entrance is a bit trickier than at Puhi Bay. The best place to enter is to the left of the third pavilion, where the wall jogs toward the ocean. From there, walk to the level area beyond the gap in the wall.

Richardson Ocean Park, just before the end of the road, has a small black-sand beach fronting Hilo's most popular snorkeling site. When the waves get bumpy, it's also boogie-boarding territory. On the Hilo side, the bay tends to be cooler, due to subsurface freshwater springs. The water is warmer and the snorkeling better on the eastern side of the park, which also has a lava shoreline for exploring. There are restrooms, showers, picnic tables and a lifeguard.

On the northern side of town, the cove at **Honoli'i Beach Park** is a protected pocket with Hilo's best surfing. The park has showers and toilets. To get there, take Hwy 19 north out of Hilo. Between the 4- and 5-mile markers, make a right onto Nahala St and a left onto Kahoa St. Join all the other cars parked on the side of the road and head down to the park. For a little variety, you can return to Hwy 19 by following Kahoa St downhill onto a one-lane road that winds through an enchanting forest.

ACTIVITIES
Swimming
Hilo is not exactly a drawcard for swimmers, as the beaches are rocky and often rough. Along Kalaniana'ole Ave, **James Kealoha Beach** (Map pp160–1) offers the calmest waters for swimming; for toddlers and young kids, **Onekahakaha Beach** (Map pp160–1) is shallow and ideal for learning to swim.

For lap swimming, the **Ho'olulu Complex** (Map pp160-1; ☎ 961-8698) contains an impressive, Olympic-sized, open-air pool that is generally uncrowded during the day. One swimmer per lane for lap swimming (no circle swimming). Bring your own towel and phone ahead for opening hours.

Diving
For diving, the best spot near Hilo is **Leleiwi Beach** (Map pp160–1), with depths of 10ft to 70ft. You can see lava arches, coral reef, turtles, dolphins, fish and whales in season. In the nearby Puna district, **Pohoiki Bay** is the best dive site in east Hawai'i, with depths of 20ft to 100ft and impressive marine life.

For equipment and first-hand advice, **Nautilus Dive Center** (Map pp164-5; ☎ 935-6939; www .nautilusdivehilo.com; 382 Kamehameha Ave; scuba package

or kayak per day $25) is a reliable outfit that organizes dives and courses in the Hilo area at competitive rates.

Surfing
By far the best surfing spot near Hilo is Honoli'i Cove at Honoli'i Beach Park (p167), which draws crowds when the surf's up.

Stroll into **Orchidland Surfboards** (Map pp164-5; ☎ 935-1533; www.orchidlandsurf.com; 262 Kamehameha Ave; 9am-5pm Mon-Sat, 10am-3pm Sun) for board rentals (per day $20) or surf gear. Owner Stan Lawrence is an expert surfer, and he opened the Big Island's first surf shop in 1972. Check his website for surf reports and cool videos.

To learn to surf, especially if you're female, **Big Island Girl Surf** (☎ 326-0269; www.big islandgirlsurf.com; 1hr group/private lesson $50/60, day camp $55-125) offers safe lessons and day camps at Honoli'i Beach. Week-long overnight camps (for both novices and advanced surfers) include accommodations, healthy meals, yoga classes, surf lessons and island excursions. Lessons are offered for boys, too, but the overnighters are all *wahine* (women). The average age range is 14 to 30 but they say 'attitude is more important than age!'

Golf
In Hilo, you can golf practically for nothing at **Hilo Municipal Golf Course** (Map p179; ☎ 959-7711; 340 Haihai St; Mon-Fri $29, Sat & Sun $34), the locals' favorite, nicknamed the 'Muni.' The nine-hole **Naniloa Country Club Golf Course** (Map pp160-1; ☎ 935-3000; Mon-Fri 9-/18-hole green fees $20/25, Sat & Sun $25/30) is located right across Lili'uokalani Park.

Fitness Centers
Spencer Health & Fitness Center (Map pp164-5; ☎ 969-1511; 197 Keawe St; per day $10; 5am-9pm Mon-Fri, 5am-3pm Sat, 6am-noon Sun) Fully equipped gym with free weights and full range of resistance and aerobic machines. Facility is well worn but clean and well located, with a steady clientele of all ages and fitness levels. Offers aerobic, stretch and yoga classes.

Orchid Isle Fitness (Map pp164-5; ☎ 961-0003; 29 Shipman St; per day $10; 4:45am-9pm Mon-Fri, 8am-3pm Sat, 8am-noon Sun) Another downtown option, located on the northern border.

Hawaii Naniloa Resort gym (Map pp160-1; ☎ 969-3333; 93 Banyan Dr; per day $15; 6am-9pm Mon-Fri, 10am-6pm Sat & Sun) Mediocre, but convenient if you're staying near Banyan Dr.

Yoga

Yoga Centered (Map pp164-5; ☎ 934-7233; www.yoga
centered.com; 37 Waianuenue Ave; drop-in class $12;
🕑 10am-5pm Mon-Thu, 10am-4pm Sun for boutique)
Spacious, beautifully designed studio offering Ashtanga and *vinyasa* (flowing se-
quences of poses) classes that get students
to focus (and sweat!) and attract a youthful,
fit crowd. Boutique features chic yoga fash-
ions by sweatshop-free manufacturers.

Balancing Monkey Yoga Center (Map pp160-1;
☎ 936-9590; www.balancingmonkey.com; 65 Mohouli St;
drop-in class $11; 🕑 Sun-Fri) An airy studio within
a house, Balancing Monkey has an unpretentious, welcoming vibe. Walk in and
feel at home right away. It's owned by the
youthful director of UH Hilo's nascent yoga
program. Classes are taught either in the
Ashtanga or Iyengar method, and they're
usually nice and small.

WALKING TOUR

Old Hilo town is perfect for a leisurely stroll
along historic buildings, unique shops and
the panoramic bay. This 2-mile (one way)
walking tour starts in downtown Hilo and
ends at Lili'uokalani Park near Banyan Dr.
First stop by the **Hawaiian Telephone Company**

Start Downtown Hilo
Finish Lili'uokalani Park
Duration 1 hour
Distance 2 miles

Building (**1**). Designed by renowned Honolulu architect CW Dickey in the 1920s, this
is the jewel in Hilo's architectural crown.
Influenced by Spanish, Italian and Californian missions, the building features handsome terracotta tiles, high-hipped roof and
metalwork detailing on the windows. The
East Hawaii Cultural Center (**2**; p165), next
door, is a public art gallery located in the
historic former police station.

Next cross Kalakaua St into **Kalakaua Park**
(**3**), which features a bronze statue of 19th-
century King David Kalakaua (the 'Merrie
Monarch') under a majestic banyan tree.
The taro leaf by the King's side symbolizes
his connection with the land, while the *ipu*
(gourd instrument) on his right stands for
the traditional Hawaiian cultural arts that
he helped to revive. The lily-filled pool is a
Korean War veterans memorial, and buried
under the grass is a time capsule, sealed on
the last total solar eclipse (July 11, 1991),
and to be opened on the next one (May
3, 2106).

Look further north at the neoclassical
Federal Building (**4**), across the street. Built in
1919 in a style typical of early-20th-century
government buildings, it now houses government offices and a post office. Next head
makai (seaward) on Waianuenue Ave, and
see the traditional **Burns Building** (**5**; 1911)
and **Pacific Building** (**6**; 1922) right next door
on Keawe St. Across the street is the **Toyama
Building** (**7**; 1908), which was meticulously
restored and now has become a destination,

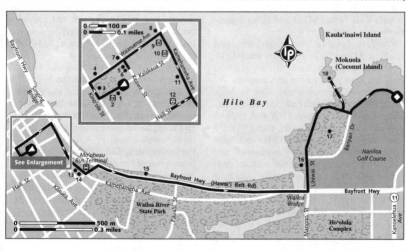

with Restaurant Kaikodo (p176) downstairs. Keep heading *makai* until you reach the **FW Koehnen Building (8)** at Kamehameha Ave. This eye-catching blue 1910 building has interior koa walls and ohia floors; since 1957 the Koehnen family has owned the building and its fine furnishings store.

Now you're on downtown Hilo's main street with a lovely view of the bay. You'll pass a handful of excellent galleries, such as the spacious **Chase Gallery (9**; p177). Just before you cross Kalakaua St, stop at the **Pacific Tsunami Museum (10**; p165) in the old First Hawaiian Bank Building. Another CW Dickey creation, this sturdy concrete building with fluted columns and wrought-iron detailing was built in 1930.

In the next block, you'll hit the art deco **SH Kress Company Building (11**; 1932), which until 1980 was a bustling department store. In the 1980s it fell into disrepair until former US Senator Hiram Fong bought and restored it in 1990. Now the building houses a first-run movie theater, a 245-student public-charter school and small shops. When you reach Haili St, turn *mauka* to see Hilo's old-time **Palace Theater (12**; p177), which in 1925 was the first deluxe playhouse on the Big Island.

Keep walking southeast along Kamehameha Ave until you reach the **S Hata Building (13**; 1912), a fine example of renaissance revival architecture that was seized from the original Japanese owner by the US government during WWII. After the war, the owner's daughter bought the building back for $100,000. Today the restored building houses Café Pesto (p175) and other restaurants, shops and offices.

On Saturday and Wednesday, the open space at Mamo St is a **farmers' market (14**; p166), teeming with more varieties of island produce than you can try on vacation.

Now cross Kamehameha Ave to walk along the **Bayfront Beach Park (15)**. The breakwater was built between 1908 and 1929 to provide a safe port for Hilo, using 951,273 tons of rock. Before the 1946 and 1960 tsunami, there were many businesses and houses on the grassy area lined with coconut palms. Watch for canoe paddlers training in the bay.

At Manono St, head left toward the unmistakable **Suisan Fish Market (16)**, where you can come back and watch fish being auctioned at 7am. Now you can picnic and hang

out at Hilo's peaceful **Lili'uokalani Park (17**; p167), which at 30 acres is rarely crowded. Just a short walk away is **Mokuola (18**; p167), easily accessible by a modern bridge. If you still have energy, a quick stroll down Banyan Dr is very scenic, past Hilo's handful of 'high-rise' hotels, giant banyan trees and a golf course.

COURSES

Island Language Center (Map pp160-1; ☎ 969-7556; www.islandlc.com; Hilo Lagoon Center, Suite 240, 101 Aupuni St; ⏰ 10am-12:30pm Mon-Fri) Learn about the language, culture and history of Hawaii in 'Hawaiian for Visitors,' a 2½-hour course ($35). Longer five- and 10-week courses are also offered. Instructors are taught by instructors of Hawaiian ancestry and classes are limited to eight students.

HILO FOR CHILDREN

All of Hilo is kid-friendly, with many outdoor spots where kids can freely romp and parents can enjoy the scenery. A day spent strolling and netting guppies at Lili'uokalani Park (p167) and crossing the footbridge to Mokuola (p167) to pole-fish is sure to please. Onekahakaha Beach (p167) is small, calm, close to town and perfect for a picnic. Kids will likely find tiny fish and shellfish in the lava tide pools. Lyman House Memorial Museum (p164) will fascinate older kids who might be interested in ancient Hawaiian culture. The grassy areas alongside Kamehameha Ave are Hilo's soccer fields and an ideal place to kick around a ball or play catch with a football or baseball. If you visit Hilo in September, the annual Hawai'i County Fair (p172) is a great, old-fashioned event with carnival rides, petting zoo, cotton candy and ring-toss games. Kids might also enjoy the following:

Tilt (Map pp160-1; ☎ 959 3444; Prince Kuhio Plaza, 111 E Puainako St; token 25¢; ⏰ 9am-11pm Mon-Fri, 7am-11pm Sat, 8am-10pm Sun) If your kid is a gamer who needs a fix, the best place is Tilt, a video-game arcade that's bustling on weekends and after school. The mall setting is nondescript, but it's clean, safe and convenient (other family members can catch a movie or shop).

Fun Factory (Map pp160-1; ☎ 935-3444; Waiakea Kai Shopping Plaza, 88 Kanoelehua Ave; token 25¢; ⏰ 10am-10pm Sun-Thu, to midnight Fri & Sat) Hilo's long-standing original arcade is unfortunately located in a commercial plaza that's lost its cinemas and become deserted over the years – a far cry from its bustling teen-hangout scene in the 1980s. At the time of writing, the arcade was closed temporarily but slated to reopen in 2005.

Pana'ewa Rainforest Zoo (Map p179; ☎ 959-9233; www .hilozoo.com; admission free; ☻ 9am-4pm, petting zoo 1:30-2:30pm Sat) Hilo's 12-acre zoo has seen better days but zoos always excite kids, and if you have an hour or two, it's a good diversion. Free-roaming peacocks have the run of the place. Caged monkeys, reptiles, a pygmy hippo and an axis deer look a bit cramped. But a white Bengal tiger (shipped in from Las Vegas) has a generous grassy arena – and if an unknowing peacock lands inside, you'll see a bloody feast worthy of a PBS documentary. You can see some of Hawai'i's endangered birds, such as nene and Hawaiian duck, hawk and owl. To get there, turn off Hwy 11 at W Mamaki St, just past the 4-mile marker; the zoo is another mile west.

TOURS
Arnott's Adventure Tours (Map pp160-1; ☎ 969-7097; www.arnottslodge.com; 98 Apapane Rd; tour per guest $50-60, nonguest $75-90), run by the same folks who run Arnott's Lodge, offers popular backpacker-oriented day tours to Mauna Kea, Waipi'o Valley and Hawai'i Volcanoes National Park. These are geared for active people who prefer to do some hiking and/or swimming during their outings, rather than just sitting on a bus.

FESTIVALS & EVENTS
For a complete listing of Big Island events, click to www.calendar.gohawaii.com.
King Kamehameha Day Celebration (Jun 11; ☎ 935-9338; Mokuola; admission free) A historic re-enactment of King Kamehameha's history at Mokuola, plus music and crafts. The Kamehameha statue will be draped with lei around this day.
Fourth of July Entertainment and food all day at Lili'uokalani Park, culminating in fireworks set off from

---

WORLD'S BEST HULA SHOW

Hilo's reputation as a low-key town is hard to believe during the annual **Merrie Monarch Festival** (Mar or Apr; ☎ 935-9168; www.merriemonarchfestival.org; 2-night admission general/reserved $5/15, 3-night admission reserved $20-25; ☻ starts Easter Sun). Established in 1964, Hilo's premier attraction lasts a week and includes a *ho'olaule'a* (celebration) at Mokuola (p167), craft fairs, a parade and a world-famous three-day hula competition. The festival honors King David Kalakaua (1836–91), who almost singlehandedly revived Hawaiian culture and arts, including hula, which had been forbidden by missionaries for almost 70 years.

Top hula troupes from all the islands vie in *kahiko* (ancient) and *'auana* (modern) categories – and if you've seen only hotel hula shows, these dancers' skill and seriousness will give you a whole new perspective. *Kahiko* performances are accompanied only by chanting and display a bent-knee stance, as it's said that dancers then can absorb the Earth's energy. *'Auana* is closer to the mainstream style, as the music incorporates string instruments and lively tunes, the arm movements are sinuous and the dancers smile.

Catching the Merrie Monarch Festival requires major advance planning, however. Order tickets by mail on December 26 (no earlier postmarks allowed). The roughly 2700 tickets sell out within a month. Only money orders or cashier's checks are accepted. Book a hotel room a year in advance, and you'll be added to a wait list. Then you'll pay a deposit in September and the balance by March. Reserve a rental car a year in advance (or as soon as they allow).

If you go, bring the following 'survival kit' items, suggested by Wanda Adams, a feature writer who covers the festival for the *Honolulu Advertiser*:

- flat, soft cushion (for folding chairs) or cushion with backrest (for bleachers)
- umbrella and *rubbah slippah* (in case of rain)
- binoculars
- sweater or jacket
- camera but no flash
- ear plugs (if you're sensitive to noise)
- sunglasses (light glare can cause headaches)
- cash (for craft fairs, food, lei and souvenirs)

For more on hula, see p37.

Mokuola. Watch from a car parked along the Bayfront Hwy or from a picnic mat at Lili'uokalani Park.

Big Island Hawaiian Music Festival (mid-Jul; ☎ 961-5711; Afook-Chinen Civic Auditorium; adult/child $10/free) A two-day concert featuring accomplished ukulele, steel-guitar and slack-key-guitar players from across the islands.

International Festival of the Pacific (throughout Aug; ☎ 934-0177; Japanese Chamber of Commerce; admission free) Celebration of island diversity with cultural events, eg craft demonstrations, a Japanese tea ceremony at Lili'uokalani Park and a lantern parade featuring up to 100 spirited Japanese sailors from the *Nippon Maru* ship, hoisting a *mikoshi* (huge portable shrine).

Hawai'i County Fair (Sep; Afook-Chinen Civic Auditorium; adult/student $3/2) The county fair is sure to spur nostalgia, with carnival rides and games and the aroma of grilled corn, popcorn, chili and cotton candy, plus only-in-Hawaii treats like *malasada*. Also featured are orchid and car shows, agricultural exhibits including live animals, and political-campaign booths during major election years.

Queen Lili'uokalani Music Festival (late Sep; ☎ 966-5416) Part of the Aloha Festival (see p229), features music and hula performances, lei and food vendors and crafts. Finale is a mass hula with 300 to 500 dancers!

Christmas Craft 'EG'stravaganza (late Nov; ☎ 959-6389; Edith Kanaka'ole Stadium, Hilo; admission $2) A two-day craft sale featuring handmade local ornaments, bags, jewelry, hats and more.

SLEEPING

The glut of resorts and 'vacation rental' condos in Kona is nonexistent here. Instead you'll find a handful of standard hotels and numerous B&Bs, including elegant old-style manors (the best option if you want a bit of extravagance).

Budget

Hilo Bay Hostel (Map pp164-5; ☎ 933-2771; www.hawaii hostel.net; 101 Waianuenue Ave; dm $18, r without/with bathroom $38/58; 🖥) In a prime location smack dab in the middle of downtown Hilo, this hostel, in the 1911 Burns Building, is clean and airy.

The crowd is diverse and from all over the world, and the vibe is low-key. Dorm rooms sleep four to eight, and there's one room with a private bathroom. Top bunk beds are singles while bottoms are doubles. All rooms have ceiling fans and windows that let in the refreshing Hilo breezes. Guests have free use of a TV (and DVDs) and a refrigerator (but no freezer). Complimentary coffee and tea. No drugs or alcohol permitted.

Arnott's Lodge (Map pp160-1; ☎ 969-7097; www .arnottslodge.com; 98 Apapane Rd; tent sites $9, dm/s/d with shared bathroom $19/39/49, r/ste $62/125; 🖨 🖥) The place for the outdoorsy, backpacking crowd, the only downside is its location at the outskirts of town. There are sex-segregated dorms, wheelchair-accessible portions, camping in the front yard and a slew of private rooms. Amenities at this laid-back hostel include a TV and DVD room (with over 200 DVDs), Internet access, air-con (in private rooms only, costing $3 per day) and coin laundry. Guests can hop cheap daily shuttles into town or rent bicycles (under $10 per day). Adventure island tours cost $50 to $60 ($75 to $90 for nonguests). Free airport pickups are available (until 8pm). If you're driving, head east of Hwy 11 on Kalaniana'ole Ave about 1.5 miles, then turn left onto Keokea Loop Rd. The lodge is about 100yd down the road. Aussies, in case you're wondering, founder Doug Arnott's grandparents started the Tim Tam biscuit company in Australia.

Midrange & Top End

The B&Bs are closer to downtown Hilo, while the hotels on Banyan Dr are adjacent to Lili'uokalani Park. Inquire with B&Bs about discounts for stays over three nights.

Bay House B&B (Map pp164-5; ☎ 961-6311, 888-235-8195; www.bayhousehawaii.com; 42 Pukihae St; r $105-

---

AUTHOR'S CHOICE

Dolphin Bay Hotel (Map pp164-5; ☎ 935-1466; www.dolphinbayhotel.com; 333 Iliahi St; r $80-90, 1-/2-bedroom ste $110/130) Located right near downtown, this popular, family-run hotel is the best deal in Hilo. All rooms resemble comfy apartment units – with full kitchen, color TV, fan and sliding glass doors. This is an ideal place for a 'home base' to explore east Hawai'i, and the down-to-earth staff are generous with insider advice. The owner is an experienced hiker and a fount of information on the entire Big Island outdoors, especially Hawai'i Volcanoes National Park – check out his photos and daily volcano update at the reception desk. Fresh-picked fruit from the backyard and free morning coffee are available to guests. Reduced weekly rates are also available.

BIG ISLAND'S TOP FIVE LUXURY B&BS

If you think all B&Bs are modest bedrooms covered with doilies and dust, think again. On the Big Island you can stay at upscale mansions catering to every creature comfort, run by hosts who add a personal touch:

Palms Cliff House Inn (p157) Pure luxury, from Italian marble fireplace to in-room Jacuzzi.

Waianuhea B&B (p148) Chic mansion smack in rolling pastureland (and run entirely on solar power).

Hawaiian Oasis B&B (p80) Spectacular gardens in tropical Kona, near top snorkeling and diving.

Shipman House B&B (below) 'Grand dame' of a mansion, the most authentically local.

Holualoa Inn (p90) Classy and private, with a sweeping view of the Kona Coast.

120) Located just across the 'Singing Bridge' from downtown Hilo, the Bay House offers three spacious rooms, literally overlooking the bay, in a separate guest wing. Each room has a private lanai, cable TV, phone and king- or queen-size beds, with a shared kitchenette and a hot tub. The hosts are friendly, longtime residents, and they serve a delicious breakfast buffet that you eat on your lanai. Rates include breakfast.

Shipman House B&B (Map pp164-5; ☎ 934-8002, 800-627-8447; www.hilo-hawaii.com; 131 Kaiulani St; r $199-219) Set on a knoll in Hilo's breathtaking 'Reeds Island' neighborhood, this graceful Victorian mansion has been in the Shipman family since 1901. Past visitors to this B&B, which is on the National Register of Historic Places, have included Queen Liliʻuokalani and Jack London. All rooms, whether in the main house or in the 1910 guest cottage, have baths (with gorgeous tubs), high ceilings, small refrigerators, hardwood floors covered with *lauhala* mats and genuine vintage furnishings. The congenial owners have added appealing touches, such as guest kimonos, fresh flowers, a library and a Steinway grand piano. Stay two or more nights and get $25 off. Rates include breakfast.

Waterfalls Inn B&B (Map pp164-5; ☎ 969-3407, 888-808-4456; www.waterfallsinn.com; 240 Kaiulani St; r $145-175) From your first glimpse of the French doors and spacious veranda, it's clear that this Reeds Island plantation home (also on the National Register of Historic Places) is magnificent. The added bonus is that it's also relaxed and unpretentious. There's a large antique soaking tub and wi-fi access, too. In the backyard, the sounds of Wailuku River and rain-forest birds add to the serenity. Rates include breakfast.

Old Hawaiian B&B (Map pp160-1; ☎ 961-2816; www .thebigislandvacation.com; 1492 Wailuku Dr; r $75-95) In a scenic neighborhood above Hilo Medical Center, a five-minute drive from downtown, these three attractive rooms with private entrances are amazing deals. A full breakfast, including homemade bread and island fruit, is served on the shared lanai, where there's a microwave and refrigerator you can use. Military discounts are also offered. Rates include breakfast.

Holmes' Sweet Home (Map pp160-1; ☎ 961-9089; www.hilohawaiibandb.com; 107 Koula St; r incl breakfast $75-85) Also a five-minute drive from downtown, this friendly, lived-in B&B provides comfy rooms with private entrances and free high-speed Internet access. The $85 room, with queen and twin beds, high ceiling and double sink, is a steal. Large common area with full-sized fridge and microwave. Wheelchair accessible. Rates include breakfast.

Hilo Hawaiian Hotel (Map pp160-1; ☎ 935-9361, 800-367-5004; www.castleresorts.com; 71 Banyan Dr; r $125-180; ❄ ❢) If you'd prefer the privacy of a hotel, the Hilo Hawaiian is definitely Hilo's best. Located on Banyan Dr, overlooking Coconut Island, the crescent-shaped building is pleasant and airy. Rooms are comfortable (with TV and phone), and most have a lanai. The popular Queen's Court restaurant (p176) is located on the lobby floor.

Uncle Billy's Hilo Bay Hotel (Map pp160-1; ☎ 935-0861, 800-442-5841; www.unclebilly.com; 87 Banyan Dr; r $85/105; ❄) This Hawaiian-owned hotel is a fixture in Hilo, and though the Polynesian decor is a cliché, the rooms are more than adequate and overlook a central courtyard of palms, red ginger and talkative mynah birds. The adjacent restaurant is popular with senior-citizen breakfast gangs and offers a free nightly hula show at 6pm. You can save over 25% if you book on the Internet.

Hilo Seaside Hotel (Map pp160-1; ☎ 935-0821, 800-560-5557; www.hiloseasidehotel.com; 126 Banyan Dr; r $100-120; ❄ ❢) A surprisingly sprawling complex of two-story motel-style buildings, the Seaside is fine if you simply want a room and a bit of anonymity. Rooms include air-con, ceiling fan, TV, louvered windows and refrigerator. Avoid those around the swimming pool and the noisy streetside Hukilau wing; better rooms in the deluxe ocean wing have balconies overlooking a carp pond. Internet specials go as low as $62.

EATING
Budget
For real local-style *grinds* (food) or late-night eats, Hilo's casual restaurants are the ticket.

Café 100 (Map pp160–1; ☎ 935-8683; specials hotline 935-6368; 969 Kilauea Ave; loco moco $2-4, plate lunches $4-6; ⏱ 6:45am-8:30pm Mon-Sat) This legendary drive-in, named for the Japanese-American WWII 100th Battalion, popularized the *loco moco*, which is rice topped with hamburger, fried egg and a cardiac-arresting amount of brown gravy, and now available in 20 different varieties (including veg). Top it off with strawberry 'goody good,' a sweet, icy dessert.

Nori's Saimin & Snacks (Map pp160–1; ☎ 935-9133; Suite 124, 688 Kino'ole St; noodle soups $4-7; ⏱ 11:30am-3pm Mon, 10:30am-3pm & 4pm-midnight Tue-Sat, to 11pm Sun) Despite the strip-mall setting, Nori's is a great place to try Japanese noodle soups such as saimin, *udon, ramen* or *soba*. Other specialties include a whole fried-fish plate ($7 to $9) and gift-ready sweets and snacks. Proprietor, Beth-An Nishijima, hosts a cooking show called *Two Skinny Chefs* (a play on restaurateur Sam Choy's 'Never Trust a Skinny Chef' motto) on the local cable channel.

Kuhio Grille (Map pp160–1; ☎ 959-2336; Suite A106, Prince Kuhio Plaza; mains $5.50-8.50; ⏱ 6am-10pm Sun-Thu, 6am-midnight Fri & Sat) Always packed at local mealtimes, Kuhio Grille is a family-run place known for filling breakfasts, for fried-rice *loco moco* and especially for 1lb *laulau* (a bundle made of pork or chicken and salted butterfish, wrapped in taro and *ti* leaves

and steamed) plates ($7) and other Hawaiian favorites such as poi, *lomilomi* salmon (minced, salted salmon, diced tomato and green onion), *kalua* (traditional-style roast pork) pig and *haupia* (coconut pudding). The *laulau* is also available packed for travel. It's behind Prince Kuhio Plaza.

Ken's House of Pancakes (Map pp160–1; ☎ 935-8711; 1730 Kamehameha Ave; meals $6-12; ⏱ 24hr) The perfect spot after Mauna Kea stargazing. A family-friendly diner, Ken's offers hundreds of menu combos, including giant Spam omelettes, macadamia-nut pancakes and milkshakes. Dinners such as *kalua* pig and cabbage come with all the trimmings.

GROCERIES
In Hilo, your best meals might be the picnics and to-go meals you cobble together yourself.

First pick up the freshest raw materials at the extensive **farmers' market** (p166), then try **Suisan Fish Market** (Map pp160–1; ☎ 935-9349; 93 Lihiwai St; ⏱ 8am-5pm Mon-Sat) for just-caught fish. You can't buy wholesale anymore, due to health regulations, but the retail store sells the whole range plus an *ono* (delicious) selection of *poke* (cubed raw fish mixed with shoyu, sesame oil, salt, chili pepper, inamona or other condiments).

O'Keefe & Sons Bread Bakers (Map pp164–5; ☎ 934-9334; 374 Kino'ole St; snacks $3-7; ⏱ 6am-5pm Mon-Fri, to 3pm Sat) Bakes gorgeous artisan breads, as well as pastries and sandwiches that will make your mouth water.

Abundant Life Natural Foods (Map pp164–5; ☎ 935-7411; 292 Kamehameha Ave; ⏱ 8:30am-7pm Mon, Tue, Thu & Fri, 7am-7pm Wed & Sat, 10am-5pm Sun) For natural foods, the best place in the downtown area and this place carries the expected cheeses, juices and bulk foods, plus a simple smoothie and sandwich bar.

Island Naturals (Map pp160–1; ☎ 935-5533; Waiakea Center, 303 Ma'akala St; smoothies $3-3.75, deli dishes

---

AUTHOR'S CHOICE

Seaside Restaurant (Map pp160–1; ☎ 935-8825; 1790 Kalaniana'ole Ave; meals $18-24; ⏱ dinner Tue-Sat) Certainly there are much swankier restaurants in Hilo, but if you want urban chic, go to New York or San Francisco. In Hilo, try the long-standing, family-run Seaside Restaurant, where you know the fish is fresh because the mullet, *aholehole* (flagtail) and other island fish are raised in Hawaiian-style fishponds right outside. The decor is unremarkable, but outdoor tables have a nice view of the aqua-farm. The simple preparation of the fish (steamed in *ti* leaves with lemon and onions) is delicious, and all meals generously include rice, salad, apple pie and coffee.

THERE'S ALWAYS ROOM FOR DESSERT

If you have a sweet tooth, Hilo won't let you down. The best ice cream and sorbet on the island comes from a Kawaihae creamery that produces two equally yummy premium lines: Hilo Home-made (classic single flavors) and Tropical Dreams (novel fusion flavors). Do your own taste test at **Hilo Homemade Ice Cream** (Map pp164-5; ☎ 933-1520; 41 Waianuenue Ave; per scoop $2; 10:30am-7:30pm Mon-Fri, noon-6pm Sat, to 4pm Sun) and **Tropical Dreams** (Map pp164-5; ☎ 935-9109; 174 Kame-hameha Ave; per scoop $2.50; 9am-6pm Mon-Thu, to 9:30pm Fri, 10:30am-9:30pm Sat).

For an island take on traditional Japanese *mochi* (sweet rice dessert) and *manju* (baked azuki bean–filled cake), stop at **Two Ladies Kitchen** (☎ 961-4766; 274 Kilauea Ave; 8-piece boxes $5.60; 11am-5pm Wed-Sat), where you can find temptingly golden *liliko'i* (passionfruit) *mochi* (Japanese sticky-rice pounded and shaped into a dumpling) made with fresh passionfruit, purple sweet-potato *mochi*, and its specialty, fresh strawberries wrapped in a sweet bean paste and *mochi* – all handmade by two Hilo-born ladies.

You haven't tasted buttermilk doughnuts until you've tried the moist, satisfying beauties from **Sputnik's** (Map pp160-1; ☎ 961-2066; 811 Laukapu St; doughnuts 80¢; 6:30am-2pm Mon-Fri), a third-generation family business. But go before 11am because they bake less than 100 doughnuts daily and they're often sold out by then!

Chocoholics can get their fix from **Big Island Candies** (Map pp160-1; ☎ 935-8890; 800-935-5510; www.bigislandcandies.com; 585 Hinano St; chocolate-dipped macadamia shortbread cookies $5.50-15, chocolate-macadamia candies $3.25-9; 8:30am-5pm), a 30-year-old company that produces perhaps the best confections in Hawaii (the chocolate-dipped shortbread is a classic). You'll be tempted to buy everything in the store, and the classy packaging makes for impressive gifts (a big cut above store-bought brands and available only at the factory or online). Free cookie, candy and coffee samples are given as you watch the white-outfitted workers hand-dipping cookies and macadamia nuts in chocolate.

And no visit to Hilo is complete without a stop at **Itsu's Fishing Supplies** (Map pp160-1; ☎ 935-8082; 810 Pi'ilani; snacks under $5; 5am-5pm) – yes, a fishing-supply store! – which sells Hilo's best ice shave (note: Hilo folks call it 'ice shave,' not 'shave ice') and concession snacks like gravy burgers and hot dogs. The ice shave is neither too fine nor too grainy, and there's no skimping on the dozens of sweet syrups that you have to choose from. And for a real blast from the past, buy a bag of sweetened, colored popcorn ($2.50 to $4.50 per bag).

---

per lb $7; 8:30am-8pm Mon-Sat, 10am-7pm Sun) Near the malls toward the airport, Island Naturals is considerably larger and newer (and also a bit more expensive), with a smoothie counter, and a deli serving hot selections such as 'ahi (yellowfin tuna) with coconut, vegetarian pad thai and curries.

KTA Super Store Downtown (Map pp164-5; ☎ 935-3751; 323 Keawe St; 7am-9pm, to 6pm Sun); Puainako Town Center (Map pp160-1; ☎ 959-9111; 50 E Puainako St; 5:30am-midnight) By far the best grocer on the Big Island. It carries appetizing *bento* such as grilled mackerel or salmon, teriyaki beef or *maki* (rolled) sushi, plus hot selections and an amazing variety of *poke*. But don't go there after mid-morning – all the good stuff is sold out by then!

Midrange

Miyo's (Map pp160-1; ☎ 935-2273; Waiakea Village, 400 Hualani St; mains $8-12; lunch & dinner Mon-Sat) On the inland bank of Waiakea Pond, Miyo's resembles a rustic Japanese teahouse. The fish specials are excellent and all mains, from tempura to *tonkatsu* (lean pork cutlets), include fresh baby-lettuce salad, miso soup, rice, pickles and tea. Savory tofu and vegetable selections will satisfy any vegetarian. Save room for the homemade ice cream.

Café Pesto (Map pp164-5; ☎ 969-6640; 308 Kamehameha Ave; lunch $8-12, dinner $10-30; 11am-9pm Sun-Thu, to 10pm Fri & Sat) It's impossible not to like Café Pesto. Located in a beautifully renovated historical building, Pesto uses local ingredients to create inspired dishes, like a seafood risotto featuring Kona lobster tail and charbroiled Kamuela beef tenderloin. There are 10 flavors of crispy-crust pizza, plus numerous vegetarian selections. If you peer through the expansive windowed facade, it looks rather fancy, but the core local crowd is casual and very diverse.

Ocean Sushi Deli (Map pp164-5; ☎ 961-6625; 239 Keawe St; 6-piece rolls $4, 2-piece nigiri $2.50; ☺ 10am-2pm & 4:30-9pm Mon-Sat) It's fantastic: scores of inventive specials include sushi rolls made with macadamia nuts plus *poke* or *'ahi* and avocado. If you're craving a hot meal, try the curry roll, which includes chicken *katsu* (fried cutlets) and curry. Vegetarian options are also plentiful. Also recommended is Ocean Sushi Deli's sister restaurant across the street, **Tsunami Grill & Tempura** (☎ 961-6789; 250 Keawe St; mains $7-9; ☺ 10am-2pm & 5-9pm Mon-Sat). You can order from either menu and servers will dodge traffic to bring you your meal!

Hilo Bay Café (Map pp160-1; ☎ 935-4939; Waiakea Center, 315 Maka'ala St; mains $10-24; ☺ 11am-9pm Mon-Sat, 5-9pm Sun) Don't be deterred by the Wal-Mart outside or by the incongruous 'urban chic' decor that's inside. The gourmet cuisine speaks for itself. The eclectic menu is not only health-conscious (organically grown produce and free-range meats) but also delicious and creative, from asparagus, watercress and feta with mint-flax dressing to bacon-infused chicken breast. Delectable veg options include spinach ravioli and grilled polenta Napoleon.

Restaurant Miwa (Map pp160-1; ☎ 961-4454; Hilo Shopping Center, 1261 Kilauea Ave; sushi $2.75-5.50, meals $6-13; ☺ lunch & dinner) This is another restaurant serving good, quality food at decent prices, located in a mall setting. It has a sushi bar, good sashimi and a full range of Japanese dishes. They serve filling *teishoku* (complete meal) at lunch and dinner, and a children's menu is available. The servers dressed in kimono are a nice touch.

Reuben's (Map pp164-5; ☎ 961-2552; 336 Kamehameha Ave; combination plates $8-9.50; ☺ 11am-9pm Mon-Fri, noon-9pm Sat) Resembling an Oaxaca cantina, with festively painted cinder block, piñatas galore and folding tables and chairs, Reuben's keeps the locals coming back with authentic Mexican fare, including classic enchiladas and rellenos (chilies stuffed with cheese), freshly fried chips, salsa that'll make you speechless, and an unforgettable fish taco-and-tamale combination plate.

Top End

Restaurant Kaikodo (Map pp164-5; ☎ 961-2558; Toyama Bldg, 60 Keawe St; lunch $10; dinner $22-27; ☺ lunch & dinner) The most talked-about restaurant in years, Kaikodo brings a touch of upscale elegance (plus inevitable yuppie-

ism) to formerly sleepy Hilo. Executive chef Michael Fennelly is meticulous about quality and presentation, with inspired dinner entrées such as *'opakapaka* (pink snapper) steamed in lemongrass and sake, and grilled mint-and-pomegranate rack of lamb. For such a lavish setting, however, service can be unpolished. The owners have a Manhattan art gallery, and they've filled the restaurant and banquet rooms with antiques.

Queen's Court (Map pp160-1; ☎ 935-9361, 800-367-5004; www.castleresorts.com; ground fl, Hilo Hawaiian Hotel, 71 Banyan Dr; ☺ breakfast, lunch & dinner) This restaurant offers local-favorite buffets: seafood ($28) on Friday, Hawaiian ($28) on Saturday and Sunday, and prime rib and crab ($25) from Monday to Thursday.

DRINKING

Kope Kope Espresso Café (Map pp160-1; ☎ 933-1221; www.kopekope.com; 1261 Kilauea St; ☺ 6:30am-9pm Mon-Fri, 7:30am-9pm Sat & Sun) While it's a *coffee* bar (in a shopping mall, no less) and closes at *nine*, Kope Kope is a great local hangout that avoids the usual touristy, divey or retro clichés. In a casual coffee-bar setting, you can enjoy light meals and *kope* (coffee) and live music on Friday nights. Local edible gifts sold online and at the café.

Cronies Bar & Grill (Map pp164-5; ☎ 935-5158; 11 Waianuenue Ave; ☺ 11-2am Mon-Sat) One of Hilo's few late-night hangouts, Cronies's bayfront location, live local music and dirt-cheap drink specials are worth checking out.

ENTERTAINMENT

Past 9pm, Hilo nightlife is scarce except for dancing at two clubs that cater to folks in their 20s. Locals tend to entertain at home or throw outdoor parties at parks and beaches. Here, you make your own fun. On clear nights, do as teens do: park around Lili'uokalani Park, fully stocked with snacks and drinks, and just hang out, 'talk story' and admire the gleaming lights of Hilo.

Live Music & Nightclubs

Uncle Mikey's Video Dance Club (Map pp160-1; ☎ 933-2667; Waiakea Village, Bldg 22, 400 Hualani St; admission $5; ☺ 9pm-1:30am Wed, Fri & Sat) Tucked in a woodsy condo-and-commercial complex, Uncle Mikey's is jammed with 600 people on Saturday nights. DJs play everything from 'old' 1970s tunes to current hits, and Wednesday night is 'college night'

BIG ISLAND'S TOP TEN ENTERTAINMENT SPOTS

Aloha Theatre (p91) Eclectic mix of film, theater, music and thought-provoking lectures.
Honoka'a People's Theater (p150) Retro wooden theater in a real-life cowboy town.
Huggo's (p83) Live music almost nightly, idyllic oceanfront setting.
Kahilu Theatre (p135) World-renowned music and dance performances.
Kanaka Kava (p83) Lively outdoor 'awa bar where the locals hang out.
Kona Brewing Company (p74) Live music, fun pizzas and da bes' brewskis.
Kona Village Resort luau (p108) Taste of ancient Hawaii.
Lava Zone (p185) Casual, gay-friendly, tourist-friendly hangout.
Outrigger Keauhou Beach Hotel (p87) Pleasantly low-key, if rather sedate, venue for live music.
Palace Theater (below) Artsy and indie films, plus live music.

(with a separate room for the under-21s). If you're above 30, however, the scene is likely to resemble a high-school dance.

Uncle Billy's Hilo Bay Hotel (Map pp160-1; ☎ 935-0861; 87 Banyan Dr; live-music & hula show 6-7:30pm & 8-9:30pm) The standard hula show offered during dinnertime at the restaurant (which serves mains comparable to the fare at a low-budget wedding) at least features enthusiastic performers. This is pure tourist entertainment, but sweet, sincere and very 'Hilo.'

Shooters Bar & Grill (Map pp160-1; ☎ 969-7069; 121 Banyan Dr; admission $5; ☯ 3pm-2am Mon-Wed, to 3am Thu-Sat) Let's face it, Shooters is a dive. Under the glare of daylight (or the unflattering fluorescent lights) the tattered furnishings, sticky floor and handful of pool tables are downright depressing. But from 10pm it's popular with the local 20-somethings because the bar turns into a nightclub. Thursday is 'college night,' permitting 18-to-20 year olds to join the party (no alcohol is served to minors).

Cinemas

If the bars and clubs are too much like campy '80s throwbacks, head to the cinemas. The two located downtown offer a pleasantly old-fashioned atmosphere, while Stadium Cinemas is the shopping-mall standby you'd find anywhere in the USA.

Kress Cinemas (Map pp164-5; ☎ 935-6777; 174 Kamehameha Ave; tickets $1) An atmospheric place to take in a little celluloid (after 6pm you pay only 50¢). It screens standard first-run Hollywood films, as does **Stadium Cinemas** (Map pp160-1; ☎ 961-3456; Prince Kuhio Plaza, 111 E Puainako St; tickets adult/child/matinee $8/5/5.50).

Palace Theater (Map pp164-5; ☎ 934-7010; box office 934-7777; 38 Haili St; tickets adult/student $6/5) Shows foreign films, documentaries and director's cuts. The local intelligentsia comes

out of the woodwork for special events including concerts, plays and readings.

SHOPPING

Most locals do the bulk of their shopping at **Prince Kuhio Plaza** (Map pp160-1; ☎ 959-3555; 111 E Puainako St; ☯ 10am-9pm Mon-Fri, 9:30am-7pm Sat; 10am-6pm Sun), a standard suburban mall with a Wal-Mart, Macy's, Longs Drugs, Safeway, OfficeMax and Borders Books Music & Café. It's located on Hwy 11, just south of Hilo airport. Downtown Hilo (Map pp164–5) makes for much better browsing, with a host of fine galleries and unique boutiques.

Chase Gallery (Map pp164-5; ☎ 934-9101; www.chase designs.com; 100 Kamehameha Ave; ☯ 11am-5pm Tue-Sat) Exquisite original art including koa furniture, island-influenced sculpture, artistic glass pieces and bronzes.

Sig Zane Designs (Map pp164-5; ☎ 935-7077; 122 Kamehameha Ave; ☯ 9am-5pm Mon-Fri, to 4pm Sat) Unique Hawaii attire featuring custom-designed fabrics and styles.

Alan's Art & Collectibles (Map pp164-5; ☎ 969-1554; 202 Kamehameha Ave; ☯ 10am-5pm Mon & Wed-Fri, 1-5pm Tue, to 3pm Sat) Get a glimpse of Hawaii 'back in the day' amid this eye-popping collection of vintage island artifacts of glassware, household doodads, plantation-era clothing, aloha shirts and old magazines and records.

Fabric Impressions (Map pp164-5; ☎ 961-4468; 206 Kamehameha Ave; ☯ 9:30am-5pm Mon-Fri, to 4:30pm Sat) Wide selection of fabrics, including cotton Hawaiian prints hard to find elsewhere, for clothing and quilts. Also carries handsewn items, including quilts, clothing, bags, potholders and placemats.

Most Irresistible Shop (Map pp164-5; ☎ 935-9644; 256 Kamehameha Ave; ☯ 9am-5pm Mon-Fri, to 4pm Sat) This long-running gift shop lives up to its name by offering handcrafted jewelry, kids' books, soaps and candles, koa objects, artsy greeting cards and much more.

Orchidland Surfboards (Map pp164-5; ☎ 935-1533; 262 Kamehameha Ave; ⊙ 9am-5pm Mon-Sat, 10am-3pm Sun) A great selection of shorts, swimsuits, rash guards and other gear, plus one of a kind boards in back.

GETTING THERE & AWAY
Air
Although most Big Island visitors fly into the Kona airport, the **Hilo International Airport** (p235), located off Hwy 11, just under a mile south of the intersection of Hwys 11 and 19, is also busy with interisland commuters. The small airport includes a lei stand and store selling magazines, snacks and sundries.

Bus
The main Hilo station for the **Hele-On Bus** (☎ 961-8744; www.co.hawaii.hi.us/mass_transit/heleon bus.html; ⊙ 7:45am-4:30pm Mon-Fri) is at **Mo'oheau bus terminal** (Map pp164-5; 329 Kamehameha Ave). All intra-island buses stop here, though some routes start at other locations in Hilo. Routes include the following:

16 Kailua-Kona Goes once a day, Monday to Saturday, departing at 1:30pm.

23 Ka'u Goes once a day, Monday to Friday, departing at 2:40pm.

9 Pahoa Goes five times daily, Monday to Friday, departing at 8:45am, 1:30pm, 2:40pm, 4:45pm and 9pm (leaves once on Saturday at 7:15am).

Waikoloa Goes once a day, daily, departing at 3:30am.

31 Honoka'a Goes five times a day, Monday to Friday, departing at 3:30am, 5:20am, 1:30pm, 2:30pm and 4:30pm.

Buses stop at towns, such as Waimea, along the way. See p239 for more on the Hele-On bus system.

GETTING AROUND
To/From the Airport
Car rental booths are located right outside the baggage-claim area. Taxis can also be found curbside; the approximate fare from Hilo airport to downtown Hilo is $15. The airport is located off Kanoelehua Ave.

Bus
The **Hele-On Bus** (☎ 961-8744; www.co.hawaii.hi.us /mass_transit/heleonbus.html) has a few intracity routes, all costing 75¢ and operating Monday to Friday only:

No 4 Kaumana Goes five times a day (from 7:35am to 2:20pm), stopping at Hilo Public Library and Hilo Medical Center (near Rainbow Falls), among other stops.

No 6 Waiakea-Uka Goes five times daily (from 7:05am to 3:05pm), stopping at the University of Hawai'i and Prince Kuhio Plaza, among other stops.

No 7 Downtown Hilo Goes twice a day (at 8am and 9:45am) to Prince Kuhio Plaza.

To return to Hilo, catch the No 7 Downtown Hilo bus. But bear in mind the last runs depart in mid-afternoon.

Bicycle
Getting around by bike is doable, if you don't mind occasional rain showers.

Da Kine Bike Shop (Map pp164-5; ☎ 934-9861; 12 Furneaux Lane; ⊙ 1-6pm Mon-Sat) Rents $5-a-day rusty cruisers and $50 pro models. It also offers island cycling tours.

CLOWN PRINCESS OF HAWAII

In 1936 Clara Inter was a Hawaiian schoolteacher on a glee-club trip to Canada when she first performed 'Hilo Hattie (Does the Hilo Hop)' to a delighted Canadian crowd. One year later in the Monarch Room at Waikiki's Royal Hawaiian Hotel, Clara approached bandleader (and the song's composer) Don McDiarmid Sr and asked him to play it. McDiarmid wondered whether the 'low-class hula' was appropriate at the ritzy hotel, implying it was a dance that 'no law would allow.'

With a taste of applause under her muumuu from her Canadian hit, Clara would not be deterred. She convinced him to play the tune and the rest, as they say, is history. Clara Inter rose to international stardom on the wings of this song (with worldwide tours and appearances in movies such as *Song of the Islands* and *Ma & Pa Kettle in Waikiki*), legally changed her name to Hilo Hattie and eventually lent it to the now-famous chain of Hawaiian stores.

Today the **Hilo Hattie** (Map pp160-1; ☎ 961-3077; www.hilohattie.com; Prince Kuhio Plaza, cnr Kanoelehua Ave & Maka'ala St; ⊙ 8:30am-6pm) chain is a guaranteed stop for tour groups, but beware: the merchandise is often overpriced and mediocre (or outright fake). You can find cheaper prices for Mauna Loa macadamia nuts at Longs Drugs (p162) and the souvenirs made in China or the Philippines are just plain ridiculous.

Hilo Bike Hub (Map pp160-1; ☎ 961-4452; 318 E Kawili St) Rents out cruisers and rock hoppers, as well as full-suspension mountain bikes for $20 to $45 per day. Ask about the phenomenal weekly discounts.
Mid-Pacific Wheels (Map pp160-1; ☎ 935-6211; 1133C Manono St; ☺ 9am-6pm Mon-Sat, 11am-5pm Sun) Rents 21-speed bikes for $15 per day.

Car & Motorcycle
Hilo is certainly a car-oriented town, so shopping malls and businesses usually have ample parking lots. Downtown, all street parking is free but limited to just two hours. On most days, it's easy to find a space, but the entire bayfront area is jam-packed during the Sunday and Wednesday farmers' market.

Taxi
In Hilo, call **Marshall's Taxi** (☎ 936-2654) or **Percy's Taxi** (☎ 969-7060).

AROUND HILO

Just a quick drive outside downtown Hilo will bring you to impressive waterfalls tucked away in the residential neighborhoods on Waianuenue Ave. On the other side of town, along Hwy 11 toward Puna, you'll find a couple of tourist attractions worth seeing only if you are truly bored. Another sight along Hwy 11 is the Pana'ewa Rainforest Zoo (p170).

RAINBOW FALLS
Just a five-minute drive outside Hilo, Rainbow Falls is worth seeing for the massive banyan tree alone. You can get a straight-on view of the falls from the lookout in front of the parking lot. The falls are usually seen as a double drop, with the two streams flowing together, before hitting the large pool at the bottom.

Waianuenue, which literally means 'rainbow seen in water,' is the Hawaiian name for this lovely 80ft cascade ringed by palm, ohia and African tulip trees. The gaping cave beneath the falls is fit for a goddess, and is said to have been the home of Hina, mother of Maui. The best time for seeing rainbows is during the morning, although they are by no means guaranteed – both the sun and mist need to be somewhat accommodating.

PE'EPE'E FALLS & BOILING POTS
Up Waianuenue Ave, about 1.5 miles past Rainbow Falls, Pe'epe'e Falls drops over a sheer rock face. The water cascades downstream in a series of waterfalls, swirling and churning in bubbling pools (hence the 'boiling pots' name). The viewpoints here are accessible by wheelchair. Swimming is tempting but not advised. You'll see locals trekking to the water on a well-beaten path just past the 'No Swimming' sign, but frequent drownings occur here.

MAUNA LOA MACADAMIA-NUT VISITOR CENTER
While essentially a 'tourist trap' that caters mainly to bus tours, this **visitor center** (☎ 966-8618, 888-628-6256; www.maunaloa.com; Macadamia Rd; ☺ 8:30am-5:30pm) is a decent diversion. On the grounds you'll see a working factory with windows that allow visitors to view the large, fast-paced assembly line, where the nuts are roasted and packaged. The little garden behind the visitors center, with labeled fruit trees and flowering bushes, is worth strolling through, if you've come this

AROUND HILO
0 — 5 km
0 — 3 miles

HILO

DETOUR: KAUMANA CAVES

Most locals venture far into **Kaumana Caves**, which are actually a large lava tube formed by an 1881 lava flow from Mauna Loa. As the flow subsided, the outer edges of the deep lava stream cooled and crusted over to form a tube. When the hot molten lava inside then drained out, these caves were created. The caves are wet, mossy and thickly covered with ferns and impatiens. Bring a flashlight and wear hiking boots if you want to explore them, although they tend to be quite drippy. They are signposted, about 3 miles up Kaumana Dr (Hwy 200) on the right, en route to Mauna Kea via Saddle Rd. Locals don't consider this a major attraction and the area seems rather abandoned and lackadaisically maintained (the parking lot across the entrance might be strewn with litter). But clearly the caves remain intact and un-touristy, which is always a plus.

---

far. C Brewer Co, which owns the Mauna Loa company, produces most of Hawaii's macadamia nuts. To get there, take the left turn off Hwy 11 just over 5 miles south of Hilo. A 2.5-mile access road, Macadamia Rd, then cuts across row after row of macadamia trees, as far as the eye can see.

NANI MAU GARDENS

Encompassing more than 20 acres of flowering plants, the rather-contrived **Nani Mau Gardens** (☎ 959-3500; 421 Makalika St; adult/child $10/6; ⏰ 8am-5pm) are yet another stop on the tour-bus circuit. Nevertheless, the orderly plots set aside for different flowers (including the hibiscus, anthurium, orchid, bromeliad and gardenia) and fruit trees might impress people who are unfamiliar with such species. About 3 miles south of Hilo town, the turnoff from Hwy 11 onto Makalika St is marked with a reasonably small sign.

Puna

Pocketed with hidden treasures, the Puna district is the easternmost point of the Big Island. Its main attractions revolve around lava: the black-sand beaches, the lava-rock tide pools, the ancient forests of lava-tree molds, the thermal ponds – and the red-hot molten stuff flowing this way. Active volcano Kilauea's lively East Rift Zone zigzags its way through Puna, and today Hwy 130 ends abruptly at the 1990 lava flow that buried the village of Kalapana.

Its sultry air and hang-loose attitude make Puna a great place to ditch your guidebook and poke around. There's an eclectic vibe surrounding the town of Pahoa, a central Puna hub where being open to chance can lead you in new directions. The land and sea are rich with abundant flora and fauna. In fact, the whole Puna region has a vitality about it, which probably stems from its proximity to Kilauea. The movement of Pele is ever present, producing opposing views: a profuse creative energy for some, and uncertainty and destruction for others. This tension keeps out big business as well as the faint of heart. New-Age retreats, alternative culture and tropical plants thrive on Puna's fringe, making the cycle of change exceedingly fresh.

The light and weather change often here, as the easterly trade winds bring passing Pacific storms, and the region's pure air is some of the freshest in the world. Rainbows are a common sight over the ocean, and the strong currents can provide an opportunity to spot the venerated dolphins and sea turtles that frequent the area.

HIGHLIGHTS

- Kicking it on a clothing-optional **black-sand beach** (p188)
- Relaxing in the volcanically heated natural sauna of a **hot pond** (p187)
- Catching waves over a black-lava reef at **Pohoiki Bay** (p187)
- Snorkeling in **Kapoho tide pools** (p187) thick with coral and fish
- Taking in the eclectic vibe at the alternative **Pahoa farmers' market** (p183)

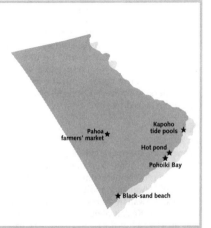

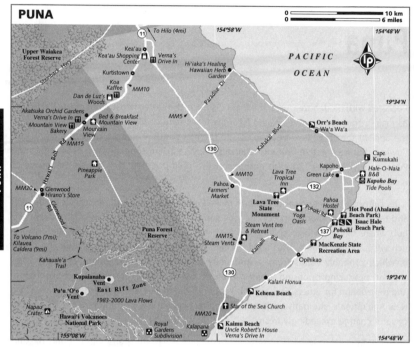

PUNA

0 ——— 10 km
0 ——— 6 miles

To Hilo (4mi)
11
154°58′W   154°48′W

Upper Waiakea
Forest Reserve

Keaʻau
Keaʻau Shopping
Center
Verna's
Drive In

Hiʻiaka's Healing
Hawaiian Herb
Garden

PACIFIC

OCEAN

Kurtistown

Koa
Kaffee
MM10

Dan de Luz's
Woods

19°34′N

Akatsuka Orchid Gardens
Verna's Drive In
Mountain View
Bakery

Bed & Breakfast
Mountain View

Mountain
View

MM5

Kahakai Blvd

Orr's Beach
Waʻa Waʻa

Cape
Kumukahi

MM15

Hawaiʻi Belt Rd

Pineapple
Park

130

MM10

Lava Tree
Tropical
Inn

Kapoho

Green Lake

Hale-O-Naia
B&B
Kapoho Bay
Tide Pools

MM20
Glenwood
Hirano's Store

132

11

Glenwood Rd

Puna Forest
Reserve

Pahoa
Farmers
Market

Lava Tree
State
Monument

Steam Vent Inn
& Retreat

Yoga
Oasis

Pohoiki Rd

Pahoa
Hostel

Hot Pond (Ahalanui
Beach Park)

Isaac Hale
Beach Park

To Volcano (7mi);
Kilauea
Caldera (9mi)

MM15
Steam Vents

Kamaili Rd

137
Pohoiki
Bay

MacKenzie State
Recreation Area

Kahaualeʻa
Trail

Opihikao

130

19°24′N

Kupaianaha
Vent

Puʻu ʻOʻo
Vent

East Rift Zone

1983-2000 Lava Flows

Kalani Honua

Kehena Beach

Napau
Crater

Hawaiʻi Volcanoes
National Park

MM20

Star of the Sea Church

155°08′W

Royal
Gardens
Subdivision

Kalapana

Kaimu Beach
Uncle Robert's House
Verna's Drive In

154°48′W

Orientation

From Hwy 11 the first town in Puna is Keaʻau. If you continue southwest along Hwy 11 you'll pass a few small towns before reaching Hawaiʻi Volcanoes National Park. From Keaʻau Hwy 130 (also known as Keaʻau–Pahoa Rd, Pahoa–Kalapana Rd and the Kalapana Hwy) goes south to Pahoa and continues almost to the coast, ending at Kaimu and Kalapana, the latter of which was buried under the 1990 lava flow.

To reach a few sights mentioned in this section, you'll pass 'No Trespassing' signs that folks seem to ignore, but do respect landowners if you're on private property and you're asked to leave.

KEAʻAU

pop 2000

Formerly known as Olaʻa, Keaʻau is the main town in Puna. While Keaʻau's population is small, it serves the burgeoning nearby subdivisions of Hawaiian Paradise Park, Hawaiian Beaches, Hawaiian Acres and Orchidland Estates. The Keaʻau Shopping Center, situated off Hwy 11 at the main crossroads, has

a post office, a laundry and an ATM. Across the street is the island's cheapest gas station.

Hiʻiaka's Healing Hawaiian Herb Garden (☎ 966-6126; www.hiiakas.com; 15-1667 2nd St, Hawaiian Paradise Park; adult/senior & child $10/8, with guided tour $15/10; ☽ 1-5pm Tue, Thu & Sat) is a lovingly tended acre of Hawaiian, Western and Ayurvedic herbs in a sprawling dirt-road subdivision southeast of town. The good-humored herbalist sells tinctures, teaches workshops and rents out a fully equipped **cottage** (s/d $50/75).

If you're hungry, **Keaʻau Natural Foods** (☎ 966-8877; Keaʻau Shopping Center, 16-586 Old Volcano Rd; ☽ 8:30am-8pm Mon-Fri, 8:30am-7pm Sat, 9:30am-5pm Sun) is convenient. For a sit-down meal, **Charley's Bar & Grill** (☎ 966-7589; Keaʻau Shopping Center, 16-586 Old Volcano Rd; pub grub $5-10; ☽ 11am-midnight Mon & Tue, 11-2am Wed-Sat, 9-1am Sun) serves decent burgers, pizza and ice-cold beers. From Thursday to Saturday it offers live music (admission $3) at night, which attracts folks all the way from Hilo.

Verna's Drive In (☎ 966-9288; 16-566 Hwy 130; lunch $2.50-7.50; ☽ 6am-10pm) is the original of four Verna's locations island-wide, serving the same artery-clogging-but-very-popular breakfasts and plate lunches. The Internet terminal at the library is usually available for walk-in appointments.

PAHOA
pop 1000

Deep in Puna's funky heart, Pahoa is a ragamuffin kind of town complete with raised wooden sidewalks, cowboy architecture and an untamed bohemian edge. It's caught in a wrinkle in time, where alternative vibes left over from the 1960s mix with the beeps of ATMs and the convenience of drive-thru espresso shacks.

Orientation & Information

Roads in and around Pahoa are known by many names. For example, the main road through town is signposted as Pahoa Village Rd but is also called Government Main Rd, Old Government Rd, Main St, Puna Rd and Pahoa Rd – but Hwy 130 is also known as Pahoa Rd! It's quite easy to hitchhike in and around Pahoa, and if you have room for hitchers in your rental car you might make a few friends.

In town you'll find a convenience store and **post office** (☎ 965-1158; 15-2859 Pahoa Village Rd; ☒ 8:30am-4pm Mon-Fri, 11am-2pm Sat). The Bank of Hawaii and First Hawaiian Bank in the town center have ATMs. In the Pahoa Village Center, **Pahoa Home Video** (☎ 965-1199; 15-2872 Pahoa Village Rd; ☒ 9am-8pm Mon-Thu, 9am-9pm Fri & Sat, 11am-8pm Sun) sells new and used

Hawaiiana books, local activity guides and maps.

For a quick Internet connection and plenty of terminals, try the **Aloha Outpost Internet Café** (☎ 965-8333; www.alohaoutpost.com; Pahoa Village Rd; per hr $8; ☒ 8am-5pm Mon-Fri, 9am-4pm Sat). This is a great Puna hub of information. Word of mouth is the best way to find out about local happenings. Owner LaMont Carroll usually knows the scoop, but if not you can check the bulletin board out front. The café also serves organic baked goodies, soups, ice cream, coffee and tea. No complaints here.

Sights & Activities

Pahoa's weekend **farmers' market** (☒ 8am Sat & Sun) is truly an event. Sip a cup of kava, indulge in a massage or palm reading, buy quality used books and organic goat cheese or boogie to a local band well into the afternoon. Ask around for the location.

Pahoa has an Olympic-size **swimming pool** (☒ 1:45-4:30pm) in the heart of town. There's also a **kiddie pool** (admission free).

Sleeping

Pahoa Hostel (☎ 965-0317; www.pahoahostel.com; 13-3345 Kumukahi, Leilani Estates; campsites $7.50, d with shared bath $15) Just 6 miles from Pahoa down Pohoiki Rd you'll find this hostel, situated on a 5-acre organic farm. The atmosphere is communal, with shared kitchen, private rooms in two converted buses, one small cottage, and covered platforms for camping. There are also possibilities for WOOFing

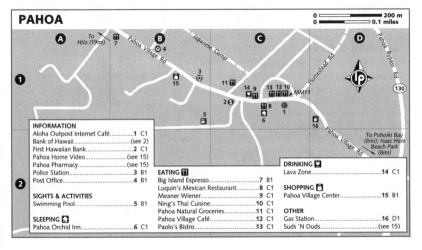

PAHOA

| 0 | 200 m |
| 0 | 0.1 miles |

To Hilo (19mi)

Pahoa Village Rd

Japanese Camp

Homestead Rd

Pahoa Bypass Rd

130

Pahoa Village Rd

To Pohoiki Bay (8mi); Isaac Hale Beach Park (8mi)

INFORMATION	
Aloha Outpost Internet Café............**1** C1	
Bank of Hawaii.................................(see 2)	
First Hawaiian Bank........................**2** C1	
Pahoa Home Video.......................(see 15)	
Pahoa Pharmacy............................(see 15)	
Police Station..................................**3** B1	
Post Office......................................**4** B1	

| SIGHTS & ACTIVITIES | |
| Swimming Pool................................**5** B1 | |

| SLEEPING | |
| Pahoa Orchid Inn.............................**6** C1 | |

| EATING | |
| Big Island Espresso...........................**7** B1 |
| Luquin's Mexican Restaurant............**8** C1 |
| Meaner Wiener.................................**9** C1 |
| Ning's Thai Cuisine.........................**10** C1 |
| Pahoa Natural Groceries.................**11** C1 |
| Pahoa Village Café..........................**12** C1 |
| Paolo's Bistro.................................**13** C1 |

| DRINKING | |
| Lava Zone.......................................**14** C1 |

| SHOPPING | |
| Pahoa Village Center.......................**15** B1 |

| OTHER | |
| Gas Station.....................................**16** D1 |
| Suds 'N Duds................................(see 15) |

(Working On Organic Farms) in exchange for board. There's plenty of beach equipment when you get the urge to head a mile down the road to Isaac Hale Beach Park (see p187) for some of the best waves on the island.

Pahoa Orchid Inn (☎ 965-9664; www.pahoaorchid inn.com; 15-2942B Pahoa Village Rd; r with shared bathroom $35-50, r $60) In a historic wooden building smack bang in the heart of town (right above Luquin's Mexican Restaurant, see right), the inn offers small but nicely furnished antique-filled rooms arranged around an inner lanai. Most have cable TV.

Steam Vent Inn (☎ 965-2122; www.steamventinn .com; 13-3775 Kalapana Hwy, Pahoa, Hawaii 96778; steam vent camping $53, equipment provided $80, d with private bath $98-125, cottages with private bath $15) Perched on 25 acres with views overlooking the ocean, this all-natural environment is an opportunity to take a retreat from yourself. The main-house rooms are tiled, clean and comfortable; the pricier rooms have ocean-facing lanais. Guests can use the kitchen (though rates include an organic breakfast) and hot tub. Downhill a bit is a basic, funky cabin with bunk beds and one private room sharing a bath and kitchen, but it's pretty good value considering the location. There are also nicely furnished, private 'jungalos', one with garden and one with ocean view. Perhaps the greatest part of this place is the on-site volcanic vent and steam house. Ask about work-exchange possibilities.

Eating

Pahoa Village Café (☎ 965-0072; 15-2471 Pahoa Village Rd; mains $8; 8am-8pm Wed-Sat, 8am-2pm Tue & Sun)

AUTHOR'S CHOICE

Ning's Thai Cuisine (☎ 965-7611; 15-2955 Government Main Rd; dishes $4.95-$11.95; lunch & dinner Mon-Sat, dinner Sun) Good Thai food is not hard to find island wide, but Ning's – with its interesting varieties of curry, such as Muslim, panang and pineapple – takes the cake. Also vying for your attention are fresh salads and sublime appetizers. Organic produce, locally raised meat and poultry, and homegrown herbs are used whenever possible. The presentation is gorgeous and the service so friendly that you can eat here two nights in a row guilt-free. It also does take-out.

This place has a pleasant café atmosphere with delicious custom omelets, organic waffles and ample veggie sandwiches with Brie, plus steak and prime rib for meat eaters.

Paolo's Bistro (☎ 965-7033; Pahoa Village Rd; mains $10-20; dinner Tue-Sun) Paolo's offers decent Northern Italian fare in an intimate atmosphere, but the waitstaff can get overwhelmed quickly. Save room (and time) for dessert.

Pahoa Natural Groceries (☎ 965-8322; 15-1403 Government Main Rd; 7:30am-7:30pm Mon-Sat, 7:30am-6pm Sun) The nexus for Pahoa's hippy-and-healthy contingent. This natural-foods shop is stocked fo' days with *da' kine veggie grinds*. The prices are a bit steep, but the hot-food bar ($6 per pound) switches regional cuisines daily, and those with the sweet-tooth munchies will be delighted with the baked items. There's a respectable wine selection as well.

Big Island Espresso (no phone; Government Main Rd; drinks $2-4.50; 6:30am-noon Mon-Fri, 7am-3pm Sat & Sun) You can't miss this little yellow-and-green shack near the post office on the way into town. The folks here make generous milkshakes, espresso drinks, shaved ice, and even maté and chai tea! There are special $1 espresso shots for those who need a quick pick-me-up. The chocolate-covered frozen bananas are a refreshing sweet treat.

Meaner Wiener (☎ 965-6644; 15-2929 Government Main Rd; hot dogs $2-4; lunch & dinner Mon-Fri, dinner Sat & Sun) If you want massive hot dogs nestled in a potato bun and buried under a mound of chili and parmesan cheese, that's the Meaner Wiener ($2.75). Too much? Try the turkey sausage Leaner Wiener or the veggie Beaner Wiener (both $2.50). Coffee here is just 50¢ a cup, with three free refills. Nice!

Luquin's Mexican Restaurant (☎ 965-9990; 15-2942 Pahoa Village Rd; breakfast $4-7, mains $8-15; 7am-9pm) This Pahoa institution can't be beat for hanging out and talking story, but do locals think this is real Mexican food? Never you mind. The atmosphere and cocktail bar let you check out a slice of life, Puna style.

Drinking & Entertainment

Pahoa's nightlife is practically nonexistent, except when a special event flares up. Full-moon parties exemplify events that travel under the radar. Locals know what's going on, so ask around.

LEE FOSTER

Water lillies in Nani Mau Gardens (p180), near Hilo

King Kamehameha statue (p166), Hilo

ANN CECIL

KAMEHAMEHA

Palace Theater (p177) on Hilo's main drag

ANN CECIL

PALACE

Ceremonial offering (p200) to the fire goddess Pele, Halema'uma'u Crater

ANN CECIL

JOHN ELK III

Lava Tree State Monument (p185), near Pahoa

Lava flow (p202), near Chain of Craters Road, Hawai'i Volcanoes National Park

For everyday hanging out, the **Lava Zone** (☎ 965-2222; 15-2929 Pahoa Village Rd; ⏰ noon-midnight Sun-Thu, noon-2am Fri & Sat) is a lively, eclectic bar with outdoor pool tables and a mixed gay-and-straight crowd. The music alternates between karaoke, DJs and live bands, and the bartenders are great sources of information about local secret spots.

Getting There & Away

The **Hele-On Bus** (☎ 961-8744; www.co.hawaii.hi.us/mass_transit/heleonbus.html) goes from Hilo to Kea'au and Pahoa on the No 9 Pahoa route ($2.25, one hour).

It's a pretty easy hitch to either Hilo or Volcano from Pahoa.

AROUND PAHOA

The usual route for exploring the Pahoa area is a triangle heading down Hwy 132 past Lava Tree State Monument to Kapoho, then continuing on the Red Rd (Hwy 137) along the shore to the lava flow at Kalapana, returning to Pahoa via Hwy 130 (with a detour to the active lava flow at the end of that road). If possible, try to time it so you arrive at the flow near sunset so you can see it firing up the night. Conveniently, the Red Rd and Hwy 130 still connect, but who knows? Pele could get frisky and change it all by the time you read this book.

From Pahoa, Hwy 132 passes through a tropical reserve. It's like an enchanted forest and will give you an idea of Puna's allure. This entire area presents a great opportunity to poke around and explore under your own steam. But always respect any 'Private Property' and 'No Trespassing' signs – you'll see lots of them. Perhaps one of the best ways to gain access around the area is to stay in one of the inns around the region and avail yourself of your host's insider status.

Lava Tree State Monument

The approach to this place, through a tight-knit canopy of trees, is like a dreamscape. Arching overhead, the forest subtly opens to let a rhythm of sunlight guide you on this beautiful stretch, known as the Tree Tunnel.

Once in the park, a 20-minute trail loops through thickets of bamboo and orchids, past 'lava trees' created in 1790, when a rain forest was engulfed in *pahoehoe* (smooth-flowing lava) from Kilauea's East Rift Zone. A flood of lava up to 10ft deep flowed through the forest, enveloping moisture-laden ohia trees and then receding. The lava hardened around the trees, which burned away, creating molds of lava that remain today. In this 'ghost forest' of lava shells, you'll see some 10ft high and others so short that you can peer down into the ferns and frogs sheltered inside their hollows. Be careful if you walk off the path, as in places the ground is crossed by deep cracks, some hidden by new vegetation.

Recently, most of the dense foliage was woefully thinned when locals tried to eradicate the proliferating coqui frog and other invasive species. To get there, follow Hwy 132 about 2.5 miles east of Hwy 130. Be advised that the mosquitoes can be dense here. There are public toilets in the area.

Lava Tree Tropical Inn (☎ 965-7441; 14-3555 Puna Rd; d $65-95, d with Jacuzzi $125) With a prime location and a quiet, peaceful setting, this two-story inn is a nice option. The entrance road is just past the park, providing lush views. All the rooms have distinct character and charm. There's a wraparound lanai, a living area with TV, VCR, fax and Internet access, and a laundry room. Room rates include breakfast and an afternoon snack.

Kapoho

pop 300

Hwy 132 heads east through orchards of papaya and thick ohia forest to Kapoho, a former farming town. The old lighthouse is less than 2 miles down a dirt road east of 'Four Corners,' where Hwy 132 and the Red Rd (Hwy 137) intersect.

On January 13, 1960, a fissure opened and a half-mile-long curtain of fire shot up in the midst of a sugarcane field just above Kapoho. The main flow of *pahoehoe* ran toward the ocean, but a slower moving offshoot of *'a'a* (rough, jagged lava) crept toward the town, burying orchid farms in its path. Two weeks later, the lava entered Kapoho and smothered the town. A hot-springs resort and nearly 100 homes and businesses vanished beneath the flow.

When the lava approached the sea at **Cape Kumukahi**, it parted into two streams around the lighthouse, sparing it from destruction. *Kumukahi* means 'first beginning' in Hawaiian, and the cape is the easternmost point in the state. Breathe deeply: the air here is among the freshest in the world.

Wa'a Wa'a

At the intersection of Hwy 132 and the Red Rd (Hwy 137), most people hook a right to explore the Red Rd's coastal diversions. If you go left, instead, you'll be spirited away to a time when the land was thick with breadfruit too tall to topple and no sound was heard but offshore breezes. Although there are lots of folks living an off-the-grid lifestyle back in here, it really feels like you're in a different century. Consequently, Wa'a Wa'a is loaded with 'Keep Out' signs, and you will be adversely affected if you fuss around here where you shouldn't.

Driving the mellow dirt road is worth the scenery, especially to enjoy the solitude and beauty of some of this hidden coast. **Orr's Beach**, accessed a further mile or so down the road, is worth a look.

RED ROAD (HWY 137)

Known to locals almost exclusively as the Red Rd because it was originally paved with red cinders from the 1960 Kapoho lava flow, the route is now mostly basic black tarmac. You can still see ribbons of scarlet along the shoulders, and a short stretch near the 8-mile marker remains red. Skirting the eastern shores of Puna, Hwy 137 (running from Kalapana hugging the coast and then to Kapoho) provides access to many of the area's most treasured sights. Driving this scenic route you'll pass lava, and milo and hala (pandanus) trees densely converging overhead, creating a natural tunnel.

In low-lying parts the road floods during winter storms and at high tide. There are many little tracks leading from the road to the cliffs and coast in this area. They might net you generous rewards if you feel like exploring.

Green Lake

Placid green waters surrounded by breadfruit, guava, avocado and bamboo make this freshwater crater lake seem ideal for swimming, but beware: the water is stagnant. In spite of this, people can't seem to resist the clothing-optional swimming hole. The draws must be the rope swing and wooden raft for your aquatic romping pleasure.

To get here, park just after the 8-mile marker, opposite the unmarked Kapoho Beach Rd. On the inland side of the road, you'll see a locked gate marked 'Keep Out,' although you can enter from an unlocked entrance on the right. Once you're inside, walk along the grassy road for five minutes,

---

PUNA & PELE

Hawaiian proverbs are profound metaphors that transcend culture. They're an expression of truths found on the cusp of life's transitions and amongst the localities of a particular environmental setting. Pele's Chant warns:

The woman comes forth from the pit
Forth from the river with yellow tide
What ravage!
Rocky strata up-torn
Deep gullied streams
Toothed are the cliffs
Like an oven glows the face of the rocks

An example of this, showing the delicate relationship of Puna with Pele, is found in an expression of anger: *Ke lauahi maila o Pele ia Puna* (Pele is pouring lava out on Puna).

Common in the region are historic and modern stories of a mysterious woman traveling through Puna with only the company of her white dog. Sometimes she's young and attractive, and at other times she's old and wizened. She's often seen just before a volcanic eruption; those who stop and pick her up while she's hitchhiking or show some other kindness to her are spared from the lava flow.

After the 1960 eruption destroyed the village of Kapoho, stories circulated about how the keeper in the spared Kapoho lighthouse (p185) had offered a meal to an elderly woman who had shown up at his door on the eve of the disaster.

always bearing right. Once you pass between the garden and the homestead, the downhill path turns muddy and overgrown. It's slippery toward the bottom, where the lake is. Be courteous and respectful in this area.

Hale O Naia (☎ 965-5340; www.hale-o-naia.com; Kapoho Beach Rd; r $75, ste $150) This sanctuary, in the gated community down Kapoho Beach Rd opposite Green Lake, is a little slice of paradise. There are three rooms in Sally Whitney's beautifully detailed home, which is right on the lip of Kapoho Bay. The two basic rooms feature a lovely canopy bed, private sea-facing lanai and a detached bath with a Jacuzzi. The suite is incredible, with a king-size bed, his-and-hers baths, a sitting room, a sauna and a huge lanai. There are hammocks and a hot tub, and you have access to kayaks, snorkeling gear and boogie boards. Rates are based on double occupancy and include breakfast. Reservations are a must.

Kapoho Tide Pools

Spend a lazy afternoon by exploring the sprawling network of tide pools formed in Kapoho's lava-rock coastline. Some of the pools are deep enough for snorkeling (except during low tide). Known to have the best snorkeling on the windward side of the island, the coral gardens here support saddle wrasses, Moorish idols, butterfly fish, sea urchins and sea cucumbers.

The nearby houses form the Kapoho Vacationland subdivision, where everyone seems to have a swimming pool. To get there, turn off the Red Rd (Hwy 137) a mile south of the lighthouse onto Kapoho Kai Dr, then left at the end on Wai Opae, and park near the house festooned with found art objects and coconut shells. Take the rocky trail across smaller pools for about 75ft to a large cove that flushes to the ocean. If you follow the rocky channel along the left-hand side it will minimize the effect of the currents, which can be really strong. Inside the various pools the water is generally calm, which makes this a good spot for novice swimmers.

Ahalanui Beach Park

Known simply as 'the hot pond' to locals, the star attraction here is a spring-fed thermal pool set in lava rock and edged by swaying palms. It's deep enough for swimming, with water temperatures averaging 90°F.

The pool has an inlet to the ocean, which pounds upon the seawall, bringing in many tropical fish during high tide and keeping the water clean. Nighttime soaks under the moon and stars are always a possibility.

The park is located along the Red Rd a mile north of Isaac Hale Beach Park. It has picnic tables, pit toilets and a lifeguard. There's plenty of parking but, as always, don't leave valuables in your car.

Isaac Hale Beach Park

Isaac Hale (*ha*-lay) Beach at Pohoiki Bay is mainly a locals' hangout. On weekends there's usually a frenzy of local activity, with family picnics and fishing. Local kids like to swim inside the breakwater near the boat ramp, which is the only place to launch in Puna. The rocky lava coast here creates an excellent offshore reef and the best place for surfing and scuba diving in the district. Surfers will find breaks to the north and south of the point. Due to rough conditions and *wana* (sea urchins) everywhere, this spot is for experienced riders only.

Soaking fans are in for a treat, as there's a small hot pond hiding in the undergrowth along the shore. To reach this spot, pick up the beaten path just beyond the house bedecked with 'No Trespassing' signs. Ask permission at the house before continuing, and moments later you'll see the pond gleaming to your right.

The park has toilets but no drinking water or showers. Camping is allowed (see p223 for information on permits), but it's not a very attractive option as the campground is virtually in the parking lot and is subject to long-term squatters.

Pohoiki Road

As you veer around the bend on the Red Rd, you can choose to continue straight on Pohoiki Rd, which is a good shortcut to Pahoa. Yet another of Puna's shaded, mystical roads, Pohoiki Rd winds through thick forest dotted with papaya orchards and wild *noni*.

Yoga Oasis (☎ 965-8460, 800-274-4446; www.yoga oasis.org; 13-678 Pohoiki Rd; s/d $75/100, cabins $100-145) For a personalized retreat, Yoga Oasis is the ticket. On average, there are just eight to 12 guests (the maximum is 18), and the 26-acre retreat center is sprawling and utterly secluded. All rates include daily yoga and an organic breakfast. The finely furnished rooms share a spectacular marble bath, and the cabins have equally impressive private facilities. The founder, a yogi since 1972, is a professional acrobat who studied mime with Marcel Marceau and Etienne Decroux. He's also trained in Tibetan Buddhism and Thai massage; retreats are offered monthly. To get there, keep your eyes peeled for a driveway on your left, 2 miles up from Red Rd, with colorful flags over the driveway and a yellow fire hydrant on the opposite side.

MacKenzie State Recreation Area

Set in a grove of ironwood trees, this park is eerily quiet and secluded. There's no beach here, only dramatic 40ft cliffs and pounding surf far below. Fishing from the cliffs may land you some *ulua*, a big old jackfish that favors turbulent waters. It's a peaceful picnic spot, and the fallen ironwood tips underfoot provide a spongy carpet. There are some lava tubes worth exploring a short walk north of the parking area. Follow the old King's Hwy trail along the coast, and you'll find the entrance after about 500ft. The tube goes *mauka* (inland) and passes an opening before coming out on the far side of the highway. Bring a good flashlight and some sturdy shoes for this short excursion.

Crime has been a problem here, however, and locals tend to steer clear of the area. Locals believe night marchers (see p150) like to prowl around here, so if you start hearing drums and seeing torches bobbing along in the distance, show your reverence by lying face down while they pass.

Camping is allowed with a state permit (p223), but facilities are shabby, trash cans are often overflowing and drinking water is unavailable.

Opihikao & Around

A little Congregational church and a handful of houses mark the village of Opihikao.

Kalani Oceanside Retreat (☎ 965-7828, 800-800-6886; www.kalani.com; tent sites $20, r & cottage d $105-155, tree house s/d $210/240) Located between the 17- and 18-mile markers, Kalani is the Big Island's largest New Age retreat center, offering a range of yoga, meditation, dance, adventure and alternative-healing classes and workshops. The setting feels like a casual resort, with a café, 25m pool, sauna and Jacuzzis (clothing optional after 5pm).

While this retreat caters mostly to groups, it welcomes individual travelers when space is available. There are dozens of rooms, most in two-story cedar lodges with exposed-beam ceilings; a screened common area contains a shared kitchen. Also available are private cottages containing one bedroom, a bath and a living room, and there are three tree houses.

Many programs are geared exclusively to gay guests. Nature tours taking in waterfalls, caves or remote beaches and valleys are on offer as well. The retreat also has daily classes that can be attended on a drop-in basis. The dining room serves healthy buffet-style meals (mostly vegetarian but also with fish and chicken options) and is open to anyone who drops by.

The center organises volunteer-resident programs. Included with the programs are room, board, pool and spa access, and yoga retreat classes, in exchange for a two-week to three-month commitment. Prices vary depending on the ratio of work to free time. This is a great alternative for those willing and able to work while they learn and play. There's a fairly rigorous application process. Kalani also has an artist-in-residence program that's open to artists of nearly all media (stipends are available).

The **dining room** (buffet breakfast $11, lunch $12, dinner $22; ⏱ 7:30-8:30am, noon-1pm, 6-7:30pm) serves buffet-style vegetarian meals and is open to the public. The food is divine, but the opening hours are short and sweet.

Kehena Beach

At the base of a cliff, this black-sand beach was created by a 1955 lava flow. Shaded by coconut and ironwood trees, it's a free-spirited, nude-sunbathing spot that attracts a mixed crowd of hippies, Hawaiians, families and seniors. On Sundays it pulsates to the beat of an open drum circle, and musicians of all shapes, sizes and abilities jam and dance among wafts of blue smoke. The nearby subdivisions of Puna Beach Palisades, Kalapana Seaview Estates and Kehena Beach Estates are all budding gay communities.

Even when it rains in Pahoa it's usually sunny here. In the morning it's not unusual for dolphins to venture close to shore. When the water is calm, swimming is usually safe, but mind the currents and undertows. Good, strong swimmers die at Kehena every year, especially in winter. Do not venture beyond the rocky point at the southern end. Rip currents, undertows and rogue waves are all possibilities, especially in winter.

Kehena is on Red Rd, immediately south of the 19-mile marker. Look for the little parking lot on the right, and you'll see the path down to the beach; it's a five-minute walk over jagged lava rock. Don't leave any valuables in your car.

Kalapana (Former Village)

For years the village of Kalapana sat precariously down shore of Kilauea's restless East Rift Zone. When the latest series of eruptions began in 1983, the main lava flow moved down the slope west of Kalapana. Lava flows are quick to change direction, however, and it changed course toward Kalapana in 1990. It's also believed that the earlier flow had passed through a series of lava tubes, which shunted the molten lava toward the sea. But, during pauses in the 1990 eruption, the tubes feeding lava to the ocean had cooled long enough to harden and block up. Thus, when the eruption resumed, the flow was redirected toward Kalapana. By the end of 1990 most of the village, including 100 homes, was buried.

Today the Red Rd (Hwy 137) abruptly ends at **Kaimu Beach** on the eastern edge of what used to be Kalapana. Formerly Hawai'i's most famous black-sand beach, Kaimu is now buried under a sea of hardened lava that flowed clear into the bay. A few houses were spared, including **Uncle Robert's house**, where you can *talk story fo' days* about the event as well as the intricacies of Hawaiian tradition. Take a nature walk (admission by donation) and peruse photos of the devastating volcanic event. Uncle Robert also sells some great local honey, *'awa* (kava) drinks, organic fruits and souvenirs.

Tourist buses arrive constantly, and a handful of shops and a branch of **Verna's Drive In** (☎ 965-8234; burgers/plate lunches $2/6; ⊙ 10am-5pm), at the end of the Red Rd, have joined Uncle Robert's. From here, a 10-minute walk across lava leads to a new black-sand beach. At the end of the flow, the *pahoehoe* turns to coarse granules, and hundreds of baby coconut palms form a natural promenade to the sea. The lonely beach is only an apostrophe of sand. Wear shoes, otherwise glass-sharp lava shards will cut your feet. While the walk is easy, the midday sun is punishing.

HWY 130

The Red Rd intersects with Hwy 130 (Old Kalapana Rd), which leads north to Pahoa. At the 20-mile marker on Hwy 130, you'll see **Star of the Sea Church**, a tiny 1929 Catholic church that's noted for its interior trompe l'oeil murals, which give visitors the impression of being in a large cathedral. The style is primitive but the illusion of depth amazingly effective. The church also has an accomplished stained-glass window of Father Damien, who was with the parish before he moved to the leprosy colony on

---

FRAGILE PARADISE

Kilauea is famous worldwide for being the newest and most active volcano. Its continual growth means that the mountain is slowly transforming its surrounding landscape. To live along the East Rift Zone in Puna is to be directly in the path of Kilauea's expansion.

Numerous lava flows from Pu'u 'O'o reached the sea at three locations on the Puna coast in 1983–6, 1986–92 and 1992–2002, destroying the village of Kalapana and the Royal Gardens subdivision, along with miles of former coastline. In Hawai'i Volcanoes National Park, the Mauna Ulu vent has only been dormant since 1977 (lava from it reached the sea in 1973), and as recently as 45 years ago lava reached the sea as far north as Cape Kumukahi.

The effect of the region's activity is paradise for some, as the thermal activity provides rich topsoil for farming, an abundant energy resource for the island and natural therapeutic practices for its people. The flip side is the geologic instability that can shake (or engulf) even the most solid foundation. Subdivisions with names like Hawai'i Beaches Estates or Hawaiian Paradise Park create a shaky identity with such idyllic language. How would you feel if your beach estate in paradise were buried by fiery lava next week? As the Hawaiian proverb says: *Aia no i ke ko a keau* – only time will tell.

Molokai. Even if the church is locked, you're free to walk up and peek at the interior through the front windows. The church was originally in Kalapana, but community members moved it just before the 1990 lava flow moved through town. Recently deconsecrated, the building is now being turned into a community cultural center by the **Kalapana Ohana Association** (☎ 965-7429). Contact the association for visiting hours information.

At the 15-mile marker, roughly 3.5 miles south of Pahoa, a big blue 'Scenic View' highway sign points into the undergrowth. There's absolutely zilch to view unless you know what you're looking for: puffs of steam from several low spatter cones, signaling natural steam baths. Follow the well-beaten track for a few minutes, taking the right fork for a two-person sauna with wooden planks. Further back there's a much larger hollow that can accommodate a few people lying down. Beware of bugs, including hundreds of voracious cockroaches after dark. In spite of this, it's relaxing and – in the spirit of Puna – clothing is optional.

ALONG HWY 11

Heading from Kea'au to Volcano on Hwy 11, the first 'burb you come to is Kurtistown. There isn't much to it apart from a gas station and a post office, but there are some affordable places to stay on the back roads. Further along is Mountain View – oops! You missed it. You'll probably notice the two gas pumps and minimart receding in your rearview mirror at the 14-mile marker. You guessed it: there's another **Verna's Drive In** (☎ 968-8774) next to the minimart, which is good for saimin or plate lunch if you're peaked. Next up is Glenwood, yet another one-store town. But, as with the towns before it, there are reasons to stop and poke around here. Hirano's Store, just before the 20-mile marker, has gas and foodstuffs, but the real reason to pull over is to see the fuming Pu'u 'O'o vent from the clearing across the way. On a clear day you can see this active vent letting off some steam. An alternative trail to see the Pu'u 'O'o vent starts in the Glenwood subdivision (see p207).

Sleeping

Pineapple Park (☎ 968-8170, 800-865-2266; www.pineapple-park.com; dm $20, r with shared/private bathroom $45/85) This hostel is very basic, but it's a soothingly quiet escape. Amenities include a big guest kitchen, laundry facilities, a common room with TV, VCR and pool table, and outdoor horseshoes and badminton. Pineapple Park has a sister hostel in Captain Cook on the Kona Coast (see p94).

Bed & Breakfast Mountain View (☎ 968-6868, 888-698-9896; www.bbmtview.com; r $55-95) Just across

---

DETOUR: HWY 11 TO VOLCANO

Why stop along the highway from Kea'au to Hawai'i Volcanoes National Park? Aside from a few sleeping options, there's no reason unless you want to see sleek koa bowls and eye-popping orchids, and sample tried-and-true 'stone cookies.' The stops in the villages of Kurtistown, Mountain View and Glenwood might not be major, but this is the real Big Island.

Just after the 12-mile marker, **Dan De Luz's Woods** (☎ 968-6607; Hwy 11; ⏰ 9am-5pm) sells hand-turned bowls, platters and furniture made from native hardwoods, such as koa, sandalwood, mango and banyan, by a master craftsman. The adjacent **Koa Kaffee** (☎ 968-1129; Hwy 11; ⏰ 5am-8pm Wed-Mon, 5am-2pm Tue) is a home-style diner cooking up excellent Portuguese bean soup and hearty breakfasts.

If you want to stock up on treats for the road, **Mountain View Bakery** (☎ 968-6353; Old Volcano Rd; ⏰ 7:30-11am Thu, 7:30am-1pm Sat), near the 14-mile marker, bakes glazed doughnuts that put Krispy Kreme to shame, along with its iconic 'stone cookies' ($4.50 per bag). Yes, they are rock hard but now come in original, soft, extra-crispy and chocolate-chip flavors! The bakery's only open twice a week.

Though just another conventional tour-bus stop, **Akatsuka Orchid Gardens** (☎ 967-8234, 888-967-6669; www.akatsukaorchid.com; Hwy 11; admission free; ⏰ 8:30am-5pm) is the best place to order orchids that can be shipped to your door (cut flowers $30 to $40, plants $40 to $54). Inside the store, cattleyas, dendrobiums and phalaenopsis orchids are perennially in bloom. The nursery's halfway between the 22- and 23-mile markers.

the way from Pineapple Park, the B&B offers clean, peaceful rooms in the home of two well-known Big Island artists, Jane and Linus Chao. At the four-acre estate you can wander around a sprawling lawn and a custom-made fishpond filled with mullet.

Butterfly Inn (☎ 966-7936, 800-546-2442; www .thebutterflyinn.com; PO Box 6010 Kurtistown, HI 96760; s/d $55/65) Here you'll find a friendly women's retreat with a tranquil Hawaiian feel. The two comfortable rooms are situated on the top floor of a house and they share an ample kitchen and sitting room. The adjacent shared bath features a tub with a good view of the gardens, but the real prize is a hot tub tucked away in the landscaped grounds. The off-the-beaten-track location makes for a nice private getaway, but you'll need a car to get out there. Inquire about the work-exchange program: you do 20 hours per week for a minimum of one month in exchange for lodging.

Hawai'i Volcanoes National Park

Hawai'i Volcanoes National Park (HAVO) is unique among US national parks. The huge preserve contains two active volcanoes and terrain ranging from tropical beaches to the sub-Arctic Mauna Loa summit. The centerpiece is steaming Kilauea Caldera, at the summit of the youngest and most-active volcano on earth. An entire day can easily be spent exploring the sights along Crater Rim Dr. At the center of the caldera is Halema'uma'u Crater, home of Pele, the Hawaiian Goddess of the volcano.

The park's landscape is phenomenal, with dozens of craters and cinder cones, hills piled high with pumice, and hardened oceans of lava. Here and there, amid the bone-cracking lava, new thickets of green life take root in the rugged black rock. Or look for islands of vegetation (kipuka) that have been spared by lava flows, all protected habitats for native bird species.

Completing the scene are the massive blue flanks of Mauna Loa in the distance. Things have been almost too quiet recently and scientists are constantly monitoring Mauna Loa. The last eruption in 1984 demonstrated that Mauna Loa, while known for taking short catnaps, is far from asleep. If you are lucky enough to spend a few days hiking to the summit you will be awestruck by the almost alien landscape. It is easy to lose yourself in the immensity of the mountain. The layers of lava fields and continually steaming cinder cones are constant reminders that you are at the pulse of the entire Hawaiian Island chain.

HIGHLIGHTS

- Catching a possible glimpse of the active **lava flow** (p202)
- Hiking **Mauna Loa** (p205), the world's most massive volcano
- Visiting **Kilauea Caldera** (p197), the world's most active volcano, and the home of Pele
- Relaxing at **secluded coves** (p208) on the rugged lava coast
- Staying at a cozy **B&B** (p210) in misty Volcano Village

CLIMATE

Get a **recorded weather forecast** (☎ 961-5582). The park has a wide range of climatic conditions that vary with elevation. Chilly rain, wind and fog typify the moody weather; on any given day it can change from hot and dry to a soaking downpour in a flash. Near Kilauea Caldera, temperatures average 15°F cooler than in Kona. Add a layer of long pants and a jacket, just in case.

DANGERS & ANNOYANCES

The park's **hotline** (☎ 985-6000; ☽ 24hr) tells you what the volcanoes are doing that day, and where to best view the action. Updates on eruptions, weather conditions and road closures are available at 530AM on your radio. During periods of prolonged drought, both Mauna Loa Rd and Hilina Pali Rd are subject to closure due to fire-hazard conditions. Also Hwy 11 is prone to flooding, washouts and closures during tempestuous storms. Drivers should note that the nearest gas is in Volcano town.

Several violently explosive eruptions are known to have occurred at Kilauea, but the most recent was in 1924. Fatalities are rare but they do happen. The most-recent deaths happened because people ventured too close to the flow – onto unstable 'benches' of new land that collapse, or near steam explosions where lava is flowing into the ocean. Other potential hazards include deep cracks in the earth and thin lava crust, which mask hollows and unstable lava tubes.

For your own safety, follow the rules: stay on marked trails and take all park warning signs seriously. Don't venture off on your own, as you're almost certain to get lost. Watch your step on undulating terrain; if you fall, you'll definitely suffer abrasions from the glass-sharp lava rock.

Another hazard, if lava reaches the sea, is the toxic cocktail of sulfuric and hydrochloric acid. Everyone should take care, but especially those with respiratory and heart conditions, pregnant women and those with infants or young children. High concentrations of sulfuric fumes (which smell like rotten egg) permeate the air at Halema'uma'u Overlook and Sulphur Banks.

If you're hiking and planning to walk over lava rock, it's important to come prepared: wear hiking shoes, long pants and a hat. Park officials are often amused, if not exasper-ated, when tourists show up in tanks and *rubbah slippah*, or wrapped in beach towels. Drink lots of water, as dehydration is another common-but-preventable malady. The park service suggests each person carry a minimum of 1L water, a flashlight with extra batteries, binoculars, a first-aid kit and sunscreen.

HISTORY

The park is one of Hawai'i's best places for camping and hiking. It has 140 miles of amazingly varied hiking trails, and both drive-up campsites and backcountry camping. HAVO encompasses roughly 333,000 acres of land – more than the entire island of Molokai – and it's still growing, as lava pouring from Kilauea has added more than 600 acres in the past 15 years. The most recent expansion of the park oddly enough was not the work of Pele. Instead, the government lent a helping hand by annexing 116,000 new acres of land spanning the southeastern flanks of Mauna Loa, formerly private ranchlands in Ka'u.

Kilauea's East Rift Zone has been erupting since 1983, destroying everything in its path. The coastal road to Puna was blocked by lava in 1987. The Waha'ula Visitor Center on the south coast was buried the next year, and the entire village of Kalapana disappeared under lava in 1990. Since that time, the flows have crept further west, engulfing Kamoamoa Beach in 1994, and later claiming an additional mile of road and most of sacred Wahaula Heiau.

The current series of eruptions, which is the longest in recorded history, has spewed out more than 2.5 billion cubic yards of new lava. Central to the action is the Pu'u 'O'o Vent, a smoldering cone in the northeastern section of the park. Although many visitors expect to see geyser-like fountains of lava, this is certainly the exception rather than the rule. Hawai'i's shield volcanoes lack the explosive gases of the more dramatic strato volcano (commonly found on the Pacific Ocean's ring of fire) that spew ash or lava into the air. Here lava is hotter and more fluid, so it mostly seeps and creeps along. In Hawai'i, people generally run to volcanoes, not away from them. When Pele sends up curtains of fire, bright-red spattering and flaming lava orbs, cars stream in from all directions.

Don't visit the park with a set idea of what you'll see. Lava flows are unpredictable, and your vantage point depends on current volcanic activity. From near the end of Chain of Craters Rd, you might see ribbons of lava pouring into the sea or only steam clouds billowing above. After sunset, you might see the mountainside glow in the sky.

ORIENTATION

The park's main road is Crater Rim Dr, which circles the moonscape of Kilauea Caldera. You can buzz through the drive-up sites in an hour – and if that's all you have time for, it's unquestionably worth it.

The park's other scenic drive is Chain of Craters Rd, which leads south 20 miles to

HAWAI'I VOLCANOES NATIONAL PARK

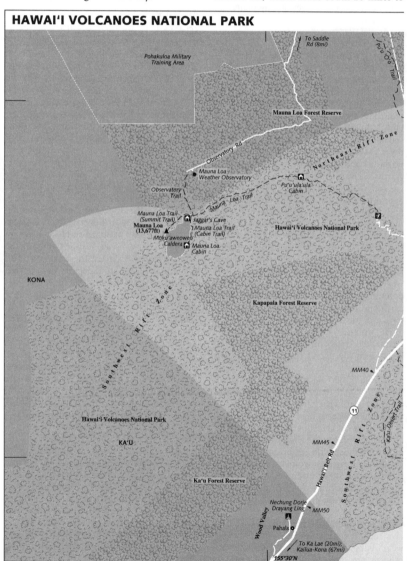

the coast, ending at the site of the most-recent lava activity. Allow about three hours down and back, with stops along the way.

While you can get a feel for the place in a full day, you'll probably want more time to explore this vast and varied park. Escaping the crowds is often as simple as leaving your car in the nearest lot. If you can, take

advantage of the fact that the price of admission allows you access for a full week. Some of the sites and shorter trails are accessible by wheelchair.

Hikers and campers will want to flip right to the Hiking section (p203). In addition to camping, there are a couple of places to stay within the park boundaries.

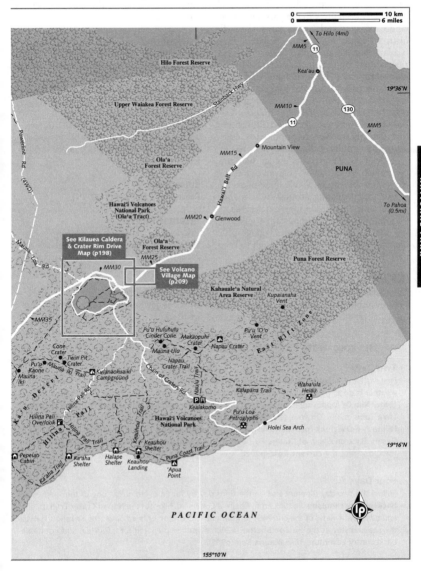

See Kilauea Caldera & Crater Rim Drive Map (p198)

See Volcano Village Map (p209)

The village of Volcano, a mile east of the park, is a mystical place of giant ferns, giant *sugi* (Japanese evergreen) and ohia trees full of puffy red blossoms. The cool mist and pristine air are invigorating, and many artists seclude themselves here.

Maps

Blame Mother Nature, but topographical maps can't keep up with the park's dynamic landscape. *National Geographic's Trails Illustrated Hawai'i Volcanoes National Park* is a large-format, prefolded, waterproof and rip-resistant topographic hiking map. It covers the most-popular hiking and wilderness areas and adds features of interest, such as campsites and trail distances. For specific hikes, the USGS 1:24,000 maps *Kilauea, Volcano* and *Ka'u Desert* are helpful. Remember that all maps are likely to be outdated, especially hiking trails in the active rift zones.

A free full-color visitors guide, that contains basic driving maps, is given out at the park entrance station. While these maps are meant for navigating around by car, they also outline the park's major networks of hiking trails, showing important trailheads, key junctions and distances. Topographic detail is lacking, but it's just enough to keep most hikers getting lost.

INFORMATION

The **national park** (☎ 985-6000; www.nps.gov/havo; 7-day pass per car $10, per person on foot, bicycle or motorcycle $5) never closes, allowing all-night views of the spectacular stars and lava flows. An annual HAVO pass will set you back only $20, and the toll station also sells annual national-parks passes ($50). US citizens with disabilities can obtain a Golden Access Passport (free), and people aged 62 or older can purchase a Golden Age Passport ($10); both allow unlimited and free lifetime access to all of the national parks in the USA.

Bookstores

Jaggar Museum (Map p198; ☎ 985-6049; ☺ 8:30am-5pm) Offers books on natural history, Hawaiian mythology and volcanoes.

Kilauea Visitor Center (Map p198; ☎ 985-6017; ☺ 7:45am-5pm) An excellent selection of books, maps and videos on volcanoes, flora and hiking.

Volcano Art Center (Map p198; ☎ 967-7565; www .volcanoartcenter.org; ☺ 9am-5pm) Find art and children's books on volcanoes as well as good fiction and nonfiction inspired by the park.

Emergency

Police, Fire & Ambulance (☎ 911)

Internet Access

Lava Rock Café (Map p209; ☎ 967-8526; ☺ 7:30am-5pm Mon, 7:30am-9pm Tue-Sat, 7:30am-4pm Sun; per 20min $3) Coming from the park there's Internet access here, next to the Volcano General Stores.

Internet Resources

www.nps.gov/havo Hawai'i Volcanoes National Park official site.

HAWAI'I VOLCANOES NATIONAL PARK IN...

Two Days

First visit the **Kilauea Visitor Center** (opposite) to gather some information. If the morning weather is good go for a hike on the varied **Kilauea Iki Trail** (p204). From there, take a tour of **Crater Rim Dr** (opposite) to get the big picture. End the day by taking the kids through **Thurston Lava Tube** (p200). On your second day go down **Chain of Craters Rd** (p201) and detour to the **Hilina Pali Overlook** (p201) and hiking part of the **Mauna Iki Trail** (p205) for a taste of the Ka'u Desert. Back on Chain of Craters Rd be at the end of the road by nightfall for a chance to see the glow from the **current flow** (p202).

Four Days

Follow the two-day itinerary and on the third day try for an overnight at one of the shelters or **backcountry campsites** (p206). From Chain of Craters Rd, hike out the **Napau Crater Trail** (p206), and camp with views of the currently erupting Pu'u 'O'o Vent, or head down the Keauhou Trail to the sea and stay at the **Halape Shelter** (p208). If you are prepared for a four-day unforgettable backcountry adventure, hike **Mauna Loa** (p205).

DISABLED TRAVELERS

Many of the park sites – including the Visitor Center, Jaggar Museum, Volcano Art Center and Volcano House hotel – are wheelchair accessible. Many of the pull-ups along Crater Rim Dr and the Chain of Craters Rd are curb-free. Other sites, including Devastation Trail (p201) and Keala-komo Overlook (p201) are wheelchair accessible as well. Hand rails or rope cordons are also used to demark short paths like the one to the Halema'uma'u Overlook and Steam Vents.

A couple of campsites are also accessible including: Namakani Paio, with restrooms, water and moderate accessibility, Kulanaokuaiki with two sites, an accessible toilet, but no water.

Restrooms can also be found at Thurston Lava Tube, Kilauea Overlook, Kipukapuaulu picnic area, and at the Ranger's Station at the end of Chain of Craters Rd.

---

www.volcanoartcenter.org Available art and event listings as well as books related to the park.

Money

There are no banks or ATMs in the park, but in Volcano Village there are a couple of ATMs at the following:

Kilauea General Store (Map p209; ☎ 985-7555; Old Volcano Rd; ⏱ 7am-7:30pm Mon-Sat, 7am-7pm Sun)
True Value Hardware (Map p209; ☎ 967-7969; Old Volcano Rd)

Post

Post office (Map p198; ☎ 967-7611; 19-4030 Old Volcano Rd; ⏱ 7:30am-3:30pm Mon-Fri, 11am-noon Sat)

Telephone

Public telephones are available in the park at Kilauea Visitor Center, Volcano House and the Jaggar Museum; in Volcano Village, there are payphones at the Volcano Store and Kilauea General Stores.

Tourist Information

You can obtain the main park brochure in advance, along with camping and hiking information if you specifically request it, by writing to Hawai'i Volcanoes National Park, PO Box 52, Hawai'i National Park, HI 96718. The park's website is also a fountain of information.

Kilauea Visitor Center (Map p198; ☎ 985-6017; ⏱ 7:45am-5pm) Rangers at the park's visitor center provide updates on volcanic activity and backcountry trail conditions. They have free pamphlets for a few of the park trails, and sell an excellent selection of books, maps and videos on volcanoes, flora and hiking. Ask about guided walks and the fun junior-ranger program for kids. There's also a 24-hour ATM here.

Volcano Visitor Center (Map p198; Volcano Rd; ⏱ 8am-5pm) Tourist and accommodation information is provided at this little shack outside the Thai Thai Restaurant,

a bit west on Old Volcano Rd. This small, unstaffed center offers just racks of glossy tourist brochures.

SIGHTS
Crater Rim Dr   Map p198

Many HAVO sights are conveniently located along Crater Rim Dr, an amazing 11-mile loop road that skirts the rim of Kilauea Caldera, and has marked stops at steam vents and steaming crater lookouts. Numerous short trails lead away from parking areas through various landscapes, including a lava tube and a native rain forest. Other longer hikes into and around the caldera are also possible.

Natural forces have rerouted the drive more than a few times. Earthquakes in 1975 and 1983 rattled it hard enough to knock sections of road down into the caldera. Quakes come with the territory: there are more than 1200 earthquakes of measurable magnitude on this island every week. If you take Crater Rim Dr in a counterclockwise direction, you'll start off at the visitor center. Unlike the Chain of Craters Rd, Crater Rim Dr is relatively level, making it a good road for cyclists. Use caution here as the road is narrow and has no shoulders.

KILAUEA VISITOR CENTER

Inside the park visitor center (left) is a tiny theater showing (on the hour from 9am to 4pm) a free 20-minute film on Kilauea Volcano. Footage includes flowing rivers of lava and some of the most-spectacular lava fountains ever to be caught on film. Commercial videos of recent eruptions run continuously in the center's equally small museum, where volcano-related exhibits are due to be upgraded.

Rest rooms, water fountains and pay phones are found outside.

HAWAI'I VOLCANOES NATIONAL PARK

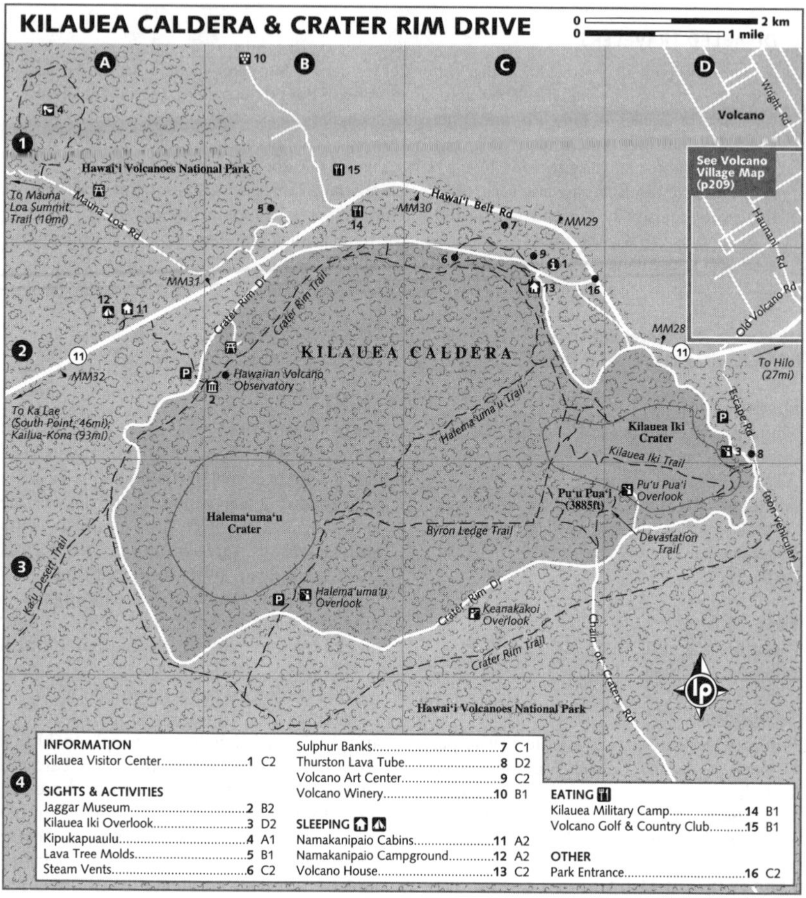
KILAUEA CALDERA & CRATER RIM DRIVE
0 2 km
0 1 mile
Hawai'i Volcanoes National Park
To Mauna Loa Summit Trail (10mi)
Mauna Loa Rd
Hawai'i Belt Rd
MM30
MM29
MM31
MM32
MM28
Volcano
Wright Rd
See Volcano Village Map (p209)
Haunani Rd
Old Volcano Rd
To Hilo (27mi)
To Ka Lae (South Point, 46mi); Kailua-Kona (93mi)
Crater Rim Dr
Crater Rim Trail
KILAUEA CALDERA
Hawaiian Volcano Observatory
Halema'uma'u Trail
Kilauea Iki Crater
Kilauea Iki Trail
Escape Rd
Pu'u Pua'i (3885ft)
Pu'u Pua'i Overlook
Halema'uma'u Crater
Byron Ledge Trail
Devastation Trail
Ka'u Desert Trail
Halema'uma'u Overlook
Keanakakoi Overlook
Chain of Craters Rd
(non-vehicular)
INFORMATION
Kilauea Visitor Center 1 C2
SIGHTS & ACTIVITIES
Jaggar Museum 2 B2
Kilauea Iki Overlook 3 D2
Kipukapuaulu 4 A1
Lava Tree Molds 5 B1
Steam Vents 6 C2
Sulphur Banks 7 C1
Thurston Lava Tube 8 D2
Volcano Art Center 9 C2
Volcano Winery 10 B1
SLEEPING
Namakanipaio Cabins 11 A2
Namakanipaio Campground 12 A2
Volcano House 13 C2
EATING
Kilauea Military Camp 14 B1
Volcano Golf & Country Club 15 B1
OTHER
Park Entrance 16 C2

VOLCANO ART CENTER

Next door to the visitor center, inside historic 1877 Volcano House lodge, this **gallery shop** (☎ 967-7565; www.volcanoartcenter.org; 9am-5pm) sells high-quality island pottery, paintings, woodwork, sculpture, jewelry, Hawaiian quilts and more. Many are one-of-a-kind items, and it's worth a visit just to admire the solid artisanship. The nonprofit arts organization that runs the gallery also puts together craft and cultural workshops, music concerts, plays and dance recitals, all listed in its free monthly *Volcano Gazette*.

SULPHUR BANKS

Continuing on a trail from the Volcano Art Center is Sulphur Banks, where piles of steaming rocks come in shades of yellow and orange. This area traditionally called **Ha'akulamanu** (gathering place for birds), is one of many areas where Kilauea lets off steam, releasing hundreds of tons of sulfuric gases daily. As the steam reaches the surface, it deposits sulfur, which crystallizes in fluorescent yellow around the mouths of the vents. The pervasive smell of rotten eggs is from the hydrogen sulfide wafting from the vents. Don't breathe deeply! Other gases in the toxic cocktail include carbon dioxide and sulfur dioxide.

STEAM VENTS

There are a few small, nonsulfurous steam vents at the next pull-off. A trail across

---

NO NO'S AT THE VOLCANO

We've all heard about folks who pocket chunks of Pele's lava, only to regret it when bad luck strikes them once they're home. Park officials receive countless boxes of lava rock, along with handwritten tales of woe, mailed back by visitors. Some pay up to $50 in postage! Hawaiians discount the bad-luck myth but emphasize that it is indeed disrespectful to take lava souvenirs without Pele's permission. Regardless, it is illegal to remove anything from a national park, so whatever your superstition quotient, don't touch the rocks. This also goes for the *ahu* (rock cairns) along the trails – don't remove any or build more.

Likewise, don't leave anything around Kilauea Caldera either. Traditionally Hawaiians leave culturally appropriate offerings of plants and animals to Pele. More recently, however, bottles of gin have appeared – apparently following the example of George Lycurgus, the owner of Volcano House during the early 20th century. Many Southeast Asians, who have adopted Pele as their goddess, burn incense and throw 'hell money' and pigs' heads into the caldera. Anonymous visitors leave 'rock laulau' – a rock wrapped in ti leaves to resemble the Hawaiian dish – at trailhead and historical sites, though the gesture holds absolutely no traditional significance. Park visitors have also started leaving white coral 'graffiti' on black lava rock, imitating what you see along Hwy 19 in Kona.

To rangers, such offerings are just litter – a case of 'monkey see, monkey do.' Take the high road and leave no trace of yourself at the park.

---

the road here is another access to Sulphur Banks. Simple rainwater that percolates into the earth is heated by the hot rocks below and released upward as steam. More interesting is the two-minute walk beyond the vents, out to a part of the crater rim aptly called **Wahinekapu** (referring to Pele the sacred woman). Go early in the morning because the steam is impressive only when the air is cool.

JAGGAR MUSEUM

At this one-room **museum** (☎ 985-6049; admission free; ⏱ 9am-5pm) you'll see real-time seismographs and tiltmeters, a mural of the Hawaiian pantheon and a short history of the museum's founder, Dr Thomas A Jaggar.

It's worth stopping, if only for the fine view of Pele's house, at Halema'uma'u Crater. Sitting within Kilauea Caldera, it's sometimes referred to as the 'crater within the crater.' Detailed interpretive plaques at the lookout explain the geological workings of volcanoes. When the weather is clear, there's a rapturous view of Mauna Loa to the west, 20 miles away.

Drivers should be careful of the endangered nene that congregate in the parking lot. Feeding them contributes to the road deaths of these endangered birds, and is strictly prohibited. After leaving the museum, you'll pass the **Southwest Rift**, where you can stop and take a look at the wide

fissure slicing through the earth, from the caldera summit out to the coast and under the ocean floor.

HALEMA'UMA'U OVERLOOK

For at least a hundred years (from 1823, when missionary William Ellis first recorded the sight in writing), Halema'uma'u was a seething lake of lava, in a state of constant flux.

This fiery lake has enchanted travelers from all over the world. Some compared it to the fires of hell, while others saw primeval creation. Of staring down at it, Mark Twain wrote in *Roughing It*: 'Circles and serpents and streaks of lightning all twined and wreathed and tied together…I have seen Vesuvius since, but it was a mere toy, a child's volcano, a soup kettle, compared to this.'

In 1924 the floor of Halema'uma'u subsided rapidly, causing groundwater to react with hot lava rock, touching off a series of explosive eruptions. Boulders and mud rained down for days. When it was over, the crater had doubled in size (to about 300ft deep and 3000ft wide) and lava activity ceased. The crust has since cooled, although the pungent smell of sulfur persists.

The last time Halema'uma'u erupted, in early morning on April 30, 1982, geologists at the Hawaiian Volcano Observatory watched as their seismographs and tiltmeters went haywire, warning of an imminent eruption. The park service quickly closed off Halema'uma'u Trail and cleared hikers from the caldera floor. Before noon a half-mile fissure broke open in the crater wall also cutting into the caldera floor before spewing out 1.3 million cubic yards of lava – and nothing since.

All of the Big Island is Pele's territory, but Halema'uma'u is her home. Ceremonial hula is performed in her honor on the crater rim, and throughout the year those wishing to appease Pele leave offerings (see p199). The overlook is at the start of the **Halema'uma'u Trail** which runs 3.2 miles across Kilauea Caldera to the visitor center and makes a terrific half-day hike. Although few people who aren't hiking the full trail venture past the overlook, it's an easy half-mile walk to a 1982 lava-flow site.

THURSTON LAVA TUBE

On the east side of the Chain of Craters Rd intersection, Crater Rim Dr passes through the rain forest of native tree ferns and ohia that covers Kilauea's windward slope.

The **Thurston Lava Tube Trail** is an enjoyable 15-minute loop walk that starts out in ohia forest and passes through an impressive lava tube. All the tour buses stop here, so don't expect peace and quiet. A soundtrack of birdsong accompanies this walk, especially in early morning. The 'apapane, a native honeycreeper, is easy to spot. With a red body, silvery-white underside and black tail and wings, it flies from the yellow flowers of the mamane tree to the red pom-pom blossoms of the lehua gathering nectar.

Lava tubes are formed when the outer crust of a river of lava starts to harden but the liquid lava beneath the surface continues to flow on through. After the flow has drained out, the hard shell remains. Dating back perhaps 500 years, Thurston Lava Tube is a grand example – it's tunnel-like and almost big enough to run a train through. If you bring a flashlight, you can walk beyond the lighted area, further into the tube.

KILAUEA IKI CRATER

When Kilauea Iki (Little Kilauea) burst open in a fiery inferno in November 1959, the whole crater floor turned into a bubbling lake of molten lava. Its fountains reached record heights of 1900ft, lighting the evening sky with a bright orange glow for miles around. At its peak, it gushed out 2 million tons of lava an hour.

From the overlook there's a good view of the mile-wide crater below, which was used for filming the 2001 remake of *Planet of the Apes*. Crossing the crater gives the sen-

---

A DELICATE BALANCE

On the lush and verdant windward shores of Puna all forms of life thrived in abundance. The plants grew with abandon, and the people prospered from nature's bounty. There, Hi'iaka, of divine lineage, lived as a mortal. Nurtured by the riches and beauty of the earth, convening with its essence, she learned its most valuable secrets. Hi'iaka thoroughly immersed herself in the cultivation and study of plants and their medicinal properties. She used her skills for healing, even performing rituals to bring back the dead. She cultivated the ohia trees, and used their vibrant red flowers for ceremonial lei. Hi'iaka herself soon blossomed into a beautiful young woman, and in a show of her grace, with her best friend Hopoe, danced the hula for the first time at Ha'ena, a beach in Puna.

Then one day Hi'iaka and her powerful sister of the volcano, Pele, got into a great argument. Pele could not stand to have her strength tested by her mortal sister. So in a jealous rage and demonstration of her superior powers Pele erupted massive amounts of lava, killing Hopoe and destroying much of the forest that Hi'iaka had so arduously looked after. Scientists have documented this enormous eruption. Occurring about 500 years ago there is evidence of a continuous outpour of new land lasting for 50 years.

To avenge this malicious act, their grandmother, Papa, co-creator of the islands, imbued Hi'iaka with divine powers. This Hawaiian myth shows Hi'iaka's power to bring new life from out of Pele's path of destruction. From death the creation cycle continues. When walking the seemingly lifeless fields of lava, stop, take a closer look, and you will see Hi'iaka's work as ohia and tree fern find their way up though the cracks to live again.

sation of walking on a paradoxical frozen surface. Plumb tests show that the lava is only about a mile beneath the surface. For more information, see p204.

DEVASTATION TRAIL

Crater Rim Dr continues across the barren Ka'u Desert, and through the fallout area of the 1959 eruption of Kilauea Iki Crater.

The **Devastation Trail** is a half-mile walk across a former rain forest that was devastated by cinder and pumice from that eruption. Everything green was wiped out. What remains today are dead ohia trees, stripped bare and sun-bleached white, and some tree molds. You just can't keep good flora down, however; ohia trees, native '*ohelo* berry bushes and ferns have already started colonizing the area anew.

The trail is paved and has parking lots on each end. The prominent cinder cone along the way is Pu'u Pua'i (Gushing Hill), formed during the 1959 eruption. The northeastern end of the trail looks down into Kilauea Iki Crater.

Chain of Craters Rd intersects Crater Rim Dr opposite the west-side parking area for the Devastation Trail.

Chain of Craters Road   Map p198

Chain of Craters Rd winds 20 miles down the southern slopes of Kilauea Volcano, ending abruptly at the latest East Rift Zone lava flow on the Puna Coast. It's a good paved two-lane road, although there are no services along the way. Allow a few hours for the round trip, to navigate around curves and slow-moving sightseers.

From the road you'll have striking vistas of the coastline far below, and for miles the predominant view is of fingers of lava, which cooled before reaching the sea. You can sometimes find thin filaments of volcanic glass, known as Pele's hair, in the lava cracks and crevices. The best time to photograph the unique landscape is before 9am or after 3pm, when sunlight slants off the lava.

In addition to endless lava expanses, the road takes in an impressive collection of sights, including a handful of craters that you can literally peer into. Some are so new there's no sign of life, while others are thickly forested with ohia, ferns and other native plants.

Chain of Craters Rd once connected to Hwys 130 and 137, allowing traffic between the volcano and Hilo via Puna. Lava flows closed the road in 1969, but by 1979 it was back in service, albeit slightly rerouted. Then Kilauea's active flows cut the link again in 1988, burying a 9-mile stretch of the road to date.

HILINA PALI RD

Descending Chain of Craters Rd, the 2.2-mile approach to Hilina Pali Rd hosts pit craters of varying size and age. The forested oasis of Koko'olau Crater is the most interesting example of this feature and is located just before the turn for Hilina Pali Rd.

Hilina Pali Rd leads 4 miles to the Kulanaokuaiki Campground (p210), and just further on is the Mauna Iki Trail (p205) bisecting the Ka'u Desert. It's another 5 miles to the end of the road and the site of Hilina Pali Overlook, a lookout at 2280ft with a view of the southeast coast. Just beyond the overlook is the trailhead for the Ka'u Desert Trail and for the Ka'aha and Hilina Pali Trails, which lead down to the coast. They are all hot, dry, backcountry trails.

MAUNA ULU

In 1969, eruptions from Kilauea's east rift began building a new lava shield that now rises above its surroundings. It was named Mauna Ulu (Growing Mountain). By the time the flow stopped in 1974, it had covered 10,000 acres of parkland and added 200 acres of new land to the coast.

It also buried a 12-mile section of Chain of Craters Rd in lava. From the parking area you can follow a trail to the lava flow by taking the turnoff on the left, 3.5 miles down Chain of Craters Rd. Just beyond this is Mauna Ulu itself.

The **Pu'u Huluhulu Overlook Trail**, a 3-mile round-trip hike, begins at the parking area, crosses over lava flows from 1974, and climbs to the top of a 150ft cinder cone, where you'll have a panoramic view of Mauna Loa, Mauna Kea, Pu'u 'O'o vent, Kilauea, the East Rift Zone and ocean. This beautiful, moderate hike takes about two hours return.

KEALAKOMO

As you continue down Chain of Craters Rd, you'll be passing over Mauna Ulu's extensive flows. About halfway along the road, at an elevation of 2000ft, is this covered shelter with picnic tables and a superb ocean view. In 1975, a 7.2-magnitude earthquake rocked the southeast coast and portions of the south flank subsided up to 12ft, touching off a tsunami that killed two people at Halape.

After Kealakomo, the road begins to descend more steeply, making one prominent switchback and winding through lava flows. This is the trailhead for the Naulu-Napau Crater Trail leading to the Pu'u 'O'o vent (see p206).

PU'U LOA PETROGLYPHS

The gentle Pu'u Loa Trail leads less than a mile to a field of petroglyphs laboriously pecked into *pahoehoe* (smooth-flowing lava) by early Hawaiians. The site, which is along an ancient trail that once ran between Ka'u and Puna, has more than 20,000 images. The marked trailhead begins on the Chain of Craters Rd midway between the 16- and 17-mile markers. It makes for an interesting, easy 1¼-hour return walk.

At the site, make sure you stay on the boardwalk at all times – the views of the petroglyphs are good, and there's no need to wear them down by trampling over the rocks. At **Pu'u Loa** (Long Hill), toward the southeast, ancient Hawaiians pecked out thousands of dimpled depressions in the petroglyph field to serve as receptacles for the umbilical stumps of their babies. By placing the umbilical stumps inside the cupules and then covering them with stones, they hoped to bestow their children with longevity.

HOLEI SEA ARCH

Just before the 19-mile marker, look for the sign marking the Holei Sea Arch. This rugged section of the coast has sharply eroded lava cliffs, called Holei Pali, which are constantly being pounded by crashing surf. The high rock arch, carved out of one of the cliffs, is quite impressive, although the wave action of Namakaokaha'i, goddess of the sea and sister to Pele, has numbered its days.

GO TO THE FLOW

The National Park Service welcomes visitors to go see the active lava when it is flowing at the end of Chain of Craters Rd, but officials also emphasize the dangers of the hike and the proximity to molten lava. The trek toward the flow is strenuous, crossing hardened lava, and the 'trail' is not only unmarked, except for temporary reflectors, but it's unpatrolled and potentially dangerous. Hikers should stay at least 400yd inland because of unstable land at the coastline.

The trek leads as close to the lava as safety allows, and often toward the point where lava flows into the sea. However, what you'll find at the end of the trek is unpredictable. You might hike *mauka* (inland) or *makai* (seaward) of Chain of Craters Rd, and you might see molten lava just a few feet away, or only steam rising in the distance. The return hike can take anywhere from 20 minutes to several hours.

During the day, the black lava reflects the sun's heat and temperature, often reaching the high 90s (°F). Many visitors begin late in the afternoon, to view the orange glow after dark, but it's inadvisable to be on the trail after sunset without a knowledgeable guide. Many adventure tour companies, such as Arnott's Lodge (p172) or Hawaii Forest & Trail (p138), lead guided treks a few days a week.

While the steam plumes are impressive to see from afar, they are extremely dangerous up close. The explosive clash between seawater and 2100°F molten lava can spray scalding water hundreds of feet into the air and can throw chunks of lava up to 500yd inland.

The lava crust itself forms in unstable ledges called lava benches, which can collapse into the ocean without warning. In 1993, a collapsing lava bench sent one islander to his fiery death and burned more than a dozen people in the ensuing steam explosion. In March 1999, the scene almost repeated itself when seven onlookers scattered to safety, after a series of explosions began blasting lava bombs into the air and then collapsed the 25-acre lava bench they'd been standing on.

Volcanic activity and viewing conditions are always subject to change, so call the park visitor-center's **hotline** (☎ 985-6000) for updates.

END OF THE ROAD

Chain of Craters Rd ends abruptly wherever hardened lava covers the road. Park rangers try to mark a trail over the hardened lava with small reflectors leading to a safe observation point. There's a simple info board and portable toilets here, but no water or other facilities.

Mauna Loa Rd   Map pp194–5

Also known as the 'Bird Park,' **Kipukapuaulu** is a unique 100-acre sanctuary for native flora and fauna, and worth the short drive 1.5 miles up Mauna Loa Rd. Visitors often overlook this peaceful, easy walk because it's outside the park entrance. On clear days, the panoramic view of Mauna Loa will make you appreciate its size.

Along the 1-mile loop trail, you'll hear only silence and birdsong, especially in early morning. Native species include the inquisitive *'elepaio* and three honeycreepers – the *'amakihi, 'apapane* and *'i'iwi*. All of these birds are sparrow-size and brightly colored. The trees soar here, so bring your binoculars or you'll see little.

About 400 years ago, a major lava flow from Mauna Loa's northeastern rift covered most of the surrounding area. Pele spared this bit of land when the flow parted, creating an island forest in a sea of lava. In Hawaiian, it's known as a *kipuka,* though the term can mean any variation in form, such as a fertile oasis, a patch of blue sky amid clouds or even the constructed resorts on the South Kohala lava terrain.

Today Kipukapuaulu is an official Special Ecological Area of rare endemic plants, insects and birds, where there is intensive management to remove alien plants and to restore native plant species. You'll see lots of koa trees, which provide a habitat for the ferns, and peperomia that take root in its moist bark. You'll also pass a lava tube where a unique species of big-eyed spider was discovered in the dark depths of 1973. A free flora-and-fauna trail guide is available at the visitor center inside the park.

Near the start of Mauna Loa Rd there's a turnoff to some lava tree molds. These deep, tube-like apertures were formed when a lava flow engulfed the rain forest that stood here. Because the trees were so waterlogged, the lava hardened around them instead of burning them on contact. As the trees disintegrated, deep holes where the trunks once stood were left in the ground.

If you keep driving on Mauna Loa Rd, you'll pass other heavily forested *kipuka* as you approach Mauna Loa, the world's most-massive active volcano. Mauna Loa has erupted more than 18 times in the past century – the last eruption, in March 1984, lasted 21 days. The onerous Mauna Loa Summit Trail (p205) begins at the end of the road after 13.5 miles.

Volcano

Just 2 miles east of the park Volcano Village is tucked among giant sugi (Japanese evergreen), ohia forest and giant tree ferns unraveling their spiral fronds. In this mystic mountain setting it is easy to lose yourself in the eternal green and the cool enchanting mist. Many artists have found this to be the perfect balance of solitude and inspiration where the imagination has no bounds.

Being so close to the volcano this place resonates mana. On the surface the picturesque B&Bs set in the tropical forest make for a storybook hamlet. But stay a while and you will find, like many before you, that there is enough here for a lifetime. Make a stop at the island's unique **Volcano Winery** (Map p198; ☎ 967-7772; www.volcanowinery.com; 35 Pi'i Mauna Dr; ☺ 10am-5:30pm) and taste the locally made wines in the shadow of Mauna Loa. These friendly folks make a selection of interesting grape, tropical fruit and honey wines ($14 to $16 per bottle).

ACTIVITIES

To join a ranger-led guided walk, see the bulletin board at the Kilauea Visitor Center (p197). You can also join a guided hike with outdoor-adventure companies Hawaii Forest & Trail or Hawaiian Walkways (p58).

If you're not a hiker and golf's your pleasure, the **Volcano Golf & Country Club** (☎ 967-8228; Pi'i Mauna Dr; green fees $62.50, Kama'iana rate $37.50) is just up the road from the winery. Receiving plenty of moisture the setting is lush beneath the grand Mauna Loa and Mauna Kea volcanoes. The course is straightforward but enjoyable and well maintained.

Hiking

If your form of exploration involves a pack of provisions and your own two feet, you will find some of the secluded riches that

---

TOP FIVE HIKES IN HAWAI'I VOLCANOES NATIONAL PARK

Keauhou Trail (p208) Follow historic lava flows to the sea and stay at one of the secluded coastal shelters.
Kilauea Iki Trail (below) A condensed look at the many intriguing environments in the park.
Mauna Iki Trail (opposite) Find solitude among a multicolored desert of sun-drenched lava.
Mauna Loa Trail (opposite) For its vast volcanic landscapes and unhindered views.
Napau Crater Trail (p206) See petroglyphs, camp and glimpse the active Pu'u 'O'o Vent.

---

are only found on the Big Island. Of the numerous climates on the island, many can be explored within the boundaries of the park on an extensive network of hiking trails, rising from sea level to over 13,000ft. Trails strike out in a number of directions – across crater floors, down to secluded beaches, through native forests, around the Ka'u Desert and up to the snowcapped summit of Mauna Loa. The trails often intersect, so you can create your own loops and paths, but the most common are described here.

The following hikes range from an easy 1-mile walk to multiday backcountry treks. Remember that except at the cabins and shelters, no drinking water is available. Trail signs are unreliable, and often contradict each other in distance and direction.

HALEMA'UMA'U TRAIL   Map p198

One of the park's best day hikes, this 6-mile loop starts in a moist ohia forest, descends almost 400ft to the floor of Kilauea Caldera, and crosses the surface of the active volcano. The trailhead is located diagonally across the road from the visitor center. Most of the counterclockwise loop is entirely exposed, making it either a hot, dry hike or chillingly damp.

You'll traverse flow after flow, beginning with one from 1974 and continuing over others from 1885, 1894, 1954, 1971 and 1982, each distinguished by changing hues from age and exposure to the elements. The trail, marked by *ahu* (lava rock cairns), ends about 3 miles from the visitor center at the steaming Halema'uma'u Overlook. On the way back, you'll take the Byron Ledge Trail, heading toward Pu'u Pua'i and the Devastation Trail (p201), which you can add as a side trip. On the last stretch, you'll return to damp, cool forest air.

KILAUEA IKI TRAIL   Map p198

Perhaps the most-popular hike, this trail leads you though a microcosm of the park.

The 4-mile, clockwise loop begins near the Thurston Lava Tube parking lot, quickly descending 400ft through fairytale ohia forest and then cutting across the mile-wide crater, passing the main vent. Like many trails in the park, the way is delineated with *ahu*. On the crater surface, scattered steam vents compliment the stubborn *'ohelo* berries, ohia trees and ferns that break through the hard and often iridescent surface.

Much of the trail is unshaded but heading generally northwest across the crater floor, the path over *pahoehoe* is not hard. Soft black cinders reveal the footprints of previous hikers, aiding navigation. Don't wander off-trail to explore any steaming vents, lava tubes or caves without an experienced guide.

Keep to the right to ascend the crater wall on the far side. You'll be on Byron Ledge, the ledge that separates Kilauea Iki from Kilauea Caldera. Turn around for good views of Kilauea Iki Crater and gold-topped Pu'u Pua'i, which looks much more jagged than when viewed from the Halema'uma'u Trail. From there you'll pass two junctions; if you turn right at both, you'll continue along the Kilauea Iki Trail back to the parking lot; if you turn left, you'll connect with the Crater Rim Trail or the Byron Ridge Trail, which hooks up with Halema'uma'u Trail after 1 mile.

CRATER RIM TRAIL   Map p198

There are obvious advantages to being out on a trail versus seeing sites from a car. Following a similar circuit to Crater Rim Dr, this 11-mile trek gives you direct contact with the impressive Kilauea Caldera while avoiding some crowds at the more accessible drive-up sites. This approach allows the process of the volcano to be seen in stages.

Starting at the Volcano House you either skirt the crater rim to the north, gaining a bird's eye view of the landscape, or drop into misty ohia and fern forest passing Kilauea Iki Crater to the south and crossing a number of historic lava flows along the way. Either way the loop will take about six hours, allowing time for a leisurely lunch. From the Southwest Rift Zone area, you should also take the short 1.2-mile side trip to see Halema'uma'u Crater, if you haven't already seen it. Be prepared for changeable weather at this altitude. A hot sunny stroll can turn to a cold downpour slosh in an instant.

MAUNA IKI TRAIL   Map pp194–5
The Ka'u Desert is a land of arid beauty and expansive horizons. Most hikers find the trails here to be long, hot and rather dull – though the sense of solitude and oneness with nature can be mesmerizing. But the 7-mile Mauna Iki Trail is doable and exceptionally varied.

To reach the trailhead, go down Chain of Craters Rd for 2 miles and turn right on Hilina Pali Rd, which can be hazardous due to blind curves, sharp rises and fog. About 4.5 miles down Hilina Pali Rd, shortly after Kulanaokuaiki Campground, look for a trailhead sign on the right. A large *ahu* signals the trail's beginning.

The trail crosses *pahoehoe* that appear in a range of colors, from shiny gray to muted brown to metallic red. Mind the lava crevices and cracks. From a distance to your left you'll see the double-peaked Pu'ukoa'e (3250ft) and on the right, a tawny cinder cone with a rust-colored 'chimney' formation on its top.

As you approach a set of twin pit craters, you'll see warning signs reading 'Danger Overhanging Edge, Stay Back.' Carefully peer into the pits, which hide a surprising amount of plant life.

The trail 'ends' around Pu'ukoa'e, though you can venture further down the trail, turning left at the Ka'u Desert Trail junction to reach Mauna Iki (3032ft) lava shield, about 3 miles away. If you continue west along the trail, you'll hit Hwy 11, which is another starting point.

MAUNA LOA SUMMIT TRAILS

Only those who are extremely fit and prepared for winter mountaineering should attempt to climb Mauna Loa, for the high elevation and sub-arctic conditions can be surprisingly daunting. The summit trail (Map pp194-5) begins at the end of Mauna Loa Rd, about an hour's drive from the visitor center. The road is occasionally closed due to fire danger but if you have a backcountry permit you'll be allowed access.

This rugged 19-mile trail gradually ascends 6600ft. It takes a minimum of three days, but four is better for proper acclimatization and time exploring the summit area. Two simple cabins, with a dozen or fewer bunks, are available on a first-come, first-served basis at Pu'u'ula'ula (Red Hill) and Mauna Loa summit. Potable water might be available and must be treated (inquire at the visitor center, p197).

At first the trail rises through an ohia forest and above the tree line. After 7.5 miles and about four to six hours, you reach **Pu'u'ula'ula** at 10,035ft. There are fine views of Mauna Kea to the north and Maui's venerable Haleakala to the northwest.

The 11.6-mile hike from Pu'u'ula'ula to the summit cabin at 13,250ft is a full day. The route crosses a stark, stirring landscape of multicolored cinder fields, *'a'a* and *pahoehoe*, with gaping fissures cleaving the landscape that includes spatter cones. If you look closely, you'll see amazing variations in the lava, ranging from iridescent black to matte clay red to olivine green.

After 9.5 miles, you come to **Moku'aweoweo Caldera** and a fork in the trail. It's another 2 miles along the **Cabin Trail** to your night's resting place. If you absolutely can't push on, **Jaggar's Cave** (just beyond the fork) can serve as a windbreak – but it's a small niche rather than an actual cave.

The other fork is for the 2.5-mile **Summit Trail**. The last 2 miles are especially challenging and will seem to last forever (no one can believe it's only 2 miles!). At 13,677ft, Mauna Loa's summit has a sub-arctic climate, and temperatures normally drop to freezing every night. Winter snowstorms can last for days, bringing whiteout conditions. Snow can fall any time of year and occasionally it falls as low as Pu'u'ula'ula, covering the upper end of the trail. Consult park rangers about weather conditions before setting out. Getting a permit at the visitor's center is essential, not only as a regulation but also to register in case of an emergency.

HAWAI'I VOLCANOES NATIONAL PARK

BACKCOUNTRY TRAILS

These trails over and around the world's most active volcano provide a wild and unparalleled Hawai'i experience. Free hiking shelters and rustic cabins are available along some of the park's backcountry trails. At Kīpuka Pepeiao along the Ka'u Desert Trail there's a small cabin and primitive three-walled shelters on the coast at Keauhou, Halape and Ka'aha. On the Mauna Loa Trail there is a cabin at Pu'u'ula'ula (Red Hill) as well as the Mauna Loa summit cabin. All have pit toilets and limited catchment water that must be treated before drinking. The current level of water at each site is posted on a board at the visitor center. There are also two primitive campgrounds, which have pit toilets, but no shelter or water, at 'Apua Point along the Puna Coast Trail, and Napau Crater campground, 3 miles west of the Pu'u 'O'o vent, reached via the Napau Crater Trail. Over lava flows you'll be relying on *ahu* to find your way. So if you are easily distracted by the wonders of nature make sure to pack the compass.

Before heading out, overnight hikers are required to register for permits, which are free, at the visitor center. Rangers have updates on trail and cabin conditions. Permits are issued on a first-come, first-served basis, beginning no earlier than noon on the day before your intended hike. There's a three-day limit at each backcountry campsite, and each site has a limit of eight to 16 campers.

Essential backpacking equipment includes a first-aid kit, a trail map, a flashlight with extra batteries, a minimum of a gallon of water, an extra stash of food, a mirror (for signaling), a cooking stove with fuel (open fires are prohibited), biodegradable soap and toilet paper, broken-in boots, sunglasses, sunscreen, rain gear and a hat. Minimum impact camping is always the rule, so pack out what you pack in, including trash. Note that the desert and coastal trails can make for extremely hot hiking. More information on backcountry hiking, including basic trail maps and hiking books, can be obtained at the visitor center.

On the Mauna Loa Summit, Observatory, and Ainapo Trails (p205), it's critically important to acclimatize. Altitude sickness is a danger (see p245 for more information). The high altitude can produce extreme environmental conditions of which

hypothermia from the cold and wind is a hazard. A good windproof jacket, wool sweater, winter-rated sleeping bag and rain gear are all essential. Sunglasses and sunscreen will provide protection from snow glare and the strong rays of the sun that prevail in the thin atmosphere.

Observatory Trail   Map pp194–5

This steep, strenuous alternative approach to the Mauna Loa summit starts at the Mauna Loa Weather Observatory (11,055ft; see p144). The Observatory is reached from a 19-mile paved spur off Saddle Rd. An Abrupt elevation gain of 2620ft in just 6.4 miles warrants proper acclimatizing (see p245). Heavy weather conditions (including freezing wind, fog, snow and other mountaineering conditions) are also considerations in assessing this hike.

Napau Crater Trail   Map pp194–5

For spectacular views of Pu'u 'O'o, the source of Kilauea's current spectacle, the 18-mile Napau Crater Trail can't be beat. Day trippers will see giant plumes of steam arising from the active vent, while fiery red 'skylights' allow glimpses of the molten lava to campers. Due to ongoing volcanic activity, however, this trail is subject to change. Note: if you've got only a couple of hours, you can do just the first leg of this hike, the Pu'u Huluhulu Overlook Trail (p201), without a permit. Otherwise the hike is about nine hours round trip.

The Napau trailhead is at the 3.5-mile marker along Chain of Craters Rd, near the Mauna Ulu parking area. The trail's first 5 miles follows what was formerly Chain of Craters Rd, before *pahoehoe* lava covered it in 1973. There are great examples of reticulite and Pele's hair strewn all over the flows.

You'll pass lava trees and the 150ft Pu'u Huluhulu (Shaggy Hill) cinder cone before veering left toward the east. On clear days the view is magnificent, with Mauna Loa off to the northwest, Mauna Kea to the north and the ever-changing Pu'u 'O'o vent straight ahead. After descending across *pahoehoe* terrain, you'll reach the south rim of Makaopuhi crater, a jaw-dropping 1 mile wide and 500ft deep.

After less than half an hour cooling off in a fern forest of purple fiddleheads, you

---

DETOUR: 'AINAPO TRAIL

The 'Ainapo Trail is the most rustic and challenging of all the marked trails to summit Mauna Loa. It combines a lengthy 10.2 miles at altitude and a steep incline rising up the southeastern flank of Mauna Loa. Pre-historic Hawaiians are thought to have originally used the 'Ainapo Trail for ceremonies honoring Pele. This route to the summit was the preferred route until volcanologist Thomas A Jaggar lobbied to have the Mauna Loa Trail built in 1915, to provide a more gradual, less strenuous incline suitable to hauling equipment on horseback.

Aside from being physically difficult, this route also provides some major logistical planning, but if you want an adventure that very few people have done, this is one of the most untouched spots on Hawai'i. Day hikers do not need a permit, but anyone interested in using the 'Ainapo trail must call **Kapapala Ranch** (☎ 928-6206; ⏱ 6:30-7:30pm or 6-7am prior to your hike) to obtain the combination (which is changed daily) for the gate providing access. If you plan on staying overnight you must obtain a permit from the Division of Forest and Wildlife to stay at the 'Ainapo Shelter, which is on the Kapapala Forest Reserve. Then if planning to summit Mauna Loa you must also register at the Kilauea Visitor Center (see p197).

To arrive at the trailhead take the *mauka* side 4WD road, at the cattle guard between mile markers 40 and 41, off of Hwy 11, south of Hawai'i Volcanoes National Park. The 8-mile road (only open during daylight hours) enters the Kapapala Ranch gate after about 2 miles. Departure from this public corridor is considered trespassing.

Beginning at 5650ft, ascend 2100ft in 2.7 miles to reach the 'Ainapo Shelter at Halewai. This moderate to challenging portion of the trail passes through Koaohia, and subalpine ohia/shrub forest. The cabin has six bunks, a composting toilet and limited catchment water (drinkable only if treated). Fires are prohibited. Above Halewai the trail is challenging, rising 5500ft in 7.5 miles to the Mauna Loa Cabin. The trail is above the tree line and exposed to the elements including the sub-arctic climate at the summit. Be equipped for winter mountaineering on this rugged adventure.

---

reach the Naulu Trail fork, leading to the Kealakomo parking area on Chain of Craters Rd. However, you should continue straight across this junction. Upon exiting the fern forest, you'll come to the rock walls of an old depository for *pulu,* the golden, silky 'hair' found at the base of *hapu'u* (tree fern) fiddlehead stems. The ancient Hawaiians used *pulu* to embalm their dead. In the late 19th century, *pulu* was exported for use as mattress and pillow stuffing, until it was discovered to quickly decompose and turn to dust.

Ten minutes past the *'pulu* factory' there are fantastic views of the partially collapsed Pu'u 'O'o cone. Beyond the junction for the **Napau Crater lookout** is a primitive campground. Hike up past this toward the toilet, swing around it to the right, and follow the almost indistinguishable trail to the floor of the Napau Crater. The *ahu* here are hard to distinguish from natural piles of lava. Keep an eye out for where the indistinct 'trail' plunges over the crater wall in a daringly steep fashion. There, crumbling switchbacks have been forced onto *'a'a* rockslides and intermittent scree. Although relatively short, the switchbacks are not painless – and they're even more difficult to scale on the way back, so keep that in mind as you plunge onward.

After making this precipitous descent, there's a barely discernible trail snaking across Napau Crater. Step lightly and keep as close to the *ahu* as possible. On the far eastern side of the crater, another set of short but steep switchbacks ascend the crater wall. Wherever the *ahu* end is the de facto terminus of the trail. Use your best judgment in deciding how closely to approach this extremely active volcanic area. Don't linger too long, to avoid more exposure than necessary to hazardous fumes.

Kahaualeʻa Trail

Park officials strongly discourage hikers from taking this unofficial trail-of-use toward the Pu'u 'O'o vent, mainly because people seeking 'adventure' are frequently unprepared and get lost or injured. The 8.5-mile hike (nicknamed the 'Pu'u 'O'o Trail') is not located on HAVO land but on the

Kahauale'a Natural Area Reserve. The trail is barely marked and poorly maintained; expect both mud and glassy *pahoehoe* terrain. Dense fog often shrouds the trail, disorienting hikers who end up unexpectedly spending the night outside and spurring an embarrassing rescue.

To get to the trailhead, take Hwy 11 north of Volcano Village and turn east onto S Glenwood Rd immediately before the 20-mile marker. Wind through the Fern Forest subdivision to the end of the dirt road. Beyond the Kahauale'a Natural Area Reserve sign, a footpath wanders for about 4.5 miles through lush ohia-*hapu'u* forest, then forges ahead one last mile over desolate volcanic desert toward Pu'u 'O'o. Don't go further than the edge of the forest – the terrain is unstable and treacherous.

Before starting out, check to see if the winds are blowing predominantly toward the trailhead – if that's the case, don't hike, since volcanic fumes can seriously impair breathing. Lock your car doors as break-ins are common. Get an early start and be aware of your progress. Wear bright clothing, as the trail passes through an area that's open year-round for game hunting. Be cautious and don't proceed beyond the sign at the end of the trail.

Keauhou Trail   Map pp194–5

The most desirable way to visit the coastal shelters is from the Keauhou Trail off of Chain of Craters Rd or from the Puna Coast. The hike has little strenuous sections, although be prepared for hot weather. After 4.8 miles the trail meets ups with the Halina Pali Trail heading southwest, splitting off to the coast and the Halape Shelter, or continuing onto the Ka'aha shelter and Ka'u Desert Trail (right). Of all the coastal shelters Halape is the most pleasant and storied.

On November 29, 1975, the strongest earthquake in 100 years shook the Big Island. Just before dawn, rockslides from the upper slopes sent most of the 36 campers at Halape running toward the sea, where the coastline suddenly sank. What moments before was an idyllic beachfront campground bordered by coconut trees had been submerged beneath their feet. A series of tsunamis swept the campers up, carrying them first out to sea and then coughing them back on shore. Miraculously, only two people died.

The earthquake left a fine sandy cove inland of the former beach, and despite its turbulent past, Halape is still a lovely spot. Swimming is good in the protected cove, but there are strong currents in the open ocean beyond.

Halape is one of only eight Big Island nesting sites for the endangered hawksbill sea turtle. Show respect when camping in these areas. Some guidelines to observe include: not setting up tents in areas identified as turtle nesting sites, keeping sites clean of food scraps and minimizing the use of night lighting, which can disorient the turtles. Hawksbill turtles also nest at the park's Keauhou and Apua Point backcountry camping areas.

If you follow the Keauhou Trail for 2 miles on to the coast you will be at the Keauhou Shelter. Head northeast on the Puna Coast Trail (below) to 'Apua Point and Chain of Craters Rd.

Ka'u Desert Trail   Map pp194–5

The Ka'u Desert Trail network is the most extensive in the park and there are many ways to approach its vastness while complimenting the trip with connecting trails. It's best to pick up the trail midway along Hilina Pali Rd. From Hilina Pali Rd, follow the Mauna Iki Trail (p205) across the Twin Pit Crater and the Mauna Iki Lava Shield en route to the Pepeiao Cabin. Take in the expanse of the arid landscape and see the effects of the searing heat on aging lava. Get lost in the sense of solitude and enjoy subtle hues shifting in the changing light.

As with all the trailheads in the park, there is no water here, though there is catchment water at the cabin. Get an early start and be prepared for intense sun on this 14.3-mile day. Continue the next day onto the Ka'aha Shelter on the coast, or push onto the more desirable Halape Shelter connecting on a loop with the Halina Pali Trail. To avoid the hot switchbacks going up Halina Pali Trail continue onto the Keauhou Trail and hitchhike back up Chain of Craters Rd to the car.

Puna Coast Trail   Map pp194–5

This trail starts almost at the end of the Chain of Craters Rd, at about the 19.5-mile mark at the Pu'u Loa Petroglyphs. The entire stretch of this hike is generally both hot and windy and crosses miles of barren *pahoehoe* from Mauna Ulu's early-1970s eruptions,

While not as colorful as the other hikes, the volcanic textures are interesting. The draw here is seeing where the lava meets the sea. You'll also pass *kipuka* along the way. 'Apua Point campground is 6.5 miles along a flat, well-marked trail. Remember that this is an endangered turtle-nesting ground. Further west, the Keauhou and Halape hiking shelters could be incorporated into a multi-day loop returning via the 7-mile Keauhou Trail (opposite). Untreated water is available only at the shelters, not the campground.

HAWAI'I VOLCANOES NATIONAL PARK FOR CHILDREN

Inside Hawai'i Volcanoes National Park you will find that it is more of a playground for grown-ups than for kids, but the process and landscape of the volcano is intriguing for all ages. There are a number of sites where children can get a first-hand look at Pele's work. Taking a tour of Crater Rim Dr (p197) is an easy way to explore what the park has to offer without getting too involved. The Kilauea Visitor Center (p197) has a short film that will capture the imagination with its images of the eruption. Sulphur Banks (p198) and Steam Vents (p198) are terrific visual examples of the thermal activity where children can feel and smell the effects. Eww, who let one! For a more scientific approach coupled with an understanding of the Hawaiian mythology, go to the Jaggar Museum (p199). The other Crater Rim sights may or may not intrigue your child, but Thurston Lava Tube (see p200) is a consummate highlight. It provides the thrill of exploration with instant gratification.

FESTIVALS & EVENTS

Regular park programs include **After Dark in the Park** (Kilauea Visitor Center Auditorium; admission free; ⏰ 7pm Tue), a series of free talks by experts on cultural, historic and geological matters. It is held two or three times monthly.

Annual special events that are free with park admission include the following:

Annual Dance & Music Concert (last weekend in Mar) An event hosted by the Volcano Art Center, presenting works by Big Island choreographers, dancers and musicians.

Kilauea Volcano Wilderness Runs (late Jul) Held at Hawai'i Volcanoes National Park. There are four separate events: a 10-mile run around the rim of Kilauea Caldera; both a 5-mile run and a 5-mile walk that go down into Kilauea Iki Crater; and a 26-mile marathon through the Ka'u Desert. For information, contact the **Volcano Art Center** (☎ 985-8725; www.volcanoartcenter.org).

Aloha Festivals Ka Ho'ola'a o Na Ali'i (Sep) A brilliant royal court procession and celebration on the Halema'uma'u Crater rim during the Aloha Festival.

Na Mea Hawaii Hula Kahiko Series A series of outdoor hula *kahiko* performances four times throughout the year.

SLEEPING

There are so many B&Bs and rental cottages in Volcano town that you might want to consult an island-wide booking service to help focus your search (see p222).

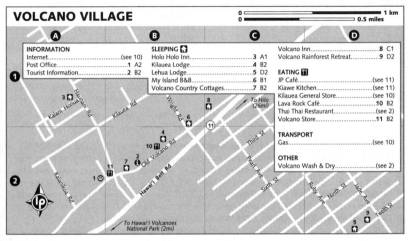

VOLCANO VILLAGE		
INFORMATION	**SLEEPING**	Volcano Inn....................................**8** C1
Internet....................................(see 10)	Holo Holo Inn.............................**3** A1	Volcano Rainforest Retreat...........**9** D2
Post Office..................................**1** A2	Kilauea Lodge............................**4** B2	
Tourist Information.....................**2** B2	Lehua Lodge...............................**5** D2	**EATING**
	My Island B&B............................**6** B1	JP Café......................................(see 11)
	Volcano Country Cottages...........**7** B2	Kiawe Kitchen...........................(see 11)
		Kilauea General Store................(see 10)
		Lava Rock Café.........................**10** B2
		Thai Thai Restaurant.................(see 2)
		Volcano Store..........................**11** B2
		TRANSPORT
		Gas...(see 10)
		OTHER
		Volcano Wash & Dry.................(see 2)

Budget

Holo Holo Inn (Map p209; ☎ 967-7950, 800-671-2999; www.enable.org/holoholo; 19-4036 Kalani Honua Rd; dm $17-19; r $44-60; 🖳) This small, sociable lodge, affiliated with Hostelling International, has clean but darkish dorms. Owner Yahuki Satoshi recently renovated two private rooms with private bath. One has a queen bed, the other a queen and a double. There's a shared kitchen, free Internet for guests and a TV room, complimentary coffee and tea, laundry facilities and a sauna. Call for reservations after 4:30pm.

Kulana Artist Sanctuary (Map p198; ☎ 985-9055; www.panpolynesia.net/kulana; Volcano Village; camping per person $15, s/d $30/40) Guests share the main house bathroom, kitchen and library, and in the cooperative spirit of the founder's vision, you're required to participate in easy caretaking tasks. It has a contemplative, communal atmosphere geared toward the creative, or spiritual seekers. Kulana truly lives up to its motto: 'no smoking, alcohol, drugs or drama.' Ask about monthly artist-in-residence rates from $300.

CAMPING

The park has two free drive-up campgrounds that are relatively uncrowded outside summer. Sites are first-come, first-served, with a limit of one week at each campground. Because of the elevation, nights can be crisp and cool. Additionally, there is backcountry camping in cabins, shelters and campsites.

Kulanaokuaiki Campground (Map pp194-5; Hilina Pali Rd; free) About 3.5 miles off Chain of Craters Rd, is newer and less developed. It has three campsites plus toilets and picnic tables, but no water.

Namakanipaio Campground (Map p198; free) The park's busiest campground is between the 32- and 33-mile markers off Hwy 11, 3 miles west of the visitor center. Tent sites are in a small meadow that offers little privacy, but

is surrounded by fragrant eucalyptus trees. There are rest rooms, water, fireplaces and picnic tables.

Namakanipaio Cabins (Map p198; bookings at Volcano House ☎ 967-7321; 4-person cabins $40) Cabins are windowless A frame plywood palaces. Each of the 10 cabins has a double bed, two single bunks and electric lights, but no power outlets or heating. Volcano House provides linen but bring a sleeping bag to warm you through cold nights. Showers and toilets are shared. Check-in requires refundable deposits for keys ($12) and linen ($20).

Midrange & Top End

Lehua Lodge (Map p209; ☎ 800-908-9764; www.volcanogallery.com; 11-3873 12th St; house $145) This airy, cedar loft is so perfect that you'll be tempted to stay indoors for your vacation. Downstairs, you'll find a bedroom, full kitchen and charming living room with rocking chair and soaring 20ft ceiling. The porch overlooks the lush ohia-fern forest that secludes the house. Upstairs, the romantic master bedroom features a sleigh bed, from which you can gaze through windows at the moon. Washer and dryer are available, and kids are welcome.

Volcano Rainforest Retreat (Map p209; ☎ 985-8696, 800-550-8696; www.volcanoretreat.com; 11-3832 12th St; cottage d $125-245) With four beautiful, private cedar cottages, this B&B is distinct in its focus on spiritual, restorative practices. Each cottage harmonizes functional structure with nature – one shaped into a cedar and redwood octagon, and two with a Japanese-style soaking tub. Reservations are a must. Massage, energy healing, counseling, personal-growth workshops and guided spiritual retreats are also offered. Rates include breakfast.

Kilauea Lodge (Map p209; ☎ 967-7366; www.kilauealodge.com; Old Volcano Rd; r $135, cottage d $155-175) This longtime B&B offers a variety of solid

---

AUTHOR'S CHOICE

My Island B&B (Map p209; ☎ 967-77216; www.myislandinnhawaii.com; 19-3896 Volcano Rd; s $50-85, d $65-100, house $135) On 7 acres of verdant rain forest, the owners, who are longtime residents, run an old-style B&B in an historic 1886 house that's filled with fine art, koa furniture and over 300 record albums. The best options, especially for families, are the six spacious houses scattered across the property and in Volcano Village (extra adult $20 per day). The rooms in the main house are rather cramped. The sociable hosts once ran a tour company and are more than willing to share their knowledge of Hawai'i. Rates include breakfast.

accommodations with the country comfort you'd expect to find: working fireplaces, high ceilings, quilts and bathtubs. None of the rooms on the main property have private TVs or phones, but who needs them with a beautiful garden hot tub? Kilauea Lodge also features a fine restaurant (see p212) run by owner-chef Albert Jeyte. Rates include breakfast.

Volcano Inn (Map p209; ☎ 967-7293, 800-997-2292; fax 985-7349; www.volcanoinn.com; PO Box 963, Volcano, HI 96785; cottages s $75-95, d $95-145, r $55-105) This wooden beauty has cozy rooms ensconced in an ohia forest. Take a delicious breakfast on the covered lanai or chill out in a hammock. The self-contained cedar cottages tucked away in the fern forest feature loads of windows and views. Stained glass, skylights, fireplaces, quilts, robes and heat are among the perks. Even the affordable Lava Room ($55) is inviting, despite being on the ground floor and next to the laundry room. Rates include breakfast.

Hale ohia (☎ 967-7986, 800-455-3803; fax 967-8610; www.haleohia.com, PO Box 758, Volcano, HI 96785; d $95-120, cottages $125-165, artist cottages $109-379) This classic 1930s establishment continues to shine with its open and beautifully maintained gardens. All the units are tastefully decorated. The cottages are lovely and have fireplaces, lanais, kitchen facilities and a hot tub in the backyard. Cottage No 44 ($165) is particularly sweet and secluded. Rates include breakfast.

Volcano Country Cottages (Map p209; ☎ 967-7960, 888-446-3910, www.volcanocottages.com; Old Volcano Rd; cottages $95-120) Located among a grove of giant sugi trees the Artist House and Ohelo Berry Cottage have a lush, secluded setting, yet remain within walking distance of Volcano Village. Centered around a 1901 home these cottages have a quaint old Hawai'i feel. Both accommodations provide a fridge filled with breakfast items, a kitchenette and private bath. The Artist House is especially equipped for families or small groups and can sleep up to eight people. The space has plenty of light and comes equipped with easel and art supplies for the budding artist. Enjoy the hot tub in the backyard after hiking in the park.

Volcano House (Map p198; ☎ 967-7321; www.volcanohousehotel.com; 1 Crater Rim Dr; r $85-185) Perched right on the rim of Kilauea Caldera, opposite the visitor center, Volcano House has a long and venerable history – and it's the

only hotel inside the park. Most lower-level rooms, however, look out onto a walkway, and even rooms on the upper floor might have only a partial view of the crater. The small rooms have a pleasant character, with koa furniture, vintage stationery and, most importantly, heating. There are no TVs, but the hotel has a terrific game library. Reserve at least two months ahead.

Other recommendations:

Chalet Kilauea Collection (☎ 967-7786, 800-937-7787; www.volcanohawaii.com; PO Box 998 Wright Rd, Volcano Village, HI 96785) The Chalet Kilauea Collection is a group of accommodations – from affordable rooms with shared bath to exclusive honeymoon suites – around town. The contact information above applies to all its properties.

Kilauea Military Camp (Map p198; ☎ 967-8334; fax 967-8343; www.kmc-volcano.com/; Crater Rim Dr; 1-bedroom apt $45-86, 3-bedroom apt $69-101, 1-bedroom cottage $48-89, 2-bedroom cottage $57-109, 3-bedroom cottage $85-117) This is a resort for active and retired military personnel. Price depends on your division and rank; some units have Jacuzzis.

EATING & DRINKING

The dining room and snack bar at **Volcano House** (Map p198; ☎ 967-7321; www.volcanohousehotel.com; 1 Crater Rim Dr) are the only restaurant options within the park, but the cafeteria-quality fare is overpriced. Go to Volcano Village to eat and just warm yourself by the living-room fire (which has been burning since the 1870s!) or just order drinks at **Uncle George's Lounge** (☼ 4:30-9pm).

It's a long haul from the park to Volcano Village restaurants, but you have no choice. For groceries, pickings are slim at **Volcano Store** (Map p209; ☎ 967-7210; cnr Old Volcano & Haunani Rds; ☼ 5am-7pm) and **Kilauea General Store** (Map p209; ☎ 967-7555; Old Volcano Rd; ☼ 7am-7:30pm Mon-Sat, 7am-7pm Sun). Stop in at the **farmer's market** (☼ 8-10am Sun) where the selection of local crafts, catering and produce is 'ono. Get there early if you want da'kine goods.

Thai Thai Restaurant (Map p209; ☎ 967-7969; 19-4084 Old Volcano Rd; mains $12-16; ☼ dinner) The owners, who hail from Thailand, offer tangy curries and noodles with plenty of vegetarian choices. Go wild: it's all fresh, tasty and spicy (if you like) and apportioned generously.

Kiawe Kitchen (Map p209; ☎ 967-7711; cnr Old Volcano & Haunani Rds; mains $9-12; ☼ lunch & dinner) A modern café with pleasant outdoor seating and a nice list of fine wines and Big Island

HAWAI'I VOLCANOES NATIONAL PARK

microbrews. The house specialties are gourmet crispy-crust pizzas and baguette sandwiches featuring wood-fired meats.

Lava Rock Café (Map p209; ☎ 967-8526; Old Volcano Rd at 27-mile marker; mains $6-12; ✆ 7:30am-5pm Mon, 7:30am-9pm Tue-Sat, 7:30am-4pm Sun) Located behind Kīlauea General Store, this is the favored breakfast spot in town. Steer clear of the saimin and order the French toast with *liliko'i* butter instead. Kids' menu available.

JP Café (Map p209; ☎ 985-7456; 19-4005 Haunani Rd; breakfasts $5, sandwiches & burgers $5-8; ✆ 6:30am-5:30pm Mon-Sat, 9am-5pm Sun) Just the basics, cooked in a kitchen smaller than your own, but it's decent for a quick meal or take-out.

Kilauea Lodge (Map p209; ☎ 967-7366; www.kilauea lodge.com; Old Volcano Rd near Wright Rd; mains $19-39; ✆ dinner) In a rustic dining room with stone fireplace, amid a misty fern forest, Kilauea Lodge perfectly suits Volcano Village. This is the only fine-dining restaurant in town, and you can expect upmarket mains like braised rabbit, venison, Parker Ranch steaks and fresh fish in papaya-and-ginger sauce. Reservations are advised.

Volcano Golf & Country Club (Map p198; ☎ 967-7331; Pi'i Mauna Dr; breakfast $3.50-5.95, lunch $7.25-9.25; ✆ 8am-2pm Mon-Fri, 6:30am-2pm Sat & Sun) The local golfing crowd convenes here to talk story over their game. Standard egg and pancake breakfast fare is suitable to get started on the links. Things get a little more interesting at lunch when there's *saimin* (local-style noodle soup), *mahimahi* (white-fleshed fish, also called 'dolphin') and *kalua* pork (pork cooked in the traditional *kalua* method) available.

Kilauea Military Camp (KMC; Map p198; ☎ 967-8333, Crater Rim Dr; breakfast & lunch $3-7, dinner $9.25-12.95; ✆ breakfast, lunch & dinner) This military installation in the park is open to civilian diners. It's cafeteria style, but better than the mess you might remember. Call ahead to get your name on the list at the guardhouse. This isn't always necessary, but with certain recent events, they're pretty skittish these days.

GETTING THERE & AROUND

Driving nonstop, the national park is 29 miles (45 minutes) from Hilo and 97 miles (two hours) from Kailua-Kona. Either way, you'll drive on Hwy 11. Volcano Village is a couple of miles east of the park entrance.

The public bus running between Hilo and Ocean View in Ka'u stops at the Volcano Village visitor center once in each direction Monday to Friday. It leaves the visitor center for Hilo at 8:10am and returns from Hilo at 3:45pm ($2.25, one hour).

Ka'u

The district is sparsely populated, with only about 5000 people. Its three towns transmit the local tranquility in tempo with nature. You'll pass desert-like expanses of hardened lava and beautiful plantations where macadamia nuts and island-favorite Ka'u oranges are grown. The lush forested slopes of Mauna Loa are equally stunning and represent one of the *wahi pana* (celebrated lands) of Hawai'i.

Ka'u recently celebrated the protection of these lands at the acquisition by the National Park Service of the 116,000 acres at Kahuku Ranch *mauka* (inland). In an area that has recently felt the pressure of urban sprawl this is considered a major victory and the largest single conservation effort in Hawaii since the creation of Hawai'i Volcanoes National Park 100 years ago.

Traveling here is like going back in time – after all, this is where it all began. Ka Lae (South Point) is considered to be the first landing point for the Polynesians and carries a great significance for the Hawaiian people. The mana found in this raw and windy portion of the island is powerful. An idea of the Hawaiian legacy here is summed up with the local proverb, *Aha'i la i ka pupuhi* ('travel with the speed of the wind').

Exotic beaches of green-and-black sand are the cornerstones that put Hawai'i's southern coastline on the travelers' map. However, if you let yourself be seduced by the rural seclusion, the handful of unique B&Bs here can distinguish your entire Hawai'i experience.

HIGHLIGHTS

- Getting close to history and the spiritual mana at **Ka Lae** (South Point) (p218)
- Hiking to see the semiprecious granules of **Green Sands Beach** (p219)
- Sunning with green sea turtles at **Punalu'u Beach Park** (p215)
- Relaxing at one of Wai'ohinu's unique **B&Bs** (p217)
- Finding true island solitude on the **Road to the Sea** (p221)

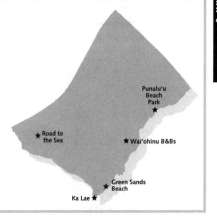

Orientation

The Ka'u district encompasses the entire southern flank of Mauna Loa, acting as a buffer zone between touristy South Kona and the wilderness of Hawai'i Volcanoes National Park. This stretch of Hwy 11 is prone to flooding, washouts and road closures during heavy winter storms. Your only two cross-island alternatives are Saddle Rd and Hwy 19 between Hilo and Waimea, but during the worst storms, even Hwy 19 might be closed due to rock slides.

Past the 35-mile marker you'll see fewer trees and more lava, before the terrain becomes ranchland. In 2004, Kahuku Ranch ended its cattle operations next to Hawai'i Volcanoes National Park, and the park ac-quired 116,000 acres on the slopes of Mauna Loa. Kilauea's Southwest Rift Zone runs through 20 miles of the Ka'u Desert, *makai* (seaward) of the road, all the way from the Kilauea summit to the coast. You'll know you've left the national park when the signs 'Caution: Nene Crossing' disappear.

PAHALA
pop 1400

Just past the 51-mile marker, you'll reach Pahala, a former sugar town. Ka'u Agribusiness once had 15,000 acres of cane planted for 15 miles in either direction from the town, but the mill closed for good in 1996. The company has since replaced the cane with groves of macadamia-nut trees.

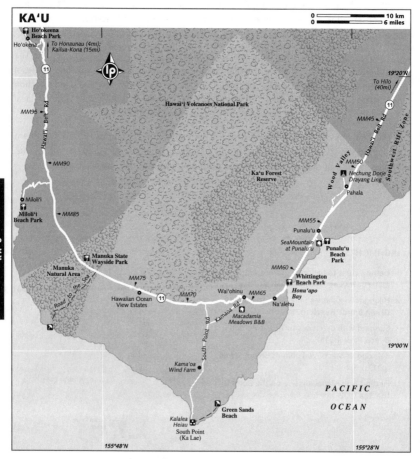

There are two entrances to Pahala. The southern access is via Maile St, which winds north past the shuttered sugar mill, rickety homes, 'Beware of Dog' signs and junker cars rusting in yards. Alternatively, turn inland off Hwy 11 at Kamani St, which passes the hospital before heading directly into the commercial part of town.

'Commercial,' however, is an overstatement. All you'll find are a fire station, a gas station, a post office, a bank with an ATM

and **Ka'u Hospital** (☎ 928-8331). The main reason to stop? Fresh, hot malasada from **Tex Drive In** (☎ 928-8200; malasada 85¢, meals $5; ☺ 7am-8pm Mon-Sat, 7am-6pm Sun). The restaurant is clean (including the rest rooms) and the egg-and-meat breakfasts will tide you over for hours.

PUNALU'U

A small bay with a black-sand beach, Punalu'u was once a major Hawaiian settlement, and after Westerners arrived it became a key

---

DETOUR: WOOD VALLEY

About 4 miles inland from Pahala is a remote Buddhist temple and retreat center, **Nechung Dorje Drayang Ling** (Immutable Island of Melodious Sound). The temple was built in 1902 by the Buddhist community of Japanese sugarcane laborers. Originally located a few miles closer to Pahala, a severe storm in 1917 caused its members to relocate the temple to higher ground and its present location.

The actual story is interesting and tells of the temple's priest and his best friends staying to guard the temple from the rising waters of the nearby stream. Soon there was no dry land around and it seemed as though the temple and the men would not survive the flood. So in desperation the men decided that if they were going to die, why not die happy. At this they broke into the sake supply that had been saved for the upcoming New Year's celebration. The following morning first light brought a break in the storm and found the temple still standing. So the people of the village, not having any sign of the men, bravely forged the swollen stream with an improvised wire bridge, and upon entering the temple, found the men roaring drunk, having the time of their lives!

The storied temple became one of the first places for the study of Tibetan Buddhism in the USA. Based on early Western pilgrims to Tibet in the 1970s, several high lamas were asked to bring their wisdom to the West. An initial visit to Oahu by His Holiness, Dudjom Rinpoche, brought this message: 'the main responsibility for religious people is to spread the teachings of peace, brotherhood and happiness to all sentient beings. Not to disturb existing religions, but spread goodwill to all faiths'.

Soon after a local anthropologist located the abandoned temple in Wood Valley and soon nonprofit organizations and volunteers helped to restore the building. In 1973 a Tibetan lama, Nechung Rinpoche, took up residence here, and in 1980 the Dalai Lama visited to dedicate the temple. Since then, many Tibetan lamas have conducted programs here and the Dalai Lama himself returned for a visit in 1994. In addition to its Buddhist teachings, the center also lets outside groups conduct meditation, yoga and **spiritual workshops** (www.nechung.org). There is a simple shop selling Buddhist inspired books and souvenirs that go to support this nonprofit religious organization. Temple monks also hand pick organic coffee that's exceptionally smooth and rich (and, at $35 per pound, likely to encourage slow sipping in the moment).

The grounds at **Wood Valley Temple & Retreat Center** (Map pp194-5; ☎ 928-8539, 928-6271; www .nechung.org; Nechung Dorje Drayang Ling; dm/s/d with shared bathroom $35/50/75) may seem deserted as peacocks roam freely about, but the peaceful forest surrounding the temple provides an ideal location for contemplation and meditation. Here you'll find a meditation hall with two peaceful guest rooms on the upper floor. One of the private quarters has a queen platform bed and Japanese decor, the other has a king bed and Hawaiian decor. There's a two-day minimum stay, and all rooms share a bath. The ground floor also has a few simpler rooms and three dormitories with a total of 14 beds. A freestanding guesthouse with five double rooms is tucked back on the grounds. Food is not provided, but a kitchen and a dining room are available. There's a library of books on Buddhist culture, and you're welcome to join in morning services. Day visitors are welcomed on weekends. For those seeking a peaceful retreat, the temple is a special place.

sugar port. Nowadays it's famous mainly for *honu* (sea turtles) that trundle out from the sea to bask in the sun after gorging on *limu* (seaweed).

Punalu'u Beach Park, a county park located just south, has rest rooms, showers, drinking water and a picnic pavilion. Be careful when walking on the sands, which are used as nesting sites by the endangered hawksbill turtle. Don't approach these gentle giants because they're both an endangered species and very sensitive to human disturbance.

Most days, the waters are hardly ideal for swimming, and it's funny to watch *malihini* (newcomers) in tropical swimwear braving the icy, spring-fed waters and strong undertow. Fierce rip currents pull seaward near the pier and lots of coconut husks and driftwood float about. The most popular part of the beach is the northern pocket, lined with coconut palms and backed by a duck pond. The ruins of the Pahala Sugar Company's old warehouse and pier lie slightly to the north. The Kane'ele'ele Heiau ruins sit on a small rise.

The campground at Punalu'u Beach Park sits on a flat, grassy area overlooking the beach, but there's zero privacy. At night, you can drift off to sleep to the sounds of crashing surf. Come daybreak, it's overrun with picnickers. Permits (p223) are required.

To reach the beach, take either the turnoff to SeaMountain, Ka'u's only condo complex, or the one marked Punalu'u Park, less than 1 mile east.

Sleeping & Eating

SeaMountain at Punalu'u (☎ 928-6200, 800-344-7675; fax 928-8075; www.viresorts.com; PO Box 460, Pahala, HI 96777) This condominium complex is a bit scary, there's no restaurant and the **golf course** (18 holes & cart $42; kama'iana $24) could use some upkeep. The seaside location and proximity to the national park seems to be the only draw. There's also a pool, Jacuzzi and tennis courts. Prices are all through Vacations International point system, check the website for bookings.

Supposedly, the golf course pro shop serves snacks and sandwiches from 10:30am to 2:30pm, but it looked like something from *The Shining* at the time of research. Good luck.

WHITTINGTON BEACH PARK

Not far before Na'alehu there's a pull-off with a scenic lookout above Honu'apo Bay. From here you can see the cement pilings

---

HONU HAUNT

The Hawaiian Islands have an extensive marine ecosystem. Almost directly in the middle of the vast Pacific Ocean, they are unique in their location and ability to provide the proper habitat for local and migrating sea life. With so many beaches and warm tropical waters, Hawai'i is especially known for its *honu* (sea turtle) population, providing some of the few nesting sites for these magnificent creatures.

The Hawaiian culture sees its role in *malama 'aina* (nourishment of the land and oceans), which sustain life. Hawaiians traditionally had limitations on hunting and harvesting from nature's bounty. *Honu* were highly respected for their mana. You will see the turtle as an ingrained Hawaiian icon, from ancient petroglyphs to modern T-shirts, it is an enduring symbol of the islands.

In more recent times the beaches these turtles depend on to reproduce have been encroached upon and overrun by human impact, development and tourism. Coupled with over-hunting and harvesting of their shells, sea turtle populations have dwindled. These factors have disrupted their ability to mate on their ancestral beaches and severely cut their chances for successful reproduction. Any further disadvantages we create could lead to extinction.

Honu are now quite common in Hawaii, but the *honu'ea* (hawksbill sea turtle) is smaller and the rarest sea turtle in the Pacific Ocean. It is characterized by the delicate pattern on its shell, similar to the tortoise. An endangered species, only one in 5000 survive the hatch and the open sea, mature, and return to reproduce. The black-sand beach at Punalu'u is one of the few spots on the southeastern coast of Hawai'i that they call home.

So needless to say be very conscious when visiting a turtle nesting area and give them ample space so as not to disturb the nests.

KARL LEHMANN

Green sea turtle (p216), Punalu'u

Flamingoes are a common sight

WOODWARD PAYNE & BEVERLY ANDERSON

ANN CECIL

The endangered nene

Golden spotted day gecko

WADE EAKLE

The travelers palm thrives in tropical conditions

The colorful cover leaves of the heliconia

Orchids abound on the Big Island

Coconut leaf at sunset, Kohala Coast

of the old pier, which was used for shipping sugar and hemp until the 1930s.

The turnoff to Whittington Beach Park is 1 mile beyond the lookout. Although there are tide pools to explore, there's no beach and the ocean is usually too rough for swimming. Endangered *honu* can sometimes be seen offshore; apparently they've been frequenting these waters for a long time, as Honu'apo means 'caught turtle' in Hawaiian.

Camping is allowed with a county permit (p223). The proximity of the park to the highway offers little privacy, but it makes a pretty good choice for camping midweek; it will probably just be you. Camp beyond the reach of the streetlight by the parking lot, as the light burns all night. There are rest rooms and sheltered picnic tables, but there's no potable water.

NA'ALEHU

pop 1000

Na'alehu is tiny, but it's famous for being the southernmost town in the USA. This town has special character and has a cultural vibe more potent than other Hawaiian towns of its size. **Jackie's Plantation House** (☎ 929-8134; Hwy 11; ☯ noon-5pm Tue-Sun) is a nice gift shop with custom island apparel, and local and international crafts. Just in front of Jackie's get a quick bite on your way through at Arrianna's Mexican Food Stand, the most authentic Mexican on the island. Who would have thought you'd find real tamales in Hawai'i.

Otherwise Na'alehu is the Ka'u district's commercial and religious center, with a grocery store, a library, a police station, a post office, a gas station, an ATM and six churches. Na'alehu closes up early, so you shouldn't count on finding food or gas here if you're driving past at night.

Eating

Na'alehu Fruit Stand (☎ 929-9009; Hwy 11; sandwiches under $5; pizza $8-10; ☯ 8am-7pm Mon-Thu, to 8pm Fri-Sun) Don't be fooled by the name: it's actually a one-stop produce store, bakery and deli. The ovens crank out bread in the morning, and pizzas to order starting at 11am. Local papaya, oranges and macadamia nuts are reasonably priced. At a few picnic tables out front, you can eat and *talk story* with the good-natured proprietor and other locals.

Punalu'u Bakeshop & Visitor Center (☎ 929-7343; Hwy 11 near Ka'alaiki Rd; ☯ 9am-5pm) The Big Island's best-known sweet-bread bakery has become a tourist landmark. You can indulgently sample many flavors of sweet bread, which can be mailed to you back home. The lunch counter serves sandwiches, soups, salads and desserts. The onslaught of tourist paraphernalia is relentless, but the public bathrooms are clean (what a find!).

Shaka Restaurant (☎ 929-7404; Hwy 11; breakfast & lunch $5-8, dinner $10-15; ☯ 10am-9pm Tue-Sun) This casual diner serves full, hearty meals, including eggs Benedict and French toast (made from Punalu'u sweet bread) for breakfast and meaty dinners. It offers a *keiki* (children's) menu, a full bar and live music on weekends.

Hana Hou Coffee Shop (☎ 929-9717; 95-1148 Spur Rd; meals $5-10; ☯ 7am-9pm Mon-Fri, 10am-7pm Sat) This home-style diner has tasty breakfast omelettes, pancakes and French toast. It serves a variety of sandwiches, burgers and Hawaiian style plates, plus stir-fry and specials on weekends. The food is good, but go for the homemade pies and cakes. Yum!

WAI'OHINU

Before reaching South Point Rd, Hwy 11 winds down into a pretty valley and the sleepy village of Wai'ohinu, which sits nestled beneath green hills. The town is known for its landmark **Mark Twain monkeypod tree**, which was planted by the author in 1866. The original tree fell in a 1957 hurricane, but hardy new trunks have sprung up and it's once again full grown.

Sleeping

Most tourists stay along the Kona Coast or in Hilo, but you might be surprised at the B&B gems you'll find in Wai'ohinu.

South Point Banyan Tree House (☎ 929-8515; reservations 949-492-1258; www.southpointbth.com; cnr Pinao St & Hwy 11; r $150) A gargantuan banyan tree envelops this studio house on stilts, giving the impression you're in a tree house. Inside, the room is suffused with light from glass doors, skylights and windows face to face with the magnificent banyan. The airy room includes a queen-size bed, sofa, full kitchen, washer/dryer, outdoor hot tub and wraparound lanai. While it's located near Hwy 11, the jungle of mango, lichee, *'ulu* (breadfruit) and banana trees outside provide privacy.

KA'U

Hobbit House B&B (☎ 929-9755; www.hi-hobbit .com/Hawaii/bnb; d $190) The aptly named Hobbit House is a whimsical, custom-designed house perched high on a bluff with a spectacular ocean view. The accommodations are very comfortable, with an antique four-poster bed, a double Jacuzzi, a full kitchen and lanai – while the sloping 'mushroom' roof, stained glass and slanted windows add a fairytale touch. The hosts moved from the mainland to Hawai'i over 25 years ago, and they're especially personable and familiar with the island. The remote setting and panoramic view make for a truly unique experience – but the steep half-mile drive up requires a 4WD. It's off Hwy 11, on the Ha'ao Springs Trail.

Macadamia Meadows B&B (☎ 929-8097, 888-929-8118; www.macadamiameadows.com; 94-6263 Kama'oa Rd; d $65-85, ste $120-135) For a close-up view of a working macadamia-nut farm, why not spend a few nights on site? Just a half-mile south of town, this contemporary home features clean, spacious guest rooms with cable TV, microwave, refrigerator, private entrances and lanai. The suites adjoin two bedrooms – ideal for families or groups. An added bonus: guests receive a free orchard tour, where you'll learn about Hawaii's macadamia-nut industry from friendly insiders (and also get to pick and taste a fresh nut). Rates include breakfast.

Margo's Corner (☎ 929-9614; margos@bigisland .com; Wakea St, PO Box 447, Na'alehu, HI 96772; tent site per person $25, cottages $60-115) This establishment is open and gay friendly, offering bicyclists and backpackers a place to pitch a tent or lay their heads while exploring the Ka'u area. The Rainbow guesthouse offers unique design, queen bed and private bath in a garden setting. The Adobe suite is suitable for groups up to six. All prices include largely organic vegetarian or vegan breakfast and there's a small health food store on-site. There's a two night minimum stay for the cottages and breakfast and dinner are included in the rates. There are a couple of tent areas with pebbly mounds to allow drainage, or you can pitch your tent on the grass; tenters share a bathroom. Smoking is prohibited. Margo's is on Wakea St, a couple of miles southwest of Waiohinu center, off Kamaoa Rd. Call ahead for reservations.

Shirakawa Motel (☎ 929-7462; www.shirakawa motel.com; 95-6040 Hwy 11; s/d $43/45, r with kitchenette $55-65) For just the basics, the 'southernmost motel in the USA' might be simple and weather-beaten, but it's a bargain. The deluxe kitchenette room comes with two double beds, full kitchen, microwave, kitchen supplies and cable TV. Still family-run, the rooms sit beneath verdant hills right near the town center. The owners can tell you all about the Big Island 'back in the day.'

GETTING THERE & AWAY

The **Hele-On Bus** (☎ 961-8744; www.co.hawaii.hi.us /mass_transit/heleonbus.html) runs one bus daily to Pahala, Punalu'u, Na'alehu, Wai'ohinu and Hawaiian Ocean View Estates on the No 23 Ka'u route ($3.75 to $5.25). From Ka'u to Hilo, take the No 7 Downtown Hilo bus, which originates in Wai'ohinu.

SOUTH POINT

South Point is the southernmost spot in the USA. In Hawaiian, it's known as Ka Lae, which means simply 'the point.' South

---

THE BIG ONE

Ka'u was at the epicenter of the massive 1868 earthquake (7.9 on the Richter scale), the worst Hawaii has ever recorded. For five straight days from March 27, the earth rattled and rolled almost continuously from a series of tremors and quakes. Then, on the afternoon of April 2, at 4pm Kilauea Iki sent up a curtain of fire.

Those fortunate enough to be uphill watched as a river of lava poured down the hillsides and swallowed up everything in its path, including people, homes, trees and cattle. Within minutes, the coast was inundated by a tsunami, and villages near the shore were swept away. A total of 77 people died in the disaster, 46 due to the tsunami and 31 from the landslide.

This triple whammy of earthquakes, lava flows and tsunamis permanently changed Ka'u's landscape. Huge cinder cones came crashing down the slopes, and one landslide buried an entire village and seriously damaged parts of Ninole and Punalu'u. You can see the 1868 lava flow along the highway 2 miles west of the South Point turnoff. The old village of Kahuku lies beneath it.

Point has rocky coastal cliffs and a turbulent ocean. Yet this rugged coastline is the site where the first Polynesians landed, in desperate straits by some accounts. As one of the earliest Hawaiian settlements, they must have overcome many hardships in light of the harsh terrain here. However, Ka Lae was a sustainable place to settle, because of the fishing largesse just offshore and the fresh water available up the road at Punalu'u. Much of the area now falls under the jurisdiction of Hawaiian Home Lands. There are no facilities.

Orientation

To get here, take the South Point Rd between the 69- and 70-mile markers on Hwy 11. Along the mostly one-lane road, drivers must let each other pass (give the *shaka* – the Hawaiian hand greeting – if someone waves you ahead!). The winds are bracing here, as evidenced by tree trunks bent almost horizontal.

Sights

KAMA'OA WIND FARM

After a few miles of scattered houses, macadamia-nut farms and grassy pastureland, you'll see the wind farm: rows of high-tech windmills in a pasture beside the road. With cattle grazing beneath, it's a surreal scene. Each of these wind-turbine generators can produce enough electricity for 100 families. It's thought, theoretically at least, that by using wind energy conversion, the state could produce more than enough electricity to meet its needs, but the wind farm is not operating at capacity.

About 4 miles south of the wind farm, you'll pass a few abandoned buildings wasting away. Until 1965, this was a Pacific Missile Range station that tracked missiles shot from California to the Marshall Islands in Micronesia.

KA LAE

Ten miles down from the highway, South Point Rd forks. The road to the left goes to Kaulana boat ramp, while the right fork leads to the craggy coastal cliffs of Ka Lae.

The confluence of ocean currents just offshore makes this one of Hawai'i's most bountiful fishing grounds. Locals fish off the cliff, with some of the bolder ones leaning out over steep lava ledges. Land ruins here include **Kalalea Heiau**, usually classified as a *ko'a* (a small stone pen designed to encourage fish and birds to multiply). Look inside for a well-preserved fishing shrine where ancient Hawaiians left offerings to Ku'ula, the god of fishermen, in hopes of currying favor for a bountiful catch.

An outcropping on the heiau's western side has numerous canoe mooring holes that were chipped long ago into the lava rock. Strong currents would pull the canoes out into deep turbulent waters, where the enterprising ancient Hawaiians could fish, still tethered to the shore, without getting swept out to sea.

The wooden platforms built on the edge of the cliffs have hoists and ladders for the small boats anchored below; you may see a *honu* or two gliding around in the relatively calm waters below the hoists. This is a popular fishing spot where red snapper and ulua fish are particularly plentiful. Folks around the island boast of cliff jumping here, but it might be a real '*okole* (buttocks) squeezer!

There's a large unprotected *puka* (hole) in the lava directly behind the platforms where you can watch water rage up the sides and recede again with incoming waves. Keep an eye out for it, as it's not obvious until you're almost on top of it.

Walk down past the light beacon and continue along the wall to reach the southernmost point in the USA. It's an awesome sight, with sets of violent waves crashing into the rocks at physics-defying angles. There are no markers here, no souvenir stands, just crashing surf and lots of wind.

GREEN SANDS BEACH

Few can resist a glimpse of Green Sands Beach, traditionally known as Papakolea, formed by semiprecious olivine crystals eroded from the cliffs of the ancient littoral cone and worn smooth by a relentless and pounding surf. Olivine is a type of volcanic basalt that's rich in iron, magnesium and silica. Don't expect to see an emerald beach, however. The olivine sand is mixed with black sand, and it appears as a dull olive green. You can swim here, but when the swell is up waves are strong and pound the shore at full force.

To get here, go left where South Point Rd forks. You'll dead-end at a shack that says Ka Lae Info Center where you might see

KA'U

locals charging $5 for 'secure parking' in an impromptu lot. Avoid wasting your money, as no one can legally charge 'admission' to the public-access shoreline. The center has a tiny Ka Lae natural history exhibit with simple artifacts from early Hawaiian dwellings.

From here, passing the Kaulana boat ramp it's a 2.5-mile hike along a rutted dirt road to the beach. If you have a high-riding 4WD vehicle, you could drive in, but the road is rough and you'll probably take about 25 minutes. A couple of minutes beyond Kaulana boat ramp the trail passes the site of Kapalaoa, an ancient fishing village. It's a gentle and beautiful hike around chunky lava points, where the dry grass fronts the sea and winds can swirl incessantly.

Eventually you'll need to scramble down some cliffs to get to Green Sands Beach. Pick a calm day to visit, for the entire beach can be windswept and flooded during high surf. By now, this beautiful small beach is squarely on the beaten path. For a more remote setting, go for the Road to the Sea.

HAWAIIAN OCEAN VIEW ESTATES

Around the 76-mile marker, there's one last stop for food and gas before the long drive up to Honaunau. You won't find much more than the necessities at the 'commercial center' of Hawaiian Ocean View Estates (HOVE) and Hawaiian Ranchos, two subdivisions with just over 2000 residents. There is a gas station, post office, hardware store, supermarket and a couple of local eateries. This residential area is one of the last sunny expanses of land in Hawai'i to be totally free of resorts. Land here is relatively cheap, perhaps owing to the isolation and harsh lava-rock vista, but burglaries are frequent. Controversial proposals for large developments occasionally pop up, but so far all have been defeated, to the relief of island environmentalists. No resorts means, in part, that the places to stay here are friendly, family-owned affairs.

Sleeping & Eating

Bougainvillea Bed & Breakfast (☎ /fax 929-7089, 800-688-1763; www.bougainvilleabedandbreakfast.com; PO Box 6045, Ocean View, HI 96737; s/d incl breakfast $80/85; 🐕) This B&B, in the home of Martie and Don Nitsche, has some of the best guest amenities on the island including a nice

sitting room and outdoor lanai, and a video library. The comfortable rooms each have private bathroom, private entrance and TV/VCR. The large grounds have table tennis facilities, horseshoes, an outdoor swimming pool with ocean views and a hot tub set back behind the house. With plenty to do this is a nice family location and the stargazing is superb. These folks know the Big Island and can hook you up with tips and advice. The B&B is between the 77- and 78-mile markers on the *makai* side of Hwy 11.

Leilani Bed & Breakfast (☎ 929-7101; fax 939-7136; lynn@fastnethi.com; PO Box 6037 Ocean View, HI 96737; s/d $75/85) This unique home made of local lava rock is located on the *mauka* side of Hwy 11 at the 78-mile marker. Three rooms with private bathrooms and TV are pleasant, while the Ohana room is a nice sitting room with covered lanai. The landscaping is beautiful; there's an atrium in the center and a gorgeous stone-paved patio out back and there are some great *puka* (caves) on the property to explore.

Ohana House Rural Retreat (☎ 929-9139, 888-999-9139; www.alternative-hawaii.com/ohana; PO Box 6351, Ocean View, HI 96737; s/d $40/60; cabin per week $100) An artistic flair provides off-the-grid charm with nice perks and a divine price. The house can sleep five in nooks and crannies. The garden setting is full of birds – check out the forest view bed. There is a lanai, fireplace and a steam bath (two night minimum, third night free), with outside facilities and a solar shower. A cottage provides a more private option with a queen bed. All linens are provided, both places have full kitchens and you can rent out the entire compound for your group. There's also a cabin on the property and work-exchange possibilities.

Ocean View Pizzaria (☎ 929-9677; Ocean View Town Center; pizzas small/large $11/15, sandwiches $5-6.50; 🕙 11am-7pm Sun-Thu, 11am-8pm Fri & Sat) A nice pit stop in the middle of nowhere and just when the craving hits, there's tasty, fresh pizza made to order. This place has a little dining room, killer milkshakes, the aforementioned pizzas and submarine sandwiches.

Mister Bell's (☎ 929-7447; Hwy 11; meals $6-20; 🕙 7am-9pm) Along Hwy 11, turn *mauka* between the 75- and 76-mile markers and find your classic local roadhouse, filling the need for a bar this far south. Have a drink and sing along with karaoke on Wednesday nights. It's your only option if you are passing through much after dark. Here you'll get hearty portions and the food is fresh, especially the local fish of the day. Yummy egg breakfasts and mac-nut pancakes, burgers soups and salads for lunch, and a variety of dinner specials round out the menu.

Anuenue Natural Foods (☎ 929-7550; Ocean View Town Center; ⏰ 9am-5:30pm Mon-Fri, to 5pm Sat, 11am-4pm Sun) This natural food store has a nice bakery, deli and hot lunch bar (from 11am). It's well stocked for its size and is definitely the best choice in the area for self-catering.

ROAD TO THE SEA

The Road to the Sea is hardly traveled, and it's no wonder: the unpaved 4WD-only road crosses loose lava rock, ledges and cracks. If you brave the journey, however, you're likely to find the beaches to yourself. This is probably the most isolated coast on the island. If you want to feel the raw mana of the south coast make your way down the Road to the Sea, but bear in mind that whipping winds are not unusual (and on especially gusty days, flying sand can just about exfoliate your inner ears!).

To get here, turn *makai* at the row of three mailboxes between the 79- and 80-mile markers. Another landmark is a sign that reads 'Ka Ulu Malu Shady Grove Farm.' Set your odometer as soon as you turn. The road is private and barking dogs might give you chase.

From here you'll cross 6 miles over a rudimentary, seemingly never-ending lava road. To reach the first and smaller of the two beaches takes 30 minutes, if you drive slowly, although it can be done in 20 minutes, if you're comfortable on very rough terrain.

To reach the second beach, drive a half-mile back inland. Skip the first left fork that appears (it's a dead end) and take the second-left fork instead. Look for arrows painted on the lava rock. The road jogs inland before heading toward the shore again,

and the course isn't always readily apparent. There are many places you can lose traction or get lost. Almost 1 mile from the fork, you'll reach a red *pu'u* (hill). Park here and walk down to the ocean. If you decide to walk the whole distance, it's about 1.5 miles. Bring as much water as you can carry as it's hot and shadeless, with no potable water.

Neither beach is named, but both have exquisite black-and-green sand, similar to Green Sands Beach. There's a bit of shade here, and the cliffs looming over the beach are stunning. If you walk to the north end of the beach, you'll come to a couple of palms and a lime-green brackish pool, a beautiful place for a soak. Trekking at low tide presents some intriguing possibilities to discover new coves where it feels like the entire island is yours alone. These waters have excellent fishing, especially off the cliffs at the second beach. Along the Kona Coast, you'll find calmer waters and convenient amenities, but finding these secluded spots can be a day's adventure.

MANUKA STATE WAYSIDE PARK

Manuka State Wayside Park is a 13½-acre arboretum off Hwy 11 just north of the 81-mile marker. The trees and bushes, planted here between the mid-1930s and the 1950s, include 48 native Hawaiian species and 130 introduced species; many are labeled.

Camping is allowed by permit but your options are meager (see p223). While camping under the trees looks tempting, it's prohibited, so your only option is the cramped three-sided shelter. You're much better off at the inviting Whittington to the east or Miloli'i Beach Park to the west. There are rest rooms and picnic tables, but no drinking water.

The park is in the 25,500-acre Manuka Natural Area Reserve, which reaches from the slopes of Mauna Loa down to the sea. The reserve encompasses a couple of heiau and other ruins.

KA'U

Directory

CONTENTS

ACCOMMODATIONS

The Big Island accommodations run the gamut, from camping to condominiums to luxury resorts. Rates sometimes vary according to high- and low-season; the high season runs from mid-December to mid-April. Holidays (p230) and special events (p229) always command premium prices, and the best accommodations are booked well in advance. Off-season, rates are cheaper, except at family-friendly places during summer vacation. Rates are typically given as a range between peak and off-peak seasons. Sometimes rates fluctuate depending on weekday or weekend stays. Never pay rack rates at hotels and condos without first checking online for ongoing Internet deals. For longer stays, call one of the condo rental agencies on p78.

Our reviews indicate rates for single occupancy (s), double (d) or simply the room (r), when there's no difference in the rate for one or two people. A double room in our budget category costs about $75 or less; midrange doubles cost $75 to $195; top-end rooms start at $195. Unless otherwise noted, breakfast is *not* included, bathrooms are private and all lodging is open year-round; our rates generally don't include taxes of 11.41%. Smoking is generally prohibited indoors.

A reservation guarantees your room, but most reservations require a deposit, after which, if you change your mind, the establishment will refund your money only if your room can be re-booked within a certain period. Note the cancellation policies and other restrictions before making a deposit.

For an explanation of the icons used in this book see Quick Reference on the inside front cover.

B&Bs, Inns & Guesthouses

B&Bs range from spare bedrooms in family households to private cottages and posh mansions. Most discourage unannounced drop-ins; thus some are not mapped in our book. B&B rates start around $75, although the average is closer to $100 and swankier properties start at $150. Many require a minimum stay of two or three days. If you stay longer than two or three days, discounts often kick in.

True to their name, B&Bs offer continental or full breakfasts or provide food for guests to prepare on their own. If you're traveling with children, note that some B&Bs are not geared to accept children as guests. Be sure to ask about such policies before making reservations.

Hawaii Island Bed & Breakfast Association (hibba@stayhawaii.com; www.stayhawaii.com; PO Box 1890, Honoka'a, HI 96727) lists about 50 quality-inspected B&Bs, which you contact yourself.

Many B&Bs are also booked through agencies, including the following:

All Islands Bed & Breakfast (☎ 263-2342, 800-542-0344; www.all-islands.com) Books scores of host homes.

Bed & Breakfast Hawaii (☎ 822-7771, 800-733-1632; www.bandb-hawaii.com; Box 449, Kapa'a, HI 96746) A larger statewide service.

Hawaii's Best Bed & Breakfasts (☎ 962-0100, 800-262-9912; www. bestbnb.com; PO Box 485, Laupahoehoe, HI 96764) While selection of B&Bs is small, all are hand-picked and high-quality.

Camping & Cabins

The Big Island offers camping at all levels of 'roughin' it.' Some campgrounds, such as Laupahoehoe Point Park (p156), are within view of houses; others, such as those atop Mauna Loa (p210), are miles from civilization. For camping supplies, big-box retailers like Wal-Mart are economical and convenient. In general, national park camping is best, followed by state parks, while county parks are at the bottom. Sites are less crowded during the week than on weekends.

NATIONAL PARKS

The only national park suitable for camping on the Big Island is Hawai'i Volcanoes National Park (p210), where sites are free and available on a first-come, first-served basis.

STATE PARKS

Tent camping requires a permit and costs $5 per family campsite. Cabins cost $20 per night for the four-person, A-frame cabins at Hapuna Beach State Recreation Area (p117) and $55 per night for the eight-person cabins at Kalopa State Recreation Area (p155).

To make a reservation and get a permit, contact the **Division of State Parks** (☎ 974-6200; www.hawaii.gov/dlnr/dsp; PO Box 936, Hilo, HI 96721; ☺ 8am-noon Mon-Fri), which accepts reservations in order of priority: first walk-ins, then mail requests, then phone requests. The phone is rarely answered and no long-distance calls are returned. The maximum length of stay allowed per permit is five consecutive nights. You can obtain another permit for the same park only after 30 days have passed.

COUNTY PARKS

Camping permits are required and can be obtained by mail, online or in person from the **Department of Parks & Recreation** (☎ 961-8311; www.co.hawaii.hi.us; Suite 6, 101 Pauahi St, Hilo, HI 96720; ☺ 7:45am-4pm Mon-Fri). You can also make reservations through the Hilo office and pick up the permit at the Department of Parks & Recreation branch offices around the island. Ask whether your specific park currently offers drinking water or treatable catchment water.

Daily camping fees are $5 for adults, $2 for teens and $1 for children 12 and under; Internet booking costs $1 more. Camping is allowed for up to two weeks, except between June and August, when the limit is one week only.

Condominiums

More spacious than similarly priced hotel rooms, condominiums are individually owned apartments furnished with everything a visitor needs, including kitchen, washer and dryer. They're almost always cheaper than all but the bottom-end hotel

---

PRACTICALITIES

Electricity Voltage is 110/120V, 60 cycles, as elsewhere in the USA.

Laundry Larger accommodations have cleaning services and coin-operated washers and dryers; laundromats are available in most towns and can be found in local yellow pages.

Newspapers Hilo's daily, *Hawaii Tribune-Herald* (www.hawaiitribune-herald.com), and Kailua-Kona's daily, *West Hawaii Today* (www.westhawaiitoday.com), are available islandwide. The free bimonthly *Hawaii Island Journal* (www.hawaiiislandjournal.com), features excellent coverage of current, often controversial, Big Island issues, plus comprehensive arts and entertainment listings. Also see the Honolulu dailies: *Honolulu Star-Bulletin* (www.star bulletin.com) and the *Honolulu Advertiser* (www.honoluluadvertiser.com).

Radio & TV The Big Island has about 25 radio stations; all the major US TV networks are represented, as well as cable channels featuring locally produced shows and Japanese-language programs.

Video Video systems use the NTSC standard, which is not compatible with the PAL system.

Weights & measures Distances are measured in feet, yards and miles; weights in ounces, pounds and tons; liquid volumes in cups, pints, quarts and gallons.

rooms, especially if you're traveling with a group. Most units have a three- to seven-day minimum stay. The weekly rate is often six times the daily rate and the monthly is three times the weekly. Inquire about cleaning fees, which might be tacked onto your bill.

Most condos are rented through agencies, which are listed in the Kailua-Kona chapter (p78) because of their overwhelming concentration there. You could surf the Internet and book directly instead of arranging it through agencies – and perhaps save a few bucks. But rental agencies can be helpful in emergencies such as plumbing disasters in the middle of the night. Agencies vary greatly, however, in the extent of on-site services they provide; some run the condo like a hotel while others leave you on your own at night.

Hostels

The only Big Island hostel that is associated with **Hostelling International** (www.hiusa.org) is the Holo Holo Inn (p210) near Hawai'i Volcanoes National Park. Otherwise, there are a handful of private hostel-style places offering inexpensive digs: Hilo Bay Hostel (p172), Arnott's Lodge (p172), Hotel Honoka'a Club (p149), Pahoa Hostel (p183) and Pineapple Park (p94 & p190) are recommended. Most are spartan, offer a common kitchen and Internet access and have bulletin boards thick with useful postings. Dorm beds generally cost under $20.

Hotels

Hotels commonly undercut their standard published 'rack rates' to remain as close to capacity as possible. While some offer straightforward discounted rates, others throw in a free rental car instead. Always book by Internet, where discounts are offered most frequently. Within a particular hotel, the main thing that impacts room rates is the view and floor. An ocean view can cost 50% to 100% more than a parking-lot view (euphemistically called a 'garden' or 'mountain' view).

Resorts

Luxury resorts along the South Kohala Coast are designed to fulfill every fantasy of Hawaii, from beach sands without blemishes to gourmet cuisine to obliging staff. They strive to meet any creature-comfort

need and to keep you on site every minute of the day. If that sounds a tad contrived, well, it is. But to many repeat visitors, the pampering is well worth the cost.

ACTIVITIES

The Big Island epitomizes the great outdoors, with a range of activities for elite athletes and vacation dabblers alike. Most companies offer lessons for beginners, so don't be shy about paddling a kayak or scuba diving for the first time. Hiking can be strenuous backpacking to remote valleys and mountaintops, or it can mean trekking across paved trails or along scenic coastline. Surfing, the quintessential Hawaiian pastime, is not the Big Island's star attraction, as only a few decent surf breaks exist, but snorkeling is excellent all along the Kona Coast.

If you're not into water sports, try whale watching in winter or a sunset catamaran cruise. On dry land, Hawaiian golf courses are almost in a class unto themselves. Tennis is also a huge draw; most hotels and resorts have their own courts, and there are plenty of public courts. In the rolling pastureland of Waimea and North Kohala, horseback riding and mountain biking is spectacular.

For further details, see the Hawai'i Outdoors chapter (p50).

BUSINESS HOURS

The following are 'normal' opening hours for listings in this book (but if different by more than a half-hour in either direction, specific hours are given in individual reviews):

Banks 8:30am-4pm Mon-Fri; some banks open to 6pm Fri & 9am-noon Sat.

Bars & Clubs to midnight daily; some clubs to 2am Fri & Sat.

Businesses 8:30am-4:30pm Mon-Fri; some post offices open 9am-noon Sat.

Restaurants breakfast 6-10am; lunch 11:30am-2pm; dinner 5-9:30pm.

Shops 9am-5pm Mon-Sat, some also open noon-5pm Sun; major shopping areas and malls keep extended hours.

CHILDREN

The Big Island has adventures galore to stave off kiddy crankiness: splashy beaches, food for the finicky, video arcades, fruit falling from trees and loads of bugs to torment. The Big Island also offers accessible cross-cultural opportunities, many available through hotels and resorts. Still, successful travel with young *keiki* (children) requires planning and effort. Try not to overdo things; even for adults, packing too much into the time available only means exhaustion and overload. Include children in the trip planning; if they've helped to choose where you'll go and what you'll do, they'll more likely be gung ho when you're there. Consult Lonely Planet's *Travel with Children,* which has lots of valuable tips and interesting anecdotes. When the going gets tough, bust out the chocolate macadamia nuts or stop for shave ice.

If you're traveling with infants and come up short, **Baby's Away** (☎ 800-996-9030; www.babys away.com) rents cribs, strollers, playpens, high chairs and more.

For babysitting services, try **Sitters Unlimited of Hawaii** (☎ 674-8440; www.sittershawaii.com), an O'ahu-based company now serving the Big Island. Hourly rates run $14 to $25, for one to four children. Another way to find babysitters is to ask the hotel concierge. Of course, always be wary of leaving your children with strangers.

For specific ideas about what to do with the kids, see p170 for Hilo, p76 for Kailua-Kona and p19 for a suggested itinerary.

Practicalities

Keiki are welcome most everywhere (except at some B&Bs). Children under 17 or 18 often stay free when sharing a room with their parents and using existing bedding. But ask first. Cots and rollaway beds are usually available (for an additional fee) at hotels and resorts.

Many restaurants have children's menus with significantly lower prices. High chairs are usually available, but it pays to inquire ahead of time. Likewise, sights and activities are often discounted for kids, but applicable age ranges can vary, so inquire beforehand. Horseback riding, Mauna Kea summit tours and other potentially 'risky' adventures enforce age or height minimums.

Most car-rental companies (p241) lease child-safety seats (cost per day $8, per week $40 to $45), but they're not always on hand so reserve in advance.

CLIMATE CHARTS

The biggest climactic factor is location. On the leeward (*kona* in Hawaiian) side, it's hot

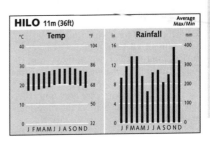

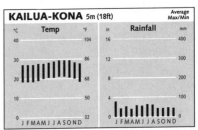

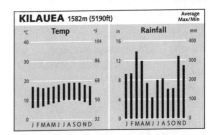

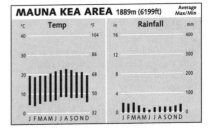

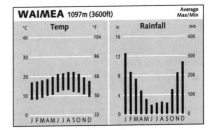

and dry, while the windward side is exposed to northeasterly tradewinds that bring abundant rainfall all year round. Occasionally, during *kona* weather, winds blow from the south, turning snorkeling spots into surfing spots and vice versa. *Kona* storms, which usually occur in winter, are very unpredictable. *Kona* winds also affect the movement of vog (p247).

The climate also varies by elevation; the higher you go, the cooler and rainier it gets. In Volcano, at 3500ft, the average daily temperature in January is 65°F, with a deluge of 160in of rainfall annually. At sea level in Hilo, the average temperature is 79°F with almost 130in of rain per year, while in Kona it's 81°F with only 64in. Hotter and drier still is South Kohala, where Waikoloa receives under 10in of rain per year (and Kawaihae's annual total might be only 3in).

Seasonally, November to March is the rainiest period but on the windward side, monthly rainfall averages 10in. Still, only during storms does it rain all day. Even in Hilo you are almost sure to see some sunshine daily. Average temperatures on Hawai'i differ by less than 10°F from winter to summer.

In Waimea and Volcano, however, the weather is chilly, foggy, and often drizzly, which often surprises visitors. And if you plan to ascend the summit of Mauna Kea, be prepared for freezing temperatures.

See also p13.

COURSES

Large hotels often offer free or low-cost classes in hula, traditional Hawaiian arts and crafts and the like. Since many schedules are unpredictable, keep your ears and eyes open. The hotel concierge is a good source of local information. Typically, the more upscale the resort, the more options you'll find; for example, **Kona Village Resort** (p107) guests can go bamboo-pole fishing, play the ukulele, make ti-leaf hula skirts and learn to hula. All this comes at steep room rates, of course.

Cooking classes are given at two top-end B&Bs, **Hawaiian Oasis B&B** (p80) in Kailua-Kona and **Palms Cliff House Inn** (p157) in Honomu. Workshops on 'alternative' or Eastern practices, eg meditation, *tai chi*, Pilates and yoga, are found islandwide. At **Island Language Center** (p170) you can learn about Hawaiian language, culture and history.

For longer-term visitors, the **University of Hawai'i at Hilo** (p163) offers both full-time university attendance and summer-school courses.

Arts & Crafts

If the Big Island awakens your creative spirit, you can find the gamut of courses – from painting and sculpture to lei making and bamboo basketry – taught by local professionals. Offerings vary widely from month to month so check websites or call in advance. Volcano Art Center has an especially varied selection, including workshops and camps for kids.

Donkey Mill Art Center (p89)
East Hawaii Cultural Center (p165)
Volcano Art Center (p198)
Wailoa Center (p166)

Hula

Unless you're staying at a resort that provides hula lessons for guests, drop-in classes are scarce, as *halau* (hula school or troupe) are for serious students only. But two B&Bs can arrange lessons if you inquire in advance, while the hotel listed following hosts classes. All require advance notice.

King Kamehameha's Kona Beach Hotel (Kulana Huli Honua; ☎ 327-0123; ⌚ 10am-2pm Mon-Fri by appointment only)
Palms Cliff House Inn (p157, per hr $40)
Shipman House B&B (p173, per hr $10)

Music

See www.taropatch.net for online forums on learning to play slack-key guitar and ukulele.

Waimea Ukulele & Slack Key Guitar Institute (p132) Annual workshops and performances.
Keauhou Shopping Center (p86) Free ukulele lessons.

Yoga & Wellness Retreats

Up until the early 2000s, yoga was pretty much an esoteric practice throughout the Big Island. Recently, however, new studios have attracted a more-diverse group of student (ie folks other than mainland haole chicks). The balmy weather and low-key atmosphere (you'll find less preening and posing here) are soothing to the soul. The two retreat centers, Kalani Oceanside Retreat and Yoga Oasis, are long-standing Puna attractions.

Balancing Monkey Yoga Center (p169)
Big Island Yoga Center (p92)

House of Motion (p125)
Kalani Oceanside Retreat (p188)
Kona Yoga (p76)
Yoga Centered (p169)
Yoga Oasis (p187)

CUSTOMS

Each visitor can bring 1L of liquor and 200 cigarettes duty-free into the USA, but you must be at least 21 years old to possess the former and 18 years old to possess the latter. In addition, each traveler is permitted to bring up to $100 worth of gift merchandise into the USA without incurring any duty.

Most fresh fruits and plants are restricted from entry into Hawaii, and customs officials are militant. To help prevent the pestilent spread of invasive alien species, it's also important to clean shoes and outdoor gear brought to the island. Because Hawaii is a rabies-free state, the pet quarantine laws are draconian, but you may be able to slice the time and expense to 30 days ($655) or five days ($225). For complete details, contact the **Hawaiian Department of Agriculture** (☎ 808-483-7151; www.hawaiiag.org).

DANGERS & ANNOYANCES

Tourism is the state's biggest industry by far, thus officials want to ensure that visitors are safe and happy. Concern about visitors' negative experiences in Hawaii has led state officials to establish the **Visitor Aloha Society of Hawaii** (VASH; ☎ 808-926-8274; www.visitoraloha societyofhawaii.org), an organization providing aid to island visitors who become the victims of accidents or crimes.

Drugs

Since the 1990s the entire state has been coping with a rampant 'ice' (crystal methamphetamine) epidemic and its ensuing crime and social problems. Be on guard for addicts, especially in rural areas. The Big Island's famous *pakalolo* (marijuana) industry remains highly profitable, and top-quality crops are cultivated mainly in Puna, despite years of government crackdowns and 'green harvests.'

Scams

The main scams directed towards visitors involve the sale of 'Hawaiian' souvenirs actually made in China, Korea, the Philippines and so forth. Such items are commonly seen in tourist-trap shops and small souvenir booths at outdoor bazaars and farmers markets. Don't waste your money on cheap fakes.

Timeshare sales booths are another scam, often disguised as tourist-information centers. Salespeople will offer enticing deals, from free luau shows to sunset cruises, if you'll just hear their 'no obligation' pitch.

Theft & Violence

The islands are notorious for break-ins into parked rental cars, whether at a secluded parking area at a trailhead or in a crowded parking lot. Best never to leave anything valuable in your car. Other than break-ins, most hassles are from addicts and alcoholics. Be tuned in to the vibes at beaches after dark and in places where folks hang out to drink, such as public campgrounds. As expected, watch your belongings in hostels.

Overall, violent crime is lower in Hawaii than in most mainland cities. However, there are some pockets of resentment against tourists and transplants. Remote beaches might be deemed 'locals-only' territory, where you'll see groups picnicking under tarps or a crowd of local surfers; don't horn in without a proper introduction. Also be wary about crossing private property, especially when 'Kapu' (No Trespassing) signs are posted.

Although theft and violence have decreased, campers should be conscious of their surroundings. People traveling alone, especially women, should be particularly cautious (p234). The less you look like a tourist, the less likely you'll be a target. Choose your park carefully; some are deserted roadside pit stops frequented mostly by troublemakers. Generally, the farther you go from population centers, the less likely you'll be hassled. (Thieves and addicts aren't big on hiking.)

Tsunami

Tsunami are generated by earthquakes, typhoons or volcanic eruptions. As evidenced by the Sumatra earthquake and massive tsunami in December 2004, they can be catastrophic. The largest tsunami ever to hit Hawaii occurred in 1946; waves reached a height of about 55ft, entire villages were washed away and 159 people died. Since that time, Hawaii has installed a warning system, aired through yellow speakers mounted on telephone poles around the islands. They're tested on the first working day each month at 11:45am.

Hawaii has had a tsunami every 10 years or so over the past century, killing more people statewide than all other natural disasters combined and causing millions of dollars in property damage. If you're in a low-lying coastal area when one occurs, immediately head for higher ground. The front section of the telephone books show maps of areas susceptible to tsunami and safety evacuation zones.

For a complete discussion of ocean safety, see p50.

DISABLED TRAVELERS

Overall, the Big Island is an accommodating destination, with many accessible activities and places to stay. The Kona side is easier to navigate than the Hilo side, which simply doesn't have comparable tourist traffic or infrastructure. However, at the Kona airport, passengers disembark directly onto the tarmac via stairs, so call ahead to make specific arrangements if necessary. Most large hotels and resorts have elevators, TTD-capable phones and wheelchair-accessible rooms, which typically must be requested in advance. Don't expect entire grounds to be accessible, however.

Seeing-eye and guide dogs are not subject to the general quarantine rules for pets, provided they meet the Department of Agriculture's minimum requirements; see www.hawaiiag.org/hdoa/ai_aqs_guidedog .htm for details. All animals must enter the state at Honolulu International Airport.

The **Disability & Communication Access Board** (☎ 586-8121; www.hawaii.gov/health/dcab; 919 Ala Moana Blvd, Rm 101, Honolulu, HI 96814) offers a three-part *Aloha Guide to Accessibility*. Part I contains general information and is obtainable free by mail. Parts II and III ($15) detail beach, park, shopping-center and visitor-attraction accessibility and list hotels with wheelchair access or specially adapted facilities.

Travelers should also pack their disabled parking placard or apply for a new one upon arrival. Placards are available, with a doctor's note, from the mayor's office in **Hilo** (☎ 961-0005; Aupuni Center, 101 Pauahi St, Suite 8, Hilo, HI 96720) and in **Kailua-Kona** (☎ 329-5226; Hanama Pl, Suite 103, 75-5706 Kuakini Hwy, Kailua-Kona 96740). Online applications are available at

www.hawaii.gov/health/dcab/resources /parking/applications/application.pdf.

Accessible Vans of Hawaii (☎ 871-7785, 800-303-3750; www.accessiblevanshawaii.com; 355 Hukulike St, Suite 121A, Kahului, Maui, 96732) is a well-regarded organization that books accommodations and personal assistants, rents accessible vans and arranges various activities for disabled travelers.

On the mainland USA, the **Society for the Advancement of Travel for the Handicapped** (SATH; ☎ 212-447-7284; www.sath.org; Suite 610, 347 Fifth Ave, New York, NY 10016) publishes a quarterly magazine and has various information sheets on travel for the disabled.

Parks are typically only partly wheelchair accessible. For example Pu'uhonua o Honaunau (p100) can be traversed by wheelchair, but not near the water or along the 1871 Trail. Walking paths at Akaka Falls State Park (p158) or into Waipi'o Valley (p151) and Pololu Valley (p126) are not accessible. Beaches are accessible to the extent one can navigate sand and rocks. See p197 for details on Hawai'i Volcanoes National Park.

DISCOUNTS

Since Hawaii is a popular destination for retirees, lots of senior discounts are available. The applicable age is constantly creeping lower so inquire about who's covered. The **American Association of Retired Persons** (AARP; ☎ 888-687-2277; www.aarp.org; Membership Center, 3200 E Carson St, Lakewood, CA 90712), an advocacy group for Americans 50 years of age and older, is a good source for travel bargains.

Students with valid identification often receive discounts into museums and other sights. For all travelers, the freebie tourist guides widely distributed around town are full of discount coupons for activities and restaurants.

EMBASSIES & CONSULATES
USA Embassies & Consulates

USA embassies abroad include:

Australia (☎ 02-6214 5600; 21 Moonah Pl, Yarralumla, Canberra, ACT 2600)

Canada (☎ 613-238 5335; 490 Sussex Dr, Ottawa, Ontario K1N 1G8)

France (☎ 33 1 43 12 22 22; 2 Av Gabriel, 75008 Paris)

Germany (☎ 030-8305 0; Neustádtische Kirchstrasse 4-5, 10117 Berlin)

Ireland (☎ 353 1 668 8777; 42 Elgin Rd, Ballsbridge, Dublin 4)

Italy (☎ 39 06 46741; Via Veneto 119/A, 00187 Rome)
Japan (☎ 03-3224 5000; 10-5, Akasaka 1-chome, Minato-ku, Tokyo)
Netherlands (☎ 070-310 9209; Lange Voorhout 102, 2514 EJ The Hague)
New Zealand (☎ 04-462 6000; 29 Fitzherbert Tce, PO Box 1190, Thorndon, Wellington)
UK (☎ 020-7499 9000; 24/31 Grosvenor Sq, London W1A 1AE)

Embassies & Consulates in the USA

All consulates in the state, including those listed below, are located in Honolulu:
Australia (☎ 524-5050; 1000 Bishop St)
Germany (☎ 946-3819; 252 Paoa Pl)
Italy (☎ 531-2277; Suite 201, 735 Bishop St)
Japan (☎ 543-3111; 1742 Nuuanu Ave)
Netherlands (☎ 531-6897; Suite 702, 745 Fort St Mall)
New Zealand (☎ 547-5117; Suite 414, 900 Richards St)
Philippines (☎ 595-6316; 2433 Pali Hwy)

FESTIVALS & EVENTS

With its multitude of cultures and pleasant weather year-round, the Big Island boasts a variety of festivals and events, summarized following. See the Festival & Events sections in individual destination chapters for more details. Surf the HVCB's complete events calendar at www.calendar.gohawaii.com. For holidays, see p230.

JANUARY
New Year New Year's Eve means massive fireworks, from backyard firecrackers and sparklers to extravagant resort displays; many businesses are closed on New Year's Day.

MARCH
Kona Brewers Festival (Kailua-Kona, p77)
Merrie Monarch Festival (Hilo, p171)
Volcano Art Center Dance & Music Concert (Volcano Village, p209)
Kona Chocolate Festival (Keauhou, p87)

MAY
Hamakua Music Festival (Honoka'a, p148)
Honoka'a Western Weekend (Honoka'a, p149)

JUNE
Great Waikoloa Food, Wine & Music Festival (Waikoloa, p113)
King Kamehameha Day Celebration (Hilo, p171)
Pu'uhonua o Honaunau Cultural Festival (Honaunau, p100)
Waiki'i Music Festival (Saddle Rd, between Waimea and Mauna Kea, p144)

JULY
Annual Kilauea Volcano Wilderness Runs (Volcano Village, p209)
Big Island Hawaiian Music Festival (Hilo, p172)
Fourth of July Events held islandwide, including a rodeo in Waimea (p133) and all-day celebration followed by fireworks in Hilo (p171).

AUGUST
Hawaiian International Billfish Tournament (Kailua-Kona, p77)
International Festival of the Pacific (Hilo, p172)

SEPTEMBER
Aloha Festival (late Aug to early Oct; ☎ 885-7786 Big Island events, 589-1771 statewide events; www.alohafestivals.com) Originally established in 1946, this Hawaiian cultural celebration now spans two months statewide; on the Big Island, the festival kicks off in late August and runs for a month. Each island selects a royal court – all of Hawaiian ancestry – introduced on the Big Island in elaborate ceremonies at Halema'uma'u Crater in Hawai'i Volcanoes National Park among other sites islandwide. Other favorite events include a *poke* (savory dish of cubed, marinated raw fish) contest (p118) at the Hapuna Beach Prince Hotel and the Queen Lili'uokalani Music Festival (p172) in Hilo.
Hawai'i County Fair (Hilo, p172)
Round-Up Rodeo (Waimea, p133)

OCTOBER
Hamakua Music Festival (Honoka'a, p148)
Hawaii International Film Festival (late Oct; O'ahu ☎ 528-3456; www.hiff.org; admission $4-6) Established in 1981, this statewide film festival features films from Asia, North America and the Pacific islands. It's an ideal venue to see locally made films that present Hawaii in a culturally accurate way. Typically, screenings take place at the Palace Theater (Hilo, p177), Honoka'a People's Theater (Honoka'a, p150) and Aloha Theatre (Kainaliu, p91).
Ironman Triathlon World Championship (Kailua-Kona, p77)

NOVEMBER
Big Island Festival (early Nov ☎ 934-9044, 866-424-3378; www.bigislandfestival.com) A culinary extravaganza featuring gourmet meals by big-name chefs, agricultural tours, wine tastings and cooking demonstrations. In the past, chefs have included 'Iron Chef' Yutaka Ishinabe and *Food & Wine Magazine*'s 'best new chefs.' Most events take place at upscale South Kohala resorts and cost between $70 and $125.
Kona Coffee Cultural Festival (South Kona, p77)
Waimea Ukulele & Slack Key Guitar Institute (Waimea, p132)

DECEMBER

Christmas Throughout December, locals celebrate with parades, craft fairs (p172), Santa Claus impersonators at shopping malls and the like. Driving in residential neighborhoods at night, you'll see many Christmas trees and quite a few elaborate outdoor displays. Most businesses are closed on Christmas day.

FOOD

Reviews in the Eating section for each destination are broken down into three price categories: budget (for those meals costing $10 or less), midrange (where most main dishes cost $10 to $20) and top end (where most dinner mains cost more than $20). These price estimates in this book do not include taxes, tips or beverages. Within each category, reviews are listed in order of author preference.

Opening hours for restaurants are: (give or take half an hour each way) breakfast 6am to 10am, lunch 11:30am to 2pm, dinner 5pm to 9:30pm. For details about local cuisine, see the Food & Drink chapter (p61).

GAY & LESBIAN TRAVELERS

Despite the contradictory attitudes of most Hawaiians – a heritage of Polynesian tolerance versus contemporary Hawaiian elders' stated prejudice against homosexuality – Hawaii remains very much an extremely popular destination for gay and lesbian travelers. And why not? The state has strong legislation to protect minority groups and a constitutional guarantee of privacy that extends to sexual behavior between all consenting adults.

Gay Hawaii is not an in-your-face kind of place; public hand-holding and other outward signs of affection between gays is not commonplace. Without question, the main gay scene is in Waikiki on O'ahu. On the Big Island, the most gay-friendly area is Puna, where you'll find Kalani Oceanside Retreat (p188), a wellness center with numerous workshops (some are clothing optional) geared for gay men, Lava Zone (p185), a lively bar for gays and straights alike, and Kehena Beach (p188), a longtime nude beach.

Pacific Ocean Holidays (☎ 923-2400, 800-735-6599; www.gayhawaiivacations.com; PO Box 88245, Honolulu, HI 96830) arranges complete vacation packages for gays and lesbians.

HOLIDAYS

The following are state holidays. Also see Festivals & Events (p229).

New Year's Day January 1
Martin Luther King Jr Day third Monday in January
Presidents Day third Monday in February
Kuhio Day March 26
Good Friday Friday before Easter Sunday
Memorial Day last Monday in May
King Kamehameha Day June 11
Independence Day July 4
Statehood Day third Friday in August
Labor Day first Monday in September
Election Day second Tuesday in November
Veterans Day November 11
Thanksgiving fourth Thursday in November
Christmas Day December 25

INSURANCE

It's expensive to get sick, crash a car or have things stolen from you in the USA. For auto insurance see p240 and for health insurance see p243). To protect yourself from car theft, consult your homeowner's (or renter's) insurance policy before leaving home.

INTERNET ACCESS

In most towns, you'll find Internet cafés or business centers offering computer and Internet access at the going rate (about $2.50 per 15 minutes). Not surprisingly, Hilo (p162) and Kailua-Kona (p70) have the most options. If you absolutely need to stay connected, bring your own computer. But don't expect the ubiquitous wireless Internet access you'd find in a big city or college campus.

A small number of accommodation options provide free or low-cost Internet access travelers without laptops; their reviews are noted with the 🖳 symbol. If B&B hosts allow you to use their computer, handle with care (and monitor kids), as some have reported damage. A larger number of top-end hotels and B&Bs provide wireless or high-speed Internet access for guests with laptops. Other options are to use your cell phone (and a cable or Bluetooth connection) to go online or to dial up using a phone line.

If you bring a laptop from outside the USA, invest in a universal AC and plug adapter. Also, your PC card modem may not work once you leave your home country – but you won't know until you try. The safest option? Buy a reputable 'global' modem before leaving home. Ensure that you have at least a US RJ-11 telephone adapter that works with your modem. For more technical help, visit www.teleadapt.com.

LEGAL MATTERS
You have the right to an attorney from the very first moment you are arrested. If you can't afford one, the state must provide one for free. The **Hawaii State Bar Association** (☎ 537-9140, 800-808-4722) makes attorney referrals, but foreign visitors may want to call their consulate for advice.

In Hawaii, anyone driving with a blood alcohol level of 0.08% or higher is guilty of driving 'under the influence,' which carries severe penalties. Driving while on any substance, be it beer, buds or barbiturates, is a bad idea. As with most places, the possession of marijuana and narcotics is illegal.

Hawaii's **Department of Commerce & Consumer Affairs** (☎ 587-1234) offers information on your rights regarding refunds and exchanges, time-share contracts, car rental and similar topics.

According to the letter of the law, hitchhiking is illegal statewide.

LEGAL AGE

The legal ages in Hawaii varies by activity:

- Drinking: 21
- Driving: 16
- Sex: 16
- Voting: 18

MAPS
If you're traveling by car, the atlas-style *Ready Mapbook* is indispensable. There are two Big Island books, for east and west Hawai'i ($11 each), in this statewide series, and they include street-by-street detail and an expansive index.

For ocean sports, see *Franko's Map of Hawai'i* (www.frankosmaps.com), a foldup, waterproof map ($6) showing snorkeling and diving spots (with a guide to tropical fish). The *Nelles Map of Hawai'i* ($6), a foldup road map, is an alternative to the Ready Mapbook if you're OK with less detail. The *UH Press Map of Hawai'i* by James Bier ($4) is a topographic map that details every bay, beach, gulch on the island.

United States Geological Survey (USGS; ☎ 888-275-8747; www.usgs.gov) publishes full-island and detailed sectional maps; note, however, that some were drawn decades ago. USGS maps can be purchased at Hawai'i Volcanoes National Park (p196). If you have a keen sense of direction and can read landmarks well, you might not need a topo map, however.

The Information sections for Hilo (p161) and Kailua-Kona (p70) list bookstores that sell maps.

MONEY
The US dollar is the only currency used in Hawaii. The dollar (commonly called a buck) is divided into 100 cents. Coins come in denominations of one cent (penny), five cents (nickel), 10 cents (dime), 25 cents (quarter) and the rare 50-cent piece (half dollar). Notes come in one-, five-, 10-, 20-, 50- and 100-dollar denominations.

See Quick Reference inside the front cover for exchange rates and Getting Started (p13) for information on costs.

ATMs
ATMs are great for quick cash influxes and can negate the need for traveler's checks entirely, but beware of ATM surcharges. Most banks charge around US$1.50 per withdrawal.

Bank of Hawaii (www.boh.com) and **First Hawaiian Bank** (www.fhb.com) have extensive ATM networks that will give cash advances on major credit cards and allow cash withdrawals with affiliated ATM cards. Most ATMs in Hawaii accept bank cards from the Plus and Cirrus systems. Look for ATMs outside banks and in large grocery stores, shopping centers, convenience stores and gas stations.

Cash
If you're carrying foreign currency, it can be exchanged for US dollars at Honolulu International Airport and at main bank branches on the Big Island.

Credit Cards
Major credit cards are widely accepted on the Big Island, but not by some restaurants, B&Bs and condominiums.

Tipping
In restaurants, tip at least 15% for good service and 10% if it's mediocre. Leaving no tip

is rare and requires real cause. Taxi drivers and hairstylists are typically tipped 10% and hotel bellhops $1 per bag.

Traveler's Checks

Traveler's checks provide protection from theft and loss. Keep a record of all check numbers separate from the checks themselves. For refunds on lost or stolen traveler's checks, call **American Express** (☎ 800-992-3404) or **Thomas Cook** (☎ 800-287-7362). Foreign visitors carrying traveler's checks will find things infinitely easier if the checks are in US dollars. Personal checks not drawn from a Hawaiian bank are generally not accepted.

PHOTOGRAPHY

For a quick but complete course on shooting great photos, consult Lonely Planet's *Travel Photography*.

Print and slide film, as well as digital cameras and storage devices, are available in Hawaii. If you're here for any length of time, have your film developed here, as the high temperature and humidity greatly accelerate the deterioration of exposed film. Don't pack unprocessed film (including the roll inside your camera) into checked luggage because exposure to high-powered x-ray equipment will cause it to fog. X-ray scanners used for carry-on baggage are less powerful and generally won't cause visible damage; to be safe, carry your film separately and submit it to airport security officials for a 'hand check.'

POST

Mail delivery to and from Hawaii via the **US postal service** (USPS; ☎ 800-275-8777; www.usps.gov) is reliable but takes a little longer than similar services across the US mainland (about 10 days for air mail and four to six weeks for parcel post).

First-class mail between Hawaii and the mainland goes by air and usually takes three to four days. For 1st-class mail sent and delivered within the USA, postage rates are 37¢ for letters up to 1oz (23¢ for each additional ounce) and 23¢ for standard-size postcards.

International air mail rates for letters up to 1oz are 60¢ to Canada or Mexico and 80¢ to other countries. Postcards cost 50¢ to Canada or Mexico and 70¢ to other countries.

You can receive mail c/o General Delivery at most post offices on the Big Island but, according to the official rule, you must first complete an application in person. Bring two forms of ID and your temporary local address. The accepted application is valid for 30 days; mail is held for a maximum of 15 days. But exceptions are made, so ask. Most hotels will also hold mail for incoming guests.

SHOPPING

Genuine Hawaiian arts and crafts, such as koa bowls by Dan De Luz (p190) and *lauhala* (woven pandanus leaves) baskets and bags from Kimura Lauhala Shop (p89), are meticulously created and worth every penny. Of course, you'll find scads of fakes. The best way to distinguish rip-offs from the real deal is to shop at respected art galleries.

Music shops, such as Mele Kai Music (p84) and Holualoa Ukulele Gallery (p90) sell Hawaiian instruments, while big-box retailers like Borders Books Music & Café (p70 and p161) and Wal-Mart (p177) carry a wide selection of Hawaiian music CDs.

Aloha shirts might seem a cliché but they're still the official male uniform. The classiest, worn by local professionals, use lightweight cotton and subdued colors, often reverse-fabric prints. As for T-shirts, Crazy Shirts (p84), that '80s icon, is still going strong with home-grown Hawaiian designs, including those dyed with island coffee, hemp, beer or red dirt.

Edibles are always a hit back home. Macadamia nuts, Kona coffee and *liliko'i* (passionfruit) or *poha* (gooseberry) preserves all make convenient, compact gift items. As for pineapples, they're heavy, bulky and likely to be just as cheap back home.

The Big Island is the anthurium capital of the world, and both cut flowers and live plants make a big splash back home. Companies such as Akatsuka Orchid Gardens (p190) pack and ship orchids, anthuriums and proteas to your door at home.

Bargaining is not the norm among locals, except at farmers markets. See p37 for more on Hawaiian arts and crafts.

TELEPHONE

Always dial '1' before toll-free (☎ 800, 888 etc), domestic long-distance numbers and interisland calls. While the area code 808 applies to all islands, it must be dialed for interisland calls (from one island to another); for intra-island calls (within island), just dial the number.

Pay phones are readily found in shopping centers, beach parks and other public places. Intra-island calls are considered local and cost 25¢ or 50¢. Interisland calls are always long distance and more expensive. Hotels often add a hefty service charge of $1 for calls made from a room phone.

Private prepaid phone cards are available from convenience stores, supermarkets and pharmacies. Cards sold by major telecommunications companies such as AT&T may offer better deals than upstart companies.

Cell Phones

The USA uses a variety of cell-phone systems, 99% of which are incompatible with the GSM 900/1800 standard used throughout Europe and Asia. Check with your cellular service provider before departure about using your phone in Hawaii. Verizon has the most extensive cellular network on the islands, but all major companies provide coverage – at least within main towns. Coverage is downright nonexistent in remote regions such as hiking trails and rural towns.

Long-Distance & International Calls

To make international calls direct from Hawaii, dial ☎ 011 + country code + area code + number. (An exception is to Canada, where you dial ☎ 1 + area code + number, but international rates still apply.)

For international operator assistance, dial ☎ 0. The operator can provide specific rate information and tell you which time periods are the cheapest for calling.

If you're calling Hawaii from abroad, the international country code for the US is ☎ 1. All calls to Hawaii are followed by the area code ☎ 808 and the seven-digit local number. As mentioned above, dial the area code when calling from one island to another.

TIME

Hawaii does not observe daylight saving time, thus the time difference is one hour greater during those months when other countries *are* observing daylight saving time (eg the first Sunday in April to the last Sunday in October in North America).

Hawaii has 11 hours of daylight in midwinter (December) and 13½ hours in midsummer (June). In midwinter, the sun rises around 7am and sets at 6pm. In midsummer, it rises before 6am and sets after 7pm.

And then there's 'Hawaiian time,' a slow-down-the-clock pace or a euphemism for being late.

TOILETS

Finding a place to go is relatively easy in Hawaii. In a pinch, duck into hotels and resorts, where you can wander freely and avail yourself of the facilities without fear of being stopped. While many beaches have decent facilities, park trailhead outhouses can be an olfactory onslaught.

TOURIST INFORMATION

The **Hawaii Visitors & Convention Bureau** (☎ 800-464-2924; www.gohawaii.com; Suite 801, 2270 Kalakaua Ave, Waikiki, HI 96815) will mail general tourist information on Hawaii. The **Big Island Visitors Bureau** (☎ 800-648-2441; www.gohawaii.com/bigisland) has a branch in Hilo (p163) and another in Waikoloa (p111).

TOURS

Bus tour operators offer around-the-island tours, which are essentially a mad dash through the main towns and Hawai'i Volcanoes National Park. Make no mistake, you'll get only an unsatisfying glimpse and might be better off watching a PBS documentary on the island instead. **Roberts Hawaii** (☎ 329-1688, 800-831-5411; www.roberts-hawaii .com), **Jack's Tours** (☎ 961-6666, 800-442-5557; www .jackshawaii.com) and **Polynesian Adventure Tours** (☎ 329-8008, 800-622-3011; www.polyad.com) offer day-long circle-island bus tours that cost from $55. Both companies pick up passengers at hotels in Waikoloa, Kailua-Kona and Keauhou; the exact time varies by location, but expect to leave at around sunrise and get back around sunset.

Specialized adventure tours like hiking down into Waipi'o Valley (p155), riding a submarine or glass-bottom boat along the Kona Coast (p77), or whale watching (p103) are listed in the Activities sections of individual destination chapters.

Elderhostel (☎ 617-426-7788, 877-426-8056; www .elderhostel.org; 1-/2-week programs $650/1300) offers educational programs on Hawaiian culture or natural environment for those aged 55 or older and includes accommodations, meals and classes. **Earthwatch International** (☎ 800-776-0188; www.earthwatch.org; 2-week programs $2400) projects in Hawaii focus on activities such as restoring mountain streams and assisting in humpback whale research. Accommodations and meals are included.

See p237 for package tours and p238 for cruises to the Hawaiian Islands.

Helicopter Tours

Though expensive, only helicopters can provide a bird's-eye view. Tours typically fly over Kilauea Caldera and live lava flows (before booking, ask whether they fly over the active Pu'u 'O'o vent). Expect to pay $120 or more for a 45-minute flight and up to $350 for a two-hour flight.

Helicopter tours are cancelled during inclement weather, but may fly when it's overcast, which limits visibility. Wait for a crystal-clear day, if possible, and remember that while it's sunny in Kona, it might be hazy over Volcano. Call around to compare prices, especially if you're willing to fly standby. **Island Hoppers** (☎ 969-2000, 800-538-7590; www.fly-hawaii.com/above) has cheaper 50-minute 'flightseeing tours' by a small prop plane.

Blue Hawaiian Helicopters (☎ 961-5600, 800-786-2583; www.bluehawaiian.com)

Safari Helicopters (☎ 969-1259, 800-326-3356; www.safariair.com)

Sunshine Helicopters (☎ 800-621-3144; www.sunshinehelicopters.com)

Tropical Helicopters (☎ 961-6810; www.tropicalhelicopters.com)

VISAS

Entering the USA can be a bureaucratic nightmare, depending on your country of origin. To make matters worse, rules change rapidly. For up-to-date information about visas and immigration, check with the **US State Department** (www.unitedstatesvisas.gov/visiting.html).

Note that the Visa Waiver Program allows citizens of 27 specified countries to enter the USA for stays of 90 days or less without first obtaining a US visa. See www.travel.state.gov/visa/temp/without/without_1990.html. Under this program you must have a machine-readable passport or a US visa, plus a return ticket (or onward ticket to any foreign destination) that is nonrefundable in the USA. Your passport should be valid for at least six months longer than your stay.

For additional information, see the website of the **Bureau of Citizenship & Immigration Service** (BCIS; www.bcis.gov).

WOMEN TRAVELERS

Hawaii presents few unique problems for women travelers and may be more relaxed and comfortable than many mainland destinations. Of course, women, especially solo travelers, might feel uneasy in local bars. If camping, women should opt for secure, well-used camping areas over isolated locales where they might be the only campers. County parks (see p223) are notorious for late-night beer binges and some are known for long-term squatting.

VOLUNTEERING

The **National Park Service** (☎ 808-985-6092; www.nps.gov/volunteer) has volunteer programs at Hawai'i Volcanoes National Park, but it's subject to change, often depending on funding, staffing levels etc. Contact the park and specify the type of work you're after. Housing is often provided, as is a minimal stipend.

Another option is volunteering at the **Mauna Kea Visitor Information Station** (☎ 808-961-2180; www.ifa.hawaii.edu/info/vis/volunteers.html; 177 Maka'ala St, Hilo, HI 96720) as visitor-center guides, trail maintenance crew, summit guides and stargazing volunteers.

The Kalani Oceanside Retreat (p188) in Puna has an established volunteer and residency program.

WORK

US citizens can work in Hawaii – the problem is finding a decent job. Foreign visitors in Hawaii on tourist visas, however, cannot legally be employed.

Finding serious 'professional' employment is difficult in the state's already-tight labor market. The biggest exceptions to this rule are for teachers and nurses. Also, residential construction is booming, and there's a shortage of licensed carpenters, plumbers, painters, electricians and roofers. Waiting on tables is probably what you can expect. Folks with language, scuba, fishing or guiding skills can investigate employment at resorts.

Check the classifieds of newspapers to get an idea of employment opportunities. For a list of government jobs available in the state, contact the **State Workforce Development Division** (Hilo ☎ 974-4126; 180 Kinoole St, Suite 205; Kona ☎ 327-4770; 74-5565 Luhia St, Bldg 3). The **State Department of Labor & Industrial Relations** (☎ 586-8700; www.dlir.state.hi.us; 830 Punchbowl St, Honolulu, HI 96813) can be a good resource.

Transportation

GETTING THERE & AWAY

No surprise: the vast majority of all visitors to Hawaii arrive by air because Hawaii is smack in the middle of the vast Pacific Ocean. Virtually all international flights and the vast majority of domestic flights arrive at Honolulu International Airport. If you are flying to the Big Island through Honolulu, make sure the ticket agent marks your baggage with Hilo or Kona as the final destination.

ENTERING THE COUNTRY

A passport is required for all foreign citizens except Canadians, who need to show only proof of residence. Residents of most other countries need a tourist visa (see opposite). It's always advisable to confirm this information since it changes rapidly.

AIR

US domestic and international air fares vary tremendously depending on the season, general tourism trends to the islands, and how much flexibility the ticket allows for flight changes and refunds. Since nothing determines fares more than demand, when things are slow, airlines lower their fares to fill empty seats. There's a lot of competition, and at any given time any one of the airlines could have the cheapest fare.

Airports & Airlines

To get to the Big Island, you'll arrive in either Hilo or Kona. Most likely you'll stop in Honolulu first, although there are quite a few direct flights into Kona now.

Hilo International Airport (ITO; ☎ 935-5707; www .state.hi.us/dot/airports/hawaii/ito; p178)
Honolulu International Airport (HNL; ☎ 836-6413; www.honoluluairport.com)
Kona International Airport at Keahole (KOA; ☎ 329-3423; www.hawaii.gov/dot/airports/hawaii/koa; p85)

Outside of Hawaii, the gateway airports for flights to and from the Big Island include the following:
Atlanta International Airport (ATL; ☎ 800-897-1910; www.atlanta-airport.com)
Chicago O'Hare International Airport (ORD; ☎ 773-686-2200; www.ohare.com)
Denver International Airport (DEN; ☎ 303-342-2000; www.flydenver.com)
Las Vegas McCarran International Airport (LAS; ☎ 702-261-5211; www.mccarran.com)
Los Angeles International Airport (LAX; ☎ 310-646-5252; www.los-angeles-lax.com)
New York JFK International Airport (JFK; ☎ 718-244-4444; www.panynj.gov)
Oakland International Airport (OAK; ☎ 510-563-3300; www.flyoakland.com)
Orange County John Wayne Airport (SNA; ☎ 949-252-5200; www.ocair.com)
Phoenix Sky Harbor International Airport (PHX; ☎ 602-273-3300; www.phoenix-phx.com)

THINGS CHANGE...

The information in this chapter is particularly vulnerable to change. Check directly with the airline or a travel agent to make sure you understand how a fare (and ticket you may buy) works and be aware of the security requirements for international travel. Shop carefully. The details given in this chapter should be regarded as pointers and are not a substitute for your own careful, up-to-date research.

TRANSPORTATION

Ronald Reagan Washington National Airport (DCA; ☎ 703-417-8000; www.metwashairports.com)
San Francisco International Airport (SFO; ☎ 650-876-2222; www.flysfo.com)
San Diego International Airport (SAN; ☎ 619-400-2400; www.san.org)
Seattle-Tacoma International Airport (SEA; ☎ 206-433-5388; www.portseattle.org)
Washington Dulles International Airport (IAD; ☎ 703-572-2700; www.metwashairports.com)

The vast majority of incoming flights from overseas and the US mainland arrive on O'ahu at Honolulu International Airport, and travelers must then catch an interisland flight on Aloha Airlines, Hawaiian Airlines or Island Air. But the following airlines do fly directly to Kona International Airport, as well as to Honolulu International Airport (none fly directly to Hilo International Airport):

American Airlines (☎ 800-223-5436; www.aa.com)
Aloha Airlines (☎ 800-367-5250; www.alohaairlines .com)
Japan Airlines (☎ 800-525-3663; www.japanair.com)
United Airlines (☎ 800-241-6522; www.ual.com)

Airlines flying into Honolulu include the following:
Air Canada (☎ 888-247-2262; www.aircanada.ca)
Air New Zealand (☎ 800-262-1234; www.airnz.co.nz)
Air Pacific (☎ 800-227-4446; www.airpacific.com)
Alaska Airlines (☎ 800-252-7522; www.alaskaair.com)
American Trans Air (☎ 800-435-9282; www.ata.com)
China Airlines (☎ 800-227-5118; www.china-airlines .com)
Continental (☎ 800-523-3273; www.continental.com)
Delta (☎ 800-221-1212; www.delta.com)
Hawaiian Airlines (☎ 800-367-5320; www.hawaiian air.com)
Korean Airlines (☎ 800-438-5000; www.koreanair.com)
Northwest-KLM (☎ 800-225-2525; www.nwa.com)
Philippine Airlines (☎ 800-435-9725; www.philippine air.com)
Qantas Airways (☎ 800-227-4500; www.qantasusa.com)
US Airways (☎ 800-428-4322; www.usairways.com)

DEPARTURE TAX

Taxes and fees for US airports are normally included in the price of tickets when you buy them, whether they're purchased in the USA or abroad. There are no state taxes to pay when leaving Hawaii.

For interisland flights, smaller commuter airlines are another option. Such airlines tend to come and go; currently there's only one decent option:
Island Air (US mainland ☎ 800-323-3345, Neighbor Islands ☎ 800-652-6541; www.islandair.com)

Tickets

There's no guaranteed formula for finding the cheapest fares, but the best deals are often found on the Internet. Recommended travel websites include the following:

- www.travelocity.com
- www.expedia.com
- www.orbitz.com
- www.cheaptickets.com
- www.lowestfare.com
- www.sta.com (for travelers under 26)

Once in Hawaii, you'll find discounted fares to virtually any place around the Pacific. Larger travel agencies that specialize in discount tickets include Kaiko'o Travel (p163) in Hilo and Regal Travel (p163) in Kona (see p71).

Round-the-world tickets (RTW) allow you to fly on the combined routes of two or more airlines and can be a good deal if you're coming from a great distance and want to visit other parts of the world in addition to Hawaii. **British Airways** (☎ 800-247-9297; www .britishairways.com) and **Qantas Airways** (☎ 800-227-4500; www.qantas.com) offer the best plans through programs called Oneworld Explorer and Global Explorer, respectively.

Circle Pacific tickets are essentially a take-off on RTW tickets, but instead of requiring you to continue moving in one general direction, they allow you to keep traveling in the same circular direction. Because you start and end at a city that borders the Pacific, these tickets are most practical for travelers who live in or near the Pacific region. Contact **Air New Zealand** (☎ 800-262-1234; www.airnz.co.nz) or **Continental** (☎ 800-523-3273; www.continental.com), whose program is called 'Circle Micronesia.' Continental's flights originate in Los Angeles, San Francisco and Honolulu.

Australia

Hawaiian Airlines flies nonstop between Sydney and Honolulu. Qantas flies to Honolulu from Sydney and Melbourne (via Sydney, but without changing planes).

Return fares range seasonally from A$900 to A$1400.

Canada

Air Canada offers direct flights to Honolulu from Vancouver and also other Canadian cities via Vancouver. The cheapest return fares to Honolulu are about C$800 from Vancouver, C$1100 from Calgary or Edmonton, and C$1400 from Toronto.

Hawaiian Airlines also flies from Vancouver, Calgary, Edmonton and Toronto, with stopovers in Phoenix and Honolulu.

Japan

Japan Airlines flies directly between Tokyo and Kona International Airport. But if you fly to Honolulu first, your starting point can be Osaka, Nagoya or Fukuoka, as well as Tokyo. Return fares vary according to departure city and season but, with the exception of busier holiday periods (particularly Golden Week in May, Obon in August and around the New Year), they're around ¥40,000 for a ticket valid for three months.

Fares to Honolulu on All Nippon Airways (ANA), which also depart from Sapporo and Kumamoto, are sometimes discounted to ¥70,000. Continental and Northwest-KLM have several flights to Honolulu from Tokyo and Osaka; ticket prices are comparable to those offered by Japan Airlines.

Micronesia & New Zealand

Continental has nonstop flights from Guam to Honolulu with return fares at about US$1100. Air New Zealand flies from Auckland to Honolulu at about NZ$1650 return.

South Pacific Islands

Hawaiian Airlines flies to Honolulu from Tahiti and American Samoa. From American Samoa return fares are about US$600; from Tahiti; they're about US$700.

Air New Zealand offers return tickets from Fiji to Honolulu via Auckland for about NZ$1370. It also flies to Honolulu from Tonga, the Cook Islands and Western Samoa for around NZ$870 (from Western Samoa) or NZ$1080 (from Tonga and the Cook Islands) return.

UK & Continental Europe

The most common route to Hawaii from Europe is west via New York, Chicago or Los Angeles. If you're interested in heading east with stops in Asia, it may be cheaper to get a RTW ticket instead of returning the same way.

The lowest return fares with American Airlines from London, Paris and Frankfurt to Honolulu are usually around €790. United, Delta and Continental have a similarly priced service to Honolulu from some European cities.

London is arguably the world's headquarters for bucket shops specializing in discount tickets, and they are well advertised. Two good, reliable agents for cheap tickets in the UK:

STA Travel (☎ 020-240 9821; www.statravel.co.uk; 33 Bedford St, Covent Garden, London)

Trailfinders (☎ 020-7628 7628; www.trailfinders.co.uk; 1 Threadneedle St, London)

US Mainland

Competition is high among airlines flying to Honolulu from major mainland cities. Typically, the lowest round-trip fares from the US mainland to Hawaii are approximately $600 from the east coast and $400 from the west coast. Sometimes package-tour companies offer the best air fare deals, even if you don't want to buy the whole 'package.'

The vast majority of mainland flights fly only into Honolulu, but can fly directly to Kona: United flies from Chicago, Denver, Los Angeles, San Francisco and Washington, DC; and American flies from Los Angeles. Aloha Airlines, which flies from Oakland and Orange County, is an ideal option because it also serves as the interisland carrier and the overall fare is quite reduced.

For those with limited time, package tours can sometimes be the cheapest way to go. Basic ones cover air fare and accommodations, while deluxe packages include car rental, island hopping and all sorts of activities. If you're going to Hawaii on a short getaway, packages may cost little more than what air fare alone would have cost. Although costs vary, one-week tours with air fare and no-frills hotel accommodations usually start around $500 from the US west coast, $800 from the US east coast, based on double occupancy. **Pleasant Hawaiian Holidays** (☎ 800-742-9244; www.pleasantholidays.com) has departures from various US mainland points. **Sun Trips** (☎ 800-786-8747; www.suntrips.com) offers packages from Oakland, California.

Then there's Air Tech's Space-Available FlightPass, which certainly can be the cheapest way to fly between the west coast and Hawaii. **Air Tech** (☎ 212-219-7000; www.airtech .com) offers super deals by selling standby seats at $129 one way. If you provide the staff with a two- to four-day travel window, they'll get you a seat at a nice price. Currently, flights to Honolulu, Kaua'i, and Maui depart from San Francisco and Los Angeles.

The nonstop flight time to Hawaii is about 5½ hours from the west coast or 11 hours from the east coast.

Within Hawaii

Only three major carriers serve interisland air travel: the two major interisland carriers are Hawaiian Airlines and Aloha Airlines. All of Hawaiian and Aloha Airlines' interisland flights require a stopover in Honolulu (except one Hawaiian Airlines flight from Kailua-Kona to Maui). The service through Honolulu is regular, with about 10 flights daily from both Hilo and Kailua-Kona; fares run almost $100 one way. Aloha Airlines offers lower interisland fares (as low as $69 one way) for those who join its 'Aloha Pass' frequent-flyer program and book tickets online.

Another option is Island Air, which flies small 18- and 37-seat planes to Honolulu and Maui. Only two to four flights are offered daily. Fares range between about $85 and $110 one way, depending on when you book your flight. (Expect an interminable wait if you call the 800 number!) If you want to fly between Hilo and Kona, Island Air is your only option, as most Big Island tourists opt to drive around the island.

If you want to visit another island while you're in Hawaii but only have a day or two to spare, consider an island-hopping tour to the Neighbor Islands. The largest company specializing in 'overnighters' is **Roberts Hawaii** (☎ 800-899-9323; www.robertsovernighters.com).

SEA

In recent years, a handful of cruise ships has begun offering tours that include Hawaii. Most cruises last 10 to 12 days and have fares that start at around US$150 a day per person, based on double occupancy – though discounts and promotions can bring that price down to under US$100 a day. Air fare to and from the departure point costs extra.

Most Hawaiian cruises include stopovers in Honolulu, Maui, Kaua'i and the Big Island. Cruise lines include the following:

Holland America Cruise Line (☎ 877-724-5425; www .hollandamerica.com) Typically departs for Honolulu from San Diego, Seattle or Vancouver.

Princess Cruises (☎ 800-568-3262; www.princess .com) Offers the most cruises; operates between Honolulu and Tahiti.

You can also get to Hawaii by private yacht. If you don't have one of your own, and you're hoping to get on a crew, start poking around the Honolulu ports in early spring. Experienced crew should try www.boat crew.net, a well-organized site with a database of boats leaving from various mainland ports. Membership is US$10 per month (or US$100 per year).

GETTING AROUND

AIR

While most visitors rent a car and gladly circumnavigate the island, Island Air offers $40 round-trip flights between Hilo and Kona. The 21-minute flight departs once daily from Hilo at 8am and from Kona at 5:10pm.

BICYCLE

It's possible to cycle around the Big Island without backtracking, but you'll encounter the gamut of terrain and weather. The Hilo side is windy and wet, while the Kona and Kohala coasts seesaw between hot and hellishly hot. What's more, the terrain is almost never flat, but presents quick, steep elevation gains that will tax even stalwart cyclists. Dedicated bicycle lanes are quite rare. Roads tend to be narrow. The main coastal routes are heavily trafficked. And the island is gigantic when navigated under pedal power! Nevertheless, determined cyclists *do* successfully traverse the island.

Bicycle-rental shops are mainly in Kailua-Kona (p85) and Hilo (p178). If you bring your own bike to Hawaii, which costs upwards of US$100 on flights from the mainland, it will cost an additional US$25 to transport it on interisland flights. The bicycle can be checked in at the counter, the same as any baggage, but you'll need to prepare the bike first either by wrapping the handlebars and pedals in foam or by fixing the handlebars to the side and removing the pedals.

In general, bicycles are required to follow the same state laws and rules of the road as cars.

BOAT

In response to the increasing costs of inter-island flights, a new ferry service will launch in early 2007. **Hawaii Superferry** (www.hawaiisuper ferry.com) will sail two state-of-the-art catamarans, each carrying up to 900 passengers and almost 300 cars, between Honolulu and Kaua'i, Maui and the Big Island. Travel time to the Big Island's Kawaihae harbor will run at four hours; the Superferry will not service Hilo because the trip would take six hours. The Big Island round-trip fares will run just over $50 per person and about the same per vehicle (higher for pickups and vans), about half of the cost of flying.

Norwegian Cruise Line (☎ 800-327-7030; www .ncl.com) is the only company that operates cruises between the Hawaiian Islands that start and end in Hawaii, launching either in Honolulu or Maui. Seven-day trips (starting in Honolulu and stopping in Maui, Kaua'i, Hilo and Kona) and three- or four-night cruises (starting in either Honolulu or Maui and excluding Kaua'i) are offered. Since 2004, NCL has sailed US-flagged cruise ships, including the *Pride of Aloha*, the *Pride of America* and the *Pride of Hawaii* (starting in 2006); so you need not travel all the way to Fanning Island in the Republic of Kiribati (foreign-registered ships must make such an international stop during their tours). But NCL does offer longer 10- or 11-day cruises that do include Fanning Island (and a much-longer time aboard ship).

Onboard there are six restaurants, 13 lounges and bars, full spa, conference rooms, a wedding chapel, golf shop and a cultural center. While customer service on the early runs of the *Pride of Aloha* was sometimes problematic, currently everything seems to be shipshape.

Prices vary depending on season (rates are approximately 50% higher in summer and winter than in spring and fall) and on type of cabin. For the seven-day cruise, an interior cabin, double occupancy, starts around US$1000 per person, while an ocean-view cabin starts around US$1700 per person.

BUS

A Big Island bus journey just isn't practical, but with a little planning you can get yourself between major towns and attractions.

Hele-On Bus (☎ 961-8744; www.co.hawaii.hi.us /mass_transit/heleonbus.html; 7:45am-4:30pm Mon-Fri), the county public bus, offers minimal islandwide service Monday to Friday, with an even more limited service on Saturday. Schedules are available at the Big Island Visitors Bureau (p163 and p111) and the information kiosk at Hilo's Mo'oheau bus terminal (p178). The individual destination chapters in the book list the main routes but if possible check the website for current information. All buses originate from Mo'oheau terminal, unless otherwise noted. The number of trips per route varies; for example, for intra-Hilo travel, there are up to eight departures on weekdays, but for longer routes, such as to Kona or Ka'u, you might be stuck with one departure time daily.

A few caveats: drivers accept only the exact fare. You can buy a sheet of 10 bus tickets (which normally cost 75¢ each) for $5. You need permission from the driver to board with a surfboard, boogie board or bicycle and you will be charged an extra $1. Luggage and backpacks also entail an extra $1. Many stops do not have signs, and the schedule does not include a map.

Bus drivers and local passengers are extremely laid-back. If you want to disembark between designated stops, just ask. Buses are rarely precisely on time, and the driver might play Hawaiian tunes during the ride!

CAR & MOTORCYCLE

Statistically speaking, over 60% of all visitors to Hawaii rent their own vehicles. And that figure rises to 85% for US visitors to Neighbor Islands. So most of you should read on.

The minimum age for driving a car in Hawaii is 18 years, though most major car-rental companies enforce a minimum age of 25. Thrifty Car Rental is one of the few renting to drivers 21 and above. If you're under age 25, you should call the car-rental agencies in advance to check their policies regarding restrictions and surcharges.

Motorcycle rental is not common in Hawaii. The minimum age to rent one at most places is 21 and you'll need to show a valid motorcycle license. The minimum age for renting a scooter or moped (the former can go highway speeds while the latter is only for around town) is 16 years.

There are no helmet laws in Hawaii and even typically cautious riders will be tempted to let loose helmet-free as they lean into turns down endless coastal stretches. This is not advised. Remember that rental agencies often provide free helmets.

Riding in Hilo, Volcano and Waimea requires hard-core rain gear, which some rental shops also supply. Snug cuffs and waterproof seams are essential, and a stash of double-sided Velcro and seam sealer will work wonders for your disposition.

State law requires mopeds to be ridden by one person only and prohibits their use on sidewalks and freeways. Mopeds must always be driven in single file and may not be driven at speeds in excess of 30mph. Bizarrely, mopeds can be more expensive to rent than cars.

Whether in a car or on a motorcycle, proceed with caution: the Big Island's per capita automobile accident rate was three times that of O'ahu and twice that of Maui and Kaua'i during 2000 and 2003. Further, Big Island drivers accounted for 30% of all car fatalities statewide between 1996 and 2003, though less than 13% of state residents live on the island.

Automobile Associations

The **American Automobile Association** (AAA; ☎ 800-736-2886; www.aaa-hawaii.com), which has its only Hawaii office in Honolulu, provides members with maps and other information. Members get discounts on car rental, air tickets, some hotels, some sightseeing attractions, as well as emergency road service and towing (☎ 800-222-4357). For information on joining, call ☎ 800-564-6222. AAA has reciprocal agreements with automobile associations in other countries, but bring your membership card from home.

Driver's License

An international driving license, obtained before you leave home, is only necessary if your country of origin is a non-English-speaking one.

Fuel & Towing

Fuel is readily available everywhere except in remote areas such as Saddle Rd. Expect to pay at least 50¢ more per US gallon than on the mainland. For example, when mainland gas costs an average of $1.90, you'll pay anywhere from $2.25 to $2.75 per US gallon in Hawaii. Still, for Europeans and Canadians, it will be less expensive than at home.

If you get into trouble with your car, towing is mighty expensive and therefore to be avoided at all costs. Figure the fees at about $65 to start, plus $6.50 per mile you must be towed. How to avoid it? Don't drive up to Mauna Kea in anything but a 4WD, for instance, and never drive 4WD vehicles in deep sand.

Insurance

Liability insurance covers people and property that you might hit. For damage to the actual rental vehicle, a collision damage waiver (CDW) is available for about $15 a day. If you have collision coverage on your vehicle at home, it might cover damages to car rentals; inquire before departing. Additionally, some credit cards offer reimbursement coverage for collision damages if you rent the

---

ROAD DISTANCES & TIMES

From Hilo

destination	distance (miles)	time (hr)
Hawi	86	2¼
Honoka'a	40	1
Kailua-Kona	92	2½
Na'alehu	64	1¾
Pahoa	16	½
Hawai'i Volcanoes NP	28	¾
Waikoloa	80	2¼
Waimea	54	1½
Waipi'o Lookout	50	1¼

From Kailua-Kona

destination	distance (miles)	time (hr)
Hawi	51	1¼
Hilo	92	2½
Honoka'a	61	1½
Na'alehu	60	1½
Pahoa	108	3
Hawai'i Volcanoes NP	98	2½
Waikoloa	18	¾
Waimea	43	1
Waipi'o Lookout	70	1¾

car with that credit card; again, check before departing. Most credit-card coverage isn't valid for rentals of more than 15 days or for exotic models, jeeps, vans and 4WDs. For recorded information on your legal rights, call the state **Department of Commerce & Consumer Affairs** (☎ 808-587-1234 ext 7222).

Rental
Rental cars are readily available, but advance reservations are highly recommended. The daily rate for a small car ranges from $30 to $50 and the typical weekly rate is $175 to $250, excluding taxes and other fees that total roughly 18% of the base estimate. Rates for 4WD vehicles average $75 to $85 per day and $400 per week. Ask for the *total* price when shopping around. Also remember that rates are extremely volatile and can significantly vary by season and availability.

If you belong to an auto club or a frequent-flyer program, inquire about discounts. It always pays to shop around between rental companies. Booking in advance assures better selection (especially if you want a 4WD), but you can also snag great last-minute deals via the Internet.

Rental rates generally include unlimited mileage, though if you drop off the car at a different location from where you picked it up, there's usually a hefty additional fee.

Having a major credit card greatly simplifies the rental process. Without one, some agents simply will not rent vehicles, while others require prepayment, a deposit of $200 per week, pay stubs, proof of return air fare and more.

The following major agencies are your best bets:

Alamo (☎ 800-327-9633; www.alamo.com)
Avis (☎ 800-331-1212; www.avis.com)
Budget (☎ 800-527-0700; www.budget.com)
Dollar (☎ 800-800-4000; www.dollarcar.com)
Enterprise (☎ 800-325-8007; www.enterprise.com)
Hertz (☎ 800-654-3011; www.hertz.com)
National (☎ 888-868-6207; www.nationalcar.com)
Thrifty (☎ 800-847-4389; www.thrifty.com)

Harper Car & Truck Rentals (☎ 969-1478, 800-852-9993; www.harpershawaii.com; 456 Kalaniana'ole Ave, Hilo) is the local car-hire agency. Only Harper puts no restrictions on driving its 4WDs to Mauna Kea's summit, or almost anywhere on the island, except Waipi'o Valley and Green Sands Beach. But bear in mind that

if you damage a vehicle you'll pay a high deductible. A mid-sized rental runs between $40 and $60 per day; a 4WD vehicle costs – brace yourself – $110 to $140 per day, all not including taxes and fees.

If you're under 21, your only option is **Affordable Rent-A-Car** (☎ 329-7766; www.bigisland autorental.com; 74-5543 Kaiwi St, Kailua-Kona) but prices are steep at $65 per day for drivers between ages 18 and 21. The agency requires pick up and drop off in Kailua-Kona.

Road Conditions & Hazards
Drivers under the influence of alcohol, marijuana or 'ice' (crystal methamphetamine) are a hazard, no matter if it's 11am or 11pm. The crime of driving while intoxicated (DWI) is legally defined as having a blood alcohol level of greater than 0.08%.

Sections of roads and bridges can be washed out after significant rainfall. Particularly prone areas include the Ka'u bridges during heavy downpours and the Hilo bayfront area. The Hamakua Coast might experience landslides near gulches, and on rare occasions Hwy 190 is closed between Waimea and Waikoloa Rd due to flooding. The most useful driving maps are the *Ready Mapbook* series (p231).

Stay alert for one-lane-bridge crossings: one direction of traffic usually has the right of way while the other must obey the posted yield sign. Downhill traffic must yield to uphill traffic where there is no sign.

Driving off-road or on 4WD-only roads like Saddle Rd is not for the faint of heart. Conditions are hazardous and in remote areas, you'll be miles from any help. If you have never driven a 4WD vehicle, don't do your trial run here.

Street addresses on major roads in west Hawai'i might seem unnecessarily long and complex, but there's a pattern. If you see hyphenated numbers, such as 75-2345 Kuakini Hwy, here's why: the first part of the number identifies the district breakdown that the post office uses; the second part identifies the street address within that district. The numbers get larger as you travel north to south along the Kona Coast.

One confusing aspect of Big Island driving is the use of common names for highways – and the way the same highway can have multiple common names, depending on the location. For example:

Hwy 11	Hawai'i Belt Rd (from Hilo to Miloli'i), Mamalahoa Hwy (from Miloli'i to Honalo), Kuakini Hwy (from Honalo to Kailua-Kona)
Hwy 19	Hawai'i Belt Rd (from Hilo to Waimea), Kawaihae Rd (from Waimea to Kawaihae), Queen Ka'ahumanu Hwy (from Kawaihae to Kailua-Kona)
Hwy 137	Red Rd
Hwy 190	Mamalahoa Hwy
Hwy 200	Saddle Rd
Hwy 250	Kohala Mountain Rd
Hwy 270	Akoni Pule Hwy

Road Rules

As in the mainland USA, drivers keep to the right-hand side of the road. On unpaved or poorly paved roads, however, locals tend to hog the middle stripe until an oncoming car approaches.

Drivers at a red light can turn right after coming to a full stop and yielding to on-coming traffic, unless there's a sign at the intersection prohibiting the turn. Island drivers usually just wait for the next green light.

Locals will tell you there are three golden rules for driving on the islands: don't honk your horn, don't follow too closely and let faster drivers pass whenever it's safe to do so. Play by the rules and drivers express their *mahalo* (thanks) by waving the *shaka* (local hand greeting) sign. Horn honking is considered rude unless absolutely necessary for safety (or for urging complacent cattle off the road).

Hawaii requires the use of seat belts for drivers and front-seat passengers. Heed this, as the penalty is stiff. State law also strictly requires the use of child-safety seats for children aged three and under, while four-year-olds must either be in a safety seat or secured by a seat belt. Most car-rental companies lease child-safety seats for around $5 a day, but they don't always have them on hand; reserve one in advance if you can.

Speed limits are posted *and* enforced. If you're stopped for speeding, expect a ticket, as the police rarely give only warnings. Most accidents are caused by excessive speed.

HITCHHIKING

Hitchhiking, though technically illegal state-wide, is not unusual (and cops have more important matters at hand). It can be an efficient, cheap way to get around, especially along well-trafficked highways, such as Hwy 11 from Hilo to Hawai'i Volcanoes National Park. Also, if you drive up to the Onizuka Visitor Information Station on Mauna Kea (p139) and need a ride to the summit, you might snag a ride from a fellow visitor or even a tour group.

That said, hitchhiking is risky anywhere in the world. Hitchhikers should size up each situation carefully before getting in cars, and women should be especially wary of hitching alone. If you do hitchhike, travel in pairs and let someone know where you plan to go.

TAXI

Locals rarely use taxicabs so you'll find them mainly in Kailua-Kona and Hilo. Fares are based on mileage regardless of the number of passengers. Since cabs are often station wagons or minivans, they're good value for groups (and strongly recommended if the designated driver joins in the partying). The standard flag-down fee is $2, plus $2 per mile thereafter. On the Big Island, cab drivers are typically locals who are familiar with the island and often act as tour guides. It's easy to find a cab at either airport during normal business hours, but cabs don't run all night or cruise for passengers; in town (and at most hotels) you'll need to call ahead. Pick-ups from remote locations (eg after long through-hikes) can be arranged by calling, and possibly paying, in advance.

See Kailua-Kona (p85) and Hilo (p179) for recommended cab companies.

Health

Hawai'i, the Big Island, encompasses an extraordinary range of climates and terrains, from the freezing heights of volcanic summits to tropical rain forests. Because of the high level of hygiene here, infectious diseases will not be a significant concern for most travelers.

BEFORE YOU GO

INSURANCE

The USA offers possibly the finest health care in the world. The problem is that, unless you have good insurance, it can be prohibitively expensive. It's essential to purchase travel health insurance if your regular policy doesn't cover you when you're abroad.

Bring any medications you may need in their original containers, clearly labeled. A signed, dated letter from your physician that describes all medical conditions and medications, including generic names, is also a good idea.

If your health insurance does not cover you for medical expenses abroad, consider supplemental insurance. Find out in advance if your insurance plan will make payments directly to providers or reimburse you later for overseas health expenditures.

INTERNET RESOURCES

There is a wealth of travel health advice on the Internet. The World Health Organization publishes a superb book, *International Travel and Health,* which is revised annually and is available online free at www.who.int/ith. Another website of interest is MD Travel Health at www.mdtravelhealth.com, which provides complete travel health recommendations for every country, updated daily, also at no cost.

It's usually a good idea to consult your government's travel-health website before departure, if one is available:

Australia (www.smartraveller.gov.au)
Canada (www.hc-sc.gc.ca/english/index.html)
UK (www.dh.gov.uk/PolicyAndGuidance/HealthAdviceFor Travellers/fs/en)
USA (www.cdc.gov/travel)

IN HAWAII

AVAILABILITY & COST OF HEALTH CARE

For immediate medical assistance, call ☎ 911. In general, if you have a medical emergency, the best bet is to find the nearest hospital and go to its emergency room. If the problem isn't urgent, you can call a nearby hospital and ask for a referral to a local physician, which is usually much cheaper than a trip to the ER. On the Big Island the nearest hospital could be a fair distance away, so the best choice may be an expensive stand-alone, for-profit urgent-care center. Keep in mind that medical helicopter evacuation may not always be possible from remote areas. Major hospitals are found in Hilo (p162) and South Kona (p93). Medical services are also available at Waimea's North Hawaii Community Hospital (p130) and Hualalai Urgent Care Clinic in Kailua (p70).

Pharmacies are abundantly supplied, but you may find that some medications that are available over-the-counter in your home country require a prescription in the USA, and, as always, if you don't have insurance to cover the cost of prescriptions, they can be shockingly expensive.

INFECTIOUS DISEASES

In addition to the more common ailments, there are several infectious diseases that are unknown or uncommon outside of the mainland. Most are acquired by mosquito or tick bites, or environmental exposure. Currently Hawaii is rabies-free.

Dengue Fever

Dengue is transmitted by aedes mosquitoes, which bite preferentially during the daytime and are usually found close to human habitations, often indoors. They breed primarily in artificial water containers such as jars, barrels, cans, cisterns, metal drums, plastic containers and discarded tires. As a result, dengue is especially common in densely populated, urban environments. In Hawaii the last outbreak of this mosquito-borne disease was in 2002, with no cases on the Big Island. For updates, check the **Hawai'i State Department of Health website** (www.state.hi.us/doh).

Dengue usually causes flu-like symptoms, including fever, muscle aches, joint pains, headaches, nausea and vomiting, often followed by a rash. There is no treatment for dengue fever except to take analgesics such as acetaminophen/paracetamol (eg Tylenol) – don't take aspirin as it increases the likelihood of hemorrhaging – and drink lots of fluids. See a doctor to be diagnosed and monitored. Severe cases may require hospitalization for intravenous fluids and supportive care. There is no vaccine. The best prevention is insect protection measures.

Giardiasis

This parasitic infection of the small intestine occurs throughout the world. Symptoms may include nausea, bloating, cramps and diarrhea, and may last for weeks. To protect yourself, you should avoid drinking directly from waterfalls, ponds, streams and rivers, which may be contaminated by animal or human feces. The infection can also be transmitted from person to person if proper hand washing is not done. Giardiasis is easily diagnosed by a stool test and readily treated with antibiotics.

Leptospirosis

Leptospirosis is acquired by exposure to water contaminated by the urine of infected animals such as rats, mongooses and feral pigs. Outbreaks often occur during floods, when sudden overflow may contaminate water sources downstream from animal habitats. Even an idyllic waterfall may be infected with leptospirosis. The initial symptoms, which resemble a mild flu, usually subside uneventfully in a few days, but a minority of cases are complicated by jaundice or meningitis. It can also cause hepatitis and renal failure, which might be fatal. Diagnosis is through blood tests and the disease is easily treated with doxycycline. There is no vaccine. You can minimize your risk by staying out of bodies of fresh water (eg waterfalls, pools, streams) that may be contaminated, especially if you have any open cuts or sores. Because hikers account for many of the cases of leptospirosis in Hawaii, the state posts warning signs at trailheads. If you're camping, water purification is essential.

West Nile Virus

These infections were unknown in the USA until a few years ago, but have now been reported in almost every state. Humans in Hawaii have not been affected so far, but the rising number of reported cases in California is cause for concern. The virus is transmitted by culex mosquitoes, which are active in late summer and early fall and

---

RECOMMENDED VACCINATIONS

No special vaccines are required or recommended for travel to the USA. All travelers should be up-to-date on routine immunizations, listed below.

vaccine	recommended for	dosage	side effects
tetanus-diphtheria	all travelers who haven't had a booster within 10 years	one dose lasts 10 years	soreness at injection site
measles	travelers born after 1956 who've had only one measles vaccination	one dose	fever; rash; joint pains; allergic reactions
chicken pox	travelers who've never had chicken pox	two doses a month apart	fever; mild case of chicken pox
influenza	all travelers during flu season (Nov-Mar)	one dose	soreness at the injection site; fever

generally bite after dusk (see p246). Most infections are mild or asymptomatic, but the virus may infect the central nervous system, leading to fever, headache, confusion, lethargy, coma and sometimes death. There is no treatment for West Nile virus.

For the latest update on the areas affected by West Nile, go to the **US Geological Survey website** (http://westnilemaps.usgs.gov).

ENVIRONMENTAL HAZARDS
Altitude Sickness

Acute Mountain Sickness (AMS), aka 'altitude sickness,' may develop in those who ascend rapidly to altitudes greater than 7500ft, as on Mauna Kea and Mauna Loa. Being physically fit offers no protection. Those who have experienced AMS in the past are prone to future episodes. The risk increases with faster ascents, higher altitudes and greater exertion. Symptoms may include headaches, nausea, vomiting, dizziness, malaise, insomnia and loss of appetite. Severe cases may be further complicated by fluid in the lungs (high-altitude pulmonary edema) or swelling of the brain (high-altitude cerebral edema).

The best treatment for AMS is descent. If you are exhibiting symptoms, do not ascend. If symptoms are severe or persistent, descend immediately. When traveling to high altitudes, it's also important to avoid overexertion, eat light meals and abstain from alcohol. If your symptoms are more than mild or don't resolve promptly, see a doctor. Altitude sickness should be taken seriously; it can be life-threatening when severe.

Bites & Stings

The Big Island has no established snake population in the wild.

Leeches are found in humid rain-forest areas. They do not transmit any disease but their bites are often intensely itchy for weeks afterwards and can easily become infected. Apply an iodine-based antiseptic to any leech bite to help prevent infection.

Bee and wasp stings mainly cause problems for people who are allergic to them. Anyone with a serious bee or wasp allergy should carry an injection of adrenaline for emergency treatment. For others pain is the main problem – apply ice to the sting and take painkillers.

Commonsense approaches to these concerns are the most effective: wear long

---

MEDICAL CHECKLIST

- acetaminophen (eg Tylenol) or aspirin
- anti-inflammatory drugs (eg ibuprofen)
- antihistamines (for hay fever and allergic reactions)
- antibacterial ointment (eg Neosporin) for cuts and abrasions
- steroid cream or cortisone (for poison ivy and other allergic rashes)
- bandages, gauze, gauze rolls
- adhesive or paper tape
- scissors, safety pins, tweezers
- thermometer
- pocket knife
- DEET-containing insect repellent for the skin
- permethrin-containing insect spray for clothing, tents and bed nets
- sun block

---

sleeves and pants, hats and shoes (rather than sandals) to protect yourself.

MAMMAL BITES

Do not attempt to pet, handle or feed any animal, with the exception of domestic animals known to be free of any infectious disease. Most animal injuries are directly related to a person's attempt to touch or feed the animal.

Any bite or scratch by a mammal, including bats or feral pigs, goats etc, should be promptly and thoroughly cleansed with soap and water, followed by application of an antiseptic such as iodine or alcohol. It may also be advisable to start an antibiotic, since wounds caused by animal bites and scratches frequently become infected.

MARINE ANIMALS

Marine spikes, such as those found on sea urchins, scorpion fish and Hawaiian lionfish, can cause severe local pain. If this occurs, immediately immerse the affected area in hot water (as high a temperature as can be tolerated). Keep topping up with hot water until the pain subsides and medical care can be reached. The same advice applies if you are stung by a cone shell.

HEALTH

Marine stings from jellyfish and Portuguese man-of-war (aka 'bluebottles,' which have translucent, bluish, bladder-like floats) also occur. Even touching a bluebottle a few hours after it's washed up onshore can result in burning stings. Jellyfish are often seen eight to 10 days after a full moon when they float into shallow waters; the influx usually lasts for three days. If you are stung, first aid consists of washing the skin with vinegar to prevent further discharge of remaining stinging cells, followed by rapid transfer to a hospital; antivenoms are widely available.

Despite extensive media coverage, the risk of shark attack in Hawaiian waters is no greater than in other countries with extensive coastlines. Avoid swimming in waters with runoff after heavy rainfall (eg around river mouths) and those areas frequented by commercial fishing operators. Do not swim if you are actively bleeding, as this attracts sharks. Check with lifeguards about local risks. Keep in mind that your chances of being hit by a falling coconut on the beach are greater than those of a shark attack, though!

MOSQUITO BITES

When traveling in areas where West Nile or other mosquito-borne illnesses have been reported, keep yourself covered and apply a good insect repellent, preferably one containing DEET, to exposed skin and clothing. In general, adults and children over 12 should use preparations containing 25% to 35% DEET, which usually lasts about six hours. Children between two and 12 years of age should use preparations containing no more than 10% DEET, applied sparingly, which will usually last about three hours. Neurologic toxicity has been reported from DEET, especially in children, but appears to be extremely uncommon and generally related to overuse. DEET-containing compounds should not be used on children under age two.

Insect repellents containing certain botanical products, including oil of eucalyptus and soybean oil, are effective but last only 1½ to two hours. Products based on citronella are not effective.

Visit the **Center for Disease Control's website** (CDC; www.cdc.gov/ncidod/dvbid/westnile/qa/prevention .htm) for prevention information.

SPIDER BITES

Although there are many species of spiders in the USA, the only ones that cause significant human illness are the black widow, brown recluse and hobo spiders. It is a matter of debate which of these species are conclusively found in Hawaii. The black widow is black or brown in color, measuring about 15mm in body length, with a shiny top, fat body, and distinctive red or orange hourglass figure on its underside. It's found usually in woodpiles, sheds, harvested crops and bowls of outdoor toilets. The brown recluse spider is brown in color, usually 10mm in body length, with a dark violin-shaped mark on the top of the upper section of the body. It is active mostly at night, lives in dark sheltered areas such as under porches and in woodpiles, and typically bites when trapped. The symptoms of a hobo-spider bite are similar to those of a brown recluse, but milder.

If bitten by a black widow, you should apply ice or cold packs and go immediately to the nearest emergency room. Complications of a black widow bite may include muscle spasms, breathing difficulties and high blood pressure. The bite of a brown recluse or hobo spider typically causes a large, inflamed wound, sometimes associated with fever and chills. If bitten, apply ice and see a physician.

Cold

Cold exposure may be a problem in certain areas. To prevent hypothermia, keep all body surfaces covered, including the head and neck. Synthetic materials such as Gore-Tex and Thinsulate provide excellent insulation. Because the body loses heat faster when wet, stay dry at all times. Change inner garments promptly when they become moist. Keep active, but get enough rest. Consume plenty of food and water. Be especially sure not to have any alcohol. Caffeine and tobacco should also be avoided.

Watch out for the 'umbles' – stumbles, mumbles, fumbles, and grumbles – which are important signs of impending hypothermia. If someone appears to be developing hypothermia, you should insulate them from the ground, protect them from the wind, remove wet clothing or cover with a vapor barrier such as a plastic bag, and transport them immediately to a warm environment and a medical facility. Warm fluids (but not coffee or nonherbal tea) may be given if the person is alert enough to swallow.

Diving & Snorkeling Hazards

Divers, snorkelers and surfers should seek specialized advice before they travel to ensure their medical kit contains treatment for coral cuts and tropical ear infections, as well as the standard problems. Divers should ensure their insurance covers them for decompression illness – get specialized dive insurance through an organization such as **Divers Alert Network** (DAN; www.diversalertnetwork .org). Have a dive medical before you leave your home country – there are certain medical conditions that are incompatible with diving that your dive operator may not always ask you about.

See p50 for general advice on ocean safety.

Heat

Travelers should drink plenty of fluids and avoid strenuous exercise when the temperature is high.

Dehydration is the main contributor to heat exhaustion. Symptoms include feeling weak, headache, irritability, nausea or vomiting, sweaty skin, a fast, weak pulse and a normal or slightly elevated body temperature. Treatment involves getting out of the heat and/or sun, fanning the victim and applying cool wet cloths to the skin, laying the victim flat with their legs raised and rehydrating with water containing one-quarter of a teaspoon of salt per liter. Recovery is usually rapid and it is common to feel weak for some days afterwards.

Heatstroke is a serious medical emergency. Symptoms come on suddenly and include weakness, nausea, a hot, dry body with a body temperature of over 106°F, dizziness, confusion, loss of coordination, fits and eventually collapse and loss of consciousness. Seek medical help and commence cooling by getting the person out of the heat, removing their clothes, fanning them and applying cool, wet cloths or ice to their body, especially to the groin and armpits.

Vog

Volcanic smog, known as 'vog,' is a visible haze composed of sulphur dioxide gas and a mixture of tiny liquid and solid aerosol particles emitted from active volcanoes. When dispersed by tradewinds, vog is not generally hazardous. But occasionally when it hangs over the island, it can create severe breathing problems for those with respiratory ailments.

Vog is typically worst in Kona because tradewinds from the northeast blow gases from Kilauea's Pu'u 'O'o vent toward Kona, then offshore across the ocean. But when the tradewinds subside and 'Kona winds' from the south take charge, vog drifts toward Volcano Village and Hilo instead.

To check on current vog conditions for Kona, call the **State Department of Health's Vog Index Hotline** (☎ 885-7143) for a recording rating of 0 (best) to 10 (worst).

HEALTH

Language

Hawaii has two official state languages: English and Hawaiian. Although English has long replaced Hawaiian as the dominant language, many Hawaiian words and phrases are commonly used in speech and in print.

Prior to the arrival of Christian missionaries in 1820, the Hawaiians had no written language. Knowledge was passed on through complex oral genealogies, stories, chants, songs and descriptive place names. The missionaries rendered the spoken language into the Roman alphabet and established the first presses in the islands, which were used to print the Bible and other religious instructional materials in Hawaiian.

Throughout the 19th century, as more and more foreigners (particularly the Americans and the British) settled in the islands, the everyday use of Hawaiian declined. In the 1890s, English was made the official language of government and education.

The push for statehood, from 1900 to 1959, added to the decline of the Hawaiian language. Speaking Hawaiian was seen as a deterrent to American assimilation, thus adult native speakers were strongly discouraged from teaching their children Hawaiian as the primary language in the home.

This attitude remained until the early 1970s when the Hawaiian community began to experience a cultural renaissance. A handful of young Hawaiians lobbied to establish Hawaiian language classes at the University of Hawai'i, and Hawaiian language immersion preschools followed in the 1980s. These preschools are modeled after Maori *kohanga reo* (language nests), where the primary method of language perpetuation is through speaking and hearing the language on a daily basis. In Hawaii's 'Aha Punana Leo preschools, all learning and communication takes place in the mother tongue – *ka 'olelo makuahine*.

Hawaiian has now been revived from the point of extinction and is growing throughout the community. Record numbers of students enroll in Hawaiian language classes in high schools and colleges, and immersion school graduates are raising a new generation of native speakers.

If you'd like to discover more about the Hawaiian language, get a copy of Lonely Planet's *South Pacific Phrasebook*.

PRONUNCIATION

Written Hawaiian has just thirteen letters: five vowels (**a, e, i, o, u**) and seven consonants (**h, k, l, m, n, p, w**). The letters **h, l, m** and **n** are pronounced much the same as in English. Usually every letter in Hawaiian words is pronounced. Each vowel has a different pronunciation depending on whether it is stressed or unstressed.

Consonants

p/k	similar to English, but with less aspiration; **k** may be replaced with **t**
w	after **i** and **e**, usually a soft English 'v;' thus the town of Hale'iwa is pronounced 'Haleiva,' After **u** or **o** it's often like English 'w,' thus Olowalu is pronounced as written. After **a** or at the beginning of a word it can be as English 'w' or 'v,' thus you'll hear both Hawai'i and Havai'i (The Big Island).

Unstressed vowels (without macron)

a	as in 'ago'
e	as in 'bet'
i	as the 'y' in 'city'
o	as in 'sole'
u	as in 'rude'

Glottal Stops & Macrons

Written Hawaiian uses both glottal stops ('), called *'okina*, and macrons (a straight bar above a vowel, eg **ā**), called *kahako*. In modern print both the glottal stop and the macron are often omitted. In this guidebook, the macrons have been omitted, but glottal stops have been included, as they can be helpful in striving to pronounce common place names and words correctly.

The glottal stop indicates a break between two vowels, producing an effect similar to saying 'oh-oh' in English. For example, *'a'a*, a type of lava, is pronounced 'ah-ah,' and Ho'okena, a place name, is pronounced 'Ho-oh-kena.' A macron inidicates that the vowel is stressed and has a long pronunciation.

Glottal stops and macrons not only affect pronunciation, but can give a word a completely different meaning. For example, *ai* (with no glottal) means 'sexual intercourse,' but *'ai* (with the glottal) means 'food.' Similarly, the word *ka'a* (with no macron over the second **a**) means 'to roll, turn or twist,' but *ka'ā* (with a macron over the second **a**) is a thread or line, used in fishing.

Compound Words

In the written form, many Hawaiian words are compound words made up of several different words. For example, the word *humuhumunukunukuapua'a* can be broken down as follows: *humuhumu-nukunuku-a-pua'a* (literally, trigger fish snout of pig), meaning 'the fish with a snout like a pig.' The place name Waikiki is also a compound word: *wai-kiki* (literally, freshwater sprouting), referring to the freshwater swamps once found in the area. Some words are doubled to emphasize their meaning, much like in English. For example, *wiki* means 'quick,' while *wikiwiki* means 'very quick.'

Common Hawaiian Words

For more Hawaiian words, see the Glossary on p548.

aloha – love, hello, welcome, goodbye
hale – house
heiau – religious temple
kane – man
kapu – taboo, restricted
lu'au – traditional Hawaiian feast
mahalo – thank you
mahimahi – dolphin fish, popular in restaurants
mauka – a directional, toward the mountains
makai – a directional, toward the sea
'ono – delicious, tasty
pau – finished, completed
poi – staple food made from taro
'ukulele – four-stringed musical instrument, used in modern Hawaiian music (literally, 'leaping flea,' because of the action of the fingers when playing)
wahine – woman

PIDGIN

Hawaii pidgin is a distinct language, spoken by over 500,000 people. It developed on sugar plantations where the *luna* (foreman) had to communicate with field laborers from many foreign countries. Early plantation pidgin used a very minimal and condensed form of English as the root language, to which elements from Cantonese, Hawaiian and Portuguese were added. It became the second language of first-generation immigrants and many Hawaiians.

As this English-based pidgin evolved, it took on its own grammatical structure and syntax. Many words were pronounced differently and combined in ways not found in English. Rather than a careless or broken form of English, it evolved into a separate language, called Hawaii Creole by linguists.

Today, there is some ongoing controversy about the validity of pidgin, with opponents saying that it erodes standard English and becomes a barrier to social and educational advancement. Proponents argue that pidgin is a rich and vibrant language that should not be looked down upon or banned from schools, and that pidgin speakers are often unjustly seen as less intelligent.

In recent years there have been many award-winning plays, books and poetry written in pidgin by local authors who are passionate in their determination to keep pidgin alive in the community.

Common Pidgin Words & Phrases

brah – shortened form of *bradah* (brother); also used as 'hey you'
broke da mout – delicious, as in 'My auntie make broke da mout kine fish!'
buggahs – guys, as in 'Da buggahs went to without me!'
bumbye – later on, as in 'We go movies bumbye den (then).'
bummahs – bummer; an expression of disappointment or regret
chicken skin – goose bumps
cockaroach – to steal, as in 'Who went cockaroach my slippahs?'
da kine – whatchamacallit; used whenever you can't think of the word you want
Fo' real? – Really? Are you kidding me?
funny kine – strange or different, as in 'He stay acking (acting) all funny kine.'
geev 'um – Go for it! Give it all you got!
Howzit? – Hi, how's it going? As in 'Eh, howzit brah?'
How you stay? – How are you doing these days?
kay den – 'OK then,' as in 'Kay den, we go beach.'
laydahs – Later on. I'll see you later, as in, 'Kay den, laydahs.'
no ack – (Literally, 'no act.') Stop showing off, cool it.
rubbah slippahs – (rubber) thongs, flip-flops
talk story – any kind of casual conversation
to da max – a suffix that adds emphasis to something, as in 'Da waves was big to da max!'

Glossary

'a'a – type of lava that is rough and jagged, and flows slowly

azuki bean – used as a sweetened paste in Japanese desserts; also added as a topping to shave ice

'ahi – yellowfin tuna

'ahinahina – silversword plant with pointed silver leaves

ahu – stone cairns used to mark a trail; or an altar or shrine

ahupua'a – traditional land division, usually in a wedge shape that extends from the mountains to the sea

aikane – friend; also refers to homosexuality

'aina – land

'akala – Hawaiian raspberry; also called a thimbleberry

akamai – clever

'akepa – endangered honeycreeper

aku – bonito (skipjack tuna)

akua – god, spirit, idol

'alae ke'oke'o – endangered Hawaiian coot

alaia – shorter, stand-up surfboard

'alala – Hawaiian crow

ali'i – chief, royalty

aloha – the traditional greeting meaning love, welcome, good-bye

aloha 'aina – love of the land

'ama'ama – mullet

'amakihi – small, yellow-green bird; one of the more common native birds

anchialine pool – contains a mixture of seawater and fresh water

'a'o – Newell's shearwater (a seabird)

'apapane – bright-red native Hawaiian honeycreeper

a'u – swordfish, marlin

'aumakua – protective deity; deified ancestor

awa – milkfish

'awa – kava, a native plant, *Piper methysticum,* from the pepper family, used to make a mildly narcotic drink

'awapuhi – wild ginger

crack seed – Chinese preserved fruit; a salty, sweet or sour snack

'elepaio – a brownish native bird with a white rump, found in the understory of native forests

goza – roll-up straw mat used at beaches and parks

grinds – food; *'ono kine grinds* is good food

hala – pandanus tree; the *lau* (leaves) are used in weaving mats and baskets

hale – house

hana – work; a bay, when used as a compound in place names

haole – Caucasian; literally, 'without breath'

hapa – portion or fragment; person of mixed blood

hau – indigenous lowland hibiscus tree whose wood is often used for making canoe outriggers (stabilizing arms that jut out from the hull)

haupia – coconut pudding

Hawai'i nei – all the Hawaiian Islands taken as a group; indicates affection (ie 'beloved' or 'cherished' Hawai'i)

he'e – octopus; also called *tako* in Japanese

he'e nalu – surfing (literally, 'wave sliding')

heiau – ancient stone temple, a place of worship in Hawaii

Hina – Polynesian goddess (wife of Ku, one of the four main gods)

hoaloha – friend

holoholo – to walk, drive or ramble around for pleasure

holua – sled or sled course

honu – turtle

honu'ea – hawksbill sea turtle

ho'olaule'a – celebration, party

ho'onanea – to pass the time in ease, peace and pleasure

huhu – angry

hui – group, organization

hukilau – fishing with a seine (a large net), involving a group of people who pull in the net

hula – Hawaiian dance form, either traditional or modern

hula 'auana, hula 'auwana – modern hula, developed after the introduction of Western music

hula kahiko – traditional (ancient) hula

hula halau – hula school or troupe

hula ohelo – hula style in which some of the dancer's motions imitate sexual intercourse

humuhumunukunukuapua'a – triggerfish; Hawaii's unofficial state fish

'i'iwi – a bright-orange Hawaiian honeycreeper with a curved, salmon-colored beak

'iliahi – Hawaiian sandalwood

'ili'ili – smooth pebbles

'ilima – native coastal plant, a ground cover with delicate yellow-orange flowers

imu – underground earthen oven used to cook *kalua* pig and other luau food

'io – Hawaiian hawk

issei – first-generation Japanese immigrants

kahili – a feathered standard, used as a symbol of royalty

kahuna – knowledgeable person in any field; commonly a priest, healer or sorcerer

kahuna nui – high priest

kaiseki ryōri – Japanese multicourse chef's tasting menu

kaku – barracuda
kalo – a plant with green, heart-shaped leaves; cultivated in Hawaii for its edible rootstock, which is mashed to make poi (*taro* in Tahitian)
kalua – traditional method of baking in an underground pit
kama'aina – person born and raised in Hawaii; literally, 'child of the land'
kanaka – man, human being, person; also native Hawaiian
Kanaloa – god of the underworld
kane/Kane – man; also the name of one of four main Hawaiian gods
kapa – cloth made by pounding the inner bark of the paper mulberry tree, used for early Hawaiian clothing (*tapa* in Tahitian)
kapu – taboo, part of strict ancient Hawaiian social and religious system
kaukau – food
kaukau wagon – lunch wagon
kauna'oa – a parasitic groundcover vine with yellow-orange tendrils; used to make lei
kava – see *'awa*
keiki – child, offspring
ki – common native plant; its long shiny leaves are used for wrapping food and making hula skirts; commonly called *ti*
kiawe – Algoraba tree, a relative of the mesquite tree introduced to Hawaii in the 1820s, now very common; its branches are covered with sharp thorns
ki'i – image, statue (often of a deity)
kiko'o – longer, stand-up surfboard
kilau – a stiff, weedy fern
kioe – small surfboard, belly board (2-4ft long)
kipuka – an area of land spared when lava flows around it; an oasis
ko – sugarcane
koa – native hardwood tree often used in making furniture, bowls and canoes
ko'a – fishing shrine
kohola – whale
koi – brightly colored, ornamental Japanese carp
koki'o ke'oke'o – native Hawaiian white hibiscus tree
kokua – help, cooperation
kona – leeward side; a leeward wind
konane – a strategy game similar to checkers
ko'olau – windward side
Ku – Polynesian god of many manifestations, including god of war, farming and fishing (husband of Hina)
kukui – candlenut tree and the official state tree; its oily nuts were once burned in lamps
kupuna – grandparent, elder
ku'ula – a stone idol placed at fishing shrines, believed to attract fish

Laka – goddess of the hula
lama – native plant in the persimmon family
lanai – veranda

lau – leaf
lauhala – leaves of the *hala* plant used in weaving
laulau – a bundle made of pork or chicken and salted butterfish, wrapped in taro and *ti* leaves and steamed
lei – garland, usually of flowers, but also of leaves or shells
li hing mui – sweet-sour crack seed
liliko'i – passionfruit
limu – seaweed (*ogo* in Japanese)
loco moco – dish of rice topped with a hamburger, a fried egg and gravy
lo'i – irrigated terrace, usually for *kalo* (taro)
loko i'a – fish pond
lolo – feeble-minded, crazy
lomi – to rub, soften, press or squeeze
lomilomi – traditional Hawaiian massage
Lono – Polynesian god of harvest, agriculture, fertility and peace
loulu – all species of native fan palms
luakini – a type of *heiau* (temple) dedicated to the war god Ku and used for human sacrifices
luau – traditional Hawaiian feast; modern term, formerly called *'aha'aina*

mahalo – thank you
mahele – to divide; usually refers to the Western-influenced land divisions of 1848
mahimahi – also called 'dolphin,' but actually a type of fish unrelated to the marine mammal
mai'a – banana
ma'i ho'oka'awale – leprosy; literally, 'the separating sickness'
maile – native plant with twining habit and fragrant sap; often used to make lei
mai tai – alcoholic drink made from rum, grenadine, and lemon and pineapple juices
maka'ainana – commoners; literally, 'people who tend the land'
makaha – a sluice gate, used to regulate the level of water in a fish pond
makahiki – traditional annual wet-season winter festival dedicated to the agricultural god Lono
makai – toward the sea
malama 'aina – to take care of the islands' natural resources
malihini – newcomer, visitor
malo – loincloth
mamane – a native tree with bright yellow flowers; used to make lei
mana – spiritual power
manini – convict tang (a reef fish); also used to refer to something small or insignificant, or someone who is stingy
mano – shark
mauka – toward the mountains; inland
mele – song, chant

menehune – the 'little people' who built many of Hawaii's fishponds, heiau and other stonework, according to legend
milo – a native shade tree with beautiful hardwood
moa pahe'e – a game, similar to 'ulu maika, using wooden darts and spears
mokihana – an endemic tree or shrub, with scented green berries used to make lei
mo'o – serpent, dragon, lizard, reptile
mu – a 'body catcher' who secured sacrificial victims for the heiau altar
mu'umu'u – a long, loose-fitting dress introduced by the missionaries

naupaka – a native shrub with delicate white flowers
Neighbor Islands – the term used to refer to the main Hawaiian Islands other than O'ahu
nene – a native goose; Hawaii's state bird
nisei – second-generation Japanese immigrants
niu – coconut palm
noni – Indian mulberry; a small tree with yellow, smelly fruit that is used medicinally
nui – large, great, many, much; aloha nui loa means very much aloha
nuku pu'u – a native honeycreeper with a bright yellow-green underbelly

ogo – Japanese for seaweed (limu in Hawaiian)
'ohana – family, extended family
'ohi'a lehua – native Hawaiian tree with tufted, feathery, pom-pom-like flowers
'ohelo – low-growing native shrub with edible red berries related to cranberries; said to be sacred to the goddess Pele
'okole – buttocks
olo – traditional longer, wooden surfboard
onaga – mild-tasting red snapper
one hanau – birthplace, homeland
'ono – delicious
ono – wahoo fish
'ono kine grinds – good food
'opae – shrimp
'opakapaka – blue snapper
'opelu – pan-sized mackerel scad
'opihi – edible limpet

pahoehoe – type of lava that is smooth and undulating, and flows quickly
pakalolo – marijuana; literally, 'crazy tobacco'
palaka – Hawaiian-style plaid shirt made from sturdy cotton
pali – cliff
palila – endemic honeycreeper
paniolo – cowboy
pau – finished, no more
Pele – goddess of volcanoes; her home is Halema'uma'u Crater in Kilauea Caldera

pad thai – rice noodles stir-fried with tofu, vegetables, egg and peanuts
pho – a Vietnamese soup of beef broth, noodles and fresh herbs
piko – navel, umbilical cord
pili – a bunchgrass, commonly used for thatching houses
pilo – native shrub in the coffee family
pipi kaula – salted, dried beef that is served broiled; Hawaiian-style beef jerky
pohaku – rock
pohuehue – morning glory
poi – staple Hawaiian starch made of steamed, mashed taro
poka – member of the passionfruit family; also banana poka
poke – cubed raw fish mixed with shoyu, sesame oil, salt, chili pepper, inamona (kukui nut relish) and other condiments
Poliahu – goddess of snow
po'ouli – endangered endemic honeycreeper
pua aloalo – a hibiscus flower
pueo – Hawaiian owl
puhi – eel
pu'ili – bamboo sticks used in hula performances
puka – any kind of hole or opening; small shells that are made into necklaces
pukiawe – native plant with red and white berries and evergreen leaves; used to make lei
pulu – golden, silky 'hair' found at the base of hapu'u (tree fern) fiddlehead stems
pupu – snack food, hors d'oeuvres; also Hawaiian word for shell
pu'u – hill, cinder cone
pu'uhonua – place of refuge

raku – a style of Japanese pottery characterized by a rough, handmade appearance

saimin – a Hawaiian version of Japanese noodle soup
sansei – third-generation Japanese immigrants
shaka – hand gesture used in Hawaii as a greeting or sign of local pride
shoyu – soy sauce
soba – buckwheat noodles

tabi – Japanese reef-walking shoes
talk story – to strike up a conversation, make small talk
tapa – see kapa
taro – see kalo
teppanyaki – Japanese style of cooking with an iron grill
ti – see ki
tiki – see ki'i
tutu – grandmother or grandfather; also term of respect for any member of that generation

'uala – sweet potato
'ua'u – dark-rumped petrel, an endangered sea bird
ukulele – a stringed musical instrument derived from the *braguinha*, which was introduced to Hawaii in the late 19th century by Portuguese immigrants
'ulu – breadfruit
'ulu maika – ancient Hawaiian bowling game using stones

unagi – eel
wahine – woman
wikiwiki – hurry, quick
wiliwili – the lightest of the native woods, balsa-like

zazen – Zen meditation
zendo – communal Zen meditation hall

Behind the Scenes

THIS BOOK

This 2nd edition of *Hawai'i the Big Island* was written by coordinating author Luci Yamamoto and assisting author Alan Tarbell. Luci wrote almost all of the front and back chapters, except for Itineraries (co-written with Alan) and Hawai'i Outdoors (sole author Alan Tarbell). Nanette Napoleon wrote the History and Language chapters. Dr Scott Rowland (The Land) and Samuel M 'Ohukani'ōhi'a Gon III (Wildlife, Environmental Issues) co-wrote the Environment chapter, which was coordinated by Luci Yamamoto (chapter introduction and National, State & County Parks section). The Health chapter was based upon text written by Dr David Goldberg. Some text and maps for this title were updated and adapted from: *Hawaii 7* by Kim Grant (coordinating author), Ned Friary & Glenda Bendure (Maui and Lana'i chapters) and Conner Gorry (Moloka'i chapter), as well as *Hiking in Hawaii 1* by Sara Benson and Jennifer Snarski. Conner Gorry and Julie Jares wrote the previous edition of this book.

THANKS FROM THE AUTHORS

LUCI YAMAMOTO

Mahalo nui loa to my commissioning editor Sam Benson for giving me an invaluable gift: to be local again. Bobby Camara deserves my highest gratitude for being an expert source on the Big Island and for holding me to impeccable standards. Thanks to specialist author Nanette Napoleon, to *Kahuna Nui* Leimomi Mo'okini Lum and to Maile Napoleon of Lapakahi State Historical Park for teaching me Hawaiian history from an insider's perspective; to Doug Codiga, Glenn Kunimura and Grant Matsushige for first-ever adventures around the island; and to Jan Takasaki for answering my countless queries. To Kim Grant, with whom I co-authored Lonely Planet's 7th edition *Hawaii* book, your work as coordinating author guided me well. I thank my co-author Alan Tarbell for joining this project with enthusiasm and fresh eyes. Love to my parents Tom and Nancy Yamamoto and to my sister Judi for endless support and patience. I dedicate this book to MJP, who helps me see – in Hawai'i, in my past and in my present – the truths I overlook. *Aloha nui loa.*

ALAN TARBELL

I'd like to give a special thanks for the warm aloha I received on my trip to the Big Island. The hospitality was enormous! *Mahalo* to Scott Lee for healing my foot so quickly so I could continue working. *Mahalo* to Sam Benson for so patiently bringing me up to speed. *Mahalo* to Luci Yamamoto for guiding me along with her island wisdom. *Mahalo* to Lamont Carroll for the local Puna dirt. *Mahalo* to Martie and Don Nitsche down in Ka'u and Pattie Cook in Waimea. To Elizabeth Sanders in Honoka'a and Beth Encencio and Bryan Green in Hilo. To Lorant at HAVO and all of the people who dropped some local knowledge and took the time to talk story. To my folks for the love and support, always. A big *mahalo* to Leo Hansen for all he gave, RIP. And to my bro for lending a helping hand. And finally to Pele and the keepers of the land and sea, let the cycle continue. Aloha and *mahalo nui loa*!

THE LONELY PLANET STORY

The story begins with a classic travel adventure: Tony and Maureen Wheeler's 1972 journey across Europe and Asia to Australia. There was no useful information about the overland trail then, so Tony and Maureen published the first Lonely Planet guidebook to meet a growing need.

From a kitchen table, Lonely Planet has grown to become the largest independent travel publisher in the world, with offices in Melbourne (Australia), Oakland (USA) and London (UK). Today Lonely Planet guidebooks cover the globe. There is an ever-growing list of books and information in a variety of media. Some things haven't changed. The main aim is still to make it possible for adventurous travelers to get out there – to explore and better understand the world.

At Lonely Planet we believe travelers can make a positive contribution to the countries they visit – if they respect their host communities and spend their money wisely. Every year 5% of company profit is donated to charities around the world.

CREDITS

Commissioning Editors: Sara Benson and Erin Corrigan
Coordinating Editor: Justin Flynn
Coordinating Cartographer: Helen Rowley
Coordinating Layout Designer: Jim Hsu
Managing Cartographer: Alison Lyall
Assisting Editors: Sarah Bailey and Diana Saad
Assisting Cartographers: Piotr Czajkowski
Cover Designer: Candice Jacobus
Color Designer: Jacqui Saunders
Project Manager: Celia Wood
Language Content Coordinator: Quentin Frayne

Thanks to Sally Darmody, Kate McDonald, Katherine Marsh, Rebecca Lalor, Nick Stebbing, Mark Germanchis, Chris LeeAck, Lachlan Ross, Paul Piaia, Ray Thompson, Alan Murphy, Melanie Dankel and Wayne Murphy.

THANKS FROM LONELY PLANET

Many thanks to the travelers who used the last edition and wrote to us with helpful hints, useful advice and interesting anecdotes. Your names follow:

Wendy Bat-Sarah, Daniel Bleaken, Catherine Breen, Yee Cheng, Katrina Corcoran, Tony DeYoung, Esrb Esrbcal, Ann Fielding, Jonathan Gaines, Tom Ganz, Mark Gomes, Jack Gordon, Gretchen Guidotti, Simon Huang, Cheryl Jones, Lindsay Jones, Shella Keilholz, Karen Kissileff, Yolanda Levy, Sarah Lieberman, Gunilla Lindblad, Michael Marquardt, Akiko Masuda, Susan Ramiro, Walter Rask, Rosemarie Richards, Tuuli Rossi, Mark Schlagboehmer, Kimberly Senior, Lorraine & Murray Sinderberry, Liz Walter, Sally Wood, Satoshi Yabuki, Tim Zeb

SEND US YOUR FEEDBACK

We love to hear from travelers – your comments keep us on our toes and help make our books better. Our well-traveled team reads every word on what you loved or loathed about this book. Although we cannot reply individually to postal submissions, we always guarantee that your feedback goes straight to the appropriate authors, in time for the next edition. Each person who sends us information is thanked in the next edition – and the most useful submissions are rewarded with a free book.

To send us your updates – and find out about Lonely Planet events, newsletters and travel news – visit our award-winning website: **www.lonelyplanet.com/feedback**.

Note: we may edit, reproduce and incorporate your comments in Lonely Planet products such as guidebooks, websites and digital products, so let us know if you don't want your comments reproduced or your name acknowledged. For a copy of our privacy policy visit www.lonelyplanet.com/privacy.

ACKNOWLEDGMENTS

Many thanks to the following for the use of their content:
Globe on back cover © Mountain High Maps 1993 Digital Wisdom, Inc.

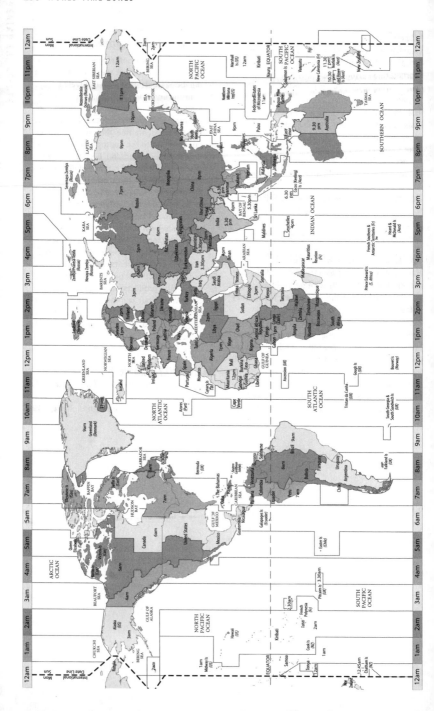

Index

INDEX

000 Map pages
000 Location of colour photographs

INDEX

MAP LEGEND

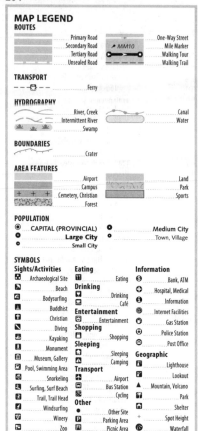

ROUTES

Primary Road
Secondary Road
Tertiary Road
Unsealed Road
One-Way Street
MM10 ... Mile Marker
Walking Tour
Walking Trail

TRANSPORT

Ferry

HYDROGRAPHY

River, Creek
Intermittent River
Swamp
Canal
Water

BOUNDARIES

Crater

AREA FEATURES

Airport
Campus
Cemetery, Christian
Forest
Land
Park
Sports

POPULATION

CAPITAL (PROVINCIAL)
Large City
Small City
Medium City
Town, Village

SYMBOLS

Sights/Activities
Archaeological Site
Beach
Bodysurfing
Buddhist
Christian
Diving
Kayaking
Monument
Museum, Gallery
Pool, Swimming Area
Snorkeling
Surfing, Surf Beach
Trail, Trail Head
Windsurfing
Winery
Zoo

Eating
Eating

Drinking
Drinking
Café

Entertainment
Entertainment

Shopping
Shopping

Sleeping
Sleeping
Camping

Transport
Airport
Bus Station
Cycling

Other
Other Site
Parking Area
Picnic Area

Information
Bank, ATM
Hospital, Medical
Information
Internet Facilities
Gas Station
Police Station
Post Office

Geographic
Lighthouse
Lookout
Mountain, Volcano
Park
Shelter
Spot Height
Waterfall

LONELY PLANET OFFICES

Australia
Head Office
Locked Bag 1, Footscray, Victoria 3011
☎ 03 8379 8000, fax 03 8379 8111
talk2us@lonelyplanet.com.au

USA
150 Linden St, Oakland, CA 94607
☎ 510 893 8555, toll free 800 275 8555
fax 510 893 8572, info@lonelyplanet.com

UK
72–82 Rosebery Ave,
Clerkenwell, London EC1R 4RW
☎ 020 7841 9000, fax 020 7841 9001
go@lonelyplanet.co.uk

Published by Lonely Planet Publications Pty Ltd
ABN 36 005 607 983